BRIERLY'S LAW OF NATIONS

GW00578227

BRIERLY'S LAW OF NATIONS

An Introduction to the Role of International Law in International Relations

SEVENTH EDITION

ANDREW CLAPHAM

OXFORD
UNIVERSITY PRESS

Great Clarendon Street, Oxford, OX2 6DP,
United Kingdom

Oxford University Press is a department of the University of Oxford.
It furthers the University's objective of excellence in research, scholarship,
and education by publishing worldwide. Oxford is a registered trade mark of
Oxford University Press in the UK and in certain other countries

British Library Cataloguing in Publication Data

Data available

Library of Congress Cataloging in Publication Data

Data available

ISBN 978-0-19-965793-3
978-0-19-965794-0 (pbk)

Printed in Great Britain by
CPI Group (UK) Ltd, Croydon, CR0 4YY

PREFACE TO THE FIRST EDITION

ANY intelligent study of the problems of international relations must raise the question of the role, if any, to be assigned in them to law. Unfortunately current discussions of the matter too often assume that this question can be determined by *a priori* methods, to the neglect of any serious examination either of the part that law is actually playing in the relations of states to-day, or of the conditions upon which an effective legal order in any society depends. This method of approach to the law of nations has made possible two popular misconceptions about its character: one that it exists solely or mainly in order to make war a humane and gentlemanly occupation, from which some critics deduce the futility of the whole science, and others the supreme need for devising a system of overwhelmingly powerful 'sanctions'; the other that, inasmuch as law within a state is normally an instrument of peace, nothing but the wickedness of governments prevents us from recognizing the law of nations as a mighty force by which war might be 'outlawed' immediately from international relations.

In this small book I have tried to give reasons for my belief that the law of nations is neither a chimera nor a panacea, but just one institution among others which we have at our disposal for the building up of a saner international order. It is foolish to underestimate either the services that it is rendering to-day, or the need for its improvement and extension.

J. L. B.

OXFORD,
February, 1928.

PREFACE TO THE SEVENTH EDITION

'Whether fairly or not, the world regards international law today as in need of rehabilitation; and even those who have a confident belief in its future will probably concede that the comparatively small part that it plays in the sphere of international relations as a whole is disappointing.'[1] Brierly's critical voice, present in the opening paragraph of his Inaugural Lecture at Oxford University in 1924, seems to speak to us in a very direct way. My aim in this new edition of *The Law of Nations* is to help Brierly explain again the role of international law in international relations, and, with him, to demystify the operation of international law today. The new subtitle reflects Brierly's preoccupation with the role played by international law, as well as the idea that international law is 'just one institution among others which we can use for the building of a better international order'.[2]

Brierly was comfortable writing that law exists for certain ends, and he saw that there exists a 'purpose in law'. This purpose can be

---

1. 'The Shortcomings of International Law' (first published in the *British Year Book of International* Law, 1924) reprinted in J.L. Brierly *The Basis of Obligation in International Law and Other Papers*, H. Lauterpacht and C.H.M. Waldock (eds), (Oxford: Clarendon Press, 1958) 68–80 at 68.
2. J.L. Brierly (ed.), *The Law of Nations: An Introduction to the International Law of Peace*, 5th edn (Oxford: Clarendon Press, 1955) preface at v. See also the opening line of the preface to the 1st edn (above).

seen as simultaneously, to provide a stable, reasonable and ordered framework for interaction, and 'to embody social justice in law (giving to that term whatever interpretation is current in the thought of our time)'.[3] The obvious tension between stability and change is the theme that runs through this approach to international law. Brierly suggested in 1924 that international law 'has attempted to maintain existing values, but rarely to create new ones'.[4] For international law to play a role in international relations the concepts used need to relate to, and reflect, the changes taking place in the world. Brierly saw an 'urgent need' to consider what words such as 'sovereignty' or 'independence' mean in 'modern conditions'.[5] He wanted us to recognize that 'as the bonds of international society have become closer, the words have changed, and are continually changing, their content.'[6]

It is hoped, therefore, that Brierly would approve of this attempt to update his book to provide the general reader with some idea of the role we expect international law might play in international relations today. Providing the reader with an accessible text means, not only examining the changing content of the relevant concepts, but also finding examples and phrases that resonate. I have tried to use a prose style which reflects what Brierly and I might have agreed on had we gone through the text together. This means I have rewritten and supplemented, imagining a co-author with opinions developed over a lifetime's writing. Consequently I have

---

3. Ibid 23.

4. 'The Shortcomings of International Law' (above) at 72.

5. Ibid 75.

6. Ibid 76.

sometimes inserted passages from Brierly's other works, where I feel these help to develop the argument. More generally, the other writings have helped me to try to imagine what Brierly would say during our virtual negotiations over certain new passages (and deletions).

In order to keep this a two-way conversation I decided to work from Brierly's fifth edition, rather than Sir Humphrey Waldock's sixth edition, published in 1963. I have, however, taken into consideration some of Waldock's alterations, and on occasion, where the phrasing and ideas built on Brierly's approach, I have incorporated Waldock's passages verbatim or referenced his General Course delivered at the Hague Academy of International Law around the time of the publication of the sixth edition of *The Law of Nations*.

The footnotes retain and expand some of Brierly's original references, but I felt the reader now expects indications for further reading. Moreover it was sometimes necessary to reference significant treaties and judgments that have appeared since 1963. In the last fifty years international law scholarship has burgeoned. The references are mostly aimed at students looking for a clear explanation of the law going beyond the outline presented in this introduction. In several cases I have deliberately emphasized the contribution of those writing in what I consider to be a similar tradition to Brierly's. I have felt comfortable liberally referring to Vaughan Lowe's *International Law*, bearing in mind that Lowe himself has self-consciously described Brierly's book as 'the ancestor' to his own.[7]

---

7. (Oxford: OUP, 2007) at 4.

Over the last fifty years there have been several attempts to bridge the gap between the fields of international law and international relations. Influential international relations scholars have sought to challenge the notion that international law has any meaningful role or effect in international relations. Brierly had little patience for those who doubted whether international law operated in the real world as a set of real obligations, and he asserted that: 'Those who act in international affairs (in contrast to those who speculate about them), statesmen, diplomatists, judges, advocates, regularly and unhesitatingly assume the existence of a juridical obligation in international law.'[8] Today there is an increasing awareness not only of the existence of international law as law, but also of international lawyers as lawyers.[9]

Brierly's empirical approach was grounded in his exposure to the day-to-day application of international law as legal advice to governments. This knowledge that international law is discussed and applied every day was matched with a rejection of abstract

---

8. 'The Basis of Obligation in International Law' in Lauterpacht and Waldock (eds) (above) at 19.

9. P. Sands, *Torture Team: Uncovering War Crimes in the Land of the Free* (London: Penguin, 2009). In 2010, the Legal Adviser to the US State Department, Harold Hongju Koh, addressed the American Society of International Law in the following terms: 'But in addition to being counselors, we also serve as a conscience for the U.S. Government with regard to international law... That means that one of the most important roles of the Legal Adviser is to advise the Secretary when a policy option being proposed is "lawful but awful." As Herman Pfleger, one former Legal Adviser, put it: "You should never say no to your client when the law and your conscience say yes; but you should never, ever say yes when your law and conscience say no."' 'The Obama Administration and International Law', 25 March 2010.

political science interpretations of notions such as 'sovereignty' and 'independence', which he saw as misleading and counterproductive. In the past half-century there have been considerable attempts at rapprochement between the fields of international law and international relations,[10] and the present volume seeks to reinforce Brierly's arguments about the real role played by international law in international affairs.

Much of the most recent interdisciplinary scholarship refers to the importance of analysing discourse, finding common meanings in vocabulary, and developing a grammar, which enables, not just scholars to understand better the developing international order, but also international law to play a greater role in international relations. The linguistic approach can be seen to build on Brierly's assertion that actors unhesitatingly assume that international law exists, and suggests that understanding international law is essential to the conduct of international relations due to the means of communication used. International law can be seen today as having been internalized by the main actors, who increasingly meet in institutionalized settings such as the United Nations and other international organizations. This socialization through the language of international law is a real phenomenon (witnessed by the

---

10. See further A.-M. Slaughter Burley, 'International Law and International Relations Theory: A Dual Agenda', 87 *AJIL* (1993) 205–39; A.M. Slaughter, A.S. Tulumello, and S. Wood, 'International Law and International Relations Theory: A New Generation of Interdisciplinary Scholarship', 92 *AJIL* (1998) 367–97 R.O. Keohane, 'International Relations and International Law: Two Optics', 38 *Harvard International Law Journal* (1997) 487–502; M. Byers (ed.), *The Role of Law in International Politics: Essays in International Relations and International Law* (Oxford: OUP, 2000).

present editor) and explains in part much of the impact of international law.

Legal methods have been described as 'styles of argument, of linguistic expression' which are adapted by the actor to the circumstances.[11] Although legal methods may indeed vary, understanding the deeper structures and the legal labels used to explain them is essential to seeing how international law works.[12] Moreover understanding the legal lexicon helps disentangle what is happening in international relations. A recent interdisciplinary study explains that: '[i]n the international context, the "official language" of interstate relations is frequently the language of international law. This means not only that legal norms increasingly become part of international discourse but that standard forms of legal reasoning creep into international "conversation".'[13]

Although Brierly has been portrayed as presupposing that states were the sole concern of international law, and overly focusing on the enforcement of law by states,[14] I would suggest that we can find evidence that he was concerned, not only with the role of the

---

11. M. Koskenniemi, 'Letter to the Editors of the Symposium', 93 *AJIL* (1999) 351–61 at 359.

12. M. Koskenniemi, *From Apology to Utopia: The Structure of International Legal Argument* (Cambridge: CUP, 2005).

13. D. Armstrong, T. Farrell, and H. Lambert, *International Law and International Relations* (Cambridge: CUP, 2007) at 30.

14. A. Carty, 'Why Theory?—The Implications for International Law Teaching', in British Institute of International and Comparative Law, *Theory and International Law: An Introduction* (London: BIICL, 1991) 75–99, at 80. In fact Carty himself says: 'Brierly objected, against his predecessors in the discipline, that the State is not a moral entity. It is merely an institution, "a relationship which men establish as a means of securing certain objects".'

individual and certain organizations, but also with the apparent failure of the dominant doctrine to recognize such non-state actors as subjects of international law. In 1928 he wrote:

> The law of any state has for its subjects both individuals and institutions, and there is no reason why international law should not become, if it is not already, a law of which the subjects are indifferently either states, or other institutions such as the League of Nations, the Bureau International de Travail, the Union Postale Universelle, &c., or finally, individuals. Such a conception of the international juridical community would in a sense be merely a return to that of Grotius; it would be a community of *Civitates*, but it would also be a community of *genus humanum*.[15]

There is a good argument for retaining the title *The Law of Nations* rather than 'updating' this to international law. Although highlighting the nation might be seen as opening the gates to reinforcing unsavoury forms of nationalism, there is an attraction in reverting to the original sense of this legal order as encompassing some universal norms that apply to a multiplicity of actors. The question lies on the fault lines of the debate about the scope of the discipline. Ironically the old-fashioned historical term (law of nations) may open up the possibility of comprehending this legal order in a way that reflects the contemporary reality and more easily allows for a progressive development of the law. Mark Janis has appealed for such a shift in the following terms:

---

15. 'Basis of Obligation' (above) at 52.

I would like to ask whether the denomination of our subject, 'international law', still makes sense. Positivist international law is rooted in the concept that relevant rules are those that address the interests of competing sovereign states. However, non-state actors now help to shape the global legal system. Arguably, it would be more appropriate and useful to re-adopt the term 'law of nations'. 'Law of nations' was used in legal discourse until Bentham's criticism of the term replaced it with 'international law'. Bentham felt that 'law of nations' did not clearly indicate that the subject had only to do with relations among sovereign states. Since 'international law' does not now solely concern 'sovereign states'—and indeed may never have—it is time to put Bentham's term to rest. Now that the practical and intellectual mould of international law is broken, why not announce a new paradigm for the discipline using older terms, 'law of nations' or 'droit des gens', which more readily signal the diversity and complexities of the subject?[16]

Sir Hersch Lauterpacht reflected that some of the doctrine Brierly was exploring in 1924 could have been seen as 'iconoclastic', even if by 1958 aspects had become 'almost orthodox'.[17] Paradoxically the book today is considered an icon among textbooks. How then can the text retain the mould breaking approach yet remain

---

16. Footnote omitted. M.W. Janis, 'International Law?' 32 *Harvard Journal of International Law* (1991) 363–72, at 371–2.

17. H. Lauterpacht, 'Brierly's Contribution to International Law', in J.L. Brierly, *The Basis of Obligations in International Law and other Papers* (1958) xv–xxxvi at xvi.

revered? This is the conundrum at the heart of this project. Lauterpacht distilled Brierly's themes down to the following:

- The moral foundation of international law
- The individual as subject of international law
- The unity of international and municipal law
- The independence and sovereignty of states.

We can nuance this list of themes by emphasizing that Brierly often downplayed the role of states. In his quest to reduce the focus on the state, and emphasize the rights and obligations of individuals that make up the state, he attacked the doctrine which sought to exclude other actors as subjects of international law and played with the concept of personality:

> Even the state, great and powerful institution as it is, can never express more than a part of our personalities, only that part which finds expression in the purpose or purposes for which the state exists; and however important these purposes may be, however true it may be that they are in a sense the prerequisite condition of other human activities in a society, they never embrace the whole of our lives.[18]

Brierly foresaw other entities becoming subjects of international law, just as 'the law of any state has for its subjects both individuals and institutions'.[19] And Brierly's sense of community was not a

---

18. 'The Basis of Obligation' (above) at 51.
19. Ibid 52.

community of sovereign states but rather a community which drew on a sense of solidarity across traditional borders. Writing at a time when the League of Nations system seemed incapable of stemming the resort to force and aggression by Italy in Abyssinia, Brierly contrasted material links across borders with the need to find a 'spiritual as well as a material basis' for society: a Rousseauian *volonté générale*.[20] And he suggested that individuals from different nations are not strangers in the sphere of the 'deeper essentials of morality'.[21] He wrote in 1936:

> These common standards, too, do sometimes issue in common action, and though the action may be half-hearted and its results meagre, it is evidence of the general acceptance of at least some degree of common responsibility for the common welfare. The Mandates system, the Minorities treaties, the Nansen office for refugees, the international Red Cross organization, the manifold social and humanitarian work of the League of Nations—these things are not enough, but they are not negligible. Moreover, the acid test of the reality of a community is that common standards of conduct should be held with a conviction strong enough to induce its members to take common action, even at the cost of sacrifices to themselves, in defence of the law.[22]

---

20. 'The Rule of Law in International Society', reprinted in *The Basis of Obligations in International Law and other Papers* (above) at 250, 251. Cf P. Allott, *Eunomia: New Order for a New World* (Oxford: OUP, 2001) at xx, who asks us to look for an 'emerging *public mind of international society*' and highlights the emergence of the '*infrastructure* of international social consciousness'; see also Carty (above) esp. at 79ff.

21. Ibid 252.

22. Ibidem.

Perhaps by putting these topics in relief there is the possibility of taking Brierly's original approach forward. Key to reconsidering Brierly's style is an understanding that he was not really seeking to state the law; rather he sought to highlight how to explore the development of international law. To demonstrate the point let us return to Lauterpacht's appreciation:

> [Brierly's] distinct contribution to the science of international law…lay not so much in the solutions which he propounded—for he often admitted, or implied, that there was no solution or no easy solution—as in the way in which he pointed to the difficulties involved and, after apparently propounding an answer to them, proceeded to develop the theme of the deceptiveness and the insufficiency of the answer thus given. It would almost appear that what weighed with him was not the result of the search, but the search itself; that he was content to be an exponent of difficulties and not a provider of solutions; and that it did not matter to him that in fact he left the problem unresolved.[23]

This new edition seeks to preserve this aspect of Brierly's approach, as well as his emphasis on the natural law origins of international law, the need to recognize that international law touched entities beyond the state, and the sense that international law provides the vocabulary for international relations.

---

23. 'Brierly's Contribution' (above) at xxx–xxxi.

I have tried to keep the prose straightforward and fluent with a view to preserving these qualities that made Brierly so readable.[24] Part of the story about Brierly's book was actually the suggestion that students might be reading it in one go. In his 1963 book review Norman Marsh started out: 'In the bad old days it was commonly said among undergraduates in at least one British university that an all-night reading of Brierly immediately before the examination in international law would ensure a satisfactory mark.'[25] Vaughan Lowe tells us that the book was helpful 'for a student to read in the vacation before starting the subject, or for an interested lay reader'.[26] All these audiences have been borne in mind. International law will become more and more meaningful as it becomes better appreciated. One aim of this book is to render international law more accessible so that it starts to belong to us all.

A.B.C.,
Graduate Institute of International and
Development Studies,
Villa Moynier, Geneva

---

24. I have chosen to revert to the universal pronoun 'they' rather than using 'he or she'. Brierly was comfortable using 'he' throughout, but this no longer seems appropriate. I was emboldened in this stylistic manoeuvre by O'Conner and Kellerman who recently pointed out that 'for centuries the universal pronoun was *they*. Writers as far back as Chaucer used it for singular and plural, masculine and feminine.' 'Anybody who's everybody', *International Herald Tribune*, 27 July 2009.

25. N.S. Marsh, 'Book review of J.L. Brierly *The Law of Nations,* 6th ed. H. Waldock (ed) (1963)', 12 *International and Comparative Law Quarterly* (1963) 1049–50.

26. *International Law* (above) at v.

CONTENTS

ACKNOWLEDGEMENTS

Whenever I mentioned to colleagues that I was working on a new edition of Brierly's *Law of Nations* their faces would invariably light up, and they would first offer effusive encouragement, usually adding that it was their 'favorite law book', and then would come the inevitable 'promise me you won't change anything'. Nevertheless, the wave of enthusiasm, especially among teachers of international law, has sustained me and I should like to thank all those whose enthusiasm helped to keep this project on track. In particular I should like to thank Georges Abi-Saab, Zachery Douglas, Marcelo Kohen, Eibe Riedel, David Scheffer, Elizabeth Wilmshurst, and Valentin Zellweger for reading various passages and for their very helpful suggestions on the manuscript. Of course it goes without saying that I alone am responsible for any errors or deficiencies in the text. Michelle Healy's advice and painstaking work on the manuscript improved the text considerably and I was fortunate to have a collaborator who was so finely attuned to Brierly's approach. I should also like to acknowledge the invaluable encouragement and advice I received from Andrea Bianchi, Lucius Caflisch, Laurence Boisson de Chazournes, Robert Cryer, Pierre-Marie Dupuy, Ben Emmerson, Guy Goodwin-Gill, Peter Haggenmacher, Kate Jones, Susan Marks, Fréderic Mégret, Theodor Meron, Philippe Sands, and Brigitte Stern.

I am especially grateful to the Graduate Institute of International and Development Studies for providing such a stimulating environment, and for granting me the sabbatical that allowed me to concentrate on producing this book. Paola Gaeta took on more than her fair share of directing the Geneva Academy of International Humanitarian Law and Human Rights while I have been working on this; and I am very appreciative of her unfailing friendship and substantive suggestions related to the book. I should like to thank here the students from the Institute's Master's Programmes as well as the students from the Academy's LL.M Programmes. Their comments and suggestions in class and on the earlier drafts have undoubtedly improved the text and shaped the way I see the contemporary challenges to international law. I was lucky to have had the help of committed teaching assistants for these courses over the past few years, and their engagement with the project has been priceless. I should like to express my thanks to Fiona Le Diraison, Bérénice Schramm, Armelle Vessier, Elise Hansbury, and Céline Bauloz. Thanks also go to the students of a class of Judge Simma at the University of Michigan Law School in Ann Arbor in the fall of 2011.

From the outset John Louth at Oxford University Press provided the sort of constant guidance and support essential for the completion of such a project. I should also like to thank all those at Oxford University Press who put in so much effort to finalize the eventual book, particular thanks to Merel Alstein, Gwen Booth, Anthony Hinton, Fiona Stables, and Caroline Quinnell. Thanks also go to the anonymous reviewers for their very helpful suggestions and encouragement.

Finally I need to thank two members of my family, first my mother Margaret Clapham for reading the whole manuscript, pointing out ambiguities, and challenging any infelicitous use of legal jargon; and second, very special thanks are owed to my wife Mona Rishmawi—not only has she been an enthusiastic ally at every stage, but her careful reading of the manuscript has improved it immeasurably.

These acknowledgements would be incomplete without recognizing the huge debt I owe to the late Antonio Cassese, who inspired my initial interest in international law, and showed us how to develop the potential of the international legal order.

ABBREVIATIONS

AJIL	American Journal of International Law
ARSIWA	ILC Articles on Responsibility of States for Internationally Wrongful Acts
BYBIL	British Year Book of International Law
CERD	Convention on the Elimination of All Forms of Racial Discrimination
CTC	Counter-Terrorism Committee
CUP	Cambridge University Press
DSB	Dispute Settlement Body
DSU	Dispute Settlement Understanding
ECtHR	European Court of Human Rights
EEZ	Exclusive Economic Zone
EFZ	Economic Fisheries Zone
EJIL	European Journal of International Law
FAO	Food and Agriculture Organization
FCO	Foreign and Commonwealth Office
GAVI	Global Alliance for Vaccines and Immunization
IBRD	International Bank for Reconstruction and Development
ICANN	Internet Corporation for Assigned Names and Numbers
ICAO	International Civil Aviation Organization
ICC	International Criminal Court
ICJ	International Court of Justice

ICLQ	International & Comparative Law Quarterly
ICRC	International Committee of the Red Cross
IDA	International Development Agency
IFAD	International Fund for Agricultural Development
IHRR	International Human Rights Reports
ILC	International Law Commission
ILO	International Labour Organization
ILQ	International Law Quarterly
IMF	International Monetary Fund
IMO	International Maritime Organization
ITLOS	International Tribunal for the Law of the Sea
ITU	International Telecommunication Union
JICJ	Journal of International Criminal Justice
LOSC	Law of the Sea Convention
MICIVIH	Mission Civile Internationale en Haïti
MINUGUA	United Nations Verification Mission in Guatemala
MUP	Manchester University Press
NATO	North Atlantic Treaty Organization
NGO	non-governmental organization
OAS	Organization of American States
OHCHR	Office of the United Nations High Commissioner for Human Rights
ONUC	Opération des Nations Unies au Congo
OUP	Oxford University Press
PCIJ	Permanent Court of International Justice
RCADI	Recueil des Cours de l'Académie de la Haye
RIAA	Reports of International Arbitral Awards
UNEF	United Nations Emergency Force

UNESCO	United Nations Educational, Scientific and Cultural Organization
UNGA	United Nations General Assembly
UNIDO	United Nations Industrial Development Organization
VCCR	Vienna Convention on Consular Relations
VCDR	Vienna Convention on Diplomatic Relations
VCLT	Vienna Convention on the Law of Treaties
WHO	World Health Organization
WIPO	World Intellectual Property Organization
WMO	World Meteorological Organization
WTO	World Trade Organization
ZaöRV	Zeitschrift für ausländisches öfentliches Recht und Völkerrecht

TABLE OF CASES

TABLE OF TREATIES, OTHER INTERNATIONAL INSTRUMENTS, AND NATIONAL LEGISLATION

International Treaties and Other International Instruments

National Legislation

South Africa

I | The Origins of International Law

§ 1. The rise of modern states

EVER since human beings began to organize their common life in political communities they have felt the need of some system of rules, however rudimentary, to regulate their inter-community relations. Rules which may be described as rules of international law are to be found in the history of the ancient and medieval worlds.[1] But as a definite branch of jurisprudence, the system now known as international law is relatively modern. It dates only from the sixteenth and seventeenth centuries. Its special character was determined by that of the modern European state system, which was itself shaped in the ferment of the Renaissance and the Reformation. Some understanding of the main features of this European state system is therefore necessary for an understanding of the nature of international law.[2]

---

1. For an introduction see S.C. Neff, 'A Short History of International Law' in Evans (ed.) *International Law* 2nd edn (Oxford: OUP, 2006) 29–56, *War and the Law of Nations: A General History* (Cambridge: CUP, 2005).

2. What follows is admittedly a very European perspective, Onuma Yasuaki encourages us all to consider our viewpoint in his 'pocketbook' *A Transcivilizational Perspective on*

1

For present purposes what most distinguishes the modern post-Reformation from the medieval state is the much greater strength and concentration of the powers of government in the modern state. The national and territorial state, with which we are familiar today, is provided with institutions of government which normally enable it to enforce its control at all times. This type of state, however, is the product of a long and chequered history; and throughout the Middle Ages the growth of strong centralized governments met many obstacles such as: problems with communication, sparsity of population, and basic economic conditions. But two retarding influences deserve special attention because of the imprint they have left on the modern state.

The first of these was feudalism. Modern historical research has taught us that, while it is a mistake to speak of a feudal *system,* the word 'feudalism' is a convenient way of referring to certain fundamental similarities which, in spite of large local variations, can be discerned in the social development of all the peoples of Western Europe from about the ninth to the thirteenth centuries. Bishop Stubbs, speaking of feudalism in the form it had reached at the Norman Conquest, says:

> it may be described as a complete organisation of society through the medium of land tenure, in which from the king down to the lowest landowner all are bound together by obligation of service and defence: the lord to protect his vas-

---

International Law (Leiden: Nijhoff, 2010) ch. IV; he reminds us that other peoples should not really be seen as being 'admitted' to international society, but rather that European international law was imposed and absorbed and 'came to be globalized in the geographical sense around the end of the twentieth century'. At 302.

sal, the vassal to do service to his lord; the defence and service being based on and regulated by the nature and extent of the land held by the one of the other. In those states which have reached the territorial stage of development, the rights of defence and service are supplemented by the right of jurisdiction. The lord judges as well as defends his vassal; the vassal does suit as well as service to his lord. In states in which feudal government has reached its utmost growth, the political, financial, judicial, every branch of public administration is regulated by the same conditions. The central authority is a mere shadow of a name.[3]

Thus to speak of a feudal 'state' is almost a misuse of terms; in a sense the feudal organization of society was a substitute for its organization in a state, and a perfectly feudal condition of society would be, not merely a weak state, but the negation of the state altogether. Such a condition was never completely realized at any time or anywhere; but it is obvious that the tendency of feudalism to disperse among different classes those powers, which, in modern times, we regard as normally concentrated in the state, or at any rate as under the state's ultimate control, had to pass away before states in our sense could come into existence.

On the other hand, there were elements in the feudal conception of society capable of being pressed into the service of the unified national states, which were steadily being consolidated in Western Europe from about the twelfth to the sixteenth centuries, and influential in determining the form that those states would

---

3. *Constitutional History of England*, 6th edn, vol. i, (Oxford: Clarendon Press, 1903) 274.

take. Thus when feudalism's disintegrating effects on government had been eliminated, the duty of personal loyalty of vassal to lord, which feudalism had made so prominent, was capable of being transmuted into the duty of allegiance of subject to monarch in the national state. The intimate association of this personal relation with the tenure of land made the transition to *territorial* monarchy easy and natural; and the identification with rights of property with rights, which we regard as properly political, led to notions of the absolute character of government, of the realm as the 'dominion' or property of the monarch, and of the people as his 'subjects' rather than as citizens. Feudalism itself had been an obstacle to the growth of the national state, but it left to its victorious rival a legacy of ideas which emphasized the absolute character of government.

The other influence which retarded the growth of states in the Middle Ages was the Church. It is not necessary here to speak of the long struggle between Pope and Emperor, although one incidental effect of this was to assist the growth of national states by breaking up the unity of Christendom. More significant in the present context is the fact that no civil authority in any country was regarded as supreme until after the Reformation. Governmental authority was always divided; the Church claimed and received the obedience of the subjects of the state, and its claims were not always limited to the purely spiritual sphere. Even in England, always somewhat restive under papal interference, the idea of the omni-competence of the civil power would have been unthinkable.

Scholars might dispute exactly how far the powers of each of the rival authorities extended; but it was clear that there were limits to the powers of the state, and it was certain that the Church had *some* powers over the members of the state which it neither derived from, nor held by the sufferance of, the state. States might often act as arbitrarily as any absolute state of the post-Reformation world; they might struggle against this or that claim of the Church; but neither in theory nor in fact were they absolute. But just as the state was gradually consolidating its power against the fissiparous tendencies of feudalism within, so it was more and more resisting the division of authority imposed upon it by the Church from without; and this latter process culminated in the Reformation, which, in one of its most important aspects, was a rebellion of the states against the Church. It declared the determination of the civil authority to be supreme in its own territory; and it resulted in the decisive defeat of the last rival to the emerging unified national state. Over about half of Western Europe the rebellion was completely and evidently successful; and even in those countries which rejected Protestantism as a religion, the Church was so shaken that, as a political force, it could no longer compete with the state. The Peace of Westphalia, which brought to an end in 1648 the great Thirty Years War of religion, marked the acceptance of the new political order in Europe.

This new order of things gave the death-blow to the lingering notion that Christendom, in spite of all its quarrels, was in some sense still a unity, and there was a danger that the relations between states would be not only uncontrolled in fact, as they had often been before, but henceforth uninspired even by any unifying ideal. The modern state, in contrast with the medieval, seemed likely to become the final goal of unity, and Machiavelli's *Prince,* written in 1513, though it formulated no theory of politics, had already given to the world a relentless analysis of the art of government based on the conception of the state as an entity which was entirely self-sufficing and non-moral. Fortunately, however, at the very time when political development seemed to be leading to the complete separateness and unaccountability of every state, other causes were at work which were to make it impossible for the world to accept the absence of bonds between state and state. These causes would bring states into closer and constant relations with one another than in the days when their theoretical unity had been accepted everywhere.[4] Among these causes were (1) the impetus to commerce and adventure as a result of the discovery of America and the new route to the Indies; (2) the common intellectual background fostered by the Renaissance; (3) the sympathy felt by co-religionists in different states for one another, from which arose a loyalty transcending the boundaries of states; and (4) the common feeling of revulsion against war, caused by the savagery with which the wars of religion were waged.

All these causes co-operated to make it certain that the separate state could never be accepted as the final and perfect form of human association, and that, in the modern as in the medieval world, it would be necessary to recognize the existence of a wider unity. These truths were reflected in the rise of international law, which accepted the abandonment of the medieval ideal of a world-state, and took instead as its fundamental postulate the existence of a number of states: secular, national, and territorial. But international law denied their absolute separateness and unaccountability,

---

4. Cf J. Westlake, *Collected Papers*, L. Oppenheim (ed.), (Cambridge: CUP, 1914) 55. Westlake also mentioned 'the intimate relationship between the literatures of different countries which sprang from their enjoyment of a common Renaissance, and from the identity of the problems which were occupying the minds of all.'

and proclaimed that states were bound to one another by the supremacy of law. Thus it reasserted the medieval conception of unity, but in a form which took account of the new political structure of Europe.

§ 2. The doctrine of sovereignty

Out of the new kind of state, which developed from the Reformation, there arose a new theory of the nature of states—the doctrine of sovereignty. This was first explicitly formulated in 1576 in the *De Republica* of Jean Bodin, and since then sovereignty has become the central problem in the study, both of the nature of the modern state, and of the theory of international law. It is necessary to examine the origins of sovereignty and its later development with some care.

Like all works of political theory, even when they profess to be purely objective, Bodin's *Republic* was deeply influenced by the circumstances of its time, and by its author's sentiments towards them; indeed one of Bodin's merits is that he drew his conclusions from observation of political facts, and not, as writers both before and since have too often done, from supposedly eternal principles concerning the nature of states as such. France in Bodin's time had been rent by faction and civil war. Bodin was convinced that the cause of France's miseries was the lack of a government strong enough to curb the subversive influences of feudal rivalries and religious intolerance, and that the best way to combat these evils was to strengthen the French monarchy. He saw, too, that a process of this kind was actually taking place at that time in his own day throughout West-

ern Europe; unified states were emerging out of the loosely com-
pacted states of medieval times, and the central authority was
everywhere taking the form of a strong personal monarchy, supreme
over all rival claimants to power, secular or ecclesiastical.

Bodin concluded therefore that the essence of statehood, the
quality that makes an association of human beings a state, is the
unity of its government; a state without a *summa potestas,* he says,
would be like a ship without a keel. He defined a state as 'a multitude of families and the possessions that they have in common
ruled by a supreme power and by reason' (*respublica est familiarum
rerumque inter ipsas communium summa potestate ac ratione mod-
erata multitudo*), and he dealt at length with the nature of this
summa potestas or *majestas,* or, as we call it, sovereignty. But the
idea underlying it is simple. Bodin was convinced that a confusion
of uncoordinated independent authorities would be fatal to a state,
and that there must be one final source, and not more than one,
from which its laws proceed. The essential manifestation of sovereignty (*primum ac praecipuum caput majestatis*), he thought, is the
power to make the laws (*legem universis ac singulis civibus dare
posse*), and since the sovereign makes the laws, they clearly cannot
be bound by the laws that they make (*majestas est summa in cives ac
subditos legibusque soluta potestas*).

We might suppose from this phrase that Bodin intended his
sovereign to be an unaccountable supra-legal power, and some of
the language in the *Republic* does seem to support that interpretation. But that was not his real intention.[5] For he went on to say

---

5. See on this point C.H. McIlwain, *Constitutionalism and the Changing World* (New
York: Macmillan, 1939).

that the sovereign is not a *potestas legibus omnibus soluta;* there are some laws that do bind him: the divine law, the law of nature or reason, the law that is common to all nations, and also certain laws which he calls the *leges imperii,* the laws of the government. These *leges imperii,* which the sovereign does not make and cannot abrogate, are the fundamental laws of the state, and in particular they include the laws which determine in whom the sovereign power itself is to be vested, and the limits within which it is to be exercised; today we would call them the laws of the constitution.

The real meaning of Bodin's doctrine can only be understood if we remember that the state he is describing is one in which the government is, as he calls it, a *recta* or a *legitima gubernatio,* that is to say, one in which the highest power, however strong and unified, is still neither arbitrary nor irresponsible, but derived from, and defined by, a law which is superior to itself. In that he was following the medieval tradition of the nature of law, for in the Middle Ages, law was not seen as something wholly man-made; it was believed that, behind the merely positive laws of any human society, there stood a fundamental law of higher binding force embodying the wisdom of the past, and that positive laws must conform to this higher law if they were to have validity.

The notion that legitimate power could ever be purely arbitrary is alien to all the legal thought of the Middle Ages, and in this respect Bodin's work made no break with the past. Medieval rulers might, and no doubt often did, behave arbitrarily; but that could not alter the fact that the rightfulness or otherwise of their conduct must be judged by the law; it was law that made the ruler, and not, as later theories of sovereignty have taught us to believe, the will of rulers that made the law. Where Bodin broke away from the medieval tradition of law was in making his sovereign a legislator, for legislation was a function which that tradition did not readily admit; when a medieval ruler made new law, it was regarded as an act of interpreting, or of restoring the true construction of, the law as it had been handed down from the past.

In the form in which Bodin propounded the doctrine of sovereignty, it raised no particular problem for the international lawyer. Sovereignty for him was an essential principle of internal political order, and he would certainly have been surprised if he could have foreseen that later writers would distort it into a principle of international disorder, and use it to prove that, by their very nature, states are above the law. Bodin evidently did not think so, for he included in the *Republic* a discussion of those very rules for the conduct of states out of which other writers of his day were already beginning to build the new science of international law. It certainly never occurred to him that, through his writing on sovereignty, he was cutting away at these foundations of international law. Yet this is what we are told that the doctrine of sovereignty has done, and, though the story is long and tangled, there have been two main developments which have brought about this astonishing reversal of its original effect. One is that sovereignty came later to be identified with absolute power above the law, and the other is that, what was originally an attribute of a personal ruler inside the state, came to be regarded as an attribute of the state itself in its relations to other states. The causes that led to these changes lie in the history of the modern state, and the theory has followed, as it generally does, in the wake of the facts.

We have seen that Bodin intended his sovereign to be a constitutional ruler subordinate to the fundamental law of the state. But there had always been grave weaknesses in the medieval concept of the fundamental law as a defence against absolutism. There was no authentic text of this law, and no means therefore of determining whether a particular ruler had transgressed it, and even if he had, there was usually nothing that could be done about it. But throughout the Middle Ages the power of rulers was always limited in fact, and, so long as that state of things endured, it was possible to go on believing that law did set some limitations on ruling power.

In the sixteenth century, however, the barriers against absolutism were giving way, and the consolidation of strong governments, with no effective checks on the powers of rulers, was breaking down the medieval idea of law as a customary rule which set limits to all human authority. And such consolidation of power made it natural to think of law as man-made—the manifestation of a ruler's superior will. The reverence everywhere paid to Roman law encouraged this tendency, for Roman law taught that the will of the prince is law. But in the main it was new political facts that were turning the ruler into a supra-legal power, and accustoming people to think of the sovereign not, as Bodin had envisaged, as the ruler established by law, but as the holder of the strongest power in the state, no matter how that power might have been acquired.

This development reached its culmination in the *Leviathan* of Thomas Hobbes, which was published in 1651. It is interesting to note that Hobbes, like Bodin, was writing with his eyes on the events of his own time; for he, too, had seen a civil war, and for him, as for Bodin, sovereignty was an essential principle of order. Hobbes believed that men need for their security 'a Common Power, to keep them in awe, and to direct their actions to the Common Benefit',[6] and, for him, the person or body in whom this power resides, however it may have been acquired, is the sovereign. Law neither makes the sovereign, nor limits his authority; it is might that makes the sovereign, and law is merely what he commands. Moreover, since the power that is the strongest clearly cannot be limited by anything outside itself, it follows that sovereignty must be absolute and unrestricted; 'it appareth plainly, to my understanding, both from Reason, and Scripture, that the Soveraign Power, whether placed in One Man, as in Monarchy, or in one Assembly of men, as in Popular, and Aristocraticall Commonwealths, is as great, as possibly men can be imagined to make it.'[7] This, of course, is what today we call totalitarianism pure and simple.

One result of identifying sovereignty with might, instead of legal right, was to remove it from the sphere of jurisprudence, where it had its origin and where it properly belongs, and to import it into political science, where it has ever since been a source of confusion. So long as the sovereign is the highest *legal* authority, there is usually no difficulty in identifying him or her. But to identify the strongest power involves us in an investigation of all those extra-legal forces, political, social, psychological, and so on, which determine how the institutions of the state shall operate in practice. That is a hopeless quest, for as a rule there is no person or body of persons in a society whose will always prevails; in fact, as has been truly said, the real rulers of society are never discoverable. Yet so strong had the hold of sovereignty upon the imaginations of

---

6. *Leviathan*, R. Tuck (ed.) (Cambridge: CUP, 1991) 120, ch. xvii.
7. Ibid 144, ch. xx.

political scientists become, that when it became obvious, as it soon did, that the personal monarch no longer fitted the role, they started a hunt for the 'location' of sovereignty; almost as if sovereignty, instead of being a reflection in theory of the political facts of a particular age, were a substance which must surely be found somewhere in every state—if only one looked for it carefully enough. With the coming of constitutional government Locke, and after him Rousseau, propounded the theory that the people as a whole were the sovereign; and in the eighteenth century this became the doctrine which was held to justify the American and the French Revolutions. As a fighting slogan, as a protest against arbitrary government, and a demand that government should serve the interests of the governed and not only of the governors, the doctrine of popular sovereignty has had beneficent results; but as a scientific doctrine it rests on a confusion of thought. It tries to combine two contradictory ideas; that of absolute power some-where in the state, and that of the responsibility of every actual holder of power for the use to which they put it.

It is possible to locate a sovereign in Bodin's sense in a constitutional state, though Bodin went too far in holding that the supreme power of making law must always be concentrated in a single hand; he could not foresee that the device of federation would make it possible to divide that power between different holders without producing chaos in the state.[8] But it is not possible to locate a Hobbesian sovereign in a constitutional state, and the political philoso-

---

8. Cf *U.S. v Lanza*, 260 U.S. 377 (1922), where Taft C.J. speaks of 'two sovereignties, deriving power from different sources, capable of dealing with the same subject matter [prohibition] within the same territory'. At 382.

phers failed to see that, with the coming of democracy, a new theory of the nature of governing power was called for. In any case, the whole people cannot be the sovereign in either sense; they do not rule, for the work of government is a skilled and a full-time job which the law cannot avoid entrusting to particular individuals or organs, and as the whole people are incapable of acting as a body, they are not even the strongest power; a politically conscious minority, a military clique, a communist party controlling the police, or a pressure group of some sort, may well be stronger than the people as a whole and better able to make its will prevail. The sovereignty of the people is not even, as soon as we begin to examine its implications more closely, a genuine democratic ideal, for the people can only act by a majority, and a majority rarely is, and never ought to be, all-powerful. No democrat, true to their principles, can believe that there ought to be somewhere in the state a repository of absolute power, and to say that such a power resides in the people, is to deny that either minorities or individuals have any rights except those that the majority allow them. That is totalitarianism, for autocracy is autocracy whoever the autocrat may be.

Still another modern development of the theory of sovereignty has been to give up the attempt to locate absolute power in any specific person or body within the state, and to ascribe it to the state itself, regarded as a juristic person. Here, again, we can see how changes in the doctrine of sovereignty reflect changes in political facts, for the sovereignty of the state gave expression in theory to the growing strength and exclusiveness of the sentiment of nationality during the nineteenth century. By so doing, it raised a formidable difficulty for international law. For if sovereignty means absolute power, and if states are sovereign in that sense, they cannot at the same time be subject to law. International lawyers have tried to escape from the difficulty in various ways, which we shall have to consider later, but, if these premises about sovereignty are correct, there is no escape from the conclusion that international law is nothing but a delusion.

§ 3. The influence of the doctrine of the Law of Nature

Though the system of international law is modern, it had, like the modern state itself, a medieval foundation. The early writers on international law developed their systems from their conception of the law of nature. And this foundation, as Sir Frederick Pollock says, has always and everywhere been treated as sound, except by one insular and unhistorical school.[9] Modern legal writers, especially in England, have sometimes ridiculed the conception of a law of nature, or, while recognizing its great historical influence, they have treated it as a superstition which the modern world has rightly discarded. Such an attitude proceeds from a misunderstanding of the medieval idea; for, under a terminology which has ceased to be

---

9. As Sir Frederick Pollock has shown in the first part of his 'History of the Law of Nature'. In part two he explains 'in the course of the seventeenth century the classical tradition of the Law of Nature was broken up after the Reformation controversies, with the result that in this country it has been forgotten or misunderstood ever since. Oblivion went so far that it was possible for Bentham and his followers to suppose quite honestly that the Law of Nature meant nothing but individual fancy. But at the same time that the Law of Nature ceased to be honoured among us in speculation, it was entering on new spheres of practical power.' *Essays in the Law* (London: Macmillan, 1922) at 62.

familiar to us, the phrase stands for something which no progressive system of law can ever discard. Some knowledge of what a medieval writer meant by the term is necessary if we are to understand either how international law arose, or how it develops today. A long and continuous history,[10] extending at least as far back as the political thought of the Greeks, lies behind the conception; but its influence on international law is so closely interwoven with that of Roman law that the two may here be discussed together. The early law of the primitive Roman city-state was able to develop into a law adequate to the needs of a highly civilized world empire, because it showed a peculiar capacity of expansion and adaptation which broke through the archaic formalism that originally characterized it, as it characterizes all primitive law.

In brief, the process of expansion and adaptation took the form of admitting, side by side with the *jus civile,* or original law peculiar to Rome, a more liberal and progressive element, the *jus gentium,* so called because it was believed or feigned to be of universal application; its principles being regarded as so simple and reasonable that they must be recognized everywhere and by everyone. This practical development was reinforced towards the end of the Republican era by the philosophical conception of a *jus naturale* which, as developed by the Stoics in Greece and borrowed from them by the Romans, meant, in effect, the sum of those principles which ought to control human conduct, because founded in the very nature of man as a rational and social being. In course of time *jus gentium,* the new progressive element which the practical genius of the Romans had imported into their actual law, and *jus natu-*

---

10. Ibid ch. ii.

rale, the ideal law conforming to reason, came to be regarded as generally synonymous. In effect, they were the same set of rules looked at from different points of view; for rules which were everywhere observed, i.e. *jus gentium,* must surely be rules which the rational nature of man prescribes to him, i.e. *jus naturale,* and vice versa. Medieval writers later developed this conception of a law of nature—sometimes elaborating it in ways which appear to the modern mind both fanciful and tedious; but so powerful was its influence that the Church accepted it into the doctrinal system. St Thomas Aquinas, for example, taught that the law of nature was that part of the law of God which was discoverable by human reason, in contrast with the part which is directly revealed. Such an identification of natural with divine law necessarily gave the former an authority superior to that of any merely positive law of human ordinance, and some writers even held that positive law which conflicted with natural law could not claim any binding force.

The effect of such a conception as this, when applied to the theory of the relations of the new national states to one another, is obvious, for it meant that it was not in the nature of things that those relations should be merely anarchical; on the contrary they must be controlled by a higher law, not the mere creation of the will of any sovereign, but part of the order of nature to which even sovereigns were subjected. As against the theory of sovereignty, standing for the new nationalistic separation of the states of Europe, was set the theory of a law of nature denying the irresponsibility of states and negating the finality of their independence from one another. No doubt it was impossible to point to any authentic text of this law, and different interpretations of it were possible; but in spite of all appearances, the belief remained that the whole universe, and included in it the relations of sovereigns to one another, must be ruled by law. Moreover, the difficulty of discovering the dictates of this law presented itself to medieval writers with much less force than it does to the modern mind. They already had a handy guide in the form of Roman law.

The position of Roman law in Europe in the sixteenth century has an important bearing on the beginnings of international law. There were some countries, such as Germany, in which a 'reception' of Roman law had taken place; that is to say, it had driven out the local customary law and had been accepted as the binding law of the land. In other countries the process had not gone so far; but even in these countries the principles of Roman law were held in great respect, and were appealed to whenever no rules of local law excluded them. Everywhere, in fact, Roman law was regarded as the *ratio scripta,* written reason; and a medieval writer, seeking to expound the law of nature, had only to look around to see a system of law, actually operative in the world, which was the common heritage of every country, revered everywhere as the supreme triumph of human reason. Moreover, this law had a further claim to respect due to its close association with the Canon Law of the Church.

Thus Roman law reduced the difficulty of finding the contents of natural law almost to vanishing-point; in fact the founders of international law turned unhesitatingly to Roman law for the rules of their system wherever the relations between ruling princes seemed to them to be analogous to those of private persons. Thus, for example, rights over territory, when governments were almost everywhere monarchical and the territorial notions of feudalism were still powerful, bore an obvious resemblance to the rights of a private individual over property, with the result that the international rules relating to territory are still in essentials the Roman rules of property. It is not difficult, therefore, to see how the belief in an ideal system of law inherently and universally binding, coupled with the existence of a cosmopolitan system of law revered everywhere, should have led to the founding of international law on the law of nature. We now have to inquire whether this foundation is valid for us today.

The medieval conception of a law of nature is open to certain criticisms. In the first place, even taking into account the aid afforded by Roman law, it has to be admitted that natural law implied a belief in the rationality of the universe which seems to us to be exaggerated. It is true that when medieval writers spoke of natural law as being discoverable by reason, they meant that the best human reasoning could discover it, and not, of course, that the results to which any and every individual's reasoning led was natural law. The foolish criticism of Jeremy Bentham: 'A great multitude of people are continually talking of the Law of Nature; and then they go on giving you their sentiments about what is right and what is wrong: and these sentiments, you are to understand, are so many chapters and sections of the Law of Nature',[11] merely showed a contempt for a great conception which Bentham had not taken the trouble to understand. Medieval controversialists might use arguments drawn from natural law to support almost any case, but there

---

11. *An Introduction to the Principles of Morals and Legislation*, (1789) ch. ii.
But Bentham himself, as Sir Frederick Pollock points out was unconsciously 'as much a dogmatist as any propounder of *Naturrecht* [natural law]'. (*History of the Science of Politics* (London, Macmillan, 1890) at 109–10). He constructed a universal theory of legislation based on abstract considerations of human motives in general, such as they appeared to him, and without taking the slightest trouble to consult history or specific facts.

was nothing arbitrary about the conception itself, any more than a text of Scripture is arbitrary because the Devil may quote it. But what medieval writers did not always realize was that what is reasonable, or, to use their own terminology, what the law of nature enjoins, can rarely receive a final definition: it is always, and, above all in the sphere of human conduct, relative to conditions of time and place. We realize, as they hardly did, that these conditions never stand still. For us as for them, a rational universe, even if we cannot prove it to be a fact, is a necessary postulate both of thought and action; and the difference between our thought and theirs is mainly that we have different ways of regarding the world and human society. When modern lawyers ask what is reasonable, they only look for an answer that is valid here and now, and not for one that is finally true; whereas a medieval writer might have said that if ultimate truth eludes our grasp, it is not because it is undiscoverable, but because our reasoning is imperfect. Some modern writers have expressed this difference by saying that what we have a right to believe in today is a law of nature *with a variable content.*

In the second place, when medieval writers spoke of natural law as able to overrule conflicting positive law, they were introducing an anarchical principle which we must reject. But this was a principle which died hard, and even in the eighteenth century Blackstone could write: 'This law of nature, being coeval with mankind and dictated by God himself, is of course superior in obligation to any other. It is binding all over the globe in all countries, and at all times; *no human laws are of any validity, if contrary to this.*'[12]

---

12. *Commentaries on the Laws of England*, Book I, Introduction (emphasis added) (1765–1769).

In Blackstone, however, such words were mere lip-service to a tradition, and had no effect on his exposition of the law. To hold, however, that unreasonableness can invalidate a rule of law is to confuse the function of legislation with that of ascertaining what existing law is. Law could never perform its proper function of a controlling force in society if courts of law did not hold themselves bound to subordinate their own ideas of what is reasonable to an assumed superior reasonableness in the law; that assumption may not always be well founded, but it is necessary to our social security that it should be acted upon until the law is altered.

These are valid criticisms, but they do not affect the permanent truths in the conception of a law of nature, and though today we generally use a different terminology, we recognize the validity of those truths as fully as ever. For one thing, the law of nature stands for the existence of *purpose* in law, reminding us that law is not a meaningless set of arbitrary principles to be mechanically applied by courts, but that it exists for certain ends, though those ends may have to be differently formulated in different times and places. Thus where we might say that our aim is to embody social justice in law (giving to that term whatever interpretation is current in the thought of our time), a medieval thinker might have said that the validity of positive law must be tested by its conformity or otherwise to a law of higher obligation, the law of nature.

Natural law, therefore, or a similar principle under some other name, is an essential underlying principle of the art of legislation. But that is not all; it is also a principle that is necessarily admitted into the actual administration of law. This is so because any system of law has to deal with life which is too complicated, and human foresight too limited for law to be completely formulated in a set of rules. Situations perpetually arise which fall outside the rules as formulated. Law cannot, and does not, refuse to solve a problem because it is new and unprovided for. Law meets such situations by resorting to a principle, outside formulated law, whose presence is not always admitted. In fact it falls back on the solution which the court or the jury think is reasonable under the circumstances. The English Common Law is perpetually appealing to reason as the justification of its decisions, asking what is a reasonable time, or what is a reasonable price, or what a reasonable person would do in given circumstances. We do not suppose that our answers to those questions will be scientific truths; it is enough if they are approximately just; but on the other hand we do not attempt to eliminate this test of reasonableness by substituting fixed rules, because it would be impossible to do so. But this appeal to reason is merely to appeal to a law of nature. Sometimes, indeed, English law still uses the term 'natural justice', and our courts have to do their best to decide what 'natural justice' requires in particular circumstances. For example, in 1924 the Northern Rhodesia Order in Council, providing for the administration of that protectorate, enacted that, in civil cases between natives, Rhodesian courts were to be guided by native laws as far as applicable and *not repugnant to natural justice*. The Rhodesian courts would have had little difficulty in interpreting this instruction.[13]

'The grandest function of the Law of Nature', Sir Henry Maine wrote, 'was discharged in giving birth to modern International Law and to the modern Law of War';[14] and even if such a founda-

---

13. Cf C. Huntington, 'Law and Anthropology', 31/1 *Columbia Law Review* (1931) 32–55 at 55.

14. *Ancient Law*, ch. iv.

tion had not been a sound one, no other would have been possible in the sixteenth century. Afterwards, in the seventeenth and eighteenth centuries, the medieval tradition of a law to which man's rational nature bids him everywhere, and always, to conform, became obscured, and later writers returned to another meaning of the term, traces of which are also to be found in Stoic and early Christian writers. They used the law of nature to denote a law under which men are supposed to have lived in a *state of nature,* that is to say, in an imaginary pre-political condition of human society which they are supposed to have left behind when they formed themselves into political societies.[15] This development had unfortunate effects on international law, but let us first turn to the men whose writings gave that law systematic form.

§ 4. The classical writers on international law

The recognition of international law as a separate object of study dates from the latter part of the sixteenth century. Earlier writers had written on some of the topics which fall within modern international law, especially on the usages of war and on the treatment of ambassadors, but they did not separate the legal from the theological and ethical, or the domestic from the international aspects of such questions. Thus side by side with questions such as whether war is ever justified, what causes for going to war are lawful and what unlawful, what means of waging war are permissible, and the like, they discussed questions of tactics, of military discipline, or the duties of a

---

15. Below, 34–5, 51–2.

vassal to help his lord, without any sense that they were lumping together topics which properly belonged to different subjects.

Theological writers especially were concerned with the perplexing ethical problems to which the practice of warfare gives rise, and a series of great Spanish Churchmen of the fifteenth and sixteenth centuries made important contributions to the progress of thought on these matters. Perhaps the greatest of these was Francisco de Vitoria, Professor of Theology at Salamanca from 1526 to 1546, whose *Relectiones theologicae,* published after his death, contained, in two courses of lectures, the *Relectiones De Indis* and *De jure belli Hispanorum in Barbaros,* an examination of the title of the Spaniards to exercise domination over the inhabitants of the New World. The work is remarkable for its courageous defence of the rights of the indigenous people being conquered. In this, Vitoria's teaching marks an important step in the expansion of international law into a world system; for it meant that a law which had its rise among the few princes of European Christendom was not to be limited to them, or to their relations with one another, but was universally valid, founded as it was on a natural law applying equally to all men everywhere. The work of these early Spanish writers has been unfairly neglected, especially in Protestant countries, but, interest in them has been revived, and their importance is now properly appreciated.[16]

Alberico Gentili, commonly known as Gentilis, an Italian Protestant who fled to England to avoid persecution and became Pro-

---

16. See J.B. Scott, *The Spanish Origin of International Law* (Oxford: Clarendon Press, 1935); and C.R. Rossi, *Broken Chain of Being: James Brown Scott and the Origins of Modern International Law* (The Hague: Nijhoff, 1998).

fessor of Civil Law in Oxford, was perhaps the first writer to make a definite separation of international law from theology and ethics, and to treat it as a branch of jurisprudence. He wrote, in his most important work, *De jure belli,* published in 1598: 'Let the theologians keep silence about a matter which is outside their province.'[17] Gentili's more famous successor, Hugo de Groot, or Grotius, was, as he himself admitted, greatly indebted to this book, but otherwise it appears to have exercised little influence, and the very name of Gentilis is often forgotten.[18]

Grotius was born in Holland in 1583, and died in 1645. Even as a boy he acquired a European reputation for learning, and as a man he became master of every subject to which he turned his interest. He was a lawyer, an historian, a poet, as well as a theologian whose great desire was to see the reunion of the Christian Church. Yet he lived the life, not of a student, but of a man of affairs, practising the law and serving in official positions. He became involved in disputes which were nominally concerned with matters of theology, but in which the real issue was a political one—the question whether the provinces of Holland should form

17. *Silete theologi in munene alieno,* Book I, ch. XII, *in fine. Classics of International Law,* J.C. Rolfe tr. (Oxford: Clarendon Press, 1933) vol. II at 57; Peter Haggenmacher has suggested that the significance of this sentence has sometimes been exaggerated. He reminds us that Gentili was prepared to abandon certain questions relating to religion to the *theologians,* and that there was 'a division of competences, rather than a general secularization of law, which seems to be at the bottom of Gentili's celebrated exclamation.' He also adds: 'The sentence is probably also an echo of the bitter quarrel that had opposed him to the puritan faction in the University of Oxford.' 'Grotius and Gentili: A Reassessment of Thomas E. Holland's Inaugural Lecture', in H. Bull, B. Kingsbury, and A. Roberts (eds), *Hugo Grotius and International Relations* (Oxford: Clarendon Press, 1990) 133–76, at 171.

18. On the reasons for the comparative success of Grotius see P. Haggenmacher, ibid.

a loose federal union or be consolidated under the House of Orange. Grotius supported the former and the losing cause. After being imprisoned for over two years, he escaped, thanks to the devotion of his wife, in a box which his captors supposed to contain books, and eventually became Ambassador of Sweden at the French Court.

Few books have won so great a reputation as Grotius's *De jure belli ac pacis,* but to regard its author as the 'founder' of international law is to exaggerate its originality and to do less than justice to the writers who preceded him; neither Grotius, nor any other single writer, can properly be said to have 'founded' the system. The reputation of the book was not wholly due to its own merits, though these are great; it was partly due to the time and circumstances of its publication. When he wrote it in 1625 Grotius was already so eminent that anything from his pen would have attracted attention. Further, he had the advantage of belonging to the country which at that time was in many ways the leading country in Europe.

The successful war of liberation by the Dutch against Spain in the previous century had heralded the rise of the modern state system; it had been the first great triumph of the idea of nationality, and the successful assertion of the right of revolt against universal monarchy. In the seventeenth century the Dutch were the leaders of European civilization, teaching other countries, not only new methods of commerce, but also new conceptions of government based on freer institutions and on a measure of religious toleration. While the issue of absolutism or liberty was still in doubt in England, and when everywhere else absolutism was triumphant and destined to remain so until the French Revolution, the Dutch had settled the issue in their own country in favour of liberty.

Some of the qualities which render Grotius's book tedious to a modern reader, especially the voluminous citation of authorities from ancient history and the Bible, and the excessively subtle distinctions, commended the book to the taste of his contemporaries still familiar with the tradition of scholasticism. Grotius's purpose was, however, practical. He explains his aim as follows:

> Fully convinced, by the considerations which I have advanced, that there is a common law among nations, which is valid alike for war and in war, I have had many and weighty reasons for undertaking to write upon this subject. Throughout the Christian World I observed a lack of restraint in relation to war, such as even barbarous races should be ashamed of; I observed that men rush to arms for slight causes, or no cause at all, and that when arms have once been taken up there is no longer any respect for law, divine or human; it is as if, in accordance with a general decree, frenzy had openly been let loose for the committing of all crimes.[19]

In contrast with this anarchy, he proclaimed that even states ought to regard themselves as members of a society, bound together by the universal supremacy of justice. Man, he said, is not a purely selfish animal, for among the qualities that belong to him is an *appetitus societatis,* a desire for the society of his own kind, and the need to preserve this society is the source of the law of nature, which he defines in the first book as:

---

19. Prolegomena, 28. *The Classics of International Law*, J.B. Scott (ed.), F.W. Kelsey (trans.) (Washington: Carnegie Institution, 1913–25) vol. II at 20.

a dictate of right reason, which points out that an act, according as it is or is not in conformity with rational nature, has in it a quality of moral baseness or moral necessity; and that, in consequence, such an act is either forbidden or enjoined by the author of nature, God.[20]

Besides being subject to natural law, he says, the relations of peoples are subject to *jus gentium;* for just as in each state the civil laws look to the good of the state, so there are laws established by consent which look to the good of the great community of which all, or most, states are members, and these laws make up *jus gentium.* It is obvious that this is a very different meaning from that which the term bore in the Roman law; there, as we saw, it stood for that part of the *private* law of Rome which was supposed to be common to Rome and other peoples; whereas in Grotius it has come to be a branch of *public* law, governing the relations between one people and another. It is important, Grotius tells us, to keep the notions of the law of nature and the law of nations (to adopt a mistranslation of *jus gentium* which its new meaning makes almost necessary) distinct; but he failed to do so himself. Nor was it possible for him to do so, as is apparent from his own statement of how their respective contents are to be discovered. He used, he tells us, the testimony of philosophers, historians, poets, and orators, not because they were themselves conclusive witnesses, but because when they were found to be in agreement, their agreement could only be explained in one of two ways: either what they said must be a correct deduction from the principles of reason, and so a rule of the

---

20. Book I, ch. X § 1. Ibid 38–9 (footnote omitted).

law of nature; or else it must be a matter on which common consent existed, and so a rule of the law of nations. Thus in effect the two terms, as we have already seen, still express the theoretical and the practical sides of the same idea.

Like all thinkers who try to understand the meaning and bases of law, Grotius had to meet the perennial and plausible arguments of those who would identify justice with mere utility. His answer was clear and convincing. Justice, he said, is indeed the highest utility, and, merely on that ground, neither a state nor the community of states can be preserved without it. But it is also more than utility, because it is part of our true social nature, and that is the basis of our obligation to ensure justice.

Grotius's work consisted in the application of these fundamental principles to war; for he says:

> Least of all should that be admitted which some people imagine, that in war all laws are in abeyance. On the contrary war ought not to be undertaken except for the enforcement of rights; when once undertaken, it should be carried on only within the bounds of law and good faith. Demosthenes well said that war is directed against those who cannot be held in check by judicial process. For judgements are efficacious against those who feel that they are too weak to resist; against those who are equally strong, or think they are, wars are undertaken. But in order that wars may be justified, they must be carried on with not less scrupulousness than judicial processes are wont to be.
>
> Let the laws be silent, then, in the midst of arms, but only the laws of the State, those that the courts are concerned with,

that are adapted only to a state of peace; not those other laws, which are of perpetual validity and suited to all times. It was exceedingly well said by Dio of Prusa, that between enemies written laws, that is laws of particular states, are not in force, but that unwritten laws are in force, that is, those which nature prescribes, or the agreement of nations has established.[21]

The first book, therefore, inquires whether war can ever be *justum,* lawful or regular; and as Grotius was of the opinion that one requirement necessary to make a war lawful was that it should be waged under the authority of one who held supreme power in the state, he was therefore led to inquire into the nature of sovereignty. His treatment of this subject was unsatisfactory and confused. By denying that government necessarily exists for the sake of the governed, and treating sovereignty as a proprietary right, a *jus regendi* capable of vesting in sovereigns as fully and in the same way as rights over things vest in private persons, Grotius encouraged the unfortunate trend of opinion towards a view of sovereignty as absolute and unaccountable power. He had to admit, too, writing when he did, that wars waged by subordinate feudatory princes, who could only be regarded as holding *summa potestas* by a transparent fiction, might be lawful, and this made much of his treatment of the subject inconsistent with his own definition. In the second book Grotius dealt with the causes of war, and in effect reduced the causes of lawful wars to two, the defence of persons or property and the punishment of offenders.

---

21. Prolegomena, §§ 25, 26, ibid 18–20 (footnote omitted).

Grotius then proceeded to examine such questions as for example: what constitutes the property of a state, how much of the sea is the state's property, how property is acquired and lost, and other questions which a modern writer would either place under the international law of peace, or exclude from international law altogether. In the third book he dealt with topics which fall under the modern laws of war, that is to say, with questions such as what acts are permissible and what are forbidden in the conduct of war. Here his plan was not only to state the strict laws of war, but to add what he called *temperamenta,* alleviations or modifications designed to make war more humane.

It is usual in estimating the work of Grotius to speak of its remarkable and instantaneous success; and if it is a proof of success that within a few years of its author's death his book had become a university textbook, that it has often since been appealed to in international controversies, that it has been republished and translated scores of times, and that every subsequent writer treats his name with reverence, however widely he may depart from his teaching, then Grotius must be accounted successful. But, if by success is meant that the doctrines of Grotius as a whole were accepted by states and became part of the law which since his time has regulated their relations, then his work was an almost complete failure.

It is true that some of his doctrines have since become established law. For instance, the doctrine that the open sea cannot be subjected to the sovereignty of any state, and many of the *temperamenta* of war that he suggested have been incorporated into international law; but these particular changes were due at least as much to changes in the character of navigation, and in the technique of war, respectively, as to Grotius. At the heart of his system lay the attempt to distinguish between lawful and unlawful war, *bellum justum* and *bellum injustum*. He saw that international order is precarious unless that distinction can be established, just as national order would be precarious if the law within the state did not distinguish between the lawful and the unlawful use of force. But this distinction never became part of actual international law.

In attempting to establish this distinction Grotius was following a tradition which the classical writers on international law had inherited from the theologians and canonists of the Middle Ages; indeed it goes back as far as to Saint Augustine in the fourth century of the Christian era. But he was well aware of the difficulties of making it prevail in view of the obstinate fact that states persisted in treating the making of war as a matter of policy and not of law. He summed up these difficulties under two main heads.[22] One was that of knowing which of the parties to any particular war had the right on his side; the other was the danger that other states incur if they presume to judge of the rights and wrongs of a war and take action to restrain the wrong-doer. Any scheme for eliminating war has still to grapple with these two difficulties; the first is our modern problem of determining the 'aggressor', and the second is that of 'collective security', of somehow placing behind the law the united force of the society of states, while ensuring at the same time protection to the states which lend their help. Neither Grotius nor the writers who followed him in the seventeenth and

---

22. *De jure belli ac pacis*, Book III ch. XII and ch. XXIII.

eighteenth centuries could see any way of overcoming these difficulties, and he fell back on the lame conclusion that the only practical course was not to ask third states to judge the lawfulness or
otherwise of a war, but to leave that question to the conscience of
the belligerents.

It has to be admitted, therefore, that the attempt to establish a
distinction in law between lawfully and unlawfully making war was
largely unreal, and it was retained by most of Grotius's successors
more as an ornament to their theme, than as a doctrine in which they
seriously believed. Later, it disappeared even from theory, and international law came frankly to recognize for a while that all wars are
equally lawful. The foundation of the League of Nations in 1919
marked the first real attempt to falsify this confession of weakness
and to embody in actual law the cardinal principle of Grotius's system. The eventual adoption of the UN Charter of 1945 finally heralded a principle on the non-use of force to be respected by its
members with the promise that the UN would ensure respect for this
principle by all states.[23] We will discuss this principle in detail later on
in this book. Let us finish now our survey of the classical writers.

Richard Zouche (1590–1660), Professor of Civil Law in
Oxford University and judge of the Court of Admiralty, produced a number of works on legal subjects, including one on
international law, the *Jus et judicium feciale, sive jus inter gentes,*
published in 1650.[24] This has been called 'the first manual of

---

23. Although Article 2(4) is addressed to member states, Article 2(6) states that the UN
shall ensure that non-member states act in accordance with the principles of the UN in
the context of the maintenance of international peace and security.
24. *The Classics of International Law*, T.E. Holland (ed.), J.L. Brierly (trans.) (Washington: Carnegie Institution, 1911).

international law',[25] for it discusses briefly, but clearly, almost every part of the subject. Without abandoning the law of nature as one of the bases of international law, Zouche preferred to deduce the law from the precedents of state practice, and he is sometimes regarded as a precursor of the 'positive' school of international lawyers, who regard the practice of states as the only source of law. Zouche introduced one important improvement of method, for he was the first writer to make a clear division between the law of peace and the law of war, and to make the former the more prominent of the two. This was necessary before war could be regarded, as it ought to be, as an abnormal relationship between states.

Samuel Pufendorf (1632–94), Professor at Heidelberg, and afterwards at Lund in Sweden, published his *De jure naturae et gentium* in 1672, and may be regarded as the founder of the so-called 'naturalist' school of writers. He denied any binding force to the practice of nations, and based his system wholly on natural law, but on a natural law in the new and debased form of a law supposed to be binding upon men in an imaginary *state of nature*.

Cornelius van Bynkershoek (1673–1743), a Dutch judge, was the author of works on special topics of international law, of which the most important was the *Quaestiones juris publici*, published in 1737. Bynkershoek had an intimate knowledge of questions of maritime and commercial practice, and he has an important place in the development of that side of international law. He belongs to

---

25. Scelle, 'Zouche' in *Les fondateurs du droit international* (Paris: Giard and Brière, 1904) at 322.

the 'positive' school of writers, basing the law on custom, but holding also that custom must be explained and controlled by reason, which he refers to as *ratio Juris Gentium magistra*.[26] He held also that the recent practice of states was more valuable evidence of custom than the illustrations from ancient history with which his predecessors had generally adorned their works, since, 'as the habits and customs of nations change, so does the law of nations';[27] but he attached more weight to the stipulations of particular treaties as evidence of the existence of custom than modern practice would allow.

Emerich de Vattel (1714–69), whose work *Le Droit des gens* was published in 1758, was a Swiss who served in the diplomatic service of Saxony. He intended his work as a manual for men of affairs, and was a popularizer of other men's ideas rather than an original thinker; yet he has probably exercised a greater permanent influence than any other writer on international law, and his work is still sometimes cited as an authority in international disputes. He accepted the doctrine of the *state of nature*: 'Nations being composed of men naturally free and independent, and who, before the establishment of civil societies, lived together in the state of nature;—nations or sovereign states are to be considered as so many free persons living together in the state of nature'; and since men are naturally equal, so are states. 'Power or weakness does not in this respect produce any difference. A dwarf is as much a man as a giant; a small republic is no less a sovereign state than the most

---

26. *Quaestiones*, vol. I, ch. 12 (Oxford: Clarendon, 1930) at 95.
27. Ibid vol. II, T. Frank (trans.), 'To the Reader' at 7.

powerful kingdom.'[28] Thus the doctrine of the equality of states, a misleading deduction from unsound premisses,[29] was introduced into the theory of international law.

According to Vattel, the law of nations *in its origin* is merely the law of nature applied to nations, it is not subject to change, and treaties or customs contrary to it are unlawful. But other elements have been admitted into the law; for, says Vattel, natural law itself establishes the freedom and independence of every state, and therefore each is the sole judge of its own actions and accountable for its observance of natural law only to its own conscience. Other states may *request* it to reform its conduct; but what they may actually *demand* from it is something much less. This lower standard of *enforceable* duties Vattel calls the *voluntary* law of nations, because it is to be presumed that states have agreed to it, in contrast with the other element of natural, or as he calls it, *necessary* law. 'Though the *necessary* law be the rule which he invariably observes in his own conduct, he should allow others to avail themselves of the *voluntary* law of nations.'[30]

This exaggerated emphasis on the independence of states had the effect in Vattel's system of reducing the natural law, which Grotius had used as a juridical barrier against arbitrary action by states towards one another, to little more than an aspiration for better relations between states; yet for the *voluntary* law, which was the

---

28. E. de Vattel, *The Law of Nations, or Principles of the Law of Nature, Applied to the Conduct and Affairs of Nations and Sovereigns* (1797), B. Kapossy and R. Whatmore (eds), T. Nugent (trans.) (Indianapolis: Liberty Fund, 2008) Preliminaries § 4, at 68.

29. Ibid § 18, at 75.

30. Ibid Book III, ch. 12, § 189, at 590.

only part of Vattel's system which had a real relation to the practice of states, he provided no sound basis in theory, for he was unable to explain the source of the obligation of states to observe it. The results of this unsatisfactory division were unfortunate. For instance, Vattel tells us that by the *necessary* law a state has a duty to maintain free trade, because this is for the advantage of the human race; but by the *voluntary* law that state may impose any restrictions it wants in any proposed trading treaty, for its duties to itself are more important than its duties to others.[31] By *necessary* law, again, for Vattel there are only three lawful causes of war: self-defence, redress of injury, and punishment of offences; but by *voluntary* law we must apparently always assume that each side has a lawful cause for going to war, for 'princes may have had wise and just reasons for acting thus: and this is sufficient at the tribunal of the voluntary law of nations.'[32]

In some respects, however, Vattel's system was an advance on those of his predecessors. He stood for a more humane view of the rights of nations in war. He rejected the patrimonial theory of the nature of government which Grotius had held: 'this pretended proprietary right attributed to princes is a chimera, produced by an abuse which its supporters would fain make of the laws respecting private *inheritances*. The state neither is nor can be a patrimony, since the end of patrimony is the advantage of the possessor, whereas the prince is established only for the advantage of the

---

31. Ibid Book II, ch. 2, § 25, at 275 and see also Book 1, §§ 92 and 98.
32. Ibid Book II, ch. 18, § 335, at 457.

state.'[33] He recognized in certain circumstances the right of part of a nation to separate itself from the rest,[34] a doctrine which partly explains his great popularity in the United States, where a copy of the work was first received in 1775.[35] Professor De Lapradelle justly wrote of him that:

before the great events of 1776 and 1789 occurred, he had written an international law, based on the principles of public law which two Revolutions, the American and the French, were to make effective. Although his work is dated 1758, it is in full accord with the American principles of 1789. It has encountered the same resistance, has undergone the same temporary set-backs, and finally has shared the same success. Vattel's *Law of Nations* is international law based on the principles of 1789 – the complement of the *Contrat social* of Rousseau, the projection upon the plane of the Law of

---

33. Ibid Book I, ch. 5, § 61, at 114–15, the paragraph continues: 'The consequence is evident: if a nation plainly perceives that the heir of her prince would be a pernicious sovereign, she has a right to exclude him.'

34. Book I. 1 ch. 7, although Vattel demands that if the city or province is overcome by force then 'necessity' frees it from its former duty of loyalty. The examples he gives are the country of Zug coming under attack from the Swiss (Uri, Schwyz, and Unterwalden) and then choosing to join the Swiss Confederation in 1352, and the city of Zurich similarly opting to join the Confederation in 1351.

35. Interestingly different Justices of the Supreme Court in the *Dred Scott Case* relied on Vattel both in support of slavery and against it. For the *independence* of states was said to lead to the inherent right in nature for a State of the Union to be free to make its own laws, while on the other hand the law of nations suggested an international morality inspired by natural rights. As explained by M.W. Janis, *America and the Law of Nations 1776–1939* (Oxford: OUP, 2010) at 105–9.

Nations of the great principles of legal individualism. That is what makes Vattel's work important, what accounts for his success, characterizes his influence, and, eventually, likewise, measures his shortcomings. Grotius had written the international law of absolutism, Vattel has written the international law of political liberty.[36]

All the same, the survival of Vattel's influence into an age when the 'principles of legal individualism' are no longer adequate to international needs, if they ever were, has been a disaster for international law. By teaching that the 'natural' state of nations is an independence which does not admit the existence of a social bond between them, he made it impossible to explain or justify their subjection to law; yet their independence is no more 'natural' than their interdependence. Both are facts of which any true theory of international relations must take account. Independence is more conspicuous but not more real than interdependence. It is true that in Vattel's own day the interdependence of states was less conspicuous in international practice than it is today, and this partly excuses the overwhelming priority he gives to independence and voluntary obligations. Nevertheless by cutting the frail moorings which bound international law to any sound principle of obliga-

---

36. 'Introduction' to Vattel's *Le Droit des Gens, ou Principes de la Loi Naturelle, appliqués à la Conduite et aux Affaires des Nations et des Souverains,* C.G. Fenwick (trans.) (Washington: Carnegie Institution of Washington, 1916) at lv. For a recent reappraisal of Vattel's influence see V. Chetail and P. Haggenmacher (eds), *Vattel's International Law from a XXIst Century Perspective* (Leiden, Nijhoff, 2011).

tion, Vattel did international law an injury which has yet to be repaired.[37]

---

37. For further introduction to the early writings see C. Covell, *The Law of Nations in Political Thought: A Critical Survey from Vitoria to Hegel* (Basingstoke: Palgrave, 2009); this is not the place to give a detailed examination of later writings, but readers who are interested in the 'sensibilities' of subsequent generations of international lawyers writing later should see the fascinating account by M. Koskenniemi, *The Gentle Civilizer of Nations: The Rise and Fall of International Law 1870–1960* (Cambridge: CUP, 2001); for a sociology of twentieth century international lawyers in the United States see D. Kennedy, 'The Twentieth-Century Discipline of International Law in the United States', in A. Sarat, B. Garth, and R.A. Kagan (eds), *Looking Back at Law's Century* (Ithaca: Cornell University Press, 2002) 386–433; on the significance of Marxist concepts see S. Marks (ed), *International Law on the Left: Re-examining Marxist Legacies* (Cambridge: CUP, 2008). A very useful introduction to contemporary ways of looking at international law, or what some call 'methods', is S.R. Ratner and A.-M. Slaughter (eds), *The Methods of International Law* (Washington: American Society of International Law, 2004). This short book covers positivism, policy orientated jurisprudence (New Haven School), international legal process, critical legal studies, international law and international relations, law and economics, feminist jurisprudence, and Third World approaches to international law (TWAIL). On the last two approaches see further H. Charlesworth and C. Chinkin, *The Boundaries of International Law: A feminist analysis*, (Manchester: MUP, 2000); M. Matua, 'What is TWAIL?' 31 *American Society of International Law Proceedings* (2000) 31–8; A. Anghie, *Imperialism, Sovereignty and the Making of International Law* (Cambridge: CUP 2005); B.S. Chimini, 'Third World Approaches to International Law: A Manifesto', 8(1) *International Community Law Review* (2006) 3–27; B. Rajogopal, *International Law From Below; Development, Social Movements and Third World Resistance* 2nd edn (Cambridge: CUP, 2010); S. Pahuja, *Decolonising International Law: Development, Economic Growth and the Politics of Universality* (Cambridge: CUP, 2011).

II | The Basis of Obligation in International Law

§ 1. The international society

LAW can only exist in a society, and there can be no society without a system of law to regulate the relations of its members with one another. If then we speak of the 'law of nations', we are assuming that a 'society' of nations exists, and the assumption that the whole world constitutes some sort of single society or community needs further examination. In any event the character of the law of nations is necessarily determined by the character of the society in which it operates.

We are witnessing the growth of factors that make states mutually dependent on one another. Science and technology have eased communications and travel, while the developing international trading system facilitates commerce in goods and services between nations. Feelings of nationalism seem to have given way in part to a more integrated world. But we may not be creating a greater sense of society.

If human affairs were more wisely ordered, and if people were as focused on the interests of others as they are on their own interests, it might be that this interdependence of the nations would lead to a

41

strengthening of their feelings of community. But this interdependence is mainly in material things, and though material bonds are necessary, they are not enough without a common social consciousness; without that, material interests are as likely to lead to friction as to friendship. Some sentiment of shared responsibility for the conduct of a common life is a necessary element in any society and the necessary force behind any system of law; and the strength of any legal system is proportionate to the strength of such a sentiment.

Hobbes, in a famous passage in the *Leviathan* (1651), has described how he saw the relations of states to one another:

> But though there had never been any time, wherein particular men were in a condition of warre one against another, yet in all times, Kings and Persons of Soveraigne authority, because of their Independency, are in continuall jealousies, and in the state and posture of Gladiators; having their weapons pointing, and their eyes fixed on one another; that is, their Forts, Garrisons, and Guns upon the Frontiers of their Kingdomes, and continuall Spyes upon their neighbours, which is a posture of War.[1]

And in our times we continue to witness gross cruelty to others, and persecution on grounds of race, religion, ethnicity, or language. All this makes it hard to believe today in the reality of a

---

1. Above, ch. 13 at 90. The passage continues later: 'To this warre of every man, against every man, this also is consequent; that nothing can be Unjust. The notions of Right and Wrong, Justice and Injustice have there no place. Where there is no common Power, there is no Law; where no Law, no Injustice.'

single world society; and it would be foolish to underrate the difficulties of creating one. Those difficulties have not decreased, but may indeed have intensified.

In part this is due to a profound change in our ideas of the nature of law. We have seen how international law had its origin in natural law, that is to say, in the belief that nations must be bound to one another by law because it is a principle of nature that our world should be a system of order and not chaos; and that therefore states, despite their independence, can claim no exception to this universal rule. But with the passing of the Middle Ages, this view of the nature of law was gradually dethroned by the growth of positivist theories according to which all law is nothing but the command of a superior will over an inferior. For international law this modern view of law has been especially unfortunate, and we will return to this issue. Here it need only be pointed out that the result of positivism has been to secularize the whole idea of law, and thus to weaken the moral foundation which is essential to the vitality of all legal obligation.

A world society will not come into existence without conscious human effort. The problem of world community remains essentially a moral problem, it is also in part a problem of leadership, and that international society needs institutions through which its members can learn to work together for common social ends. The League of Nations was the first great experiment with that end in view, and we know that it failed. A second came with the United Nations, which has proven more successful, even if many will remain disappointed. But it is right that we should remember that a relatively short time has passed since the building of a world community began to be seen as a practical problem, and it is only fairly recently that most of us began to see that the problem is really urgent.

§ 2. The modern 'sovereign' state

The previous chapter traced the curious metamorphosis which transformed the doctrine of sovereignty from a principle of internal order, as Bodin and even Hobbes had conceived it, into one of international anarchy.

Sovereignty started in Bodin's writings as a formal juristic concept in the sixteenth century, the attribute of a personal monarch entrusted by the constitution with supreme authority over the ordinary laws of the state. Sovereignty, under the momentum of the historical developments which took place in the character of European governments, then came to be regarded as power absolute and above the law. Eventually, when it became impossible to fix the location of such power in any definite person or organ within the state, sovereignty became seen as the attribute of the personified state itself.

The doctrine of sovereignty was developed for the most part by political theorists who were not interested in, and paid little regard to, the relations of states with one another. And in its later forms sovereignty not only involved a denial of the possibility of states being subject to any kind of law, but became an impossible theory for a world which contained more states than one.

Writers on international law have attempted in various ingenious ways to reconcile the existence of their subject with the doctrine of the absolute sovereignty of states, but all these devices are in effect variations of the theory of the auto-limitation of sovereignty discussed below. One formula, for example, is to say that international law is a law of *co-ordination* but not of *subordination,* and even Oppenheim in the twentieth century, though he was no believer in absolute sovereignty, felt obliged to attribute to international law a specific character not shared by law in general. He told us that the law of nations is usually regarded as a law *between,* but not *above,* the several states.[2] Yet if states are the subjects of international law, as Oppenheim admits that they are, international law must surely be above them, and they must be subordinate to it.

The American judge Cardozo warned us that when we treat certain concepts as if they exist and develop them without considering their consequences, these concepts become our tyrants rather than our servants. We ought to deal with our concepts, he told us, always as provisional hypotheses, to be reformulated and restrained when their outcomes lead to oppression and injustice.[3] It would be better if international lawyers could simply invoke this reasoning and erase the nightmare of the doctrine of sovereignty. But sovereignty, however much it may need reformulating as a political doctrine, does stand today for something in the relations of states which is both true and very formidable. It expresses, though in a misleading way, the claims that states habitually make that they may act as they see fit without restraints on their freedom.

---

2. *International Law: a Treatise (the Law of Peace)*, H. Lauterpacht (ed.), 6th edn, vol. i (London: Longmans, 1947) 6.

3. B.N. Cardozo, *Paradoxes of Legal Science* (New York: Columbia University Press, 1928) 65; see also K. Popper, *Conjectures and Refutations: The growth of scientific knowledge* (London: Routledge Classics, 2002).

For the practical purposes of an international lawyer, sovereignty is not a metaphysical concept, nor is it part of the essence of statehood; it is merely a term which designates an aggregate of particular and very extensive claims that states habitually make for themselves in their relations with other states. To the extent that sovereignty has come to imply that there is something inherent in the nature of states that makes it impossible for them to be subjected to law, it is a false doctrine which the facts of international relations do not support. But to the extent that it reminds us that the challenge of subjection of states to law is an aim as yet only very imperfectly realized, it is a doctrine which we cannot afford to disregard.

The fundamental difficulty of subjecting states to the rule of law is the fact that states possess power. The legal control of power is always difficult, and it is not only for international law that it constitutes a problem. The domestic law of every state has the same problem; though usually in a less acute form. In any decently governed state, domestic law can normally deal effectively with the behaviour of individuals, but that is because the individual is weak, and society is relatively strong; but when people join together in associations or factions for the achievement of some purpose which the members have in common, the problem of the law becomes more difficult. Union always gives strength, and when the members of these bodies are numerous, when they can command powerful resources, and when they feel strongly that the interests which their combination exists to protect are vital to themselves, they may develop a tendency to pursue their purposes extra-legally, or even illegally, without much regard to the legal nexus which nominally binds them to the rest of the society. In fact, they behave inside the state in a way that is similar to the way in which sovereign states behave in the international society.

§ 3. The basis of obligation in modern international law

Traditionally there are two rival doctrines which attempt to answer the question why states should be bound to observe the rules of international law: the doctrine of the natural or fundamental rights of states, and the doctrine of their consent. Powerful attacks have been made on both these doctrines in the literature, but they have their defenders, and it is worth examining these two doctrines in turn.

The doctrine of 'natural rights' is a corollary of the doctrine of the 'state of nature', in which individuals are supposed to have lived before they formed themselves into political communities or states; for states, not having formed themselves into a super-state, are still supposed by the adherents of this doctrine to be living in such a condition. Natural rights doctrine teaches that the primary principles of international law can be deduced from the essential nature of the state. Every state, the theory goes, by the very fact that it is a state, is endowed with certain fundamental, or inherent, or natural, rights.

Writers differ in how they enumerate what these rights are, but generally five rights are claimed, namely self-preservation, independence, equality, respect, and intercourse. It is obvious that this doctrine of fundamental rights is merely the old doctrine of the natural 'rights of man' transferred to states. That doctrine played a great part in history; Locke justified the English Revolution by it, and from Locke it passed to the leaders of the American Revolution and became the philosophical basis of the Declaration of Independence. But hardly any political scientist today would regard it as a true philosophy of political relations; and all the objections to it apply with even greater force when it is applied to the relations of states. It implies that individuals or states, as the case may be, bring with them into society certain primordial rights not derived from their membership of society, but inherent in their personality as individuals, and that out of these rights a legal system is formed; whereas the truth is that a *legal right* is a meaningless phrase unless we first assume the existence of a *legal system* from which it gets its validity.

Furthermore, the doctrine implies that the social bond between individuals, or between states, is somehow less natural, or less a part of the whole personality, than is the individuality of the human being or the state, and that is not true; the only individuals we know are individuals-in-society. It is especially misleading to apply this atomistic view of the nature of the social bond to states. In its application to individuals it has a certain plausibility, because it seems to give a philosophical justification to the common feeling that human personality has certain claims on society; and in that way it has played its part in the development of human liberty. But in the society of states there is no need for individual states to enjoy greater liberty, but rather the need is to strengthen the social bond between them. Rather than providing for the vociferous assertion of the rights of states, we need to insist on reminding them of their obligations towards one another.

Finally, the doctrine of sovereignty is really a denial of the possibility of development in international relations. When the doctrine asserts that such qualities as independence and equality are inherent in the very nature of states, it overlooks the fact that such an attribution to states is merely a stage in an historical process. We know that until modern times states were not regarded as either independent or equal, and we have no right to assume that the process of development has stopped. On the contrary it is not improbable, and it is certainly desirable, that there should be a movement towards the closer interdependence of states.

The doctrine of positivism,[4] on the other hand, teaches that international law is the sum of the rules by which states have *consented* to be bound, and that nothing can be law unless they have

---

4. The background to aspects of the positivist tradition is explained by S.C. Neff: 'By "positivism" is meant such a wealth of things that it may be best to avoid using the term altogether. As originally coined in the 1830s by the French social philosopher Auguste Comte, it meant something like "scientific" or "objective" or "empirical", in contrast to speculative or religious or hypothetico-deductive modes of thought. Comte posited that the human race had gone through three great historical stages: the theological, the metaphysical, and (now) the "positive". In the theological stage, religious ideas had been dominant. In the metaphysical stage, legalistic and jurisprudential ideas had prevailed—meaning, in essence, natural law. But the third stage was now dawning. A "positive" era (as Comte called it) promised to bring the true and final liberation of the human mind from the superstitions and dogmas of the past.' Neff goes on to explain that the positivist outlook viewed voluntary law as a point of principle so that this came to be seen as the *'only* true source of law'. And there developed an 'insistence on the independent nation-State as the fundamental unit of international law. This inevitably gave to positivism a strongly pluralistic cast.' 'A Short History of International Law' in M. Evans (ed.), *International Law*, 2nd edn (Oxford: OUP, 2006) 29–55, at 38–9. See further R. Ago who explains that legal positivists determined that positive law only existed when created by a 'formal source' and that for them it is 'necessary to exclude from the formal sources of positive law all processes which cannot directly or indirectly be traced back to the will of the State. This tenet was to flourish and achieve wide currency, reducing legal positivism to mere State voluntarism.' 'Positivism' in R. Bernhardt (ed.), *Encyclopedia of Public International Law*, vol. 3 (Amsterdam: Elsevier, 1997) 1072–80 at 1073. See further M.D.A. Freeman, *Lloyd's Introduction to Jurisprudence*, 3rd edn (London: Sweet and Maxwell, 2008) esp. 'Bentham, Austin and Classical Positivism'.

consented to it. This consent may be given expressly, as in a treaty, or it may be implied by a state acquiescing in a customary rule. But this assumption, that international law consists of nothing save what states have consented to, is an inadequate account of the system we see in actual operation; and even if it were a complete account of the contents of the law, it would fail to explain why the law is binding.

First, it is quite impossible to fit the facts into a consistently consensual theory of the nature of international law. *Implied* consent is not a philosophically sound explanation of customary law, international or domestic. A customary rule is observed, not because it has been consented to, but because it is believed to be binding; and whatever may be the explanation or the justification for that belief, its binding force does not depend, and is not felt by those who follow it, to depend on the approval of the individual or the state to which it is addressed.

Further, in the practical administration of international law, states are continually treated as bound by principles which they cannot, except by the most strained construction of the facts, be said to have consented to. And it is unreasonable when we are seeking the true nature of international rules, to force the facts into a preconceived theory, instead of finding a theory which will explain the facts as we have them.

For example, a state which has newly come into existence does not in any intelligible sense *consent* to accept international law; it does not regard itself, and it is not regarded by others, as having any option in the matter. The truth is that states do not regard their international legal relations as resulting from consent, except when the consent is express. The theory of implied consent is therefore a fiction invented by the theorist. Only a certain plausibility is given to a consensual explanation of the nature of their obligations by the fact that, in the absence of any international machinery for legislation by majority vote, a *new* rule of law cannot be imposed upon states merely by the will of other states.

Second, even if the positivist consent-based theory did not involve a distortion of the facts, it would fail as an explanation. For consent cannot of itself create an obligation; it can do so only within a system of law which has already declared that consent duly given, as in a treaty or a contract, will be binding on the party consenting. To say that the rule *pacta sunt servanda* (treaties are binding on the parties) is itself founded on consent is to argue in a circle. A consistently consensual theory would have to admit that if consent is withdrawn, the obligation created by it comes to an end. So the conclusion would be that once a state decided it no longer consented to a treaty it would no longer be bound. Most positivist writers would not admit this, but to deny it, is, in effect, to fall back on an unacknowledged source of obligation, which, whatever it may be, is not the consent of the state.

We suggest there need be no mystery about the source of the obligation to obey international law. The same problem arises in any system of law and it can never be solved by a merely *juridical* explanation.[5] The answer must be sought outside the law, and it is

---

5. See also Triepel, *Droit international et droit interne* (Paris: Pedone, 1920), who considers that there comes a point when a legal explanation for the obligatory nature of law is impossible. He separates a state's consent to the application of a rule from its previous participation in the creation of a collective consent to the rule, suggesting that in the end a state *feels* bound by the rule, and that pointing to violations of the rule does not disprove this fact. 'Je crois qu'on peut se contenter d'affirmer qu'il se *sent* tenu par cette règle. C'est un fait qu'on ne peut nier en renvoyant à des violations de droit.' At 81.

for legal philosophy to provide it. The notion that the validity of international law raises some peculiar problem arises from the confusion which the *doctrine of sovereignty* has introduced into international legal theory. Even when we do not believe in the absoluteness of state sovereignty, we have allowed ourselves to be persuaded that the fact of states' sovereignty makes it necessary to look for some specific quality in this international law to which states are subject which is not found in other kinds of law. We have accepted a false idea of the state as a personality with a life and a will of its own, still living in a 'state of nature', and we contrast this with the 'political' state in which individuals have come to live.

But this assumed condition of states is the very negation of law, and no ingenuity can explain how states in a 'state of nature' and law can exist together. It is a notion as false analytically as it is historically. The truth is that states are not persons, however convenient it may be to personify them; they are merely *institutions,* that is to say, organizations which individuals establish among themselves for securing certain objects, most fundamentally a system of order within which they can carry on the activities of their common life. They have no wills except the wills of the individual human beings who direct their affairs; and they exist, not in a political vacuum, but in continuous political relations with one another. Their subjection to law is as yet imperfect, though it is real as far as it goes; the problem of extending it is one of great practical difficulty, but it is not intrinsically impossible. There are important differences between international law and the law under which individuals live in a state, but those differences do not lie in metaphysics or in any mystical qualities of an entity called 'state sovereignty'.

The international lawyer then is under no special obligation to explain why the law with which we are concerned should be binding upon its subjects. If it were true that the essence of all law is a *command*, and that what makes the law of the state binding is that for some reason, for which no satisfactory explanation can ever be given, the will of the person issuing a command is *superior* to that of the person receiving it, then indeed it would be necessary to look for some special explanation of the binding force of international law. But that view of the nature of law has long been discredited. If we are to explain why any kind of law is binding, we cannot avoid some such assumption as made in the Middle Ages, and in Greece and Rome before that, when they spoke of natural law.

The ultimate explanation of the binding force of all law is that individuals, whether as single human beings, or whether associated with others in a state, are constrained, in so far as they are reasonable beings, to believe that order and not chaos is the governing principle of the world in which they have to live.[6]

---

6. This explanation of the basis of obligation under international law has been seized on by Martti Koskenniemi to reveal how international lawyers are destined to oscillate between, on the one hand, arguments that assume that a normative code *overrides* state behaviour, will, and interests (descending arguments), and, on the other hand, 'ascending' arguments that nation states *determine* the law through their behaviour, will, and interests. Our explanation is said to rely simultaneously on both forms of argumentation: 'A descending and ascending argument are made to coincide: order is binding because no social life can exist without it. This is presented as an objective truth, independent of human will or perception. But it is also binding because human beings believe it is. It is now subjective conviction which is primary.' *From Apology to Utopia. The Structure of International Legal Argument. Reissue with new Epilogue* (Cambridge: CUP, 2005) at 169.

§ 4. The sources of modern international law

Article 38(1) of the Statute of the International Court of Justice directs the Court to apply:

(a) international conventions, whether general or particular, establishing rules expressly recognized by the contesting states;

(b) international custom, as evidence of a general practice accepted as law;

(c) the general principles of law recognized by civilized nations;

(d) subject to the provisions of Article 59,[7] judicial decisions and the teachings of the most highly qualified publicists of the various nations, as subsidiary means for the determination of rules of law.

This is a text of the highest authority, and we may fairly assume that it influences the way that other courts and tribunals approach the sources of international law.[8]

---

7. This Article provides that 'The decision of the Court has no binding force except between the parties and in respect of that particular case'.

8. One should not, however, consider these sources as exclusive sources for the role of international law in international relations. We will address unilateral undertakings by states and the texts produced by international organizations later in this chapter. For an argument which explains how the participants in the international system in practice use a much wider range of norms of international law see Onuma, Y., *A Transcivilizational Perspective on International Law* (Leiden: Nijhoff, 2010) ch. III.

(a) *Treaties as a source of law*

'Agreement is a law for those who make it, which supersedes, supplements, or derogates from the ordinary law of the land.'[9] It is natural, therefore, to find that in seeking the law applicable to the facts of a particular case the Court is first directed to inquire whether the general law, under which their rights would otherwise fall to be determined, has been excluded by an agreement between them.

Treaties are clearly then a source of law for the parties to them; they are 'special' or 'particular' law. But can we go further and describe them in any sense as a source of 'general' international law? Certainly it is only a particular class of treaty which has any claim to be so regarded. The ordinary treaty by which two or more states enter into engagements with one another for some special object can very rarely be used to establish the existence of a rule of general law; it is more probable that the very reason for the treaty was to create an obligation which would not have existed in the general law, or to exclude an existing rule which would otherwise have applied.

Still less can such treaties be regarded as actually creating new law (as opposed to new obligations). The class of treaties, which it is admissible to treat as a source of general law, are those which a large number of states have concluded for the purpose either of declaring their understanding of what the law is on a particular subject, or of laying down a new general rule for future conduct, or of creating some international institution. Such treaties are, as we

---

9. J. W. Salmond, *Jurisprudence: or The Theory of Law*, 6th edn (London, Sweet and Maxwell, 1920) 31.

shall see in the next chapter, a substitute for legislation in the international system, and they are conveniently referred to as 'law-making' treaties. This mass of law-making treaties (what could be called 'conventional law of nations') now far surpasses customary international law.

These terms are convenient, and they are not inaccurate, for it is not necessary that all the rules of a legal system should be binding on all the members of a community. But it must always be borne in mind that even a law-making treaty is subject to the limitation which applies to other treaties, that it does not bind states which are not parties to it. Thus, except in the event of every state in the world becoming a party to one of these treaties, the law which it creates will not be law for every state. Some writers have attempted to meet this difficulty by saying that the law which these treaties create is 'general' international law, but not 'universal' international law, even if certain provisions which are widely binding have 'a tendency to become universal international law';[10] but the terminology is not very happy, nor does it really address the crux of the problem.

The real justification for ascribing a law-making function to these treaties is the practical one already referred to: they do in fact perform the function which a legislature performs in a state, though they do so only imperfectly. They fulfil twin functions: both purposively adapting international law to new conditions, and strengthening the force of the rule of law between states. Moreover, there is something artificial in saying, even if it is strictly

---

10. R. Jennings and A. Watts (eds), *Oppenheim's International Law*, 9th edn, vol. i (London: Longman, 1996) at 4.

true in theory, that such important institutions of international life as the International Criminal Court or the United Nations and its International Court of Justice, along with its specialized agencies such as the Universal Postal Union, the World Health Organization, and the International Civil Aviation Organization, are nothing but contractual arrangements between certain states. It is right that we should look behind the form of these treaties to their substantial effect.

(b) *Custom as a source of law*

Custom in its legal sense means something more than mere habit or usage; it is a usage felt by those who follow it as obligatory. There must be a feeling that if the usage is not followed some sort of adverse consequence will probably, or at any rate ought to, fall on the transgressor. In technical language there must be a possible 'sanction', though the exact nature of this need not be very distinctly envisaged. Evidence that a custom in this sense exists in the international sphere can be found only by examining the practice of states.

That is to say, we must look at what states actually do in their relations with one another, and attempt to understand why they do it, and in particular whether they recognize an obligation to adopt a certain course. Or, in the words of Article 38(1)(b) of the Statute, we must examine whether the alleged custom shows 'a general practice accepted as law'.[11]

---

11. 'Not only must the acts concerned amount to a settled practice, but they must also be such, or be carried out in such a way, as to be evidence of a belief that this practice is rendered obligatory by the existence of a rule of law requiring it. The need for such a belief, i.e., the existence of a subjective element, is implicit in the very notion of the *opinio*

Such evidence will obviously be voluminous and also diverse. There are multifarious occasions on which persons who act or speak in the name of a state, do acts, or make declarations, which either express or imply some view on a matter of international law. Any such act or declaration may, so far as it goes, be some evidence that a custom, and therefore that a rule of international law, does or does not exist. But, of course, its value as evidence will altogether be determined by the occasion and the circumstances. States, like individuals, often put forward contentions for the purpose of supporting a particular case which do not necessarily represent their settled or impartial opinion; and it is that settled opinion which has to be ascertained with as much certainty as the nature of the case allows.

Particularly important as sources of evidence are diplomatic correspondence; official instructions to diplomats, consuls, and military commanders; acts of state legislation and decisions of state courts, which, we should presume, will not deliberately contravene any rule regarded as a rule of international law by the state;

---

juris sive necessitatis. The States concerned must therefore feel that they are conforming to what amounts to a legal obligation. The frequency, or even habitual character of the acts is not in itself enough. There are many international acts, e.g., in the field of ceremonial and protocol, which are performed almost invariably, but which are motivated only by considerations of courtesy, convenience or tradition, and not by any sense of legal duty.' ICJ, *North Sea Continental Shelf,* ICJ Rep. (1969) p. 44 at para. 77. Brigitte Stern has suggested that states 'feel' this obligation differently: 'According to their position of power in international society, states will voluntarily participate in the elaboration of international custom. Either with the feeling of creating *law* or with the feeling of obeying a *necessity*, which results precisely from the will of those states who feel that they are creating law.' B. Stern, 'Custom at the Heart of International Law', 11(1) *Duke Journal of Comparative and International Law* (2001) 89–108, at 108.

and opinions of law officers, especially when these are published, as they are for example in the United States and Switzerland.[12]

In applying these forms of evidence in order to establish the existence of an international custom, what we are looking for is a general recognition among states of a certain practice as obligatory. It would hardly ever be practicable, and all but the strictest of positivists admit that it is not necessary, to show that *every state* has recognized a certain practice. Just as in English law the existence of a valid local custom of trade can be established without proof that every individual in the locality, engaged in the trade, has practised the custom.

This test of *general* recognition is necessarily a vague one; but it is of the nature of customary law, whether national or international,

---

12. *Digest of United States Practice in International Law*; *Revue suisse de droit international et européen*. See also McNair's *International Law Opinions* [1782–1902] 3 vols (Cambridge: CUP, 1956); C. Parry and G. Fitzmaurice (eds), *British Digest of International Law* 8 vols [Phase 1, 1860–1914] 8 vols (London: Stevens, 1965); and the sections in yearbooks and journals such as the *British Year Book of International Law, Irish Yearbook of International Law; Australian Year Book of International Law, New Zealand Yearbook of International Law; Canadian Yearbook of International Law, the Annuaire Français de Droit International; Austrian Review of International and European Law; Baltic Yearbook of International Law; Revue belge de droit international; Finnish Yearbook of International Law; Revue Générale de Droit International Public* (France); *German Yearbook of International Law; Heidelberg Journal of International Law; Revue Hellénique de Droit International; Italian Yearbook of International Law; Netherlands Yearbook of International Law; Nordic Journal of International Law; Polish Yearbook of International Law; Spanish Yearbook of International Law; European Journal of International Law* (for EU practice); *American Journal of International Law; The Japanese Yearbook of International Law; Asian Yearbook of International Law; Chinese Journal of International Law; Indian Journal of International Law; South African Yearbook of International Law; Palestine Yearbook of International Law; Colombian Yearbook of International Law; Mexican Yearbook of International Law.*

not to be susceptible to exact or final formulation. When a system of customary law is administered by courts, which perpetually reformulate and develop its principles, as has happened in the English Common Law, the uncertainty of the customary law is so reduced, that it is no different than the uncertainty which attaches to codified law. But such a clarifying influence by courts is only now beginning to be felt in international law. It is therefore harder to formulate customary international law principles than to formulate those of a national system of law.[13] The difference, however, is not between uncertainty and certainty in formulation, but rather degrees of uncertainty.

The growth of a new custom is always a slow process, and the character of international society makes it particularly slow in the international sphere. The progress of customary international law therefore has come to be more and more bound up with that of the law-making treaty. But it is possible even today for new customs to develop and to win acceptance as law when the need is sufficiently clear and urgent. Striking illustrations of this are the rapid development of the principle of sovereignty over the air, the law of outer space, and the regime covering the moon and 'other celestial bodies'.[14]

---

13. See however the important ICRC study developed over almost ten years: J.-M. Henckaerts and L. Doswald-Beck, *Customary International Humanitarian Law—Volume 1: Rules* (Cambridge: CUP, 2005) and E. Wilmshurst and S. Breau (eds), *Perspectives on the ICRC Study on Customary International Humanitarian Law* (Cambridge: CUP, 2007).

14. Treaty on Principles Governing the Activities of States in the Exploration and Use of Outer Space, including the Moon and Other Celestial Bodies (1967); Agreement Governing the Activities of States on the Moon and Other Celestial Bodies (1979) discussed

Today, it is admitted that the activities of states within international organizations contribute to a 'more rapid adjustment of customary law to the developing needs of the international community'.[15] Moreover the activity in these organizations provides new evidence of custom: 'the concentration of state practice now developed and displayed in international organisations and the collective decisions and the activities of the organisations themselves may be valuable evidence of general practices accepted as law in the fields in which those organizations operate.'[16] This material evidence of customary international law should be distinguished from any law-making activity that one may ascribe to the international organizations themselves. Furthermore, it is increasingly clear that the existence of these organizations facilitates interaction between states and other actors, so that even where the activity cannot be seen as law-making (in the sense of treaty drafting or the formation of custom), such interaction

---

in Ch. V below. Cheng has demonstrated how the participation of the space powers has led in this field to a relatively rapid (instantaneous) development of international law, and that 'the preponderant weight of States should be behind a given norm before it can be pronounced a rule of general international law. How the weight of different States is to be calculated varies with the subject matter and probably from case to case, if it can be calculated at all.' His concludes that 'in the making of rules of international law, the weight of States certainly is not equal'. B. Cheng, *Studies in International Space Law* (Oxford: OUP, 1997) at 687. On the role of power and control in the formation of custom see Byres' stimulating book *Custom, Power and the Power of Rules: International Relations and Customary International Law* (Cambridge: CUP, 1999).

15. *Oppenheim's International Law*, 9th edn (1996) at 30–1.

16. Ibid 31. See also B.D. Lepard, *Customary International Law: A New Theory with Practical Applications* (Cambridge: CUP, 2010) ch. 14.

accelerates the process of international standard setting.[17] We shall return to organizations as a possible source of law below.

One form of customary international law that requires less evidence of acceptance is *jus cogens* (or peremptory norms of general international law). These rules have a higher status and not only do they require no evidence of general practice but they also provide no possibility for states to opt out, object, or derogate.[18] We will consider some of the effects of claiming that a norm is a rule of *jus cogens* in a later Chapter on treaties (a treaty that conflicts with such a norm is void). For present purposes it is perhaps enough to note that the list of peremptory norms is contested, all the more so because it is accepted that the norm can be modified by a new norm of *jus cogens*. We have here perhaps the continuation of a highest form of natural law by another name.

Although the International Law Commission introduced some detailed rules on the consequences that flow from certain violations of *jus cogens* in the context of state responsibility,[19] they stopped short of codifying a list. The Commission's Commentary does however provide the following: 'Those peremptory norms that are clearly accepted and recognized include the prohibitions of aggression, genocide, slavery, racial discrimina-

---

17. See J.E. Alvarez, *International Organizations as Law-makers* (Oxford: OUP, 2005) 588–601, and see further K.W. Abbott and D. Snidal, 'Why States Act through Formal International Organizations', 42 *Journal of Conflict Resolution* (1998) 3–32.

18. V. Lowe, *International Law* (Oxford: OUP, 2007) at 58–60; Lowe suggests that *jus cogens* contains only rules that are logically or morally necessary. So, for example, the rule that parties must respect treaties is logically necessary for the legal system to work.

19. For further consequences see *Oppenheim's International Law*, 9th edn (1996) at 8.

tion, crimes against humanity and torture, and the right to self-determination.'[20] Other examples included in Commentary are 'the slave trade...and apartheid...the prohibition against torture as defined in article 1 of the Convention against Torture and Other Cruel, Inhuman or Degrading Treatment or Punishment...the basic rules of international humanitarian law applicable in armed conflict'.[21] This list is carefully described as exemplary rather than definitive.

(c) *The general principles of law*

Article 38(1)(c) of the Statute directs the Court to refer to 'the general principles of law recognized by civilized nations'.[22] The phrase is a wide one; it includes, though it is not limited to, the principles of private law administered in national courts where these are applicable to international relations. Private law, being in general more developed than international law, has always constituted a sort of reserve store of principles upon which international law has drawn. Roman law, as we have seen, was so drawn upon by the early writers on international law, and the process continues, for the good reason that a principle which is found to be generally accepted by established legal systems may fairly be assumed to be

---

20. The ILC's Articles on Responsibility of States for Internationally Wrongful Acts (2001) (hereafter ARSIWA), Commentary to Art. 26, para. 5. Report of the ILC, UN Doc. A/56/10, at p. 85.

21. Commentary to ARSIWA Art. 40, paras 3–5, ibid, at p. 112.

22. See further C.H.M. Waldock, *General Course on Public International Law*, 106 *RCADI* II (1962) ch. 4, who also pointed out that 'now the emphasis on "civilized nations" seems to us both otiose and unpalatable'. He construed the clause as meaning 'simply the general principles recognised in the legal systems of independent states'. At 65.

so reasonable as to be necessary to the maintenance of justice under any system. Prescription, estoppel, *res judicata,* are examples of such principles.[23]

Article 38(1)(c) introduces no novelty into the system, for the 'general principles of law' are a source to which international courts have instinctively and properly referred in the past. But its inclusion is important as a rejection of the positivist doctrine, according to which international law consists solely of rules to which states have given their consent. It is an authoritative recognition of a dynamic element in international law, and of the creative function of the courts that administer it.[24]

---

23. Note this category of sources should not be confused with principles of general international law which include binding principles for all states such as those prohibiting the use of force (See Ch. IX), or relating to the equality of states (see Ch. IV § 3 below). See the discussion by G. Abi-Saab *Cours Général de Droit International Public,* 207 *RCADI* (The Hague: Nijhoff, 1996) at 197–203: Abi-Saab highlights how a universally applicable rule or principle of 'droit international général' may be invoked by the International Court of Justice without any apparent need to prove its origins or existence, and, how in his opinion it is the sense of obligation held by states that counts, rather than a sense of obligation derived from treaty or custom. Abi-Saab distinguishes such a principle of general international law from 'un principe général du droit international' which is general due to its roots and rank in the legal system rather than its scope of application. Such principles have been highlighted by P.-M. Dupuy who suggests that international judges see them as axiomatic and inherent in the international legal order. P.-M. Dupuy, *Droit international public,* 9th edn (Paris: Dalloz, 2008) at 358–62. Cf G. Schwarzenberger, *A Manual of International Law,* 5th edn (New York: Praeger, 1967) at 42–5.

24. For a review of how the courts have approached this issue see G. Gaja, 'General Principles of Law', <mpepil.com> (2009) who finds: 'The assertion by the ICJ of a general principle of law, whether or not it finds a parallel in municipal systems, is only rarely accompanied by an adequate demonstration of its existence in international law. A similar remark could be made with regard to the ascertainment by the ICJ of customary rules.' At para. 20; see further B. Simma and P. Alston, 'The Sources of Human Rights Law: Custom, Jus Cogens, and General Principles', 12 *Australian Year Book of International Law* (1992) 82–108.

(d) Judicial decisions and text writers

Judicial decisions are described in Article 38(1)(d) of the Statute as a 'subsidiary means for the determination of rules of law'. Such decisions are not strictly seen as precedents and are therefore not binding authorities in international law. The English law theory that judicial precedents have binding force merely elevates into a dogma a natural tendency found in all judicial procedure. When any system of law has reached a stage at which it is thought worthwhile to report the decisions and the reasoning of judges, other judges inevitably give weight, though not necessarily decisive weight, to the work of their predecessors or colleagues.

There was originally only a restricted scope for the operation of this tendency in international law, for the practical reason that since international adjudications were relatively few reports were not readily accessible. This is rapidly changing due to the proliferation of tribunals and ease of access to their rulings though the internet. Judicial decisions are taking their proper place in the system. The change is a wholly beneficial one; it is creating for international law a vast stock of detailed rules, testing abstract principles against their capacity to solve practical problems, and depriving international law of its rather academic character. According to Judge Meron, judicial decisions are in turn accelerating the formation of customary international law: 'In my experience, legal principles whose maturation into customary international law has long been in dispute become accepted as customary international law by the international community very rapidly after they have been given the imprimatur of adoption by an international tribunal.'[25]

---

25. *The Making of International Criminal Justice: A View from the Bench* (Oxford: OUP, 2011) at 242.

Text writers again are a 'subsidiary means for the determination
of rules of law'. The function of text writers in the international
system is in no way peculiar; it is a misapprehension to suppose
that they have or claim any authority to make the law. Actually
they render exactly the same services as in any other legal system.
One of those services is to provide useful evidence of what the law
is. This function is universally recognized, and it has been expressed
by Mr Justice Gray, delivering the judgment of the Supreme Court
of the United States, in these words:

> International law is part of our law, and must be ascertained
> and administered by the courts of justice of appropriate juris-
> diction, as often as questions of right depending upon it are
> duly presented for their determination. For this purpose,
> where there is no treaty, and no controlling executive or legis-
> lative act or judicial decision, resort must be had to the cus-
> toms and usages of civilized nations; and as evidence of these,
> to the works of jurists and commentators who by years of
> labour, research, and experience have made themselves pecu-
> liarly well acquainted with the subjects of which they treat.
> Such works are resorted to by judicial tribunals, not for the
> speculations of their authors concerning what the law ought
> to be, but for trustworthy evidence of what the law really
> is.[26]

Another function of text writers is referred to by Mr Justice Gray
when he speaks of their 'speculations concerning what the law

---

26. *Paquete Habana* (1899) American Prize Cases, p. 1938.

ought to be', for their writings may help to create opinion, which may influence the conduct of states, and, thus indirectly over the course of time help to modify the actual law.

Whether the speculations of any particular author are likely to have this active influence depends mainly on their prestige, and on the persuasiveness with which they present their arguments. But it is important not to confuse these two functions, providing evidence of what the law is, and the exercise of influence on its development. The notion that the position of international writers differs from that of other legal writers is perhaps due to three causes. The first is that, in the past, the influence of international writers as exponents of the law did not compete with the influence of judges. The second is that Continental lawyers neither exalt the function of the judge, nor depreciate that of the text writer, to the extent that the training of English and American lawyers leads them to do. Third, English is a language which sometimes separates 'law', i.e. the rules that *do* exist, and 'right', i.e. the rules that *ought* to exist. 'Jus' in Latin, 'droit' in French, 'Recht' in German, can combine both these meanings, and it is therefore easy for writers in these languages to pass unconsciously from the idea of international *law* to what seems to us the very different idea of what is *right*. On the other hand, language makes it easy for English writers to treat the difference as greater than it is in fact, and to forget that there is a necessary connexion between the two ideas in international law even more than in national law. For even if law and right are sometimes separated in fact, law can only be true to its purpose if it is perpetually assimilating what is felt to be right.[27]

---

27. This last sentence is reprised from the 1st edition of this book at 43.

(e) *The place of 'reason' in the modern system*

In our discussion of natural law we saw that no system of law consists only of formulated rules, for these can never be sufficiently detailed or sufficiently clairvoyant to provide for every situation that may call for a legal decision. Those who administer law must meet new situations not precisely covered by a formulated rule, by resorting to the principle which medieval writers would have called natural law, and which we generally call reason. Reason in this context does not mean the unassisted reasoning powers of any intelligent person, but rather a 'judicial' reason. This means that a principle to cover the new situation is discovered by applying methods of reasoning which lawyers everywhere accept as valid, for example, the consideration of precedents, the finding of analogies, and resorting to the fundamental principles behind established legal rules.

This source of new rules is accepted as valid, and is constantly resorted to in the practice of states, both in the decisions of international tribunals and in the legal arguments conducted by foreign offices with one another,[28] so that a positivism which refuses to accept it is untrue to its own premisses. A 'positivist' by definition recognizes as law everything that is 'posited' as law by states and nothing else; and positivists profess to discover what states have 'posited' as law by referring only to their customs, which they explain as based on their tacit consent, and their treaties, which are based on their express consent. But actually the practice of states themselves is not limited in this way, for they habitually recognize as valid and binding on themselves principles not derived from either of these sources. Almost any diplomatic legal argument, or

---

28. See further V. Lowe, *International Law* (2007) at 97ff.

the proceedings before any international tribunal, would show the search for a relevant rule of law proceeding on lines much broader than those which alone are assumed to be permissible in the positivist position.[29]

International law, like any other system of law, is, in a formal sense, though not of course in any other sense, a 'perfect' system; it ought to be able to provide a solution for any issue submitted to a court, and it can do this because it accepts the practice by which judges are required to 'find' a rule of law which is applicable to the case before them.[30] Lord Mansfield, one of the greatest judges who ever sat on the English bench, doubtless had the same principle in mind when he wrote: 'The law of nations is founded on justice, equity, convenience, and *the reason of the thing,* and confirmed by long usage.'[31]

(f) *Law-making by international organizations*

We saw above that the way in which states behave in international organizations, such as the United Nations, can provide evidence as

---

29. This paragraph reprises some of Brierly's earlier thoughts on this topic. 'The Basis of Obligation in International Law' (1928) (above) at 17.

30. Vaughan Lowe suggests that the judge develops this system of law by resorting to 'interstitial norms' or 'meta principles' which are derived from influences beyond the legal rules generated by states; see V. Lowe, 'The Politics of Law-Making: Are the Method and Character of Norm Creation Changing?' in M. Byers (ed), *The Role of Law in International Politics: Essays in International Relations and International Law* (Oxford: OUP, 2000) 207–26.

31. Emphasis added, for the occasion and reference see Pollock, *Essays in the Law* (Macmillan: London 1922) at 64 (*Case of the Silesian Loan,* 1753); cf McNair, 'The Debt of International Law in Britain to the Civil Law and the Civilians' in vol. iii *International Law Opinions* (above) Appendix II at 415–17, who suggests that Mansfield may not have been as influential in writing the report as Sir George Lee.

to the existence of a rule of customary international law. Now let us consider whether votes and texts adopted by international organizations can generate international obligations as a separate source of law. When the fifteen-member Security Council 'decides' that member states must act or refrain from acting in a certain way, this creates a binding obligation on the member states of the organization.[32] Strictly speaking one could say that the member states are simply bound by the treaty obligations that they undertook by becoming parties to the UN Charter, and one obligation they undertook was to accept to follow the decisions of the Security Council.[33] But to explain the situation in this formalistic way would be to miss an opportunity to understand the dynamics of the ways that international organizations create new obligations for their members, and indeed for themselves and other entities.[34]

Consider the work of the International Organization for Civil Aviation (ICAO); as new navigation and safety issues arise (for example in the wake of the use of civil aeroplanes to attack the

---

32. Article 25 of the UN Charter.

33. We will consider these decisions in more detail in Ch. III.

34. See further Alvarez, *International Organizations as Law-makers* (above) and Lepard, *Customary International Law* (above) ch. 20. For a thoughtful study which examines the normative effects of the acts of international organizations not only for their members but also on individuals and corporations see M. Goldmann, 'Inside Relative Normativity: From Sources to Standard Instruments for the Exercise of International Public Authority', in A. von Bogdandy et al (eds), *The Exercise of Public Authority by International Institutions: Advancing International Institutional Law* (Heidelberg: Springer, 2010) 661–711. The International Court of Justice has suggested that the Security Council has the power to impose international obligations on actors other than states and international organizations, see *Accordance with International Law of the Unilateral Declaration of Independence in Respect of Kosovo*, Advisory Opinion of 22 July 2010, paras 115–19.

World Trade Centre in New York on 11 September 2001) the ICAO Council (made up of 36 representatives from its 180 member states) can adopt a new Standard by a two-thirds majority. Unless a majority of the member states 'register their disapproval' in the following three months, this new Standard takes effect as an annex to the treaty for all member states.[35] In this way the Council, like the Security Council, can be seen to create new obligations.

Another example is the International Whaling Commission. Here the capacity to regulate for the members is more limited. A 75 per cent majority of those voting is needed to amend the regulations concerning:

> the conservation and utilization of whale resources, fixing (a) protected and unprotected species; (b) open and closed seasons; (c) open and closed waters, including the designation of sanctuary areas; (d) size limits for each species; (e) time, methods, and intensity of whaling (including the maximum catch of whales to be taken in any one season); (f) types and specifications of gear and apparatus and appliances which may be used; (g) methods of measurement; and (h) catch returns and other statistical and biological records.[36]

States have 90 days to object, and should one party object, other states have a further period in which to object. Thereafter the amendment becomes binding on those states that have not objected. Although the potential here for law-making over and

---

35. Article 90(a) of the Convention on International Civil Aviation (1944).
36. Article V(1) of the International Convention for the Regulation of Whaling (1946).

above the wishes of a state is reduced, the Commission's decisions do nevertheless create new obligations.

Waldock suggested already in 1963 that the acceptance of organizations such as the UN 'as independent international persons may now justify us in considering their acts as original sources of international law under Article 38 of the Statute, instead of a secondary source derived from their constituent treaties'. He accepted the argument that the capacity of international organizations to act on the international plane 'derives from a constituent treaty concluded between States and the treaty is therefore the origin of the legal force of their acts'. But he continued by suggesting 'once the treaty is concluded, an organization which possesses autonomous organs detached from its Member States begins a life of its own and becomes a new decision-making unit of the international community.'[37]

(g) *Unilateral declarations of states*

The International Law Commission (ILC) has adopted Guiding Principles which clarify how declarations publicly made by government authorities can create international legal obligations. The declarations must demonstrate a 'will to be bound' and the authority must be vested with the power to bind the state in this way. According to the ILC's Principles: 'By virtue of their functions, heads of State, heads of Government and ministers for foreign affairs are competent to formulate such declarations. Other persons representing the State in specified areas may be authorized to

---

37. *General Course on Public International Law*, 106 *RCADI* II (1963), 1–251, at 103.

bind it, through their declarations, in areas falling within their competence.'[38] One could therefore imagine, for example, a minister for transport or trade acting within their areas of competence, creating obligations for their state.

The declaration can be oral or written, but it must be addressed to 'the international community as a whole or to one or several States or to other entities'.[39] In a well-known case from 1974 the International Court of Justice found that France had assumed a unilateral obligation to refrain from atmospheric nuclear testing. Interestingly the Court did not rely on any one declaration in isolation but rather a series of statements by the President, members of the French Government, and the Minister of Defence, which they held 'to constitute an engagement of the State, having regard to their intention and to the circumstances in which they were made.'[40]

The ILC has been careful to offer a guideline limiting the possibilities for states to revoke their declarations. In short, the ILC suggests that arbitrary revocations should not be permitted, and that one factor to assess arbitrariness would be the extent to which others, to whom the obligations were owed, had relied on the declaration as a source of obligation.[41]

---

38. Guiding Principles applicable to unilateral declarations of States capable of creating legal obligations (2006), Principle 4.

39. Ibid. Principle 6.

40. *Nuclear Tests Case* (1974) at para. 51. Cf V. Lowe, *International Law* (2007) 88–90. See also the PCIJ Judgment in *Legal Status of Eastern Greenland, Denmark v Norway* (1933) Series A/B 22 at 71ff.

41. Principle 10(ii).

(h) *International standards and the debate over 'soft law'*

In recent years scholars have become dissatisfied with the above description of sources. Even if the Statute of the International Court of Justice apparently restricts the sources of law which that Court is bound to apply, any description of international law as it applies in contemporary international relations has to admit the influence of international standards, either as a source of law or as a set of normative developments. One of the most developed arguments for such standards as a source of law comes from Eibe Riedel who starts by admitting that: 'Traditional international lawyers of the positivist school tried to reduce legal discourse to the pure discussion of relations between norms and questions of legal validity ... By contrast, a wider conception of law will embrace relevant factual bases of norms as an empirical basis of a social and political nature, thereby taking into purview the reality of the international community.'[42] This wider conception of law represents a more realistic picture of the norms that are taken into consideration by states, organizations, and individuals on a day-to-day basis. As Riedel points out: 'the stage of final decisions binding upon the parties concerned is reached only in a very few isolated instances.'[43] In most situations international relations unfold in accordance with the international standards developed through the United Nations and other fora without too much reference as to whether such norms are 'sources of law' or even 'strictly legally binding'.

---

42. E. Riedel, 'Standards and Sources: Farewell to the Exclusivity of the Sources Triad in International Law?' 2 *EJIL* (1991) 58–84 at 64.

43. Ibid 65.

This distinction between 'hard law' and 'soft law' remains critical when a tribunal is asked to settle a dispute between two entities based on the applicable law and according to a limited set of sources of law. But, as already suggested, international law is often invoked outside the courtroom, and international soft law standards may be particularly influential in this general realm of international relations. Some international relations scholars have sought to explain how this soft law takes effect and the dynamics of its increasing impact. According to Kenneth Abbott and Duncan Snidal, rather than concentrating on the binary distinction between hard law and soft law, it makes more sense to break down the norm into three dimensions or variables and consider the different levels of *Obligation*, *Precision*, and *Delegation* developed by states in the specific context.[44] Under this hypothesis states not only choose varying degrees of Obligation (for example between a treaty and a declaration), but in addition they negotiate various levels of Precision and Delegation according to the context. Therefore the normative framework is much more complex and malleable than the simple hard–soft dichotomy suggests. For example, states may choose to develop very precise obligations but subject them to monitoring mechanisms with relatively little delegated authority—this may suit states that are worried about erosions of sovereignty and yet tie in a large number of heterogeneous states to a particular regime with detailed norms. The level of any one dimension can be adjusted over time, so for instance states may delegate more and more authority to the monitoring/adjudicatory

---

44. K.W. Abbott and D. Snidal, 'Hard and Soft Law in International Governance', 54(3) *International Organization* (2000) 421–56.

bodies, and in turn the obligations could become more and more precise through adjudication of disputes by the delegated authority.

One can add to the complexity of the picture by admitting that any one international instrument might contain both hard and soft elements. Some treaties address certain obligations through provisions with low levels of precision, while tackling other obligations through provisions with a high degree of precision or 'hardness'. Some commentators have chosen to describe certain instruments as containing 'combination standards' with hard and soft law components, a black and white combination, sometimes even known as 'zebra codes'. The composite norm is in turn developed through the influence of the soft provisions on the harder ones.

> The 70-year experience of standard-setting at the ILO, but also similar experiences at the UNESCO and WHO, to name but two further examples, have gradually built up new types of legal norms; the '*zebra codes*' which aggregate binding and non-binding norms in one single combination standard. In applying the 'zebra code', decision-makers will have to bear in mind the different degrees of normative density of the component parts of it, and the ultimate decision will usually be based on the hard law component of the combination standard. The other components serve as interpretative tools for the binding, yet highly open-ended and abstract hard law elements of the standard.[45]

---

45. Riedel (above) at 82 (footnote omitted).

This image of the two types of law interacting to influence the outcome helps us to see that non-binding 'soft-law' instruments adopted in intergovernmental organizations are certainly worth more than the paper they are written on. They will affect how treaty law is interpreted and applied, they will contribute to the formation of customary international law, and they will form the normative framework for all sorts of regimes.[46] Increased opportunities for drafting soft law in international fora mean that soft law will remain central to the role of international law in international relations. The doctrinal debate over the wisdom of referring to 'soft law' as international law will continue to engage academics. Some scholars have sought to highlight the dangers of including soft law in the study of international law, but it must be admitted that any attempt to understand the normative influences that drive international relations should take into account the influence of soft law and the normative pull of such international standards.[47]

§ 5. The legal character of international law

It has often been said that international law ought to be classified as a branch of ethics rather than of law. The question will clearly depend on the definition of law which we choose to adopt; in any

---

46. For a useful overview of the significance and varieties of soft law see A. Boyle and C. Chinkin, *The Making of International Law* (Oxford: OUP, 2007) at 211–29.

47. J. d'Asprement, 'Softness in International Law: A Self-Serving Quest for New Legal Materials', 19(5) *EJIL* (2008) 1075–93; A. D'Amato, 'Softness in International Law: A Self-Serving Quest for New Legal Materials: A Reply to Jean d'Asprement', 20(3) *EJIL* (2009) 897–910.

case it does not affect the value of the subject one way or the other, though those who deny the legal character of international law often speak as though 'ethical' were a depreciatory epithet. In fact it is both practically inconvenient, and contrary to sensible legal thinking to deny the legal character of international law.

It is inconvenient because, if international law is nothing but international morality, it is certainly not the whole of international morality, and it is difficult to see how we are to distinguish it from those other, admittedly moral, standards which we apply in forming our judgments on the conduct of states. Ordinary usage certainly uses two tests in judging the 'rightness' of a state's act, a moral test and another one which is somehow felt to be independent of morality. Every state habitually commits acts of selfishness which are often gravely injurious to other states, and yet are not contrary to international law; but we do not on that account necessarily judge them to have been 'right'. It is confusing and pedantic to say that both these tests are moral. Moreover, it is the pedantry of the theorist and not of the practical person; for questions of international law are invariably treated as legal questions by the foreign ministries which conduct our international business, and in the courts, national or international, before which they are brought. Legal forms and methods are used in diplomatic controversies and in judicial and arbitral proceedings, and authorities and precedents are cited every day in argument.

It is significant too that when one party to a controversy alleges a breach of international law, the act impugned is practically never defended by the other party claiming that this is a matter of private judgment, which would be the natural response if the issue was simply a question of morality. Rather the accusation is always met by attempting to prove that no rule of international law has been violated. This was true of the defences put forward even for such palpable breaches of international law as the invasion of Belgium in 1914.

But if international law is not the same thing as international morality, and, if in some important respects at least, it certainly resembles law, why should we hesitate to accept its definitely legal character? The objection comes in the main from the followers of writers such as Hobbes and Austin, who saw law solely as the will of a political superior. But this is a misleading and inadequate analysis even of the law of a modern state; it cannot, for instance, account for the existence of the English Common Law. Most of the characteristics which differentiate international law from the law of the state, and are often thought to throw doubt on its legal character, such as, for instance, its basis in custom, the fact that the submission of parties to the jurisdiction of courts is voluntary, and the absence of regular processes either for creating or enforcing it, are familiar features of early legal systems.

It is only in quite modern times, when we have come to regard it as natural that the state should be constantly making new laws and enforcing existing ones, that to identify law with the will of the state has become even a plausible theory. We can agree that today the only essential conditions for the existence of law are: the existence of a political community, and the recognition by its members of settled rules binding upon them in that capacity. International law seems generally to satisfy these conditions.[48]

---

48. Cf Lowe 'international law consists of that body of rules that States have decided are binding' *International Law* (above) at 27.

§ 6. Some defects of the system

It is more important to understand the nature of the system than to argue whether it ought to be called law or something else. The best view is that international law is in fact just a system of customary law, upon which has been erected, almost entirely within the last century, a superstructure of 'conventional' or treaty-made law, and some of its chief defects are precisely those that the history of law teaches us to expect in a customary system.

It is a common mistake to suppose that the most conspicuous defect of international law is the frequency of violations. Actually international law is normally observed because, as we shall see, the vast majority of demands that it makes on states are not exacting; and states generally find it convenient to observe the law. This fact receives little notice however, because the interest of most people in international law is not with the ordinary routine of international legal business, but in the rare and often sensational occasions on which it is flagrantly broken. Such breaches generally occur either when some great political issue has arisen between states, or in that part of the system which professes to regulate the conduct of war. So our diagnosis of what is wrong with the system will be mistaken if we fail to realize that most customary rules and the great majority of treaties are, on the whole, regularly observed in international relations. And this is no small service to international life, however far it may fall short of the ideal by which we judge the achievements of the system. If we fail to understand this, we are likely to assume, as many people do, that all would be well with international law if we could devise a better system for enforcing it.

But the weakness of international law lies deeper than any mere question of enforcing sanctions. It is not the existence of a police force that makes a system of national law strong and respected, but the strength of respect for the law that makes it possible for a police force to be effectively organized. When the imperative character of law is felt so strongly, and obedience to it has become so much a matter of habit within a state operating under the rule of law,[49] then national law develops a machinery of enforcement which generally works smoothly, though never so smoothly as to make breaches impossible. If the imperative character of international law were equally strongly felt, the institution of effective sanctions would easily follow. The spiritual cohesion of international society remains weak, and as long as this weakness endures we can expect a weak and primitive system of law. In sum, the shortcoming is not so much the spectacular breaches, but rather the weak cohesion of international society.

Further serious shortcomings of the present system are the rudimentary character of the institutions which exist for making and applying the law, and the restricted scope of international law. These rudimentary institutions will be described briefly in the next chapter. Here we may simply note that there is no formal legislature to keep the law abreast of new needs in international society; no executive power generally to enforce the law; and although certain administrative bodies have been created, these are unable to tackle everything that ought to be treated as matters of international concern. Machinery does exist for the arbitration of disputes, and we have a standing International Court of Justice, but

---

49. See Lord Bingham, *The Rule of Law* (London: Allen Lane, 2010).

the range of action of these entities is limited because resort to them is not compulsory.

Most recently, the models of the Nuremberg and Tokyo Military Tribunals (established after the Second World War) have been reintroduced and we have seen the creation of international criminal Tribunals to try individuals for international crimes committed, for example, in the former Yugoslavia, Rwanda, and Sierra Leone.[50] These Tribunals are limited in the scope of their jurisdiction, but they have been joined, since 2002, by the new International Criminal Court. This permanent Court can try individuals for genocide, crimes against humanity, and war crimes that fall within its jurisdiction. From 2017 it will likely have jurisdiction over the crime of aggression.[51] Such developments are welcome and significant but cannot yet claim to have instilled the instinctive respect for the international rule of law we referred to above.

It is certain that if international law is ever to become one of the pillars of a stable international order, it must make and maintain the most elementary of all legal distinctions, the difference between the legal and the illegal use of physical force. The elaboration of a definition of the international individual crime of aggression is one step in this direction. And when it comes to inter-state disputes the International Court of Justice has made some headway elaborating the difference between the legal and illegal use of force by states, yet, as we shall see in Chapter IX, several dimensions of this question remain contested.

---

50. See W.A. Schabas, *The UN International Criminal Tribunals: The Former Yugoslavia, Rwanda and Sierra Leone* (Cambridge, CUP, 2006).
51. See Ch. IX below.

The restricted scope of international law is merely the counter-part of the wide freedom of independent action which states claim by virtue of their sovereignty, and, as we have seen, it is because the demands that international law makes on states are, on the whole, rather light that its rules in general are fairly well observed. The system is still at a *laissez-faire* stage of legal development. The conduct of a state does not necessarily fall under international law merely because it may affect the interests of other states. The matter in question may fall within what is called the 'domestic jurisdiction' of a single state. For example, legislation restricting immigration is not a matter which affects the interests only of the countries of immigration; it creates serious difficulties for certain countries where economic life has come to depend on emigration facilities. This latter fact, however, may be considered irrelevant from a legal point of view, for immigration is usually a matter which international law leaves each country to determine for itself.[52]

But we should be aware that the scope for states to operate outside the reach of international law is rapidly diminishing. Two examples illustrate this development. Until relatively recently, the way in which a state treated its own citizens was considered a matter of domestic jurisdiction. Today no state would question that international human rights law regulates many aspects of a state's treatment of its own citizens; governments agreed at the 1993 World Conference on Human Rights that 'the promotion and

---

52. Of course states can depart from this state of affairs by concluding treaties, as we see in the context of the European Union where the member states have established complex rules covering free movement of persons, see also the Schengen Agreements.

protection of all human rights is a legitimate concern of the international community.'[53] Secondly, international economic relations concerning tariffs, preferences, and other restrictions on trade were worked out between states under the aforementioned *laissez-faire* approach. Today the World Trade Organization's 'covered agreements', and the multiple regional and bilateral trading arrangements, mean that international trade and investment can no longer be seen as areas of activity isolated from international law.

It is a natural consequence of the absence of authoritative law-declaring machinery that the detailed application of the principles of international law is uncertain. But, on the whole, the non-lawyer tends to exaggerate this defect. It is not in the nature of any legal system to provide mathematically certain solutions to problems which may be presented to it; for so long as different factual circumstances can arise in multiple permutations, uncertainty cannot be eliminated from law. Although there may be an important difference between international law and the law of a state in this respect, it is one of degree and not of kind. And the difference is diminishing with the increasing resort to arguments and evidence presented to international courts and tribunals.

Most people hear little of international law as a working system, for it is mostly practised within the walls of secretive foreign offices; and even if the foreign offices were inclined to be more communicative, the public would not find what they said particu-

---

53. Vienna Declaration and Programme of Action (1993), Part I para. 4. UN Doc. A/CONF.157/23.

larly sensational, any more than they would be surprised by the working of a solicitor's office. For in fact, the practice of international law proceeds on much the same lines as any other kind of law, with the foreign offices taking the place of the private legal adviser. Different foreign offices argue about the facts and the law, and later, more often than is sometimes supposed, settle the dispute with a hearing before some form of international tribunal. The volume of this work is considerable, but most of it is not sensational, and it only occasionally relates to matters of high political interest. That does not mean that the matters are unimportant in themselves; often they are very important to particular interests or individuals. But it means that international law is performing a useful and necessary function in international life by enabling states to carry on their day-to-day relations along orderly and predictable lines.

Whether the shortcomings outlined earlier force us to conclude that international law is a failure depends upon what we assume the aim of international law to be. As long as we assume the aim to be enabling international relations, creating predictability and a degree of stability, then international law has not failed to serve the purposes for which states have chosen to use it; in fact it serves these purposes reasonably well. If we are dissatisfied with this role for international law, if we believe that international law can and should be used, as national law has been used, as an instrument for promoting the general welfare, and even more if we believe that it ought to be a powerful means of preventing conflict, then we shall have to admit that it has so far failed. But it is only fair to remember that these have not been the purposes for which states have so far chosen to use international law.

§ 7. Proposals for codification

It has often been said that international law could be improved if it were properly codified. A code, it is argued, would make its provisions clearer and more easily ascertainable, would remove uncertainties, and fill existing gaps. But no actual code ever does this once and for all, for when a code is made it is never possible to foresee all the situations to which it will have to be applied. In any case, even if that were possible, it would not be desirable to give the law a form so detailed and precise as to exclude the need to adapt it to new situations through judicial interpretation. But this is only to say that no code can ever make the application of law to facts a merely automatic process.

The real difficulties in any process of codification vary with the nature of the materials with which the drafters have to work; that is to say, with the state of the law as it exists before codification. If the existing law is more or less well settled in the form of customary rules, judicial precedents, or particular acts of legislation, then the work of the drafters is mainly one of orderly arrangement; they are not required to concern themselves with the substance or policy of the law, for that is settled before their work begins. It is true that the work must inevitably involve some element of law-creation, for the drafters must exercise some discretion in eliminating minor uncertainties and in filling gaps in the existing law. But this aspect of the work is only incidental to the main task, which is to state the law in a form clearer and more convenient than that in which it previously existed, and that is a task for experts which can appropriately be entrusted to lawyers. Examples of codification which exist in the English legal system, such as the law relating to the sale of goods or to bills of exchange, have been of this type; that is to say, they have been concerned with the form of the law, and only to a very small extent with its substance. But the codification of international law is a very different task.

International codifiers cannot limit their attention to the form of the law; they are inevitably concerned throughout with its substance. They have to choose between competing rules, to fill gaps where the law is uncertain or silent, and to give precision to abstract general principles where the practical application is unsettled; in short, the codification of international law is only possible to the extent that there exist decisions about the law which the drafters are seeking to codify. In circumstances such as these, codification has ceased to be a technical task which can be entrusted to lawyers; it becomes a political matter, a task of law creation, and, in the absence of any international organ with legislative powers, the contents of the code can be settled only if the representatives of governments can agree upon them.

The difficulty involved in achieving such agreement was seen early on in the Codification Conference convened by the League of Nations at The Hague in 1930. Three subjects were before the Conference: the law of nationality, of territorial waters, and of responsibility for damage done to foreigners in the territory of a state. The preparatory work for the Conference had been exceptionally thorough, and there were high hopes, but it was a dismal failure. When governments are asked to bind themselves irrevocably to a proposed formulation of some rule of law, they inevitably (and perhaps even properly) ask themselves whether they might one day find the formulation of the rule inconvenient. Alternatively, they refrain from accepting it because it is part of a broader agreement containing other provisions to which they object. In both cases the result of their refusal in such a codification conference may be to throw doubt on something which has hitherto been generally regarded as an established rule of customary law.

Codification by government representatives has now given way to drafting exercises by the international lawyers in the UN International Law Commission (ILC) or in independent bodies such as the Institute of International Law or the International Law Association.[54] The value of such work depends on its own scientific merits alone. It has proven to be valuable to governments and others by revealing exactly where the law is clear, where it is uncertain, and where it needs amendment. The Statute of the UN ILC distinguishes between the promotion of the *progressive development* of international law, that is, its extension into new fields, which can obviously only be done by official international conventions, and its *codification,* that is, a statement of the law as it exists.[55] The ILC

---

54. For an early suggestion, in the wake of the failure of the 1930 conference, that codification be taken away from governments and conducted by independent groups of lawyers at the international level see Sir Cecil Hurst, 'A Plea for the Codification of International Law on New Lines', in *International Law: The Collected Papers of Sir Cecil Hurst* (London: Stevens, 1950) 129–51. For an examination of the commitment of international lawyers to the issue of codification in the 20th century see T. Skouteris, *The Notion of Progress in International Law Discourse* (The Hague: Asser Press, 2010) ch. 3; see also H.W.A. Thirlway, *International Customary Law and Codification* (Leiden: Sijthoff, 1972).

55. Note also Art. 13(1)(a) of the UN Charter: 'The General Assembly shall initiate studies and make recommendations for the purpose of: (a) promoting international co-operation in the political field and encouraging the progressive development of international law and its codification.'

promotes both these purposes, but when it submits a codifying draft to the General Assembly, it does not always present the text as a draft treaty; it may recommend that once the articles are published no further action should be taken. In such cases the ILC's articles may, or may not, be followed by courts and states as a codification of the law, depending on whether the article in question is considered as part of the Commission's progressive development of the law, or whether the particular article is seen as reflecting the law as it currently stands.[56]

§ 8. The application of international law in domestic courts

Each national legal order will have its own rules for the application of international law in its domestic courts.[57] The accepted doctrine in Britain is that international law is part of our law, and one practical consequence of this, which has been called the doctrine of 'incorporation', is that international law for a British court is not a foreign law. On the one hand, when British courts have to deal

---

56. Of course all aspects of such codification probably involve a degree of progressive development through the choices they make: see Abi-Saab (above) at 139–54. We will examine in later Chapters particular articles produced by the ILC on state responsibility (2001) and diplomatic protection (2006). One of the most significant examples of a draft treaty prepared by the ILC for an international conference of states, who then eventually adopted a negotiated text as a treaty, is the Vienna Convention on the Law of Treaties 1969 (dealt with in detail in Ch. VII).

57. For a systematic look at the situation in a selection of 27 states see D. Shelton, *International Law and Domestic Legal Systems: Incorporation, Transformation, and Persuasion* (Oxford: OUP, 2011).

with an issue which depends on a rule of foreign law, the rule has to be proved by evidence as a fact, like any other fact; on the other hand, because international law is part of the law of the land the courts will take judicial notice of it.

The earliest recorded judicial statement of the doctrine of incorporation is in 1735 in a dictum of Lord Chancellor Talbot in *Barbuit's Case*,[58] where he is reported to have said 'the law of nations in its fullest extent is and forms part of the law of England.' But there is nothing in the report to suggest that the Lord Chancellor thought that he was introducing a new principle; he seems to have been merely stating one that was already well established in the law. Probably for the origin of the doctrine we must remind ourselves of the original conception of international law as simply the law of nature applied to the relations between sovereign princes, and of the fact that the Common Law also professed to be an embodiment of reason. It was natural therefore that judges should think of the two kinds of law, not as two unrelated systems, but as the application to different subject-matters of different parts of one great system of law. However that may be, the doctrine survived after the natural law theories of the basis of international law had ceased to be fashionable in the nineteenth century, and after those theories were succeeded by the positivist view that the law is founded on the express or implied consent of states. The only change was that the doctrine was given a somewhat different formulation.

---

58. *Cas. t. Talbot*, 281.

It was formulated by Lord Chief Justice Alverstone in 1905 in the case *West Rand Mining Co. v The King*[59] in these terms:

Whatever has received the common consent of civilized nations must have received the assent of our country, and that to which we have assented along with other nations in general may properly be called international law, and as such will be acknowledged and applied by our municipal tribunals when legitimate occasion arises for those tribunals to decide questions to which doctrines of international law may be relevant.

Another statement to the same effect is one by Lord Atkin delivering the advice of the Privy Council in *Chung Chi Chiung v The King*: 'The courts acknowledge the existence of a body of rules which nations accept among themselves. On any judicial issue they seek to ascertain what the relevant rule is, and, having found it, they will treat it as incorporated into the domestic law.'[60]

The doctrine that the law of nations, later called international law,[61] is incorporated into national law has therefore been estab-

---

59. [1905] 2 KB 391.

60. [1939] AC 160. When applying customary international law as part of the law of England Lord Bingham suggests 'it can be argued that British judges, applying international law, are applying domestic law, whatever its origin'. T. Bingham, *Widening Horizons: The Influence of Comparative Law and International Law on Domestic Law* (Cambridge: CUP, 2010) at 31. See also J.L. Brierly, 'International Law in England', *Law Quarterly Review* (1935) 24–35 at 31: 'international law is not a part, but is one of the sources, of English law'.

61. On the significance of this change see 'Blackstone and Bentham: The *Law of Nations* and *International* Law' in M.W. Janis, *America and the Law of Nations 1776–1939* (Oxford: OUP, 2010) ch. 1.

lished in our law for nearly 300 years; but it is necessary to ask how accurately it really represents the practice of British courts. Incorporation is limited in a number of ways.

First, under the British Constitution, an Act of Parliament is paramount; international law is part of the Common Law, and in a British court any rule of the Common Law must yield before an Act of Parliament. The point arose in 1906 in the Scottish case of *Mortensen v Peters*,[62] where the appellant, a Danish national, had been fined for trawling (fishing) in the Moray Firth outside the three-mile limit under an Act which made it an offence for 'any person' to trawl in those waters. It was argued by the lawyers on behalf of the Danish fisherman that Parliament could not have intended those words to apply to a foreigner because this would run counter to international law, but the High Court of Justiciary said that the question was purely one of construction of the national law, and they refused to accept the international law arguments put forward by the Danish fisherman.

'In this Court,' said Lord Dunedin, 'we have nothing to do with the question whether the legislature has or has not done what foreign powers may consider a usurpation in a question with them. Neither are we a tribunal sitting to decide whether an Act of the legislature is *ultra vires* as in contravention of generally acknowledged principles of international law. For us an Act of Parliament is supreme, and we are bound to follow its terms … It is a trite observation that there is no such thing as a standard of international

---

62. 14 SLR 227.

law extraneous to the domestic law of a kingdom to which
appeal may be made ... International law, so far as this court
is concerned is the body of doctrine regarding the international rights and duties of states which has been adopted
and made part of the law of Scotland.

There is, however, a presumption that Parliament does not intend
to violate international law, and a statute will not be interpreted
as doing so if that conclusion can be avoided. The same presumption can be seen in the case-law of the United States Supreme
Court in an 1804 case concerning another claim by an individual, Jared Shattuck, who had moved to St Thomas (then Danish
territory, now the US Virgin Islands) and taken an oath of allegiance to Denmark, even though he had been born a US citizen
in the United States. Shattuck's vessel was seized and he was
accused of violating the law suspending commercial relations
between the United States and France. He claimed that his Danish nationality meant he should be considered a neutral under
the law of nations and the Court agreed. In the words of Chief
Justice Marshall 'an act of Congress ought never to be construed
to violate the law of nations if any other possible construction
remains, and consequently can never be construed to violate
neutral rights or to affect neutral commerce further than is war-
ranted by the law of nations as understood in this country.'[63] In
other countries the reception of international law will depend on
the particular constitutional or other arrangements laid down in

---

63. *Murray v The Charming Betsey*, 6 US (2 Cranch) (1804) 64 at 118.

that particular legal order.[64] States vary in their receptiveness,[65] and the willingness to absorb international law in the national legal order under one or another model may change over time as new polities emerge from wars and revolutions.[66]

In the United States the acceptance of the relevance of international law ebbs and flows. There is currently a lively debate on the legitimacy of resorting to international law as an aid to interpretation of the Constitution and other laws especially where these impact on how the United States is seen by others. In a recent speech Ruth Bader Ginsburg, a Justice of the Supreme Court, explained why she thought American courts should pay regard to the law of nations:

> In the value I place on comparative dialogue—on sharing with and learning from others...I draw on counsel from the founders of the United States. The drafters and signers of the Declaration of Independence showed their concern about the opinions of other peoples; they placed before the world the reasons why the States, joining together to become the United States of America, were impelled to separate from

---

64. For a comparative analysis of treaty enforcement by domestic courts see D. Sloss (ed.), *The Role of Domestic Courts in Treaty Enforcement* (Cambridge: CUP, 2009) which includes studies on Australia, Canada, Germany, India, Israel, the Netherlands, Poland, Russian Federation, South Africa, United Kingdom, and the United States.

65. For examples see M. Shaw, *International Law*, 6th edn (Cambridge: CUP, 2008) 166–79.

66. See A. Cassese, 'Modern Constitutions and International Law', 192 *RCADI* III (The Hague: Nijhoff, 1985) 341–476; E. Stein, 'International Law in Internal Law: Toward Internationalization of Central-Eastern European Constitutions?' 88(3) *AJIL* (1994) 427–550.

Great Britain. The Declarants stated their reasons out of 'a decent Respect to the Opinions of Mankind.' They sought to expose those reasons to the scrutiny of 'a candid world.'

The U.S. Supreme Court, early on, expressed a complementary view: The judicial power of the United States, the Court said in 1816, includes cases 'in the correct adjudication of which foreign nations are deeply interested... [and] in which the principles of the law and comity of nations often form an essential inquiry.' Just as the founding generation showed concern for how adjudication in our courts would affect other countries' regard for the United States, so today, even more than when the United States was a new nation, judgments rendered in the USA are subject to the scrutiny of 'a candid World.'[67]

A second qualification of the doctrine of incorporation is that a treaty, though internationally binding, does not thereby alone become part of the law of the land under the British Constitution. The making of treaties is a prerogative power which the Executive may exercise without the concurrence of the Legislature,[68] so that

---

67. '"A decent Respect to the Opinions of [Human]kind": The Value of a Comparative Perspective in Constitutional Adjudication', International Academy of Comparative Law American University, 30 July 2010.

68. As Aust explains: 'This division of powers was a product of the seventeenth-century constitutional struggle between the King of England and Parliament. It resulted in the power to legislate being almost completely vested in Parliament, although the Crown retained in common law certain "royal prerogatives" (the right to act without the consent of Parliament), including the making of treaties.' A. Aust, 'United Kingdom', in *The Role of Domestic Courts in Treaty Enforcement* (above) at 477.

if a treaty were *ipso facto* to become part of our domestic law, it would mean that the Executive could legislate for the country.

Walker v Baird illustrates the British rule.[69] The commander of a naval vessel, acting under orders to enforce a convention with France for regulating the lobster fisheries off Newfoundland, had seized certain lobster factories of the plaintiff, but it was held that this did not excuse the invasion of private rights under national law. There are possibly some exceptional cases in which the Crown, without legislative confirmation, can make treaties which will bind individuals and affect their rights,[70] but the general rule is clear. In the same way the English courts will be reluctant to grant a right and a remedy in national law for the violation of a treaty provision that has not been expressly or indirectly transformed into English law.[71]

Under the US Constitution the rule is different, for a treaty is 'the supreme law of the land ... anything in the constitution or laws of any State notwithstanding'; this is sometimes known as 'automatic incorporation'. But the US Constitution associates the Executive (the President) with one House of the Legislature (the Senate) with the making of treaties. So there is arguably less need for legislative action. The doctrine of self-executing effect means, however, that a judge adjudicating under this model will have to consider whether the provision in question is aimed at the courts

---

69. [1892] AC 491.

70. The operation of European Union law probably takes effect in this way.

71. See Aust 'United Kingdom' (above) for examples of how far English judges are prepared to apply international law in the absence of relevant legislation. The clearest example of legislation which does allow for such a remedy in English law is the Human Rights Act 1998 which incorporates rights from the European Convention on Human Rights (1950).

and can take effect without further legislative action.[72] A number of states allow international law to take effect in the national legal order in this way. Virginia Leary summarized the results of her comparative study as follows: 'in general, treaty provisions are considered by national courts and administrators as self-executing when they lend themselves to judicial or administrative application without further legislative implementation.'[73]

These sorts of qualifications are reflected in the recent South African Constitution of 1996 which contains very explicit provisions on how international law is incorporated into national law:

231. International agreements
(4) Any international agreement becomes law in the Republic when it is enacted into law by national legislation; but a self-executing provision of an agreement that has been approved by Parliament is law in the Republic unless it is inconsistent with the Constitution or an Act of Parliament.
232. Customary international law
Customary international law is law in the Republic unless it is inconsistent with the Constitution or an Act of Parliament.
233. Application of international law
When interpreting any legislation, every court must prefer any reasonable interpretation of the legislation that is consistent with international law over any alternative interpretation that is inconsistent with international law.

---

72. For the origins of this doctrine see Janis (above) at 46–8.
73. V.A. Leary, *International Labour Law and Conventions: The Effectiveness of the Automatic Incorporation of Treaties in National Legal Systems* (The Hague: Nijhoff, 1982) at 39.

A third qualification arises from the practice of British courts in accepting information from the Executive, instead of taking evidence in the ordinary way, on matters which they regard as falling within the Executive sphere. In such cases the responsibility for ensuring that the court's decision conforms to international law rests with the Executive and not with the court. For example, if the Executive informs the court that Britain has recognized Barataria as an independent state, the court will not inquire whether Barataria does or does not satisfy the international requirements of a state.[74] The doctrine of 'act of state' also may have the effect of precluding the courts from judging certain issues, such as the relations between the British Government and other states.[75]

---

74. As we shall see in Ch. IV, since 1980 the UK no longer explicitly recognizes governments in the same way that it officially recognizes states, so it may be for the courts to determine whether the people who claim to represent a government really do represent the state concerned. See *Somalia (A Republic) v Woodhouse Drake and Carey (Suisse) SA* [1993] 1 All ER 371.

75. See further I. Brownlie, *Principles of Public International Law*, 7th edn (Oxford: OUP, 2008) at 49–50; Shaw (above) at 179–92; R. Jennings and A. Watts (eds), *Oppenheim's International Law*, 9th edn, vol. i (London: Longman, 1996) at 365–71. For recent examples of English courts declining to rule in circumstances which raised issues of foreign relations see *Al Rawi and Ors, R (on the application of) v Secretary of State for Foreign & Commonwealth Affairs & Anor* [2006] EWCA Civ 1279: 'This case has involved issues touching both the government's conduct of foreign relations, and national security: pre-eminently the former. In those areas the common law assigns the duty of decision upon the merits to the elected arm of government; all the more so if they combine in the same case. This is the law for constitutional as well as pragmatic reasons.... The court's role is to see that the government strictly complies with all formal requirements, and rationally considers the matters it has to confront. Here, because of the subject-matter, the law accords to the executive an especially broad margin of discretion.' At para. 148. The Court therefore refused to review the Executive's decision not to raise with the US authorities the situation of British residents detained in Guantánamo.

A fourth qualification of the doctrine of incorporation is one that no national court can avoid. It is that a national court can only apply its own version of what the rule of international law is, and however objectively it may try to approach a question which raises an issue of international law, its views will inevitably be influenced by national factors. The Scottish Court case put this very frankly in the passage from *Mortensen v Peters* which has been quoted above, and it is interesting to contrast that passage with one from the judgment of Lord Stowell in the case of *The Maria*.[76]

> The seat of judicial authority, [he said] is indeed locally here … but the law itself has no locality … It is the duty of the person who sits here to determine this question exactly as he would determine the same question if sitting in Stockholm … If I mistake the law in this matter, I mistake that which I consider, and which I mean should be considered, as the universal law upon the question.

But when we remember that the question upon which Lord Stowell was deciding concerned the resistance on the part of a Swedish ship sailing under convoy to visit and search by a British warship, and that the right of convoy was one on which the British and Swedish views were at that time diametrically opposed, it is hard to believe that Lord Stowell really thought that a Swedish judge, sitting in Stockholm, would have been likely to decide the case in the way in which he proposed to decide it himself.

---

76. 1 C. Rob. 340.

Lastly, the highest English court has recently shown that it will not now easily incorporate an international crime into national law, where the legislature has done nothing to create such a crime. In the case of *Jones and others* the appellants were on trial for conspiracy to cause criminal damage, having broken into the Royal Air Force base at Fairford in 2003 and caused damage to fuel tankers and bomb trailers. Part of their defence was that they were acting to prevent an international crime of aggression against Iraq. The question arose whether the crime of aggression was justiciable in a criminal trial in England. Although some of the opinions of their Lordships highlighted the special nature of the crime of aggression as a crime committed by a state through its leaders, the thrust of the judgment turns on the separation of powers and the need for new crimes to be legislated:

> The creation and regulation of crimes is in a modern Parliamentary democracy a matter *par excellence* for Parliament to debate and legislate. Even crimes under public international law can no longer be, if they ever were, the subject of any automatic reception or recognition in domestic law by the courts.[77]

---

77. [2006] UKHL 16, Lord Mance at para. 102.

III | The Legal Organization of International Society

§ 1. The beginnings of international constitutional law

UNTIL relatively recently, government was seen as a purely national function, and interaction between states took place through national officials. This is still the general rule. Every state, for example, has a department of the national government corresponding to the Foreign and Commonwealth Office; and the foreign offices of the world are linked together by the practice of 'legation', or sending of representatives to other states. Since the sixteenth century there has been a general practice of maintaining standing legations (now usually known as 'missions' in other countries), but envoys are still sometimes sent for special purposes as well. Diplomatic agents abroad are appointed by 'letters of credence' from their own state, and they present these 'credentials' to the head of the state to which they are 'accredited'. A state may decline to receive any particular representative, may ask for his or her recall, or even dismiss him or her, but any of these actions is a serious step which should not be taken except for good reason. Such actions belong, however, to

the sphere of international comity (courtesy) rather than to law.[1]
International law, as we shall see, does nevertheless cover issues
relating to the immunities of envoys and their premises.

But diplomacy of this kind is only an instrument for conducting the business of one state with another, and not for conducting
general international business in which a number of states have an
interest. This latter kind of business has vastly increased in extent
and importance in modern times, and states have had to recognize
that in many departments of government none of them can serve
the interests of its own people in the best way unless it arranges to
co-ordinate its action with that of other states. This development
began about the middle of the nineteenth century, and it has led to
the development of institutions which, while they cannot yet be
regarded as giving a 'constitution' to the international society, may
not unfairly be described as a beginning of its constitutional law.[2]

These institutions operate by organizing co-operation between
national governments and not by superseding or dictating to them,
and they are, therefore, probably not so much the beginnings of an
international 'government', though the term is often convenient, as
a substitute for one. It is proper to ask how far these international

---

1. See *Oppenheim's International Law*, 9th edn, vol. i (1996) at 50–2; see further
J.A. Kämmerer, 'Comity', <mpepil.com>.

2. For a contemporary contribution to the debates on this concept see J. Klabbers,
A. Peters, and G. Ulfstein, *The Constitutionalization of International Law* (Oxford: OUP,
2009) whose aim is to 'make visible what might be called the invisible constitution of the
international community'. At p. 4, see also J.L. Dunoff and J.P. Trachtman (eds), *Ruling
the World? Constitutionalism, International Law, and Global Governance* (Cambridge:
CUP, 2009). Compare N. Krisch, *Beyond Constitutionalism: The Pluralist Structure of
Postnational Law* (Oxford: OUP, 2010).

institutions perform for international law the functions which governmental institutions perform for national law, that is to say, the legislative, administrative, executive, and judicial functions.[3]

§ 2. International legislation

An international legislature, in the sense of a body having general powers to enact new international law binding on the states of the world or on their peoples, has not been created. The idea that international law requires deliberate amendment is, indeed, quite modern. The international community was happy historically to rely on the slow growth of custom for the development of its law. Perhaps the first recognition of the need for a consciously constructive process in building up the law was the Declaration by the Congress of Paris in 1814 in favour of freedom of navigation on international rivers. This Declaration was not very effective, but it was significant, as through this conference the international community demonstrated that it had gained a sort of rudimentary legislative organ. Little use, however, was made of conferences for this purpose until after the Conference of Paris in 1856, at which a famous Declaration dealing with the laws of maritime warfare was

---

3. See also the new emphasis on applying public law principles in this context as a way to 'translate concerns about the legitimacy of governance activities into meaningful arguments about legality'. A. von Bogdandy, P. Dann, and M. Goldmann, 'Developing the Publicness of Public International Law: Towards a Legal Framework for Global Governance Activities', in von Bogdandy et al (eds), *The Exercise of Public Authority by International Institutions: Advancing International Institutional Law* (Heidelberg: Springer, 2010) 3–32 at 10.

agreed to. After this time quasi-legislation by conference became fairly frequent.

The movement took different forms. In part it was inspired by the humane desire to mitigate the horrors of war; examples of this are the Geneva Conventions for the victims of war, starting with the first in 1864 (later replaced by the more recent Conventions of 1949 and the Protocols of 1977 and 2005), and most of the Hague Conventions of 1899 and 1907. It took another form in the foundation of the international administrative system which is referred to in the next section. And conferences have often been used for the settlement of *special* political questions by action which is really legislative in character, although it generally preserves the forms of mere mediation between supposedly sovereign states. Instances are: the Conferences of London which established the independence of Belgium and Luxembourg in 1831 and 1867 respectively; and the Congress of Berlin, 1878, which dealt with the affairs of Turkey and the Balkan States. Lastly, in the second half of the twentieth century we have seen diplomatic conferences convened to negotiate and finalize conventions regarding regimes such as for the law of the sea (Geneva 1958, New York 1973–1982), diplomatic and consular relations (Vienna 1961 and 1963), the law of treaties (Vienna 1968 and 1969), and for the Statute of the International Criminal Court (Rome 1998).

The process of changing the law by means of conventions reached at international conferences has obvious disadvantages if we compare it with the work of an ordinary legislative body. The conference is not a continuous body; it meets for some special purpose and then dissolves. The conventions at which it arrives have no binding force over states which do not accept them, and unfortunately states, through apathy, or faced with domestic opposition, or for some other reason, often fail to ratify even those conventions which their representatives have signed. But more serious than the difficulties which arise from the defective nature of international legislative machinery, is the psychological difficulty of mobilizing public opinion behind proposals for international legislation. Only a small minority of the people of any country is continuously interested in international affairs, and the domestic claims upon the time and energies of leaders are so numerous that they are not easily induced to take up reform proposals which have no insistent constituency. Almost any proposal for international change by agreement involves some sacrifice or apparent sacrifice of particular interests, and in the general ignorance of the issues at stake, the sacrifice is easily made to appear greater than any corresponding advantage.

But despite all these difficulties, the volume of international legislation is considerable, and with the burgeoning number of international organizations it has become much easier for states to develop such legislation. Indeed the dynamics of such organizations mean that, in the words of José Alvarez: 'Some international organizations—such as the UN itself and the ILO—have become virtual treaty machines.'[4] Moreover, there is the insight that the continual rounds of meetings and negotiations create the conditions for 'socialisation'. Even if it is hard to see why domestic constituencies should prioritize international 'legislation', the dynamics

---

4. *International Organizations as Law-makers* (above) at 276.

of international gatherings produce a society of international law-makers driven by a certain sense of community.[5]

> [W]hen the representatives of states make official pronounce-ments, when they participate in intergovernmental organisa-tions or other meetings and when they sign international conventions and engage in numerous other formal and infor-mal actions [including networking], they are performing within a context that is sufficiently 'social' for broader hypoth-eses about social interaction to be applied. Nor should it be forgotten that those acting on behalf of states are not autom-ata but individual human beings who are susceptible to the same kinds of social pressures that help to condition all human behaviour.[6]

---

5. The reader will have noticed that we are moving here from the concept of international society to international community. Schwarzenberger saw law as an instrument of power to deal with the conflicting interests found in a society, and as a means to co-ordinate the common efforts of a community. But we should recall Schwarzenberger's injunction 'to realise that sociological terms such as society or community represent ideal or pure types of social relations. In actual life none of these groups exists in undiluted form; they are hybrids. Communities such as the family, nation or church may suffer from greater or smaller admixtures of society elements. Conversely, societies such as a joint-stock com-pany, cartel or even a gang of thieves must accept a minimum of community standards, at least in the relations between members of such groups. Otherwise they cannot even fulfil their own limited social or anti-social functions. Yet community aspirations remain nec-essarily dwarfed in such uncongenial surroundings. Relations between sovereign States, especially on the level of unorganised international society, are more typical of those to be found in a society than in a community.' G. Schwarzenberger, *A Manual of International Law*, 5th edn (New York: Praeger, 1967) at 12.

6. D. Armstrong, T. Farrell, and H. Lambert, *International Law and International Rela-tions* (Cambridge: CUP, 2007) at 29 (footnote omitted).

We might also recall that, as we saw in the last chapter in the section on 'soft law', the output of such legislative exercises is not limited to drafting binding conventions, nor is it necessarily dependent on states becoming legally bound under the law of treaties. Not only have states found it convenient to establish international institutions which can develop international treaties, they have also used such institutions to develop influential instruments. International relations scholars have emphasized how these texts influence states and others even in the absence of binding legal obligation: 'Established procedures for elaborating rules, standards, and specifications enhance cooperation even when member states retain the power to reject or opt out—as they do even in IOs with relatively advanced legislative procedures, like the ILO. Nonbinding recommendations can become de facto coordination equilibria, relied on by states and other international actors.'[7]

We can trace these developments to the formation of the League of Nations which greatly stimulated the practice of international legislation. In pre-League days, when a matter was thought to call for international regulation, it had to be taken up as a piece of business unrelated to other matters of a similar kind; a special conference would be summoned through the slow-moving channels of diplomacy, a secretariat improvised, and perhaps a special

---

7. K.W. Abbott and D. Snidal, 'Why States Act through Formal International Organizations', 42 *Journal of Conflict Resolution* (1998) 3–32, at 15. For examples of how nonbinding institutional acts may nevertheless have legal (and other) effects see P. Sands and P. Klein, *Bowett's Law of International Institutions*, 6th edn (London: Sweet and Maxwell, 2009) at 267–302, and we might note here how the 'norms contained in these acts are binding because they can be linked to other, "traditional" sources of international law such as unilateral undertakings or international customary law'. Ibid 297.

organ created to give effect to the decisions of the conference after it had broken up. The League provided a permanent organization which could be used for taking up any matter which states had decided to regulate internationally, which could collect the relevant information on which to base an agreement, and could supervise the working of an agreement if one should be concluded. In this aspect of its work the League was simply a standing conference system, and for no idealistic reasons, but merely as a matter of practical convenience, the modern world can hardly conduct its international relations without such a system. There are many functions which states cannot perform efficiently unless they act together—one of the most obvious is the control of disease— germs recognize no frontiers.

As far back as 1974 this was obvious to Sir Gerald Fitzmaurice who predicted that states will inevitably come together to tackle transnational threats through international action. For him there were:

fields in which it is becoming clear that the nation-State alone cannot assure the protection of the individual—even its own particular subjects or citizens—from the prospect of serious harm,—and where in the long run only international action, internationally organized and carried out, will suffice, since the mischief knows no natural boundaries, and cannot be kept out by any purely national barriers;—such things as overpopulation and its consequences in overcrowding, malnutrition and disease; the pollution of waters, rivers, seas and airspace; the overexploitation and potential exhaustion of the earth's mineral resources and stores of fuel and power; the extinction of species and devastation of fish stocks; problems of drought, famine and hurricane damage; problems of poverty and underdevelopment; the possible misuse of outer space; terrorist activities that cross all frontiers, and 'hi-jacking' of aircraft and other threats to the safety of communication; the traffic in arms, narcotic drugs and slavery; forced labour; migration, emigration, conditions of work and other labour problems, etc.[8]

In short, there is a contracting field of action within which any one state can develop its own policies without taking account of what other states are doing, or are likely to do. Technological developments in transport and communications are making the economy of every country, even the greatest and most self-sufficient, ever more sensitive to what happens in other countries. Today the 'standing conference system' of the League has been replaced by multiple fora for such legislative activity. We should highlight the convenience of negotiating multilateral treaties through the organs, bodies and agencies of the United Nations, as well as regional intergovernmental organizations, such as the Organization of American States, the Council of Europe, the African Union, and the League of Arab States.[9]

8. 'The Future of Public International Law and of the International Legal System in the Circumstances of Today', in Institut de Droit International, *Livre du Centenaire 1873–1973: Evolution et perspectives du droit international* (Basel: Karger, 1973) 196–329 at 260.

9. More than 500 multilateral treaties are deposited with the UN and their status and participants can be seen at <http://treaties.un.org/pages/ParticipationStatus.aspx>. Treaties deposited with other organizations or with a state can be found with the database established by the London Institute of Advanced Legal Studies: <http://ials.sas.ac.uk/library/flag/introtreaties.htm>.

Sands and Klein have helpfully reminded us that the international legislative function of international institutions is not confined to international organizations established as such. Some treaties have given rise not to separate organizations but rather to regular meetings of the states parties, such as the Convention on Certain Conventional Weapons, and in the environmental field we find Conferences of the Parties which may even take binding decisions, such as listing endangered species in the context of the Convention on International Trade in Endangered Species of Wild Fauna and Flora.[10] Other examples concern Conventions on: Migratory Species, Biological Diversity, the Protection of the Ozone, Climate Change, and Desertification. We can add for completeness that there are multiple conventions of this type on oil pollution, hazardous waste, and corruption. Similarly we are reminded that: 'International law has long sought to regulate the production of, and trade in, basic commodities. Sugar was regulated by international agreement as early as 1864, and the first rubber agreement was adopted in 1934.'[11] In the absence of a systematic regime, it is explained that single commodity agreements with their own institutional regimes were adopted after the Second World War including for 'wheat (1949), sugar (1953), tin (1954), olive oil (1956), coffee (1962), cocoa (1973), rubber (1979) and tropical timber (1986)'.[12] Recalling these multiple sites for international legislation helps to emphasize that we do not have an international

---

10. For detail on this treaty regime and others related to the environment and commodities see Sands and Klein (above) 123–38; regional institutions can be found in chs 5–10.
11. Ibid 131.
12. Ibid.

society legislating through one international organization, but rather, as the Chapter heading suggests, the Legal Organization of International Society.

§ 3. The administrative and executive functions

The administrative function, like the executive, is not provided in the international system with any centralized organ, but in the latter half of the nineteenth century a number of separate institutions with specialized administrative functions were created. They arose not from any idealistic theory of international relations, but from the compelling force of circumstances. In one national administrative department after another, experience showed that government could not be even reasonably efficient if it continued to be organized on a purely national basis. These institutions were known as 'public international unions'. The first such union was the International Telegraphic Union formed in 1865; others are the Universal Postal Union of 1874, the International Institute of Agriculture of 1905, and the Radiotelegraphic Union of 1906.

The Postal Union represents a continuing successful example of the type. It was achieved after it became obvious that bilateral treaties between different pairs of states, and an insistence on sovereign independence, were hopelessly inefficient in such a matter as international postage. This is one of the many experiments in international administrative co-operation which have arisen in response to problems which could not be solved by methods of government organized on the traditional theory that each state is a sovereign and separate unit. States are no longer separate units in such matters as commerce, labour, art, morals, inventions, health; and slowly they are being compelled to recognize that they cannot be altogether separate units in the political or economic fields. The creation of the League of Nations in 1919 was therefore not the introduction of a wholly new principle into international life, but the logical outcome of a movement which had been gathering force for many years. There is now a wide range of UN specialized agencies, programmes, and funds which tackle international cooperation in these fields.[13]

Moreover, we should recognize that these arrangements represent a nascent administration of international society rather than

---

13. The UN Specialized Agencies: International Labour Organization, Food and Agriculture Organization, United Nations Educational, Scientific and Cultural Organization, World Health Organization, the World Bank Group (International Bank for Reconstruction and Development, International Development Association, International Finance Cooperation, Multilateral Investment Guarantee Agency, International Centre for Settlement of Investment Disputes), International Monetary Fund, International Civil Aviation Organization, International Maritime Organization, International Telecommunication Union, Universal Postal Union, World Meteorological Organization, World Intellectual Property Organization, International Fund for Agricultural Development, United Nations Industrial Development Organization, World Tourism Organization. See also the International Atomic Energy Agency and the following examples of UN programmes and funds: United Nations Conference on Trade and Development, United Nations Drug Control Programme, United Nations Environment Programme, United Nations Children's Fund, United Nations Development Programme, United Nations Development Fund for Women, United Nations Population Fund, United Nations Human Settlements Programme, United Nations Relief and Works Agency for Palestine Refugees in the Near East, and World Food Programme. In addition consider the activities of the Office of the UN High Commissioner for Human Rights and the High Commissioner for Refugees.

something approaching an administrative function for an international community. These organizations for the most part provide ways for states to pursue more efficiently their interests. The type of legal organization we find in the Universal Postal Union has been described by Joseph Weiler as an expression of 'transactional law'.[14] It is 'mostly a mechanism to serve more efficiently the contractarian goals of States'.[15] This mechanism and other arrangements such as the General Agreement on Tariffs and Trade (GATT) of 1947 are 'multipartite in form', but 'in substance just more efficient structures enabling their parties to transact bilateral Agreements'.[16] For Weiler such arrangements are not emblematic of something approaching international community; for this he says we need to start to think about common assets:

> Materially, the hallmark of Community may, in my view, be found in the appropriation or definition of common assets. The common assets could be material such as the deep bed of the high sea, or territorial such as certain areas of space. They can be functional such as certain aspects of collective security and they can even be spiritual: Internationally defined Human Rights or ecological norms represent common spiritual assets where States can no more assert their exclusive sovereignty, even within their territory, [than] they could over areas of space which extend above their air-space.[17]

---

14. 'The Geology of International Law—Governance, Democracy and Legitimacy', 64 *ZaöRV* (2005) 547–62 at 533.

15. Ibid 556.

16. Ibid 533.

17. Ibidem.

The notion that certain functions carried out by international organizations represent a sort of international administrative role has in recent years led to the idea of a corresponding 'global administrative law'. These entities have taken on administrative functions which go beyond their own relationship with their members. Some agencies such as the International Civil Aviation Organization or the World Health Organization actually administer in contexts such as terrorist attacks on civil aviation or health emergencies (SARs, H5N1 (avian flu), H1N1 (swine flu) etc). In such situations administrative law principles have become more prominent. Such principles may demand: transparency, access to information, privacy of information, participation, giving reasons for decisions, review of administrative-type decisions, and accountability.[18] Moreover, we are witnessing new forms of global administration that involve not only the public international unions and specialized agencies mentioned above, but also public-private partnerships (PPPs), multi-stakeholder initiatives, and hybrid models that defy categorization as public or private. We could mention here the global mechanism that administers internet domain names: Internet Corporation for Assigned Names and Numbers (ICANN)[19] as well as the entity supervising doping in sport—the World Anti-Doping Agency (WADA). And we can look beyond such regulatory regimes to discover private institu-

---

18. See B. Kingsbury and L. Casini, 'Global Administrative Law Dimensions of International Organizations Law', 6 *International Organizations Law Review* (2009) 319–58 at 325.

19. For studies see M. Hartwig, 'ICANN—Governance by Technical Necessity', in von Bogdandy et al (above); J. Mathiason, *Internet Governance: The new frontier of global institutions* (London: Routledge, 2009).

tions under Swiss law such as the Global Fund to Fight AIDS, Malaria and Tuberculosis, the Global Alliance for Vaccines and Immunization (GAVI), and the International Olympic Committee.

In many ways these so called administrative developments contain elements of legislative activity as well as some adjudication and enforcement possibilities. Cybersquatting on Madonna.com can be challenged by Madonna herself through the ICANN dispute settlement procedure, and the eventual ruling to attach this domain name to her IP address is enforced with a few keystrokes, resulting in 99 per cent of cases never reaching a national court.[20] The regime created by the World Anti-Doping Code (WADC) is not only detailed in its regulations, but it contains its own mechanisms for enforcement against individual athletes; and appeals are to a specialized Court of Arbitration for Sport.[21] The Code even carries the threat of enforcement by excluding national Olympic committees from bidding for the Olympic Games.[22] Many of these developments now take place somewhere between the national level and the treaty-based intergovernmental organizations that developed in the

---

20. T. Schultz, 'Private Legal Systems: What Cyberspace Might Teach Legal Theorists', 10 *Yale Journal of Law and Technology* (2007) 151–93.

21. See L. Casini, 'Global Hybrid Public-Private Bodies: The World Anti-Doping Agency (WADA)', 6 *International Organizations Law Review* (2009) 421–46.

22. The International Olympic Committee has a responsibility under the Code '[t]o accept bids for the Olympic Games only from countries where the government has ratified, accepted, approved or acceded to the UNESCO Convention and the National Olympic Committee, National Paralympic Committee and National Anti-Doping Organization are in compliance with the Code'. Art. 20.1.8, and see further Arts 22.6 and 23.5.

nineteenth century. So we find 'regulation by private international standard-setting bodies and by hybrid public-private organizations that may include, variously, representatives of businesses, NGOs, national governments, and intergovernmental organizations'.[23] This is said to have created 'an accountability deficit in the growing exercise of transnational regulatory power' which has not yet been met with an extension of administrative law to these transnational decisions and regimes.[24]

Turning to the idea of enforcement through executive action, we have to admit the international system has no central organ for the enforcement of international legal rights as such; and the creation of any such general scheme of sanctions is a rather distant prospect. Nevertheless, each of the institutional regimes outlined above has various compliance mechanisms with varying degrees of effectiveness. But to understand properly the work of the agencies one has to look beyond mechanisms for the enforcement of legal obligations and examine the daily work done in the field. The High Commissioner for Refugees, for example has around 7,000 personnel working in 125 countries.

But the major change followed the end of the cold war; the Security Council and the General Assembly were able to agree to deploy large operations in the context of the UN's work on the maintenance of peace and security. By 2012 there were over 120,000 personnel serving in 16 UN peace operations. Similarly, human rights field activities have mushroomed, and now the

---

23. B. Kingsbury, N. Krisch, and R. Stewart, 'The Emergence of Global Administrative Law', 68 *Law and Contemporary Problems* (2005) 15–62, at 16.
24. Ibid.

Office of the High Commissioner for Human Rights has about 500 staff deployed around the world, with offices in Bolivia, Cambodia, Colombia, Guatemala, Mexico, Nepal, Togo, Uganda, Kosovo, and the occupied Palestinian territory. All such international personnel can be seen as indirectly enforcing international norms, through their day-to-day interaction with the local authorities and their reporting back to the relevant political bodies.

However, the enforcement problem that captures everyone's attention is how the use of force by states can be subjected to law. In the twentieth century two notable experiments, in the Covenant of the League of Nations and the Charter of the United Nations, were undertaken with this end in view. These two experiments followed different lines. The system of the League relied on the members taking certain prescribed measures against an aggressor, but it did not set up a supra-national authority—the organs of the League could merely be used for co-ordinating the actions of the individual members, the League's organs could not issue directions as to the action these members were to take. On the other hand, the UN Charter created, for the first time in 1945, an authority (the Security Council) which is to exercise a power of this supra-national kind in situations that threaten international peace and security. As we shall see later, in such circumstances the Security Council has been given the legal power to impose binding sanctions on UN member states and ultimately to authorize the use of force. Suffice it say here that the UN contains no general enforcement mechanism or executive arm to respond to 'ordinary' violations of international law where the Security Council is not operating under Chapter VII of the Charter to restore or maintain international peace and security.

This absence of a general executive power means that each state remains free, subject to the legal limitations on peaceful reprisals (countermeasures), and the prohibition on the threat or use of force,[25] to take such action as it thinks fit to enforce its own rights. This may mean that a state chooses to respond to a violation by failing to fulfil its international obligations to the state that is in violation. This is known as a reprisal or countermeasure, and such action will not be considered unlawful if certain conditions are met.[26] So we can see that it is wrong to assert that international law has no sanctions, if that word is used in its proper sense of 'means for securing the observance of the law'. But it is true that the sanctions which international law possesses are not systematic or centrally directed, and they are precarious and uneven in their operation. Today, many references to 'sanctions' tend to allude to collective measures, taken through the UN or regional organiza-

---

25. See below, Ch. IX and N. Stürchler, *The Threat of Force in International Law* (Cambridge: CUP, 2007); C. Gray, *International Law and the Use of Force*, 3rd edn (Oxford: OUP, 2008); O. Corten, *The Law Against War: The Prohibition on the Use of Force in Contemporary International Law* (Oxford: Hart, 2010); and N. Lubell, *Extraterritorial Use of Force Against Non-State Actors* (Oxford: OUP, 2010).

26. The International Law Commission's Articles on Responsibility of States for Internationally Wrongful Acts (2001) set out the limits in this context: Arts 49–54. Most importantly the countermeasures must be proportionate, allow for the resumption of performance of the obligation that has been violated, and finish as soon as the violating state has complied with its obligations. Countermeasures are not permitted if they affect obligations to protect fundamental human rights or those persons and objects protected from reprisal under the laws of war. Nor can countermeasures be used with regard to obligations owed in the context of respecting the inviolability of ambassadors, embassies and so on (see below Ch. VI § 11). For more detail on countermeasures see J. Crawford, A. Pellet, and S. Olleson (eds), *The Law of International Responsibility* (Oxford: OUP, 2010) chs 79–86.

tions such as the European Union or African Union, and these measures of course remain politically selective. This lack of system is obviously unsatisfactory, particularly to those states which are less able than others to assert effectively their own rights through resorting to countermeasures.

The difficulties of introducing any radical change into the present means of enforcing international law are formidable. The problem has little analogy with that of the enforcement of law within the state, and the idea of an 'international police force' tends to make it appear much simpler than it really is. Police action suggests the bringing to bear of the overwhelming force of the community against a comparatively feeble individual law-breaker, but such action is more problematic in the international sphere, where the potential law-breakers are states, and the preponderance of force may even be on the side of the law-breaking state.

§ 4. The judicial function

Although it seems obvious that there is a need for a court, the danger is that it may be thought to be the only institutional need for the rule of law in international society. For it is a profound, though unfortunately a common mistake to think of law as something of which the whole purpose is the maintenance of existing rights and the enforcement of existing duties. Perhaps we tend to do this because, when we look at the state, we see the work of the courts as one great department of government, distinct both from politics and administration, and are tempted to identify this with the whole of the rule of law. But actually the work of the courts is only one aspect of that rule.[27]

As we have just seen the legislative, executive, and administrative functions may operate even in the absence of a system of courts. The growth of international courts in the twentieth century, however, has been significant and should be seen alongside the multiple opportunities for binding arbitration at the international level. These possibilities now cover not only general international law disputes but also areas such as international investments, the law of the sea, international trade, intellectual property, human rights, and international criminal law.[28] The main problem, however, is that these decision-making instances are not courts of universal jurisdiction. Not all states are covered and not all fields of law are covered. In general states choose which courts they will allow to have jurisdiction over them and then only with regard to certain disputes. We will explain in more detail in Chapter VIII the ways in which states submit to the jurisdiction of the International Court of Justice for inter-state disputes. But now, in addition to the International Court of Justice exercising such jurisdiction over states, we have international criminal tribunals with jurisdiction over individuals.

As already mentioned in the 1990s the UN Security Council established *ad hoc* tribunals with regard to international crimes committed in the former Yugoslavia and with regard to Rwanda.[29]

27. This paragraph is adapted and reprised from Brierly 'The Rule of Law in International Society' (1936) reprinted in *The Basis of Obligation and Other Papers* 250–64 at 260.

28. For detail see *Bowett's Law of International Institutions* (above) ch. 13; see also the useful website of the Project on International Courts and Tribunals <http://www.pict-pcti.org/>.

29. For some of the political background, see D. Scheffer, *All the Missing Souls: A Personal History of the War Crimes Tribunals* (Oxford: Princeton University Press, 2012).

A series of internationalized tribunals were also established with regard to Sierra Leone, Kosovo, Cambodia, and Lebanon. Each of these tribunals has its own set of rules limiting its jurisdiction.[30] We will explain only the rules relating to the International Criminal Court.

The Statute of the International Criminal Court entered into force on 1 July 2002 and the Court has jurisdiction over certain crimes committed after that date: genocide, crimes against humanity, and war crimes.[31] From 2017 it will likely also have additional jurisdiction over the crime of aggression.[32] The Court, however, does not, strictly speaking, have what might be called 'universal jurisdiction', even though this was proposed during the negotiations.[33] The Statute grants the Court jurisdiction in four different ways. First, where the conduct occurred on the territory of a state party or on board a vessel or aircraft registered in a state party.[34] Second, where the accused is a national of a state party.[35] Third, any state (not a party to the Statute) can make a declaration with respect to a situation in order to bring crimes committed by its nationals, or

---

30. See C.P.R. Romano, A. Nollkaemper, and J.K. Kleffner (eds), *Internationalized Criminal Courts and Tribunals: Sierra Leone, East Timor, Kosovo, and Cambodia* (Oxford: OUP, 2004).

31. We will consider these crimes in Chapter IX. Note the preconditions for jurisdiction are different with regard to crimes which have been included in the Court's Statute through the Review Conference in Kampala 2010, see Resolutions RC/Res. 5 and 6, and Arts 15*bis* and 15*ter*, see fn 38 (below).

32. See Ch. IX § 4 below.

33. See W.A. Schabas, *The International Criminal Court: A Commentary on the Rome Statute* (Oxford: OUP, 2010) at 276–83.

34. Art. 12(2)(a).

35. Art. 12(2)(b).

on its territory, within the jurisdiction of the Court.[36] And fourth, the Security Council may decide to bring a situation within the jurisdiction of the Court; this has happened with regard to Darfur and Libya.[37]

The International Criminal Court can exercise its jurisdiction when any one of these four preconditions is satisfied but there is an additional requirement of a 'trigger' in the absence of a Security Council referral. Jurisdiction is triggered through two possibilities. First, when a state party refers a situation to the Prosecutor; or second where the Prosecutor decides to initiate an investigation.

The International Criminal Court has so far had very few defendants, and has been focused on Africa. So far, the only states that have chosen to use the trigger mechanism are the Central African Republic, the Democratic Republic of Congo, and Uganda. While the Security Council's first referrals were with

---

36. Art. 12(3). Article 12(3) has to be read in conjunction with Rule 44 of the Rules of Procedure and Evidence in essence ensuring that any such declaration covers all crimes of relevance to the situation. Note that declarations under Art. 12(3) can be retroactive back to 1 July 2002. On the Palestinian declaration see A. Pellet, 'The Palestinian Declaration and the Jurisdiction of the International Criminal Court', 8 *EJIL* (2010) 981–99; M.N. Shaw, 'The Article 12(3) Declaration of the Palestinian Authority, the International Criminal Court and International Law', 9(2) *Journal of International Criminal Justice* (2011) 301–24. Declarations have also been made by Côte d'Ivoire and Uganda.

37. Art. 13(b) See Resolutions 1593 (2005) and 1970 (2011). In these last two situations the Security Council decided that nationals and personnel from states that have not joined the ICC Statute, and that are engaged in UN authorized operations in Sudan or Libya, would come under the exclusive jurisdiction of that sending state and not that of the International Criminal Court. This was an attempt to exclude US personnel from the jurisdiction of the Court. Whether or not the Court would accept such an exclusion from its jurisdiction in this form, the Security Council does have the power under the Statute to defer an investigation or prosecution for 12 months. See Art. 16.

regard to Darfur (Sudan) and Libya. The Prosecutor has triggered jurisdiction with regard to Kenya and Côte d'Ivoire, and has announced preliminary examinations in situations such as Afghanistan, Georgia, Guinea, Colombia, Palestine, Honduras, Korea, and Nigeria.

The Court is something more than an arrangement between the states party to the Statute. It has potential universal reach. As we have just seen, the Security Council can decide to refer a situation (in the context of a threat to international peace and security) to the Court. Indeed it was as the result of such referrals that we have seen arrest warrants issued by the Court for, *inter alios*, the President of Sudan and the Head of State of Libya. But even in the absence of a Security Council referral, any state can make a retroactive declaration bringing acts committed in their territory or by their nationals within the jurisdiction of the Court. The result is that any individual who has committed acts constituting genocide, crimes against humanity, or war crimes, committed after the entry into force of the Court's Statute (1 July 2002), can potentially be tried before this international court.[38] Of course the Security Council or the relevant states may not be willing to create these preconditions for jurisdiction, and this new court cannot try everyone suspected of such international crimes (apart from issues of cost, the problems of evidence gathering, witness protection, and

---

38. Such a Declaration cannot, however, be used by a state which is not a party to the Statute with regard to the crime of aggression, following the entry into force of the relevant amendments, nor, in the absence of a Security Council referral, can the Court exercise its jurisdiction over the crime of aggression when committed by nationals from such a state or on the territory of such a state. See Art. 15*bis*(5) of the amended Statute and Ch. IX § 4 below.

capture remain insurmountable). But one may fairly state that international society now has a criminal court with potential universal jurisdiction. This criminal jurisdiction sits alongside the more established possibilities for the settlement of disputes in non-criminal cases.[39]

While the prospect of prosecution perhaps has the greatest impact on behaviour, it is the Court's interaction with national jurisdictions which will have the most concrete impact on the evolution of criminal jurisdiction in international law. Under the Statute, a case will be considered inadmissible by the Court where it is 'being investigated or prosecuted by a State which has jurisdiction over it, unless the State is unwilling or unable genuinely to carry out the investigation or prosecution'.[40] This relationship is known as 'complementarity'. The upshot has been that all states (the provision is not restricted to states parties) have an interest in legislating for national jurisdiction over these international crimes. As national legislation develops in this field, states are developing their jurisdiction to prosecute with regard to these (and other related crimes[41]) in ways which cover not only crimes committed on their territory, but also acts committed abroad by their nationals and residents (this is the case for example for the United Kingdom[42]). In some cases states (such as Switzerland[43]) have provided for national prosecutions for genocide, crimes against humanity, and war crimes even without such links; the presence of the defendant within the jurisdiction is enough.

---

39. Discussed in Ch. VIII.

40. Art. 17(1)(a).

41. See J. Bacio-Terracino, 'National Implementation of ICC Crimes', 5 *JICJ* (2007) 421–40.

42. International Criminal Court Act 2001, section 51.

43. Loi fédérale of 18 June 2010, see Code pénal Art. 264m, Code militaire Art. 10.

The debate will continue as to whether such prosecutions may hinder the prospects of peace or enhance transitional justice.[44] The International Criminal Court has two provisions to deal with the peace versus justice dilemma. First, the Security Council may defer investigation or prosecution for a renewable period of twelve months.[45] Second, the Prosecutor may decide that an investigation would not 'serve the interests of justice'.[46] At the national level, national justice systems may require political approval for the prosecution of international crimes committed abroad by foreign officials. The widening net of jurisdiction generated by the Statute of the International Criminal Court will not eliminate the tension between ensuring accountability for international crimes—and states' continuing interest in smooth international relations.[47] What is clear is that there are now multiple sites to try those

---

44. See the interesting recent study by K. Sikkink, *The Justice Cascade: How Human Rights Prosecutions are Changing World Politics* (NY: Norton, 2011).

45. ICC Statute Art. 16.

46. ICC Statute Art. 53.

47. It is perhaps worth opening a parenthesis to revisit Brierly's opposition to an International Criminal Court. 'Do We Need an International Court?' 8 *BYBIL* (1927) 81–8. We might select three misgivings he had voiced, writing in the inter-War period: first, he considered that the deterrent effect would be minimal—'the nobler class of war criminal' would probably regard the ultimate punishment as adding to a sense of patriotic duty; while the baser would regard the chances of getting caught as remote, in addition states would be unwilling to surrender their nationals to such a jurisdiction. Second, legal recriminations would hinder the work of drafting peace settlements. Third, the rules on aerial warfare, the protection of civilians, and the use of submarines were all underdeveloped, and in addition there was no scale of punishments for contraventions of the laws of war. Today we have a much more detailed law of war—but we should continue to ask how this new International Criminal Court can achieve deterrence, the presence of detainees, and assist rather than hinder effective peace settlements.

accused of international crimes and that the international law on jurisdiction is expanding these possibilities.

National courts have started to take on the role of trying those accused of these international crimes. In several cases the national courts have no particular link to the commission of the crimes other than the fact that the accused were found on their territory. Rwandese were tried in Switzerland, Belgium, Finland, Germany, and Canada; Serbs were tried in Germany; and a Bosnian Muslim was tried in Denmark. This decentralized international judiciary has only handled relatively few cases but it is becoming clearer that one cannot simply deny the existence in international society of any judicial arm for dealing with international crimes.

In fact, in considering the judicial function in international society we need to admit that away from the criminal context national courts often act as courts of international law. In the previous Chapter we saw how international law may take effect as national law through incorporation in the national legal order. But national courts may be not only applying national law but also enforcing international law. Let us consider the civil litigation unsuccessfully brought against the Saudi Arabian Government in the English courts alleging acts of torture against certain British nationals.[48] The House of Lords examined the international law of immunity and found that it applied in this case to the Saudi Arabian Government, notwithstanding the international law prohibiting torture. Lord Bingham, writing in his non-judicial capacity, concluded 'the English court was not in this case expounding and

---

48. *Jones v Ministry of the Interior of the Kingdom of Saudi Arabia* [2006] UKHL 26. We deal with this topic further in Ch. VI § 11.

applying a body of English law but was acting, to all intents and purposes, as a tribunal exploring and seeking to expound the law which prevails internationally'.[49]

§ 5. The United Nations

Our discussion of the legal organization of international society would not be complete without a brief introduction to the United Nations.[50] We have already seen how specialized agencies such as the UN World Health Organization may not only provide a forum for international legislative activity, but also play a sort of administrative role, for example by tackling health emergencies. We have suggested that the executive powers of the organization may sometimes be exercised even in the absence of the unanimous consent of the members; for example where the Security Council imposes sanctions or authorizes force against a member state. We have also seen that the UN General Assembly has been the site for the negotiation and adoption of resolutions, declarations, and treaties which make up the tapestry of written international 'legislation'; moreover these texts can be evidence of the emergence of customary international law. Let us now consider the structure of the

---

49. *Widening Horizons: The Influence of Comparative Law and International Law on Domestic Law* (Cambridge: CUP, 2010) at 49.

50. For a brief history see J.M. Hanhimäki, *The United Nations: A Very Short Introduction* (Oxford: OUP, 2008); for an introduction to the work of the various organs and bodies see T.G. Weiss and S. Daws (eds), *Oxford Handbook on the United Nations* (Oxford: OUP, 2007); and for legal issues see B. Conforti and C. Focarelli (eds), *The Law and Practice of the United Nations*, 4th edn (Leiden: Nijhoff, 2010).

United Nations by examining its nature and the procedures used in some of the principal organs.

The International Court of Justice considered the juridical nature of the United Nations in an Advisory Opinion on *Reparation for injuries suffered in the service of the United Nations.*[51] On 17 September 1948 Count Bernadotte was murdered in Jerusalem.[52] He was a Swedish diplomat who was serving as the UN Mediator in Palestine with a mandate, *inter alia*, to '[p]romote a peaceful adjustment of the future situation of Palestine'.[53] Following the murder of Bernadotte and another UN official, the General Assembly asked the Court to advise whether, in the event of an agent of the United Nations suffering injury in circumstances involving the responsibility of a state, the United Nations, as an organization, had the capacity to bring an international claim against the state responsible, with a view to obtaining reparation. The Court was of the opinion that the states which set it up, representing as they did the vast majority of the members of the international community, had the power, in conformity with international law, to bring into being an entity possessing objective international personality and not merely personality recognized by themselves alone. That does not mean that the United Nations is a state, and still less that it is a super-state, or that its rights and duties are the same as those of a state. It means that it is a subject of international law and capable of possessing international rights and duties, and

---

51. ICJ Advisory Opinion, 11 April 1949.

52. For the background see K. Marton, *A Death in Jerusalem: The Assassination by Jewish Extremists of the First Arab/Israeli Peacemaker* (NY: Pantheon, 1994).

53. GA Res. 186 (S-2), 14 May 1948; see also SC Res. 49 (1948).

of maintaining its rights by bringing international claims. In this case the claim was against a non-member state, as Israel had not yet been admitted as a member of the UN. More recently the International Court of Justice has ruled that Malaysia had to respect the immunity of a UN human rights expert who had spoken out about corruption.[54] Most disputes however between the UN and its member states will not finish before the International Court of Justice, but rather will be settled through diplomatic channels.

The United Nations itself is composed of almost all the states in the world and has five effective principal organs, the General Assembly, the Security Council, the Economic and Social Council, the International Court of Justice, and the Secretariat.[55] The Charter (the UN's constitution) distinguishes between the functions of the General Assembly and the Security Council by placing on the Council the 'primary responsibility' for the maintenance of peace, and precluding the Assembly, whose functions in other respects are very wide and general, from dealing with that subject in a way that might embarrass the Security Council.[56] But the

---

54. ICJ Advisory Opinion, *Difference Relating to Immunity from Legal Process of a Special Rapporteur of the Commission on Human Rights*, 29 April 1999.

55. We will only consider aspects of legal organization presented by the General Assembly and Security Council; for a fuller overview see M. Shaw, *International Law*, 6th edn (Cambridge: CUP, 2008) ch. 22.

56. The Charter's Article 12(1) reads: 'While the Security Council is exercising in respect of any dispute or situation the functions assigned to it in the present Charter, the General Assembly shall not make any recommendation with regard to that dispute or situation unless the Security Council so requests.' Nevertheless in practice the General Assembly does address situations before the Security Council on the grounds that the Council is not exercising its powers 'at this moment', and under the Uniting for Peace Resolution 377 (V) (1950) the Assembly determined that where the Security Council fails to

effect of this differentiation is in some respects unfortunate; it separates matters which are not intrinsically separable, for those that are given to the General Assembly, social and economic matters, for example, are often the underlying causes of the frictions which threaten international peace and security. In recent years there has been an effort to address wider issues in the Security Council, for example through the debates on AIDS; justice and the rule of law; international terrorism; the protection of civilians in armed conflict; women, peace and conflict; children and armed conflict; drug trafficking; small arms; nuclear non-proliferation and nuclear disarmament.

The General Assembly has a number of subsidiary organs such as the International Law Commission (composed of 31 individuals of 'recognized competence in international law'[57]), the Human Rights Council (with a membership of 47 states elected by the membership of the Assembly taking into account 'the contribution of candidates to the promotion and protection of human rights and their voluntary pledges and commitments made thereto'[58]), and the Peacebuilding Commission (with 31 states drawn in part from the states that contribute the most 'military personnel and civilian police to United Nations missions'[59]).

---

exercise its primary responsibility for the maintenance of international peace and security due to a lack of unanimity of the permanent members, the Assembly may make appropriate recommendations for collective measures. See further the Advisory Opinion of the ICJ *Legal Consequences of the Construction of a Wall in the Occupied Palestinian Territory,* Advisory Opinion, ICJ Rep. (2004) p. 136, paras 24–32.

57. Statute of the ILC Article 2(1).

58. A/RES/60/251, para. 8.

59. A/RES/60/180, para. 4c; S/RES/1645 (2005) para. 4c; the Commission was established by the Security Council and the General Assembly concurrently.

The specific functions of the General Assembly, which consists of all the members of the Organization, are to discuss any matter within the scope of the Charter and to make recommendations thereon, either to the members of the United Nations, or to the Security Council, or to both. But this is subject to the proviso that the Assembly must refer to the Security Council any question relating to international peace on which action is necessary, and it may not make any recommendation on a dispute or situation which is being dealt with by the Security Council. The General Assembly also approves the budget of the Organization and apportions the expenses among the members. It takes its ordinary decisions by a majority vote, but if a question is 'important' a two-thirds majority of the members present and voting is required. There is a list of these 'important' questions which includes, *inter alia*, the election of the non-permanent members of the Security Council, the admission, suspension, and expulsion of members, the budget, and any other question which by a bare majority the General Assembly decides ought to be considered as 'important'.

The introduction of majority voting for the General Assembly was a departure from the usual practice of international bodies requiring unanimity, but here the innovation does not have the vital importance that we find with regard to the Security Council. That is because, apart from the Assembly's control over the budget where its decisions are binding on the member states, all that the General Assembly can do (in executive terms) is to discuss, recommend, initiate studies, and consider reports from other bodies. It cannot *act coercively* on behalf of all the members, as the Security Council does. But while its recommendations do not bind member states in law, its actions may be quite tangible. Following a controversy over the scope of its powers, the International Court of Justice held that the General Assembly's power to recommend measures 'implies some kind of action'.[60] And so the Court held that the General Assembly is actually entitled to apportion expenditure for the maintenance of peace and security through peace-keeping operations, or other missions for investigation, observation, and supervision. This right is limited, however, to operations that are not *coercive* or *enforcement action* (which would need to be decided by the Security Council) but which are sent by the General Assembly with the consent of the state concerned.[61]

The Security Council consists of five permanent members—China, France, the Russian Federation, the United Kingdom, and the United States, and ten other members elected by the General Assembly for a term of two years. Its functions are laid down in Article 24 of the Charter in the following terms:

(1) In order to ensure prompt and effective action by the United Nations, its Members confer on the Security Council primary responsibility for the maintenance of international peace and security, and agree that in carrying out its duties under this responsibility the Security Council acts on their behalf. (2) In discharging these duties the Security Council shall act in accordance with the Purposes and Principles of the United Nations.

---

60. ICJ Advisory Opinion, *Certain Expenses of the United Nations,* ICJ Rep. (1962) p. 151 at 163.

61. The background was the financing of UNEF and ONUC peacekeeping operations deployed with the consent of Egypt (post Suez crisis) and the Congo respectively. More recently one might recall the GA's human rights operations in Haiti (MICIVIH, 1993) and Guatemala (MINUGUA, 1994).

The Charter then refers to certain 'specific powers' granted to the Security Council to enable it to discharge its duties; most of these relate to its action in the pacific settlement of disputes and with respect to threats to the peace. We will return in particular to the power to impose sanctions and authorize the use of force in Chapters VIII and IX of the present book. Article 25 provides that:

> The Members of the United Nations agree to accept and carry out the decisions of the Security Council in accordance with the present Charter.

It is clear that these provisions confer on the Security Council powers to demand that states act or do not act in certain ways. The decisions are binding on the member states. These powers far exceed those of the other organs of the United Nations. They are powers greater than anything ever previously exercised by any international body.

This binding effect of the Security Council's decisions has to be considered alongside the way its decisions are reached. The victorious powers in the Second World War, or at least some of them, would not consent to be bound by decisions which were arrived at without their concurrence. They refused to accept a system of voting under which they might be outvoted, and, in the system eventually accepted and embodied in the Charter, they insisted on a privileged position. Decisions of the Security Council require the affirmative votes of nine members, but these nine votes must include the concurring votes of all the five permanent members. Consequently each of the five permanent members has a veto on decisions.

There are some exceptions to this voting rule. For the election of judges to the International Court of Justice, there is no veto and the vote is by simple majority (i.e. only eight votes are needed).[62] Decisions on matters of procedure may be made by the votes of *any* nine members.[63] And when a member is a party to a dispute which the Security Council is investigating, that member must abstain from voting; but this rule applies to action by the Security Council outside its enforcement powers found in Chapter VII of the Charter. The Charter carries no obligation for permanent members or any states to abstain in votes concerning enforcement action under Chapter VII. Such enforcement under Chapter VII can include sanctions and the authorization of the use of force (either by UN forces or UN member states).

The Security Council has applied sanctions (e.g. with regard to Rhodesia, Iraq, Haiti, Iran, Libya, and North Korea), authorized the use of force by Member States (e.g. with regard to Korea, Iraq in 1990–1, Haiti, East Timor, and Libya), and deployed UN peace-keepers in various situations (e.g. Bosnia and Herzegovina, Democratic Republic of Congo, Liberia, Haiti, Sudan, East Timor, and Darfur). In addition, as we saw above, the Security Council has established *ad hoc* criminal tribunals and authorized referrals to the International Criminal Court. The vast bulk of this activity took place after 1990, before which the Council was paralysed by cold war rivalry and multiple uses of the veto.

---

62. Statute of the ICJ, Art. 10(2).

63. On the voting on the preliminary question of whether the issue is procedural or not see B. Simma, S. Brunner, and W. Kaul, 'Article 27', in B. Simma (ed.), *The Charter of the United Nations: A Commentary*, 2nd edn (Oxford: OUP, 2002) 476–523 at 489–92.

The Security Council has also developed new tools in the context of counter-terrorism. In 1999 the Council adopted a binding resolution in which it demanded 'that the Taliban turn over Usama bin Laden without further delay to appropriate authorities in a country where he has been indicted'.[64] The Resolution further decided that 'all States shall: (a) Deny permission for any aircraft to take off from or land in their territory if it is owned, leased or operated by or on behalf of the Taliban...(b) Freeze funds and other financial resources, including funds derived or generated from property owned or controlled directly or indirectly by the Taliban'.[65] Following the terrorist attacks of 11 September 2001 the action was extended through multiple resolutions.[66] So the Security Council has obliged all states to:

- freeze without delay the funds and other financial assets or economic resources, including funds derived from property owned or controlled directly or indirectly;
- prevent the entry into or the transit through their territories;
- prevent the direct or indirect supply, sale, or transfer of arms and related material, including military and paramilitary equipment, technical advice, assistance or training related to military activities, with regard to the individuals, groups, undertakings, and entities placed on the Consolidated List.

---

64. S/RES/1267 (1999) para. 2

65. Ibid para. 4.

66. See in particular Resolutions 1373 (2001) and 1624 (2005).

In turn the Consolidated List contains the following:

A. Individuals associated with the Taliban
B. Entities and other groups and undertakings associated with the Taliban
C. Individuals associated with Al-Qaida
D. Entities and other groups and undertakings associated with Al-Qaida.[67]

The procedures for listing and delisting are complex and controversial and the list contains hundreds of names.[68]

We could say that the Security Council has exercised its powers in ways which can be seen as quasi-legislative or quasi-executive or both. Although the Security Council has no general legislative or executive power, when it comes to threats to international peace and security, its powers are apparently far-reaching. These Resolutions which impose obligations on states in the context of counter-terrorism, have, in effect, legislated the key terms of the Convention on the Financing of Terrorism into the international legal order binding on all states. The Security Council's listing creates in effect executive orders that deny individuals the right to travel and freeze

---

67. <http://www.un.org/sc/committees/1267/consolist.shtml>.

68. An Ombudsperson has been functioning since 2010 to hear requests for delisting. For background see A. Bianchi, 'Security Council's Anti-terror Resolutions and their Implementation by Member States', 4 *Journal of International Criminal Justice* (2006) 1044–73; A. Bianchi, 'Assessing the Effectiveness of the UN Security Council's Anti-terrorism Measures: The Quest for Legitimacy and Cohesion', 17 *European Journal of International Law* (2006) 881–91.

the assets of the targeted entities.[69] Under the UN Charter, not only are member states obligated to comply with the Security Council's decisions,[70] but Security Council decisions have been interpreted as overriding other international agreements binding on the member states.[71] The Security Council's powers in this regard, however, are not boundless.[72]

Previous editions of this book concluded that the Charter has given us a body in the form of the Security Council that 'can neither decide nor act',[73] and that 'so long as the cold war remains intense, it is the Assembly which plays the chief role'.[74] The activities sketched above show that things are radically different fifty years later. This is in part due to the end of the cold war, as well as

---

69. See the work of the 1267 Committee (Al-Qaida and Taliban sanctions), Counter-Terrorism Committee (CTC, established under resolution 1373), 1540 Committee (non-proliferation of weapons of mass destruction and terrorism).

70. See Art. 25 above.

71. Article 103 of the Charter reads: 'In the event of a conflict between the obligations of the Members of the United Nations under the present Charter and their obligations under any other international agreement, their obligations under the present Charter shall prevail.' *Questions of Interpretation and Application of the 1971 Montreal Convention arising from the Aerial Incident at Lockerbie (Libyan Arab Jamahiriya v United Kingdom),* Provisional Measures, Order of 14 April 1992, para. 42.

72. On the question of whether a state would be obliged to follow a decision of the Security Council which forced the state to assist in genocide or in some way undermine a purpose of the UN see Judge E. Lauterpacht's separate opinion in the International Court of Justice's Order in *Prevention and Punishment of the Crime of Genocide (Bosnia and Herzegovina v Serbia and Montenegro)* (13 September 1993) paras 98–104; for a book length examination of this problem see A. Tzanakopoulos, *Disobeying the Security Council: Countermeasures against Wrongful Sanctions* (Oxford: OUP, 2011).

73. 5th edn at 112.

74. 6th edn at 118.

to the innovative use of peace-keeping, international criminal tribunals, targeted sanctions, and terrorist listing. The Security Council is active and relevant in the legal organization of international society. Moreover its capacity to impose a higher set of obligations needs to be carefully considered. Some commentators are coming to regard the Security Council as a supreme legislator for international society: 'Unlike any other international organisation [the Security Council has] the power to rewrite or dispense with existing international law in particular situations, and possibly in more general terms... In effect the capacity to override other treaties and general international law amounts to a claim to formal legislative capacity.'[75] Should this really be the case, it represents a departure from our previous conception of the Security Council as an executive arm of the organization. As Waldock explained:

> [A]t San Francisco the smaller Powers were afraid that the permanent members of the Council might agree together and impose settlements on smaller Powers; and they made it clear that they were not willing to entrust to it the power to dictate the terms upon which international disputes are to be settled. In other words, they conferred upon the Council the powers of a policeman, but not of a legislator.[76]

---

75. A. Boyle and C. Chinkin, *The Making of International Law* (Oxford: OUP, 2007) at 233.

76. *General Course on Public International Law*, 106 *RCADI* II (1962) at 25.

IV | States

§ 1. General notion of states in international law

A state is an *institution*; that is to say, it is a system whereby individuals establish relations among themselves in order to secure certain objects, the most fundamental being a system of order within which they can carry on their activities. Modern states are territorial; their governments exercise control over persons and things for the most part within their frontiers, and today the whole of the habitable world is divided between around 200 of these territorial states.

A state should not be confused with the whole community of persons living on its territory. The state is only one among a multitude of other institutions, such as churches and corporations, which a community establishes for securing different objects, though obviously it is one of tremendous importance. None the less it is not, except in the ideology of totalitarianism, an all-embracing institution, or something from which, or within which, all other institutions and associations have their being; certain institutions, such as the Roman Catholic Church, and multiple associations, such as federations of employers and of workers, transcend the boundaries of any single state.

Nor should a state be seen as the same thing as a *nation*, although in modern times many states are organized on a national basis, and confusingly the terms are sometimes used interchangeably, as in the title 'United Nations', which is actually a league of states, in the expression 'most favoured nation', and even in the term 'inter*national* law'. A single state may include several nations, or a single nation may be dispersed among many states, as the Poles were before 1919. There are instances where the term nation is used to denote entities which are not independent states under international law (the Six Nations Rugby Championships). We might also mention here two developments in Canada: the expression 'First Nations' has come to be used in Canada to denote the Indian peoples that together with the Inuit and Métis peoples make up the Aboriginal Peoples of Canada. And in a separate development we see the adoption on 27 November 2006 of a motion by the Canadian House of Commons: 'That this House recognize that the Québecois form a nation within a united Canada.'

Furthermore, the term 'state' is often relative, for there may be states within a state. Whether a smaller entity, having certain institutions of self-government but contained within a larger state, should be called a state or not, is generally felt to depend upon the extent of its powers; but there can be no exact rule. A state of the United States of America is invariably called a state, whereas an English county is not; Australia has states, as well as territories and the latter are not considered states under Australian law. International law is not, however, concerned with all the institutions which in common parlance are called states, it is only concerned with those states whose governmental powers extend to the conduct of their external relations. Whether a state has such powers is a question of fact which must be answered by examining its system of government. But it is usual to distinguish between a federal state and a confederation of states. A *federal state* is a union of states in which the control of the external relations of all the member states has been permanently surrendered to a central government; in this case the only state which exists for international purposes is the state formed by the union. In a *confederation of states*, although a central government exists and exercises certain powers, it does not control all the external relations of the member states, and therefore for international purposes there exists not one but a number of states.

Thus the United States since 1787, and the Swiss Confederation since 1848, each form a single federal state, whereas the United States from 1778 to 1787, and the German Confederation from 1820 to 1866, were confederations of many states. This distinction between federations and confederations would be convenient if it were always observed by clear nomenclature, but it is not; for example, Switzerland goes under the name *Confédération Suisse* in French, or, as motorists and internet users are well-aware, under the official Latin name *Confoederatio Helvetica* (CH). The European Union (EU) is not a federal state as the member states retain a considerable degree of control over their external relations (even though in certain areas such as external trade and fisheries the member states have agreed to surrender exclusive competence to the EU).[1]

§ 2. Independent and dependent states

International law is primarily concerned with those states which are 'independent'[2] in their external relations. International law is also to some extent concerned with a few states which 'depend' on other states in the conduct of those relations in a greater or less degree. The proper usage of the term 'independence' is to denote

---

1. On the issue of exclusive competence for the EU see Arts 2–6 of the Treaty on the Functioning of the European Union; on the new European External Action Service, the role of the High Representative of the Union for Foreign Affairs and Security Policy and the relationship with the diplomatic missions of the member states, following the entry into force of the Lisbon treaty on 1 December 2009, see Treaty on European Union Arts 21–46.

2. The individual opinion of Judge Anzilotti in the Permanent Court of Justice's Advisory Opinion on the *Customs Régime between Germany and Austria* contains a useful discussion of the meaning of 'independence' and the relationship between sovereignty and international law (Reports of the PCIJ, Series A/B, No. 41, 5 September 1931, pp. 57–8). 'Independence as thus understood is really no more than the normal condition of States according to international law; it may also be described as *sovereignty* (*suprema potestas*), or *external sovereignty*, by which is meant that the State has over it no other authority than that of international law.... It follows that the legal conception of independence has nothing to do with a State's subordination to international law or with the constantly increasing states of *de facto* dependence which characterize the relation of one country to other countries. It also follows that the restrictions upon a State's liberty, whether arising out of ordinary international law or contractual arrangements [treaties], do not as such in the least affect its independence. As long as these restrictions do not place the State under the legal authority of another State, the former remains an independent State however extensive and burdensome those obligations may be.'

the status of a state which controls its own external relations without dictation from other states; it contrasts such a status with that of a state which either does not control its own external relations at all, and is therefore of no interest to international law, like the State of New York, or controls them only in part. The exact significance of the term appears most clearly in such a phrase as 'declaration of independence', whereby one state throws off its control by, or its dependence on, another state.

The decolonization period was marked by a number of landmark Resolutions at the UN General Assembly that can be seen as authoritative interpretations of the UN Charter. By 1970 it was accepted that:

> The territory of a colony or other Non-Self-Governing Territory has, under the Charter, a status separate and distinct from the territory of the State administering it; and such separate and distinct status under the Charter shall exist until the people of the colony or Non-Self-Governing Territory have exercised their right of self-determination in accordance with the Charter, and particularly its purposes and principles.[3]

The Declaration explains that such a people can implement their right of self-determination through: 'The establishment of a sovereign and independent State, the free association or integration

---

3. See Resolution 2625 (1970) Declaration on Principles of International Law Friendly Relations and Co-Operation Among States in Accordance with the Charter of the United Nations; see also Resolutions 1514 and 1541 of 1960.

with an independent State or the emergence into any other political status freely determined by a people.' But the states that negotiated this Declaration were careful to recall the competing right of a state to its own territorial integrity.

> Nothing in the foregoing paragraphs shall be construed as authorizing or encouraging any action which would dismember or impair, totally or in part, the territorial integrity or political unity of sovereign and independent States conducting themselves in compliance with the principle of equal rights and self-determination of peoples as described above and thus possessed of a government representing the whole people belonging to the territory without distinction as to race, creed or colour.

In other words, although a people under colonial domination may have the right to choose to establish an independent state, a non-colonial people within an independent state will not normally enjoy an international right to declare independence and secede from such a state, unless they are excluded from government in a discriminatory way.[4] Marc Weller has concluded that today self-

---

4. For successful and unsuccessful attempts at secession leading to independent statehood see J. Crawford, *The Creation of States in International Law*, 2nd edn (Oxford: OUP, 2006) ch. 9; see also M. Kohen (ed.), *Secession in International Law: Contemporary Perspectives* (Cambridge: CUP, 2006). See further the Committee on the Elimination of Racial Discrimination General Recommendation 21 (1996) which states that in its view 'international law has not recognized a general right of peoples unilaterally to declare secession from a State'.

determination 'can be seen as something of a curse. It appears to offer a promise of independence to populations. However, governments have ensured that this promise is a hollow one.'[5]

To insist that a state (as opposed to a people) has a 'right', and particularly a 'natural right' of independence, suggests that for a state to pass from the condition of independence to that of dependence, as the American states did when they formed the Union (now the USA), necessarily involves a moral loss, instead of a mere change of legal status to be judged according to the circumstances of the case. Further, it should be noted that 'independence' is a negative term meaning that a state is not 'dependent'; we cannot legitimately infer from it anything whatsoever about the positive rights to which a state may be entitled. In particular, we have no right to argue as though an independent state had a right to determine its own conduct without any restraint at all; 'independence' does not mean freedom from law, but merely freedom from control by other states.

Unfortunately, the argument that independence means states are free from law is quite common; the associations of sovereignty have become attached in the popular mind to the notion of independence, and the word is often used as though it meant freedom from any restraint whatsoever, and appealed to as a justification for arbitrary and illegal conduct. The temptation to mistake catch-

---

5. 'Why the Rules on Self-determination Do Not Resolve Self-determination Disputes', in M. Weller and B. Metzeger (eds), *Settling Self-Determination Disputes: Complex Power-Sharing in Theory and Practice* (Leiden: Nijhoff, 2008) 17–45; see further A. Cassese, *Self-determination of Peoples: A legal reappraisal* (Cambridge: CUP, 1995); C. Tomuschat (ed.), *Modern Law of Self-Determination* (Dordrecht: Nijhoff, 1993); R. McCorquodale (ed.), *Self-Determination in International Law* (Aldershot: Ashgate, 2000).

words for arguments is strong in all political controversy; it is especially dangerous in the controversies of states.

§ 3.   The doctrine of the equality of states

The doctrine of equality[6] was introduced into the theory of international law by the naturalist writers. They argued that, because individuals in the 'state of nature' before their entry into the political arrangement were equal to one another, and because states are still in a 'state of nature', therefore states must be equal to one another. This argument, however, is based on unsound premises, and the literal conclusion is contradicted by obvious facts; for by whatever test states are measured—size, population, wealth, strength, or degree of civilization—they are not equal, but rather unequal to one another. When, therefore, this doctrine requires us to believe that states are equal in law despite these obvious inequalities, we are bound to ask what are the practical consequences which are supposed to follow from this legal equality? And then we find it difficult to draw any consequence which is not better explained by the fact that states are independent.

That at least seems to be true of the list of four consequences which Oppenheim tells us follow from the doctrine of equality of states: they are (*a*) that when a question arises which has to be settled by consent, every state has a right to a vote, but, unless it has

---

6. Cf E.D. Dickinson, *Equality of States in International Law* (Cambridge MA: Harvard University Press, 1920), and P.J. Baker 'The Doctrine of the Legal Equality of States' 4 *BYBIL* (1923–4) 1–21.

agreed otherwise, to one vote only; (*b*) that the vote of the weakest and smallest state has, unless otherwise agreed by it, as much weight as the vote of the largest and most powerful; (*c*) that no state can claim jurisdiction over another; and (*d*) that the courts of one state do not as a rule question the validity of the official acts of another state in so far as those acts purport to take effect within the latter's jurisdiction.[7] These are all true statements of the law, but no theory of equality is needed to explain or justify them.

In practice states have agreed to deviate from these general rules and the exceptions are of considerable importance.[8] Each permanent member of the Security Council can use its vote to veto a resolution. States can and do exert jurisdiction over each other in their national courts in disputes concerning commercial activity.[9] And while there may be a presumption of validity with regard to the legislative acts of other states, where these are in violation of international law they will not be accorded legitimacy. So, for example, in the context of the illegal invasion of Kuwait by Iraq, the Iraqi law authorizing the seizure of Kuwaiti airplanes was disregarded as contrary to international law by the House of Lords,[10] and discriminatory foreign legislation in violation of

---

7. *Oppenheim's International Law,* 9th edn, vol. i, 339–79.

8. Some states enjoy more votes than others in organizations such as the World Bank and the International Monetary Fund.

9. See Ch. VI § 11 below.

10. *Kuwait Airways v Iraqi Airways* [2002] UKHL 19, 'Such a fundamental breach of international law can properly cause the courts of this country to say that, like the confiscatory decree of the Nazi government of Germany in 1941, a law depriving those whose property has been plundered of the ownership of their property in favour of the aggressor's own citizens will not be enforced or recognised in proceedings in this country. Enforcement or recognition of this law would be manifestly contrary to the public

human rights will not be enforced in English courts.[11] Finally, even where there is a presumption of states treating other states equally, exceptions in the form of differentiated treatment may be used to assist developing countries in contexts such as the World Trade Organization.[12]

The equality of states is perhaps best seen as another way of referring to some general international rights that all states have accorded to each other. The UN Friendly Relations Declaration (1970) explains the 'principle of sovereign equality of States' as follows:

> All States enjoy sovereign equality. They have equal rights and duties and are equal members of the international community, notwithstanding differences of an economic, social, political or other nature.
>
> In particular, sovereign equality includes the following elements:
>
> a. States are juridically equal;
> b. Each State enjoys the rights inherent in full sovereignty;

policy of English law. For good measure, enforcement or recognition would also be contrary to this country's obligations under the UN Charter. Further, it would sit uneasily with the almost universal condemnation of Iraq's behaviour and with the military action, in which this country participated, taken against Iraq to compel its withdrawal from Kuwait. International law, for its part, recognises that a national court may properly decline to give effect to legislative and other acts of foreign states which are in violation of international law.' At para. 29.

11. Ibid para. 18 and see *Oppenheimer v Cattermole* [1976] AC 249.

12. WTO law contains many examples in which 'special and differentiated treatment' is accorded to Least Developed Countries and developing country members more generally. See, e.g. Decision of 28 November 1979 L/4903 and Doha Ministerial Declaration, adopted 14 November 2001, WT/MIN(01)/DEC 1.

c. Each State has the duty to respect the personality of other States;

d. The territorial integrity and political independence of the State are inviolable;

e. Each State has the right freely to choose and develop its political, social, economic and cultural systems;

f. Each State has the duty to comply fully and in good faith with its international obligations and to live in peace with other States.

§ 4. Commencement of the existence of a state

A new state comes into existence when a community acquires not momentarily, but with a reasonable probability of permanence, the essential characteristics of a state, namely an organized government, a defined territory, and such a degree of independence from control by any other state as to be capable of conducting its own international relations.[13] Occasionally a new state has been formed in territory not previously under the rule of any state; as when in 1836 Boers from Cape Colony trekked northwards and founded the South African Republics, or when in 1847 emancipated slaves from the United States founded the Liberian Republic. But generally in modern times a new state has been formed by the division of an existing state into more states than one.

Whether or not a new state has actually begun to exist is a pure question of fact; and as international law does not provide any

---

13. Cf Montevideo Convention on the Rights and Duties of States (1933) (not in force) Art. 1; Crawford (above) chs 2 and 3.

machinery for an authoritative declaration on this question, it is one which every other existing state must answer for itself as best it can. Sometimes the circumstances make the answer obvious; as when the union between Sweden and Norway was dissolved by agreement in 1905, and each of these countries began a separate international existence. But often the question is both difficult and delicate, especially when part of an existing state is forcibly endeavouring to separate itself from the rest; for a premature recognition of the independence of the revolting part would be an unwarrantable intervention in the internal affairs of the other existing state. It is impossible to determine by fixed rules the moment at which other states may justly grant recognition of independence to a new state; it can only be said that so long as a real struggle is proceeding, recognition is premature, whilst, on the other hand, mere persistence by the old state in a struggle which has obviously become hopeless is not a sufficient cause for withholding recognition.[14] There is some evidence that in certain situations where the criteria for statehood may not have been fully met, this defect will be offset where the people are entitled to establish a state in the exercise of their right to self-determination.[15]

The legal significance of recognition is controversial. According to one view it has a 'constitutive' effect, so a state becomes an international person and a subject of international law only through recognition. But there are serious difficulties in this view. The status of a state recognized by state A but not recognized by

---

14. See *Oppenheim's International Law* 9th edn, vol i, at 143–6.

15. D. Raič, *Statehood and the Law of Self-Determination* (The Hague: Kluwer, 2002); well known examples include Algeria and Guinea Bissau.

state B, and therefore apparently both an 'international person' and not an 'international person' at the same time, would be a legal curiosity. Perhaps a more substantial difficulty is that the doctrine would oblige us to say that an unrecognized state has neither rights nor duties at international law. Non-recognition may certainly make the enforcement of rights and duties more difficult than it would otherwise be, but the practice of states does not support the view that states have no legal existence before recognition.[16]

The better view is that the granting of recognition to a new state is not a 'constitutive' but a 'declaratory' act; it does not bring into legal existence a state which did not exist before. A state may exist without being recognized, and if it does exist in fact, then, whether or not it has been formally recognized by other states, it has a right to be treated by them *as* a state. The primary function of recognition is to acknowledge as a fact something which has hitherto been uncertain, namely the independence of the body claiming to be a state, and to declare the recognizing state's readiness to accept the normal consequences of that fact—namely the usual courtesies, rights, and obligations of international relations between states. It is true that the present state of the law makes it possible that different states should act on different views of the application of the law to the same state of facts, but this does not mean that their differing interpretations are all equally correct, but

---

16. E.g. when Israeli airmen shot down British aeroplanes over Egypt in January 1949 the British Government at once informed the Government of Israel, even though at that time Britain had not recognized the State of Israel, that they would demand compensation. For background see W.K. Pattison, 'The Delayed British Recognition of Israel', 37(3) *Middle East Journal* (1983) 412–28.

only that there exists at present no procedure for determining which are correct and which are not.[17]

In practice non-recognition does not always imply that the existence of the unrecognized state is a matter of doubt. States have discovered that the granting or withholding of recognition can be used to further a national policy. States have refused recognition as a mark of disapproval, as nearly all of them did to Manchukuo (the puppet state established by Japan in 1932); and they have granted it in order to *establish* the very independence of which recognition is supposed to be a mere acknowledgement. So in 1903 the United States recognized Panama only three days after it had revolted against Colombian sovereignty and at the same time took steps to prevent the re-establishment of Colombia's sovereignty over the emerging state of Panama. Similarly we can point to the situation in 1948 when the United States recognized Israel within a few hours of its proclamation of independence.[18]

Most recently, the issue of Kosovo continues to divide the world into those states that have recognized Kosovo as a state and those that have not. While Kosovo has been admitted to some

---

17. For a comprehensive overview of the practice see M. Fabry, *Recognizing States: International Society and the Establishment of New States Since 1776* (Oxford: OUP, 2010).

18. On the occasion of the recognition of Israel, Mr Warren R. Austin, the representative of the United States on the United Nations Security Council, asserted the political character of the act of recognition in the most unequivocal terms: 'I should regard it as highly improper for me to admit that any country on earth can question the sovereignty of the United States of America in the exercise of that high political act of recognition of the *de facto* status of a state. Moreover I would not admit here, by implication or by direct answer, that there exists a tribunal of justice or of any other kind, anywhere, that can pass upon the legality or the validity of that act of my country.' (Reported in the *New York Times* of 19 May 1948.)

international organizations such as the World Bank and the International Monetary Fund, it is not currently a member of the United Nations.[19] For those states that have recognized Kosovo, it is treated by them as if it has all the rights and obligations of a state under international law. Diplomats are accorded full diplomatic privileges and Embassies operate in the normal way. The situation is different for those states that have not so recognized Kosovo as a state, but in practice, as those states have chosen not to enter into international relations with this entity, its statehood remains a question which for them can remain unanswered.[20] Today, recognition is often seen as declaratory of the facts which suggest an independent state has emerged, yet constitutive only as far as it generates rights and duties for the new entity 'in its relations with the recognizing state'.[21]

The recognition of a new state as independent must be distinguished from the recognition as belligerent of a part of a state in rebellion against its legitimate government. Various conditions must be satisfied before an outside state is justified in acting to recognize a belligerent. The operations must have reached the dimensions of an actual war; that is to say, the rebels must be organized

---

19. For the implications of the admission of Palestine as a member of UNESCO see Ch. VII § 6 below.

20. The International Court of Justice considered that 'that general international law contains no applicable prohibition of declarations of independence'. Advisory Opinion of 22 July 2010, *Accordance with International Law of the Unilateral Declaration of Independence in Respect of Kosovo* at para. 84. The Court's Opinion does not address the questions of premature recognition, the criteria for statehood, the right to secede, or indeed the actual statehood of Kosovo. See further the symposium in 24 *Leiden Journal of International Law* (2011) 71–161.

21. *Oppenheim's International Law* 9th edn at 130.

under a government which controls a certain territory of its own, which sees that the laws of war are observed by its troops, and in general which is acting for the time being like the government of an independent state at war. There need be no assurance of this government's permanence, for that is clearly a matter which can only be determined by the issue of the war.

The effect of a recognition of belligerency is that the state giving it demands and accepts for itself all the consequences which follow from the existence of a regular war; it claims the rights of a neutral state, and accords the rights of a belligerent to the warring parties.[22] But the effects of the recognition are purely provisional; it puts both belligerent parties in the position of states vis-à-vis those who recognize the belligerency; but only for the purposes and for the duration of the war. It differs radically, therefore, from a recognition of the rebellious part of a state as an independent state. None the less, the granting of recognition of belligerency to rebels has often been resented by the state to which they belong, and that state is likely to see such recognition rather differently than the recognizing state. Today recognition of belligerency is unlikely.[23]

---

22. Whether the concept of war still exists in international law is uncertain, any rights and obligations of a neutral state towards the belligerents may therefore come to be determined by a third party's recognition of belligerency or declaration of neutrality rather than through a determination that there is a state of war. See further C. Greenwood, 'The Concept of War in Modern International Law', 36 *ICLQ* (1987) 283–306; see also S. Neff, *The Rights and Duties of Neutrals: A general history* (Manchester: MUP, 2000).

23. Note the recognition in March 2011 by France of the Libyan Interim Transitional National Council was not a recognition of belligerency but rather recognition that the Council was the 'représentant légitime du peuple libyen'.

§ 5. Continuity and termination of the existence of a state

The government of a state must not be confused with the state itself, but international relations are only possible between states if each has a government with which the others may enter into relations, and whose acts they may regard as binding on the state itself. States are concerned to know whether the person or persons with whom they propose to enter into relations are in fact a government whose acts will be binding under international law for the state which they profess to represent.

The law regarding this question was clearly stated in an award of Chief Justice Taft in an arbitration between Great Britain and Costa Rica in 1923.[24] Great Britain claimed that a number of British companies had acquired certain rights against Costa Rica by contracts entered into with one Federico Tinoco. In 1917 Tinoco had overthrown the existing government of Costa Rica and established a new constitution which lasted till 1919, when the old constitution was restored and Tinoco left power. In 1922 the restored government passed legislation nullifying all engagements entered into by Tinoco's government. The Chief Justice held that if Tinoco's government was the actual government of Costa Rica at the time when the rights were alleged to have been acquired, the restored government could not repudiate the obligations which his acts had imposed on the state of Costa Rica. The arbitrator further said that this question must be decided by evidence of the facts. It was immaterial that, by the law of Costa Rica, Tinoco's

---

24. Reported in *AJIL* (1924) 147.

government was unconstitutional. Even the objection put forward by Costa Rica that many states, including Great Britain herself, had never recognized Tinoco's government, was only relevant as suggesting, though it did not prove, that that government had not been the actual government of Costa Rica; but since Tinoco 'was in actual and peaceable control without resistance or conflict or contest by any one until a few months before the time when he retired', the arbitrator held that Tinoco's acts were binding upon Costa Rica.

This decision therefore shows that a state is bound internationally by the acts of the person or persons who in *actual fact* constitute its government. This is sometimes expressed by saying that a new government 'succeeds' to the rights and obligations of its predecessor, but the expression is a loose one, because international rights and obligations belong to states and not to governments, and a new government 'succeeds' to them only in the sense that it becomes the government of a state to which they are attached.

It follows, therefore, that the identity of a state is not affected by changes in the form or the persons of its government, or even by temporary anarchy, as in Somalia in recent years. But constitutional changes may make it difficult for other states to know who, if anyone, is in a position to bind the state, and may thus give rise to the problem of deciding whether or not they will recognize a new government. The recognition of a new government is not to be confused with the recognition of a new state, but it raises similar problems.

Recognition either of a state or a government may be recognition *de jure* or *de facto. De facto* recognition is used when a government is reluctant to recognize definitively some entity claiming to be a state or government. This may be because the position is obscure or for political reasons, but yet the recognizing government finds it necessary for practical reasons to enter into some sort of official relations. Recognition *de facto* is provisional; it means that the recognizing government offers for the time being to enter into relations, but ordinarily without cordiality, and without the usual courtesies of diplomacy. The terminology is, however, misleading in more ways than one. It is not the act of recognition that is *de jure* or *de facto,* but it is the state or the government that is recognized as existing either *de jure* or *de facto.*

Non-recognition of a foreign government is more than a refusal to enter into relations. From 1917 to 1921 Great Britain refused to recognize the Soviet Government. In 1921 she recognized that Government as the *de facto,* and in 1924 as the *de jure,* Government of Russia. In 1927 she broke off diplomatic relations with it. That action did not mean that she ceased to recognize the Soviet Government as the government of Russia; she merely declined to deal with that Government.

A separate issue is an obligation of non-recognition. Obligations of non-recognition may apply where an entity seeks to enter into existence as a state in violation of international law.[25] So with regard to the declaration of independence by Rhodesia in 1965, the Security Council adopted a resolution calling on all states 'not to recognize this illegal racist minority regime',[26] and later decided that member states must ensure that acts taken by the illegal regime

---

25. See A. Cassese, *Self-Determination of Peoples: A Legal Reappraisal* (Cambridge: CUP, 1995) at 340.
26. SC Res. 217 (1965).

are not granted any form of recognition by the organs of the member states.[27] In 1983 the Council expressed concern with regard to the declaration by the Turkish Cypriot authorities which purported to create an independent state in northern Cyprus, and called 'upon all states not to recognise any Cypriot state other than the Republic of Cyprus'.[28] And in 1992 the Council called for strict respect for the territorial integrity of the Republic of Bosnia and Herzegovina, and affirmed that any entities unilaterally declared or arrangements imposed in contravention of this territorial integrity 'will not be accepted'.[29] The International Court of Justice distinguished such situations from the unilateral declaration of independence made in the case of Kosovo by noting that:

> in all of those instances the Security Council was making a determination as regards the concrete situation existing at the time that those declarations of independence were made; the illegality attached to the declarations of independence thus stemmed not from the unilateral character of these declarations as such, but from the fact that they were, or would have been, connected with the unlawful use of force or other egregious violations of norms of general international law, in particular those of a peremptory character *(jus cogens)*. In the context of Kosovo, the Security Council has never taken this position.[30]

---

27. See Resolutions 277 and 288. The General Assembly and Security Council both called for a denial of recognition when South Africa established the Transkei (1976), Bophuthatswana (1977), Venda (1979), and Ciskei (1981).

28. SC Res. 541(1983).

29. SC Res. 787 (1992).

30. Advisory Opinion 2010 (above) at para. 81.

On the declaratory view of the nature of recognition, granting or withholding recognition does not, *so far as international law is concerned,* affect the international legal status of the state or government to which it is accorded or from which it is withheld. Yet recognition has important effects in the administration of the domestic law of the recognizing state. For example, as we shall see, the representatives and the property of a foreign state or government may be immune from legal process, and the validity of such a government's acts in its own country cannot normally be questioned in our courts.

Recognition may therefore affect how national courts treat the acts of foreign governments and their agents. In *Luther v Sagor* the English courts had to deal with a claim to a certain amount of timber which had been the property of the plaintiff company in Russia. The timber had been confiscated by legislation of the Soviet Government, sold by them, and subsequently brought to England by the purchaser. At the time when the case was heard by Roche, J., the British Government had not recognized the new Soviet Government which had taken over, and Roche J. accordingly gave judgment for the plaintiff company in Russia. But before the case was heard by the Court of Appeal, the Soviet Government had been recognized with retrospective effect as a *de facto* government, and the Court therefore reversed the decision of Roche, J., holding that the Soviet legislation had been effective to pass the title (property rights) in the timber.[31] In a number of more recent cases, issues related to commercial rights, family law issues, and the validity of certificates relating to births, marriages, and deaths have arisen in the context of the acts of unrecognized states such as the Turkish

---

31. [1921] 1 KB 456, and 3 KB 532.

Republic of Northern Cyprus. The courts and Parliament have sought to find reasonable solutions so that non-recognition, or even the non-existence of the state, does not prevent the courts from accepting the validity of the acts of these entities (even in the absence of recognition by the UK Government).[32]

A separate question is whether someone claiming to be the government is to be considered the actual government of a state. UK courts traditionally answered that question by relying on a certificate issued by the Foreign Office as to whether the UK recognizes the government in question. However, in 1980, the UK Government announced that it would no longer extend recognition to new governments (as opposed to states).[33] The question therefore falls to be decided by the courts. In *Republic of Somalia v Woodhouse* Mr Justice Hobhouse was faced with the question of whether the 'interim Government of the Republic of Somalia' (headed by Ali Mahdi Mohammed) should be regarded as the Government of Somalia for the purpose of claiming property belonging to the State of Somalia.[34] A faction led by General Aidid was fighting Mahdi Mohammed's faction for control of Mogadishu and other parts of Somalia were under the control of the Somali Defence Movement and the Somalia Patriotic Movement. According to the law report, at that time: 'No one group has established control over the country.'[35] The case had been brought by the solicitor Crossman Black on behalf of Mr Qalib (apparently

---

32. The Foreign Corporations Act 1991; *Emin v Yeldag* (2002) 1 FLR 956 (divorce); *Hesperides Hotels v Aegean Holidays* [1978] QB 205 (trespass).

33. This new policy was stated in Parliamentary answers, e.g. 408 HL Deb. Cols 1121–2, 28 April 1980.

34. *Republic of Somalia v Woodhouse Drake & Carey (Suisse)* [1993] QB 54.

35. Ibid 57.

appointed prime minister by Mahdi Mohammed). Mr Justice
Hobhouse considered that in light of the 1980 change in policy,
such inquiry could not be limited to an investigation of the attitude of the UK Government or even the degree of international
recognition granted to the claimant. He concluded:

> But any apparent acceptance of the interim government by
> the United Nations and other international organisations
> and states does not suffice in the present case to demonstrate
> that the interim government is the Government of the Repub-
> lic of Somalia. The evidence the other way is too strong.
>
> Accordingly, the factors to be taken into account in decid-
> ing whether a government exists as the government of a state
> are: (a) whether it is the constitutional government of the
> state; (b) the degree, nature and stability of administrative
> control, if any, that it of itself exercises over the territory of
> the state; (c) whether Her Majesty's Government has any
> dealings with it and if so what is the nature of those dealings;
> and (d) in marginal cases, the extent of international recogni-
> tion that it has as the government of the state.
>
> On the evidence before the court the interim government
> certainly does not qualify having regard to any of the three
> important factors. Accordingly the court must conclude that
> Crossman Block does not at present have the authority of the
> Republic of Somalia to receive and deal with the property of
> the Republic.[36]

---

36. Ibid 68; applied in *Sierra Leone Telecommunications v Barclays Bank* [1998] 2 All ER
820, where the judge found that the military junta were not the Government of Sierra
Leone.

A change in the extent of a state's territory has in principle no effect on its international identity, but in practice difficult cases may occur. Thus when two states become united, it may not always be easy to determine whether one of the two has annexed the other, or whether both have merged their separate identities so as to form a single new state. For instance, it might seem natural to regard Italy as a new state formed by the union of the several independent states of the Italian Peninsula, but in fact she saw herself as, and was accepted as being, the kingdom of Piedmont territorially enlarged by annexation of the other Italian states.[37] Germany was eventually considered to have absorbed East Germany and able to continue as a member of the European Community (and other organizations) rather than have to apply for admission as a new state. On the other hand, a Californian Court held that Yugoslavia was not the old kingdom of Serbia enlarged, but a new state which came into existence after the First World War.[38] A separate question concerns merger: so the merger of North and South Yemen led to the extinction of those states and the creation of the new Republic of Yemen.

Similarly, when an existing state breaks up it may be difficult to say whether the old state has been extinguished and its place taken by two or more new states, or whether the old state continues to exist with its territory reduced by the separation from it of a new state or states. With regard to the dissolution of the Soviet Union, James Crawford's authoritative analysis suggests this was a 'devolu-

---

37. See, for example, the case of *Gastaldi v Lepage Hemery,* Annual Digest, 1929–30, Case No. 43.

38. *Artukovic v Boyle,* 47 *AJIL* (1953) 319–21.

tion resulting in a number of new States with the "core" State Russia, retaining the identity of the Soviet Union'.[39] The situation with regard to Yugoslavia was more complex and the same author concludes that 'all the Republics should be considered successors to a State become extinct'.[40]

'Succession' is primarily a principle of private law, and suggests that the extinction of a state is in some sense comparable to the death of an individual. But states do not die in any literal sense; their population and their territory do not disappear, but merely suffer political change. Moreover, succession is a notion taken from the law of property; and it is easy to be misled by the suggestion that something analogous to the transfer of property takes place when people and territory cease to form part of one state and begin to form part of another. The rules are complex and uncertain,[41] and we will only consider here the situation with regard to treaties.[42]

---

39. *The Creation of States in International Law*, 2nd edn (Oxford: OUP, 2006) at 705.

40. Ibid 714.

41. Koskenniemi has observed that the absorption of East Germany into Germany, the break-up of Yugoslavia, the Czech and Slovak Federal Republic, and the Soviet Union can be seen as pointing to a 'heterogeneity of State practice' and demonstrates the 'open-endedness of rules' regarding the international law of state succession. But in highlighting these perceptions Koskenniemi reminds us that 'State succession doctrines are resorted to in concrete struggles about the right of representation of human communities and the division of material and spiritual values between them'. 'The Present State of Research Carried out by the English-Speaking Section of the Centre for Studies and Research', in *State Succession: Codification Tested Against the Facts* (Hague Academy) (Dordrecht: Nijhoff, 1997) 89–168 at 93.

42. Other contexts in which the issue of the succession of states arises include property, contracts, wrongs, archives, and debts. See Vienna Convention on Succession of States in respect of State Property, Archives and Debts (1983) (not yet in force). See also B. Stern

In 1962, against a background of recent decolonization and competing sets of priorities, the International Law Commission embarked on a consideration of succession of states with respect to treaties. Out of this work emerged two potentially conflicting concerns. On the one hand was the concern for the continuity of international law and the rights of those states that had entered into agreements which covered the territories which were emerging as new states on the international scene. On the other hand, the principle of self-determination and the radical nature of the changes were invoked in order to suggest that these 'new states' should start life with a 'clean slate' unencumbered by the international obligations assumed by the colonial powers. Matthew Craven has recently analysed in detail how these competing priorities ebbed and flowed in the run up to the adoption of the Vienna Convention on Succession of States in Respect of Treaties (1978). The choice is more complex than it might first appear. According to Craven:

> Many members of the Commission were of the view that self-determination implied a complete freedom of choice in respect to the treaty actions of the former colonial masters. Many were equally clear, however, that for all the benefits that might be gained from freeing themselves from inherited

---

(ed.), *Dissolution, Continuation, and Succession in Eastern Europe* (Dordrecht: Kluwer, 1998); B. Stern, *La succession d'Etats*, 262 *RCADI* (2000). For a general overview see M. Shaw, *International Law*, 6th edn (Cambridge: CUP, 2008) ch. 17. On the particular question of the rights and obligations of successor states for succession for international wrongs by the predecessor state see P. Dumberry, *State Succession to International Responsibility* (Leiden: Nijhoff, 2007).

commitments, new States might also positively benefit from being able to rely upon an existing network of agreements rather than have to conclude all afresh. Denying the possibility of succession in the name of self-determination was not necessarily an emancipatory initiative.[43]

The 1978 Convention establishes a special regime for 'newly independent states'[44] offering in general terms a 'clean slate' with no obligation to be bound by a treaty which binds the predecessor state, while for parts of states that separate into new states outside the colonial context, the treaty obligations of the predecessor state continue to be in force for the new state.

While this Convention entered into force in 2006 it has very few states parties and there is considerable doubt as to whether the bulk of its provisions can be considered as a codification of general international law. Previous editions of this book simply asserted that treaty rights and obligations are unaffected when part of an existing state breaks off and becomes a new state. It was stated that the rights and obligations 'remain with the old state, and the new state starts its career without any'. Recent practice suggests that the issue is more likely to be resolved through discrete negotiations between the new state and the relevant treaty parties than under the influence of a supposed rule of international law.[45] Moreover

---

43. M. Craven, *The Decolonization of International Law: State Succession and the Law of Treaties* (Oxford: OUP, 2007) at 141.

44. Essentially those previously under colonial rule, see Art. 2(1)(f).

45. Although it has been pointed out that the Czech Republic and Slovakia both stated that they considered that the provisions of the Convention represented rules of binding international law. Koskenniemi (above) at 94.

another established way for new states to succeed to treaty obligations is by participation in multilateral treaties through a 'declaration of continuity' or a 'notification of succession' to the depositary of the treaty.[46] This seems to contradict the idea that newly independent states were outside the treaty relations of the predecessor state and the other states parties to the treaty. However, the first ILC Special Rapporteur on this topic, Sir Humphrey Waldock (the previous editor of the present volume), established that there was no need to obtain the consent of other participating states, pointing to the practice of the United Nations Secretary-General, the Swiss Government, and the United States. Waldock expressed the view that requiring the consent of the other states would be 'unrealistic, unduly conservative and unprogressive'.[47]

Whether or not such rules can be considered general international law, we should mention here a situation whereby treaties will be binding on the new state: this is the category of treaties relating to the use of territories. So the International Court of Justice held that a 1977 treaty between Hungary and Czechoslovakia establishing third-party rights and obligations for the parties which attached to parts of the Danube was not affected by state succession, and so was binding on Slovakia as the new succeeding state with the relevant territory.[48]

---

46. Note this does not apply to joining international organizations where the new state must apply in the usual way.

47. As detailed by Craven (above) at 138; I *Yearbook of the ILC* at 135, para. 26.

48. *Case Concerning the Gabčíkovo-Nagymaros Project (Hungary/Slovakia)* ICJ Rep. (25 September 1997) at para. 123. The Court referred in this context to the ILC's finding that 'treaties concerning water rights or navigation on rivers are commonly regarded as candidates for inclusion in the category of territorial treaties'.

It has also been suggested that another exception to any notion of 'clean state' applies with regard to human rights. According to the UN Human Rights Committee the inhabitants of the new state take with them their human rights acquired under treaty obligations entered into by the predecessor state:

> [O]nce the people are accorded the protection of the rights under the Covenant, such protection devolves with territory and continues to belong to them, notwithstanding change in government of the State party, including dismemberment in more than one State or State succession or any subsequent action of the State party designed to divest them of the rights guaranteed by the Covenant.[49]

---

49. General Comment 26, 'Continuity of obligations' 8 December 1997, para. 4. Cf A. Aust, *Modern Treaty Law and Practice*, 2nd edn (Cambridge: CUP, 2007) at 371.

V | The Territory of States

§ 1. Territorial sovereignty

AT the basis of international law lies the notion that a state occupies a definite part of the surface of the earth, within which it normally exercises, subject to the limitations imposed by international law, jurisdiction over persons and things to the exclusion of the jurisdiction of other states. When a state exercises an authority of this kind over a certain territory it is popularly said to have 'sovereignty' over the territory, but that much-abused word is here used in a rather special sense. It refers here neither to a relation of one person over another, nor to the independence of the state itself, but to the nature of rights over territory; and in the absence of any better word, sovereignty is a convenient way of contrasting the full set of legal rights over territory with the minor territorial rights discussed below.

Territorial sovereignty bears an obvious resemblance to ownership in private law. Today this is less marked than it was in the days of the patrimonial state, when a kingdom and everything in it was regarded as being to the king very much what a landed estate was to its owner. As a result of this resemblance, early international law borrowed the Roman rules for the acquisition of property, and adapted them to the acquisition of territory, and these rules are still used as the foundation of the law on the subject.

§ 2. Modes of acquiring territory

Traditionally there are considered to be various modes of acquiring territory: occupation, cession, conquest, prescription, and accretion. These modes (inspired by Roman law) fail to cover satisfactorily the acquisition of title to territory when a new state comes into existence. Nor do they really reflect the complex process that occurs when a tribunal has to adjudicate between competing claims.[1]

We should also note straight away, that unlike the transfer of property in domestic law, transfers of territorial sovereignty can have serious implications for the people already living in the territory; although they may be given the choice to take the new nationality, they would normally become subjects of the acquiring state.[2] In coming to a decision regarding any acquisition of territory or boundary dispute the principle of self-determination will today therefore play a role.[3]

---

1. See I. Brownlie, *Principles of Public International Law*, 7th edn (Oxford: OUP, 2008) at 127ff.

2. See *Oppenheim's International Law*, 9th edn at 683–6.

3. For a discussion of the relevance of the principle of self-determination of peoples in this context see S.P. Sharma, *Territorial Acquisition, Disputes and International Law* (The Hague: Nijhoff, 1997) 212–53; and Shaw, 6th edn at 522–5, and 579–82; cf M. Kohen, *Possession contestée et souveraineté territoriale* (Paris: PUF, 1997) at 407–23. For a feminist

The International Court of Justice has recalled in this context the principle of *uti possedetis*, whereby newly independent states in Latin America and Africa have accepted certain colonial administrative borders in the interests of stability.[4] In the *Frontier Dispute* between Burkina Faso and Mali the Court was asked to resolve a dispute based on the 'principle of the intangibility of frontiers inherited from colonization', otherwise known as the principle of *uti possedetis*. In an oft-quoted passage it stated:

At first sight this principle conflicts outright with another one, the right of peoples to self-determination. In fact, however, the maintenance of the territorial status quo in Africa is often seen as the wisest course, to preserve what has been achieved by peoples who have struggled for their independence, and to avoid a disruption which would deprive the continent of the gains achieved by much sacrifice. The essential requirement of stability in order to survive, to develop and gradually to consolidate their independence in all fields, has induced African States judiciously to consent to the respecting of colonial frontiers, and to take account of it in the interpretation of the principle of self-determination of peoples.[5]

---

critique of traditional approaches to self-determination see H. Charlesworth and C. Chinkin, *The Boundaries of International Law: A feminist analysis* (Manchester: Manchester University Press, 2000) at 151–64 and 263–8.

4. This principle has also been applied beyond the colonial context with regard to the break-up of Yugoslavia. See Opinions 2 and 3 of the Arbitration Commission and Shaw (above) at 525–30.

5. ICJ Rep. (1986) p. 554 at para. 26. See further the Separate Opinion of Judge Abi-Saab at paras 13–15.

Occupation[6] was a means of acquiring territory not already forming part of the dominions of any state. Although it was once considered appropriate to consider land inhabited by tribal communities as *terra nullius* this view has now been authoritatively discredited.[7] Since all the habitable areas of the earth now fall under the dominion of some state or other, future titles by occupation are no longer possible.[8] But the law of the matter is still important because the

---

6. This type of occupation of land belonging to no one (*terra nullius*) should not be confused with the regime covering occupation in times of armed conflict. Although the Occupying Power in times of armed conflict may acquire some rights these are not rights to acquire title to territory.

7. 'Whatever differences of opinion there may have been among jurists, the state practice of the relevant period indicates that territories inhabited by tribes or peoples having a social and political organization were not regarded as *terrae nullius*. It shows that in the case of such territories the acquisition of sovereignty was not generally considered as effected unilaterally through "occupation" of *terra nullius* by original title but through agreements concluded with local rulers. On occasion, it is true, the word "occupation" was used in a non-technical sense denoting simply acquisition of sovereignty; but that did not signify that the acquisition of sovereignty through such agreements with authorities of the country was regarded as an "occupation" of a *"terra nullius"* in the proper sense of these terms. On the contrary, such agreements with local rulers, whether or not considered as an actual "cession" of the territory, were regarded as derivative roots of title, and not original titles obtained by occupation of *terrae nullius*.' *Advisory Opinion on Western Sahara, International Court of Justice* (1975) at para. 80; see *Oppenheim's International Law*, 9th edn, vol. i, at 687.

8. For an introduction to the claims to sectors in the Antarctic made by Argentina, Australia, Chile, France, New Zealand, Norway, and the United Kingdom see D.R. Rothwell, *The Polar Regions and the Development of International Law* (Cambridge: CUP, 1996) at 51–63; the Antarctic Treaty (1959) Art. IV(2) states that: '[n]o acts or activities taking place while the present Treaty is in force shall constitute a basis for asserting, supporting or denying a claim to territorial sovereignty in Antarctica or create any rights of sovereignty in Antarctica. No new claim, or enlargement of an existing claim, to territorial sovereignty in Antarctica shall be asserted while the present Treaty is in force.'

occupations of the past often give rise to the boundary disputes of the present.[9] The principles of law are fairly well settled; the difficulty of a boundary dispute generally arises in applying them to the facts, which may go back for centuries. In what is often considered the leading case on the subject, the *Legal Status of Eastern Greenland*,[10] it was necessary for the Permanent Court to go back to events of the tenth century AD.

The Eastern Greenland dispute arose out of the action of Norway in 1931 in proclaiming the occupation of certain parts of East Greenland. Denmark then asked the Court to declare the Norwegian proclamation invalid, on the ground that the area to which it referred was subject to Danish sovereignty, which extended to the whole of Greenland. The Court pointed out that a title by occupation involved two elements, 'the intention or will to act as sovereign, and some actual exercise or display of authority'.[11] In these words the Court affirmed a well-established principle of law, namely that occupation, in order to create a title to territory, must be 'effective' occupation; that is to say, it must be followed up by action, such as establishing a settlement or building a fort, which

---

In short the claims are 'frozen'. On the Arctic see pp. 161–220, and note now the recent various claims in the Arctic by Canada, Russia, Denmark, Norway, and the United States to the extended continental shelf under the Convention on the Law of the Sea (1982).

9. See *Sovereignty over Pedra Branca/Pulau Batu Puteh, Middle Rocks and South Ledge (Malaysia/Singapore)*, ICJ Rep. (2008) p. 12.

10. Series A/B, (1933) No. 53.

11. Professor Ross, however, seems to be correct in saying that the subjective requirement of the 'will to act as sovereign' in addition to the objective display of authority is 'an empty phantom', a sort of vestigial relic 'of the Roman animus possidendi which had itself sprung from a primitive animistic mysticism'. *A Textbook of International Law: General Part* (London: Longmans, 1947) at 147.

shows that the occupant not only desires to, but can and does, control the territory claimed. The Court was satisfied on the evidence that at any rate after a certain date, 1721, Denmark's *intention* to claim title to the whole of Greenland was established. But the areas in dispute were outside the settled areas of Greenland, and it was necessary therefore for the Court to examine carefully the evidence by which Denmark tried to satisfy the second necessary element in occupation, namely the exercise of authority. On this it pointed out that the absence of any competing claim by another state (and until 1931 no state other than Denmark had ever claimed title to Greenland) was an important consideration; a relatively slight exercise of authority would suffice when no other state could show a superior claim. It held, too, that the character of the country must be considered; the arctic and inaccessible nature of the uncolonized parts of Greenland made it unreasonable to look for a continuous or intensive exercise of authority.

Denmark was able to show numerous legislative and administrative acts purporting to apply to the whole of Greenland. Furthermore, there were a number of treaties in which other states, by agreeing with Denmark to a clause excluding Greenland from their effects, had apparently acquiesced in her claim, and there had been express recognition of Denmark's claim by many states. The Court held that in the circumstances there was sufficient evidence to establish Denmark's title to the whole of the country. The area which Norway claimed in 1931 was therefore not at that time a *terra nullius* capable of being acquired by her occupation.

From the requirement that occupation must be 'effective' it follows that mere discovery of an unappropriated territory is not sufficient to create a title, for discovery alone does not put the discoverer in a position to control the territory discovered, however they may desire or intend to do so. But on this point the law makes a concession and allows the strict rule of effective occupation to be qualified by the doctrine of 'inchoate title'. Since an effective occupation must usually be a gradual process, it is considered that some weight should be given to mere discovery, and it is regarded therefore as giving an 'inchoate title', that is to say, a temporary right to exclude other states until the state of the discoverer has had a reasonable time within which to make an effective occupation. This could be described as a sort of 'option to occupy' which other states had to respect while it lasted.

The effects of discovery were discussed by the eminent Swiss arbitrator, Max Huber, in the *Island of Palmas* award.[12] The United States, having acquired the Philippines for $20m under a treaty with Spain,[13] claimed (as Spain's successor) an island which was half-way between the Philippines and the Dutch East Indies, mainly on the ground of its discovery by the Spanish in the sixteenth century. Huber, as the sole arbitrator, held that even if the international law of that century recognized mere discovery as giving a title to territory (though there is very little reason for thinking that it did), such a title could not survive today, when it is certain that discovery alone, without any subsequent act, does not establish sovereignty. Even if the title originally acquired was 'inchoate' (as according to the modern doctrine it would be) it had not been turned into a definitive title by an actual and durable taking of possession within a reasonable time. The claimed title could

---

12. *Island of Palmas case (Netherlands/USA)*, RIAA vol. II, 829–71.

13. Treaty of Peace Between the United States and Spain, 10 December 1898, Art. III.

not therefore on either view prevail over the continuous and peaceful display of authority, which the evidence satisfied him had been exercised by Holland.

It is perhaps worth noting here that commentators on Huber's contribution to international law often highlight this award as evidence of his sociological approach.[14] In the words of Daniel-Erasmus Khan: 'The message Huber tries to convey to his learned readership is a simple and noble one: "International law, like law in general, has the object of assuring the coexistence of different interests which are worthy of legal protection."[15] And worthy of such protection are essentially those rules which reflect today's social realities and not those of a distant past—who would dare to object?'[16]

Cession is a mode of transferring the title to territory from one state to another. It resulted sometimes from a successful war, and sometimes from peaceful negotiations. Cession was sometimes gratuitous (as with Austria's gift of Venice to France in 1866), an exchange (as with the cession of the inhabited North Sea Heligoland islands by Great Britain to Germany in exchange for a protectorate in Zanzibar), or for some consideration, such as when Denmark sold the Danish West Indies (St Thomas, St John, and St Croix) to the United States in 1917 for $25m, or Russia's sale in 1867 of the Alaskan territory to the United States for $7.2m. It should be remembered that cession can only transfer legitimate title. In the *Island of Palmas* arbitration the Spanish cession of the

---

14. Symposium on Max Huber 18(1) *EJIL* (2007) 69–197.

15. *Island of Palmas case* (above) at 870.

16. D.-E. Khan, 'Max Huber as Arbitrator: The *Palmas (Miangas)* Case and Other Arbitrations' 18 *EJIL* (2007) 145–70, at 169.

Island to the United States had no legal effect as it was held that the territory at the time of the cession was Dutch. The Netherlands had successfully exercised a continuous and peaceful display of authority up to that critical date. In the words of Judge Huber: 'It is evident that Spain could not transfer more rights than she herself possessed.'[17]

Conquest (also known as *subjugation*) was the acquisition of the territory of an enemy by its complete and final subjugation and a declaration of the conquering state's intention to annex it. In practice a title by conquest was rare, because the annexation of territory after a war was generally carried out by a treaty of cession, although such a treaty might be seen as only confirming a title already acquired by conquest. A relatively modern instance of title by conquest is that of Rumania to Bessarabia in the period between the two World Wars. There is an obvious moral objection to the legal recognition of a title by conquest. But on reflection it is no greater than the moral objection to the recognition of an enforced cession of territory by treaty. That legal title has in the past been conferred by an enforced treaty is undeniable, and it would have been idle for the law to have accepted the effects of force when the formality of a forced assent had followed by treaty and not otherwise. As we shall see the following paragraphs, today, cession by force, (whether or not formalized in a treaty[18]) can no longer be considered as a valid way to acquire territory.

By 1932 Mr Stimson, then American Secretary of State, proposed what has come to be known as the *Stimson Doctrine of*

---

17. *Island of Palmas Case* (above) at 842.

18. On the question of coercion and treaties see more detail below Ch. VII § 3.

Non-Recognition. This was triggered by the Japanese occupation of Manchuria. The United States notified Japan and China that it would not 'recognize any situation, treaty or agreement which may be brought about contrary to the covenants and obligations of the Pact of Paris'.[19] The concern was to protect the treaty rights of the United States or its citizens in China. But Stimson saw this as relevant beyond US Foreign Policy, and stated in a separate note that: '[i]f a similar decision should be reached and a similar position taken by the other governments of the world, a caveat will be placed upon such action which, we believe, will effectively bar the legality hereafter of any title or right sought to be obtained by pressure or treaty violation'.[20] The Assembly of the League of Nations later the same year passed a resolution to the same effect.[21] This call for non-recognition fell on deaf ears. Within three years of the League Resolution Italy had conquered Ethiopia, and most of the League states had decided that it was expedient to recognize that Ethiopia had become Italian territory. Previous editions of this book concluded at this point that: 'the truth is that international law can no more refuse to recognize that a finally successful conquest does change the title to territory than municipal law can a

---

19. Note of 7 January 1932. The Pact of Paris 1928 condemned recourse to war, and states parties renounced war as an instrument of national policy. Art. I, see Ch. IX below.

20. Summary sent to Sen. Borah, 32 February 1932. For a detailed examination of the impact of this doctrine see D. Turns, 'The Stimson Doctrine of Non-Recognition: Its Historical Genesis and Influence on Contemporary International Law', *Chinese Journal of International Law* (2003) 105–42.

21. The Assembly declared 'that it is incumbent upon the Members of the League of Nations not to recognize any situation, treaty or agreement, which may be brought about by means contrary to the Covenant of the League of Nations or the Pact of Paris'. *League of Nations Official Journal* (1932), Special Supp. No. 101, 87–8.

change of regime brought about by a successful revolution'.[22] We must now admit this is no longer true.

Already in 1963 Robert Jennings was challenging such an approach. He wrote that reason demanded that there was only one answer to the question whether the legal right to territory may still be acquired by military conquest: 'To brand as illegal the use of force against the "territorial integrity" of a State, and yet at the same time to recognize a rape of another's territory by illegal force as being itself a root of legal title to the sovereignty over it, is surely to risk bringing the law into contempt.'[23] Jennings also addressed the conundrum we encountered above; namely, how can we forbid acquisition of territory by conquest while admitting that title can pass through a forced cession of territory by treaty? His answer is perfectly reasoned: not only are states prevented from acquiring title through conquest, they are similarly prevented from acquiring territory through a treaty of cession forced on another state. Jennings considers a number of arguments based on realism and practicality. He quotes at some length Sir Gerald Fitzmaurice's report to the International Law Commission which concluded: 'it is not practicable to postulate the invalidity of this type of treaty, and that if peace is a paramount consideration, it must follow logically that peace may, in certain circumstances, have to take precedence for the time being over abstract justice—*magna est iustitia et praevalebit* but *magna est pax: perstat si praestat*.'[24] But there is no

---

22. 5th edn at 156–7; 6th edn at 172–3.

23. *The Acquisition of Territory in International Law* (Manchester: MUP, 1963) at 54.

24. *Third Report on the Law of Treaties*, UN Doc. A/CN.4/115 of 18 March 1958, at para. 62; *Yearbook of the ILC* vol. II at 38.

reason to believe that such Latin maxims force us to prioritize peace over justice,[25] and Jennings asks us instead to consider what the law is and not what it is expedient to think it ought to be:

> It cannot be denied that the law now stigmatizes as unlawful certain uses of force or threat of force in international relations. This is a revolutionary change – far and away the most important change that has ever been brought about in international law. It is not a paper change imagined by text writers and commentators. It is one, as we have seen, wrought in the changing practice of States over half a century and now solemnly stated in [the UN Charter]...The principle of effectiveness requires that force thus proscribed should no longer be regarded either as being itself a title or as ousting the general principle of law that a genuine consent is required to create an obligation ostensibly based upon agreement.[26]

---

25. The first Latin phrase is a play on the chant '*Magna est veritas, et praevalet*' (Ezra 4.4), 'Truth is great, and it prevails.' The context is the Apocrypha, in 1 Esdra iv, 41. A competition had been organized in front of King Darius of Persia to see who could utter the wisest sentence; the winner would be heralded as the wisest advisor. The original three entrants proposed: wine is the strongest; the King is strongest; women are strongest—but above all things Truth beareth away the victory. 1 Esdra iii, 10–12. *Fortius est vinum; fortior est rex; fortiores sunt mulieres, super omnia autem vincit veritas.* After each competitor had defended his entry the crowd chose the winner (Zorobabel) with the chant *Magna est veritas, et praevalet.* Fitzmaurice's sentences apparently inspired by this biblical reference could be translated as 'Justice is great and it shall prevail'; the second phrase could be translated as 'Peace is great, put it first and it will last.'

26. Above at 60–1. See also Vienna Convention on the Law of Treaties (1969) Art. 52 'A treaty is void if its conclusion has been procured by the threat or use of force in violation of the principles of international law embodied in the Charter of the United Nations.'

We have to admit, with Jennings, that we must now start from the premise 'that neither conquest nor a cession imposed by illegal force of themselves confer title'.[27]

It remains then to address the question of whether a lawful use of force in self-defence could confer a title. Here the practicality of the rule and the paramount principle outlawing the use of force pull in the same direction. States nearly always claim that their use of force is legal under the rules of self-defence, to allow for the acquisition of territory through self-defence would rob the prohibition just outlined of much of its effect.[28] The UN General Assembly's consensus Friendly Relations Declaration leaves no room for doubt when it outlaws the acquisition of territory though any form of force (legal or illegal): 'The territory of a State shall not be the object of acquisition by another State resulting from the threat or use of force. No territorial acquisition resulting from the threat or use of force shall be recognized as legal.'[29]

Prescription as a title to territory in international law is so vague that some writers deny its recognition altogether. It has been described as 'the legitimisation of a doubtful title by the passage of time and the presumed acquiescence of the former sovereign'.[30] In

---

27. Ibid 61.

28. Ibid 55–6; *Oppenheim's International Law* vol. i, at 702–5; Kohen (above) at 394–6.

29. UNGA Declaration of Principles of International Law Concerning Friendly Relations and Co-operation Among States in Accordance with the Charter of the United Nations, Res. 2625, 24 October 1970, Principle 1 (prohibition on the use of force), para. 10; and see the affirmation of this principle as customary international law by the International Court of Justice in its *Advisory Opinion on the Legal Consequences of the Construction of a Wall in the Occupied Palestinian Territory* (2004) para. 87.

30. Shaw (above) at 504.

fact existing frontiers are often accepted by international law simply because they have existed *de facto* for a long time; they exemplify the maxim *e facto oritur jus*,[31] which is at the root of the notion of prescription in all systems of law. It is therefore no paradox to say that prescription is the commonest of all titles to territory; we only fail to recognize that it is so because the titles that depend on it are rarely called into question. On the other hand, there is a sense in which international law may be said not to recognize prescription; it recognizes the principle which lies behind prescription, but that principle has not led to detailed rules as it has in more developed legal systems. There are no fixed rules as to the length of possession which will give a good title, nor as to good faith of its origin, and it would be difficult to frame rules that could cover every situation.[32]

Accretion is the addition of new territory to the existing territory of a state by operation of nature, as by the drying up of a river or the recession of the sea. It is of little importance and the detailed rules on the matter need not here be considered.[33]

---

31. The law arises from the fact.
32. See the factors taken into consideration in the *Frontier Land case (Belgium v Netherlands)* ICJ Rep. (1959) p. 209: 'The question for the Court is whether Belgium has lost its sovereignty, by non-assertion of its rights and by acquiescence in acts of sovereignty alleged to have been exercised by the Netherlands at different times since 1843.' At 227. See also *Case concerning Kasikili/Sedudu Island (Botswana v Namibia)* ICJ Rep. (1999) at paras 94–99, where the conditions for prescription were agreed by the parties, even if the Court refrained from addressing the 'status of acquisitive prescription in international law' or the 'conditions for acquiring title to territory by prescription'. At para. 97.
33. For further references see *Oppenheim's International Law*, 9th edn, vol. i at 696–8.

§ 3. Minor rights over territory

(a) *Leases*

Leases of territory by one state to another which closely resemble
the ordinary leases of private law were not uncommon; such leases
included leases of specified areas in ports for transit purposes. But
there are other leases, political in character, in which it was usual to
regard the use of the term 'lease' as no more than a diplomatic
device for rendering a permanent loss of territory more palatable
to the dispossessed state by avoiding any mention of annexation
and holding out the hope of eventual recovery. In 1898 China
leased Kiao-Chau to Germany and other territories to Great Britain, France, and Russia, the Russian lease being transferred to
Japan in 1905, and the German in 1919. But it has been justly
pointed out that this last interpretation of the Chinese leases is
inadmissible.[34] Not only did China by the terms of the leases themselves retain and actually exercise more than a nominal sovereignty
over the leased territories, but, even if the lessee states intended the
leases as disguised cessions, this was certainly not the intention of
the lessor, China, and we are not entitled to estimate the legal
character of a transaction by conjecturing the undisclosed intentions of one of the parties only. Moreover, events seem to have confirmed the straightforward construction of these leases, for at the
Conference of Washington in 1922 China was promised the restitution of most of the territories. In 1930 the United Kingdom

---

34. H. Lauterpacht, *Private Law Sources and Analogies of International Law: With Special
Reference to International Arbitration* (London: Longmans, 1927) 183–90.

returned to China the leased territory of Weihaiwei. The British 99-year lease of territory north of Kowloon (the New Territories) was due to expire in 1997, and the 1984 Joint Declaration by Britain and China eventually covered, not only this lease, but also other parts of Hong Kong then controlled by the United Kingdom. Under its the terms the Chinese Government declared that it 'has decided to *resume the exercise of sovereignty* over all of Hong Kong with effect from 1 July 1997' while the United Kingdom declared 'that it will *restore* Hong Kong' to China on that date.[35]

The 1903 lease associated with the Guantánamo Naval Base in Cuba is well known now due to the detention centres established there by the United States and the creation of Military Commissions to prosecute suspected terrorists. While Cuba has complained of the 'illegal occupation' of her territory,[36] the terms of the lease are clear about sovereignty: 'While on the one hand the United States recognizes the continuance of the ultimate sovereignty of the Republic of Cuba over the above described areas of land and water, on the other hand the Republic of Cuba consents that during the period of the occupation by the United States of said areas under

---

35. Arts 1 and 2 of the Joint Declaration on the Question of Hong Kong (emphasis added). The Declaration and its annexes also contained commitments for the future Special Administrative Region including with regard to the rights of the inhabitants and other persons: 'The current social and economic systems in Hong Kong will remain unchanged, and so will the life-style. Rights and freedoms, including those of the person, of speech, of the press, of assembly, of association, of travel, of movement, of correspondence, of strike, of choice of occupation, of academic research and of religious belief will be ensured by law in the Hong Kong Special Administrative Region. Private property, ownership of enterprises, legitimate right of inheritance and foreign investment will be protected by law.' Art. 3(5) and see also Annex 1 Art. XIII.

36. See A. De Zayas, 'Guantánamo Naval Base' <mpepil.com>.

the terms of this agreement the United States shall exercise complete jurisdiction and control over and within said areas.'[37]

(b) *Servitudes*

It has been suggested that international law recognizes rights over territory which correspond to the servitudes of Roman law or the easements of English law. Let us recall the nature of a servitude in Roman law: it is a right enjoyed by the owner of one piece of land, the *praedium dominans*, not in their personal capacity, but in their capacity as owner of the land, over land which belongs to another, the *praedium serviens*. Its essential characteristic is that it is a right *in rem*, rather than a right *in personam*, that is to say, it is exercisable not only against the person of a particular owner of the servient tenement, but against any successor to that person in title, and not only by particular owners of the dominant tenement but also by their successors in title. It is, of course, quite common that a state should acquire rights of one kind or another over the territory of another state, the right, for example, to have an airfield or free port facilities, but ordinarily such rights are merely rights *in personam* like any other treaty-created right; they do not in any way resemble servitudes. The test of an international servitude can only be, on the analogy of private law, that the right should be one that will survive a change in the sovereignty of either of the two states concerned in the transaction.

Claims by states that they enjoy such servitudes do not usually provide much evidence that any such right exists. The leading case

---

37. Agreement Between the United States and Cuba for the Lease of Lands for Coaling and Naval Stations, 23 February 1903, Art. III.

is the award of the *North Atlantic Fisheries Arbitration* between Britain and the United States in 1910. The United States enjoys certain fishing rights off the coast of Newfoundland under a treaty of 1818, and it argued that this treaty had created a servitude in their favour; the right was a derogation from British sovereignty over the Island, and the result of this division of the sovereignty was, it was claimed, that Britain had no independent right to regulate the fishery. The Tribunal rejected this contention; the right, they thought, was not a sovereign right but merely an economic one, and there was nothing in the treaty to show that the parties had intended it to be anything else. To have held that the right was a servitude would have meant that the benefit would pass to a new sovereign over the territory of the United States, and the burden of it to a new sovereign over Newfoundland (in this case Canada after 1949). It is purely fanciful to imagine that such remote contingencies were present in the minds of those who made the treaty.

In the terminology of English real property law, the right must 'run with the land'. One case illustrates this difficulty of proving the existence of such a right. It was provided in the Treaty of Paris of 1815 that the Alsatian town of Huningue was never to be fortified. This arrangement was made in the interests of the Swiss Canton of Basle. When the treaty was made Huningue was French; in 1871 it became German; in 1919 French again. The facts are not altogether easy to ascertain, as it is said that neither France nor Germany ever fortified Huningue, and it is suggested that this proves the existence of a servitude which survived the changes of sovereignty. But, in fact, it proves nothing at all. Huningue may have been left unfortified for quite other reasons; very likely new conditions of warfare made its fortification unnecessary. It does not prove that neither Germany nor France could legally have fortified it, nor that if, for example, Switzerland had been annexed by Italy, Italy would have had a right to insist on its non-fortification.[38]

The issue is covered in the 1978 Vienna Convention on Succession of States in respect of Treaties where it is stated that rights and obligations relating to the use of any territory established by a treaty for the benefit of one or more states, and considered as attaching to that territory, are not affected by state succession.[39] Of course one still has to show that the parties to the treaty considered these rights as rights *in rem* attaching to the territory, and there is an interesting exception whereby the provisions do not apply 'to treaty obligations of the predecessor State providing for the establishment of foreign military bases on the territory to which the succession of States relates.'[40]

With regard to the establishment of servitudes through custom we might mention two more recent decisions that might suggest that servitudes are recognized under international law.[41] In the *Right of Passage Case*, Portugal successfully argued before the International Court of Justice that she enjoyed a right of passage

---

38. See A.D. McNair, 'So-called State Servitudes', 6 *BYBIL* (1925), 111–27.

39. Art. 12(2).

40. Art. 12(3).

41. For a review of the issue see M. Ragazzi, *The Concept of International Obligations* Erga Omnes (Oxford: Clarendon Press, 1997) ch. 2. Ragazzi concludes in part that '[i]nternational tribunals have been very cautious: while not rejecting the concept [of state servitudes] as a matter of principle, they have invariably decided the disputes before them on other grounds'. At 23. The Chapter also discusses the *Wimbledon case* PCIJ Series A, No. 1 (1923) and the Aaland Islands Dispute (1920).

for civilians between her territories in India. The Court found that the right had been established by custom based on the practice of Portugal and Britain as well as by the subsequent practice by India.[42] In the *Eritrea—Yemen* arbitration, the arbitral tribunal found that there was an obligation on Yemen to ensure 'that the traditional fishing regime of free access and enjoyment for the fishermen of both Eritrea and Yemen shall be preserved for the benefit of the lives and livelihoods of this poor and industrious order of men'.[43] The Tribunal refers to 'a sort of "*servitude internationale*" falling short of territorial sovereignty'.[44] Here the immediate beneficiaries were the fishermen themselves. The Tribunal found that '[s]uch historic rights provide a sufficient legal basis for maintaining certain aspects of a *res communis* that has existed for centuries for the benefit of the populations on both sides of the Red Sea'.[45] This kind of servitude, enforced for the common good of benefici-

---

42. 'The Court, therefore, concludes that, with regard to private persons, civil officials and goods in general there existed during the British and post-British periods a constant and uniform practice allowing free passage between Daman and the enclaves. This practice having continued over a period extending beyond a century and a quarter unaffected by the change of regime in respect of the intervening territory which occurred when India became independent, the Court is, in view of all the circumstances of the case, satisfied that that practice was accepted as law by the Parties and has given rise to a right and a correlative obligation.' ICJ Rep. (1960) p. 40.

43. Award of the Arbitral Tribunal (Territorial Sovereignty And Scope Of The Dispute) 9 October 1998, at para. 526 and see para. vi of the *dispositif*. See also the successful claim by Costa Rica that Nicaragua owed it a customary international law obligations with regard to subsistence fishing in Nicaraguan waters, *Dispute regarding Navigational and Related Rights (Costa Rica v Nicaragua)*, ICJ Rep. (2009) p. 213.

44. Ibid para. 126.

45. Ibidem.

aries beyond the state,[46] was in part supported by references to Islamic law,[47] and also probably owes much to the development of notions such as common heritage of mankind associated with the law of the sea and with outer space law.

§ 4. Territorial sea

Every state is entitled to regard a certain area of the sea adjacent to its coasts as its territorial sea (also known as its territorial waters), but the extent of this area and the details of its legal status have only been settled relatively recently. We shall deal here with the extent of the territorial sea, and with issues concerning jurisdiction in the following chapter.[48]

The extent of the territorial sea raises two questions:

(a) what is the base-line from which it is to be measured? and
(b) what is its width?

---

46. See especially the detailed approach outlined in *Yemen—Eritrea* Award, PCA, Award of the Arbitral Tribunal in the Second Stage of the Proceedings (Maritime Delimitation) 17 December 1999 at paras 87–111.

47. 'The basic Islamic concept by virtue of which all humans are "stewards of God" on earth, with an inherent right to sustain their nutritional needs through fishing from coast to coast with free access to fish on either side and to trade the surplus, remained vivid in the collective mind of Dankhalis and Yemenites alike.' At para. 92 of the Second Stage Award (1999). See also para. 93 of that Award and paras 130–1 and 525 of the 1998 Award (above).

48. We will also cover issues of jurisdiction related to internal waters, the contiguous zone, the exclusive economic zone, the exclusive fishery zone, the continental shelf, and the high seas.

(*a*) For some time there was considered to be an established general customary rule of law that the baseline is the line of low-water mark following all the sinuosities of the coast. This rule was the product of an overwhelming weight of authority in the practice of states, in codification projects, and in the works of authoritative writers. To this general rule the law made two exceptions: bays and islands. In the case of a bay, the base-line crosses its waters from shore to shore, and the waters between the coast and the base-line are not part of the territorial sea but rather *inland waters*. The Law of the Sea Convention (1982) (LOSC) has now defined a bay for this purpose,[49] and makes it clear that '[w]here the distance between the low-water marks of the natural entrance points of a bay exceeds 24 nautical miles, a straight baseline of 24 nautical miles shall be drawn within the bay in such a manner as to enclose the maximum area of water that is possible with a line of that length'.[50] There are certain bays, sometimes called 'historic bays', much larger than this, which are certainly inland waters.

The judgment of the International Court of Justice in the *Anglo-Norwegian Fisheries Case* addressed not only the issue of how to take into account islands, but also base-lines that linked promontories on the heavily indented Norwegian coast.[51] The case concerned the validity in international law of the provisions of a Norwegian Royal

---

49. A 'bay is a well-marked indentation whose penetration is in such proportion to the width of its mouth as to contain land-locked waters and constitute more than a mere curvature of the coast. An indentation shall not, however, be regarded as a bay unless its area is as large as, or larger than, that of the semi-circle whose diameter is a line drawn across the mouth of that indentation.' Art. 10(2).

50. Ibid Art. 10(5).

51. ICJ Rep. (1951) p. 116.

Decree defining Norwegian territorial waters with the object of excluding foreign ships from fishing off the Norwegian coast. The base-lines laid down in this Decree did not anywhere follow the low-water tide line; they were imaginary straight lines, some as much as forty-four miles long, linking selected points, some of these points being headlands on the mainland and others situated on islands, some of them at a considerable distance from the mainland, in the so-called 'skjaergaard' or 'rock rampart', the fringe of innumerable islands which lie off long stretches of the Norwegian coast. The effect was to enclose and to reserve as Norwegian internal waters some very large areas of sea lying inside those straight base-lines. The Court held by a majority that the Decree was not contrary to international law. It was not necessary that the base-line should follow the low-water mark; it was sufficient that it should follow 'the general direction of the coast',[52] and the lines drawn by Norway did.

The rule laid down by the Court was certainly an innovation in the law, and it was enunciated in a rather short judgment. It is true that the Court says that the base-line must be drawn 'in a reasonable manner',[53] and that the 'delimitation of sea areas has always an international aspect; it cannot be dependent merely upon the will of the coastal state as expressed in its municipal law. Although it is true that the act of delimitation is necessarily a unilateral act, because only the coastal state is competent to undertake it, the validity of the delimitation with regard to other States depends upon international law.'[54] But this rather half-hearted attempt to

---

52. Ibid 129.
53. Ibid 141.
54. Ibid 132.

save the ultimate authority of international law has not prevented states from putting forward extravagant claims to appropriate areas of the open sea.

The rules for the drawing of baselines are now set out in LOSC 1982 which goes some way to mitigating the effects of drawing straight baselines,[55] and entrenches a number of principles stating, for example that '[t]he drawing of straight baselines must not depart to any appreciable extent from the general direction of the coast, and the sea areas lying within the lines must be sufficiently closely linked to the land domain to be subject to the regime of internal waters'.[56] However, specific economic interests remain relevant so that: 'account may be taken, in determining particular baselines, of economic interests peculiar to the region concerned, the reality and the importance of which are clearly evidenced by long usage'.[57]

(b) The seaward limit of territorial waters has traditionally been regarded as founded on the extent to which the sea can be commanded by gunfire from the land. The principle was thus laid down by Bynkershoek in 1702. Historically, however, this origin is prob-

---

55. Where the establishment of a straight baseline 'has the effect of enclosing as internal waters areas which had not previously been considered as such, a right of innocent passage as provided in this Convention shall exist in those waters'. LOSC Art. 8(2).

56. LOSC Art. 7(3) and see *Qatar v Bahrain (merits)* ICJ Rep. (2001) p. 41 where the Court emphasizes that straight baselines should only be resorted to where exceptional conditions apply such as where 'the coastline is deeply indented and cut into' or 'there is a fringe of islands along the coast in its immediate vicinity'. At para. 212. For another detailed application of the principles in Art. 7 LOSC see the *Yemen—Eritrea* Award, PCA, Award of the Arbitral Tribunal in the Second Stage of the Proceedings (Maritime Delimitation) 17 December 1999 (above).

57. Ibid Art. 7(5).

ably mythical; a marine league (three nautical miles) was more or less generally accepted as the width at a time when the range of gunfire was much less than that. Today LOSC 1982 provides that every state has 'the right to establish the breadth of its territorial sea up to a limit not exceeding 12 nautical miles' from the baselines.[58] The vast majority of states have claimed this 12-mile breadth, while certain others have made less extensive claims (often for geographical reasons related to relations with neighbouring states).[59] The territorial sea and the airspace above it is part of the territory of a state. There are, however, rights of innocent passage for ships of all states through the territorial sea, as we shall see in the following chapter when we consider jurisdiction.[60]

Straits in territorial waters pose a separate set of issues. If a strait is less than 24 nautical miles in width it is clearly territorial; but special rules apply under LOSC 1982 to straits which are for international navigation between two parts of the seas which are not territorial sea.[61] The Dardanelles and the Bosphorus have long had a special status imposed upon them by treaty, and they remain mostly regulated by the Montreux Convention of 1936.[62] Controversies

---

58. Ibid Art. 3.

59. For a table compiled by the UN see <http://www.un.org/Depts/los/LEGISLATIO-NANDTREATIES/PDFFILES/table_summary_of_claims.pdf>.

60. A minority of states do in fact require prior authorization/notification for warships see Wolff Heintschel von Heinegg 'Warships' <mpepil.com> para. 37.

61. Art. 37 LOSC.

62. Art. 35(c) LOSC preserves the legal regime established by the Montreux Convention. The Montreux Convention's chief provisions are these: *Merchant vessels.* In time of peace, and in time of war when Turkey is not a belligerent, merchant vessels enjoy complete freedom of transit and navigation. In time of war, when Turkey is a belligerent, those of a country at war with Turkey have no rights; those of a country not at war with Turkey

continue with regard to the passage of Russian and American warships, and in 2008 Russia raised questions of compliance with regard to the presence of NATO ships in the Black Sea in the context of the conflict between Russia and Georgia.

§ 5. The continental shelf

'Continental shelf' is a geological expression and now a legal term. On most coasts of the continents there is no sudden drop to the sea-bed; the coast shelves gradually downwards underwater for a considerable distance (the 'shelf'). It then, more or less abruptly, plunges (the 'slope'), and finally there is what is known as the 'rise', a more gentle slope with sediments descending to the deep ocean floor (the

---

enjoy freedom of transit and navigation on condition that they do not assist her enemy, but they must enter the Straits by day and follow a route indicated by the Turkish authorities. Turkey may also require merchant vessels to enter the Straits by day and to follow an indicated route if she considers herself threatened with imminent danger of war.

Warships. In time of peace smaller surface vessels enjoy freedom of transit, provided it is begun in daylight, and is preceded by notification to the Turkish Government, but there are limits on the aggregate tonnage of foreign warships that may be in transit, or that non-Black Sea Powers may have in the Black Sea, at any one time. Except for courtesy visits at the invitation of Turkey, only Black Sea Powers may send capital ships or submarines through the Straits, and then only in certain circumstances. In time of war, when Turkey is not a belligerent, neutral warships have the same rights as warships in time of peace; those of a belligerent may pass only to fulfil obligations arising out of the Charter of the United Nations or to assist a state which is the victim of aggression in virtue of a treaty of mutual assistance binding Turkey and concluded within the framework of the Charter. No hostile act may be committed, or belligerent right exercised, in the Straits. When Turkey is a belligerent, or if she considers herself threatened with imminent danger of war, the passage of warships is left entirely to her discretion.

'Area'). The distance from the baseline to the end of the rise is technically known as the 'continental margin'; but the term 'continental shelf' tends to be used to cover the whole prolongation of the land under the water. (For a diagram see the next page.) The continental shelf became a matter of legal interest because technological progress made it possible to extract oil and gas by rigs and machinery installed in the open sea and unconnected with the land.

An early and important statement of a claim to exploit the continental shelf was contained in a proclamation by President Truman in September 1945.[63] This proclamation spoke of the shelf as 'appertaining' to the United States and claimed 'jurisdiction and control' over its resources. The absence of protest and the rapid proclamation of similar claims has meant that this area of the law developed relatively quickly.[64] The exclusive right to exploit the shelf for the natural resources in its subsoil and for sedentary species which are attached to it (such as oysters) is now well established. This right is, however, not the same as full territorial sovereignty and the legal status of both the superjacent waters and the air space above these waters remains unaffected.[65] Determining the limits of this continental shelf has, however, proved more tricky.

Article 76 of LOSC is perhaps one of the most complex provisions in the law of the sea. The key definition is simple and established beyond the Convention: the continental shelf comprises

---

63. For details of the various early claims that were put forward by states see H. Lauterpacht, 'Sovereignty over Submarine Areas' 27 *BYBIL* (1950), 376–433.

64. Cf *The Abu Dhabi Arbitration* (1951) 18 ILR 144.

65. Art. 78(1).

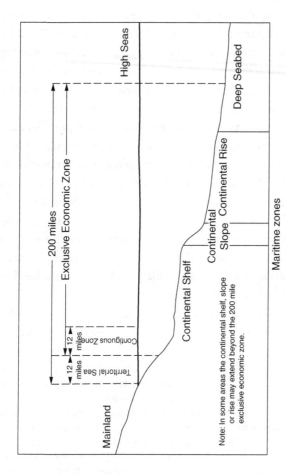

Mainland

Territorial Sea — 12 miles

Contiguous Zone — 12 miles

Exclusive Economic Zone — 200 miles

High Seas

Continental Shelf

Continental Slope

Continental Rise

Deep Seabed

Note: In some areas the continental shelf, slope or rise may extend beyond the 200 mile exclusive economic zone.

Maritime zones

R.R. Churchill and A.V. Lowe, *The Law of the Sea*, 3rd edn (Manchester: MUP, 1999) at 30.

the seabed and subsoil of the submarine areas that extend throughout the natural prolongation of its land territory to the outer edge
of the continental margin, or to a distance of 200 nautical miles
from the coastal state's baselines, whichever is the larger.[66] Under
the Convention states have a choice of methods for determining
the outer edge of the margin and have to communicate geological
data to the UN Secretary-General and their proposed limits to the
continental shelf to the Commission on the Limits of the Continental Shelf. In an innovative move the Convention provides that:
'[t]he Commission shall make recommendations to coastal States
on matters related to the establishment of the outer limits of their
continental shelf. The limits of the shelf established by a coastal
State on the basis of these recommendations shall be final and
binding.'[67] More than 50 claims have been made and the Commission has delivered over 11 recommendations, but there are a
number of pending claims and the Commission is faced with a
mound of detailed information which needs to be considered in
the light of the Convention's complex provisions.[68]

The prospect of the exploitation of the minerals found in this
area and perhaps more importantly in the adjoining deep sea bed

---

66. See generally *North Sea Continental Shelf Cases* ICJ Rep. (1969) p. 3; *Continental Shelf
(Libya v Malta)* ICJ Rep. (1985) p. 13; *Continental Shelf (Tunisia v Libya)* ICJ Rep.
(1982) p. 18. These cases concern the delimitation of the maritime boundaries, the principles to be applied with regard to the continental shelf and maritime delimitation in general
are beyond the scope of this book. For an introduction see D.R. Rothwell and T. Stephens,
The International Law of the Sea (Oxford: Hart, 2010) ch. 16; see further M.D. Evans,
Relevant Circumstances and Maritime Delimitation (Oxford: OUP, 1989) and R. Kolb,
Case Law on Equitable Maritime Delimitation (Dordrecht: Nijhoff, 2003).
67. Art. 76(8).
68. See esp. Art. 76(4)(5)(6)(7).

gave rise to a set of concerns on the part of developing states. Various forms of deep sea mining offer the prospect of access to zinc, manganese, nickel, copper, and cobalt; as well as silver, gold, and diamonds.[69] As these possibilities became known, developing states feared that the resources to be found in the continental rise would be exploited by industrialized nations to the detriment of developing countries that were either ill-equipped to mine these minerals, or were facing a threat to the price of the same commodity that they were already mining on land. The Convention therefore established a special regime for the exploitation of the deep sea bed which we will examine in the next section. With regard to the exploitation of the non-living resources of the continental shelf beyond 200 nautical miles from the baselines, the coastal state is obliged to make payments or contributions in kind to the International Seabed Authority with respect to all production at a site after the first five years of production.[70] The rate is then one per cent of the value or volume of production at the site for the sixth year, increasing by one per cent each year until the maximum of seven per cent is reached. The Convention stipulates that the Authority is to distribute these sums to the states parties to the Convention 'on the basis of equitable sharing criteria, taking into account the interests and needs of developing States, particularly the least developed and the land-locked among them.'[71]

---

69. For the methods and potential sites see D.R. Rothwell and T. Stephens, *The International Law of the Sea* (Oxford: Hart, 2010) at 120–5.

70. Art. 82.

71. Art. 82(4).

§ 6. The deep sea bed

We will discuss jurisdiction on the high seas in the next chapter; here we will limit ourselves to a brief description of the new regime which now covers what lies beneath—the deep sea bed. In the words of the Law of the Sea Convention this is the 'International Seabed Area' also known as simply 'the Area' or '*la zone*'.[72] The Area is defined as 'the seabed and ocean floor and subsoil thereof, beyond the limits of national jurisdiction', and it is now subject to a special regime administered by the International Seabed Authority, or simply 'the Authority'. As we have just seen, the limits of national jurisdiction will be 200 nautical miles from the baseline or the outer limits of the continental margin (whichever is the larger). The Area is therefore about fifty percent of the earth's surface. As noted above, the prospect of extracting valuable minerals has led developing states to ensure an international regime is created whereby the resources that are extracted are shared in equitable ways. Furthermore, it is clear that no-one can claim or acquire territory on the deep sea bed or rights over the resources. The Convention states that the 'Area and its resources are the common heritage of mankind',[73] and then explains that '[n]o State shall claim or exercise sovereignty or sovereign rights over any part of the Area or its resources, nor shall any State or natural or juridical person appropriate any part thereof. No such claim or exercise of sovereignty or sovereign rights nor such appropriation shall be recognized.'[74]

---

72. Art. 1(1).

73. Art. 136.

74. Art. 137.

Activities in the Area are to be carried out by an organ of the Authority called the 'Enterprise' together with other entities authorized under the terms of the Convention in conjunction with another treaty adopted in 1994 (the Agreement).[75] So far the costs associated with such deep sea operations have meant that this innovative scheme for exploitation and distribution has not borne significant practical results, and there are serious concerns about the environmental effects of such deep sea extraction.[76] Perhaps, for present purposes, the most significant dimension to these developments is the discernable shift in international law from an early emphasis on *co-existence* among states, through to *co-opera-tion* between states, and now to a potential *community* based approach in which precious resources are preserved and distrib-uted not only according to capacity to exploit, but also with respect to needs and fairness. These shifts may be more of theoretical inter-est than practical effect when we examine the actual operation of the Convention regime,[77] but the concept of the distribution of the benefits from this deep sea bed for the benefit of humankind[78]

---

75. Agreement relating to the Implementation of Part XI of the United Nations Conven-tion on the Law of the Sea (1994). See also the Mining Code adopted by the Authority and the Regulations on Prospecting and Exploration for: Polymetallic Nodules, Polyme-tallic Sulphides, and Cobalt-Rich Crusts.

76. Rothwell and Stephens (above) 123–5; see also Seabed Disputes Chamber of The International Tribunal for the Law of the Sea, Advisory Opinion, Case 17, *Responsibilities and Obligations of States Sponsoring Persons and Entities with Respect to Activities in the Area*, 1 February 2011.

77. For a wider examination and the shifts between co-existence and co-operation against the background of Wolfgang Friedmann's work see G. Abi-Saab, 'Whither the Interna-tional Community?' 9 *EJIL* (1998) 248–65 and the other the contributions to the sym-posium collected in the four issues of the *EJIL* (1997) nos 3 and 4, (1998) nos 1 and 2.

78. See LOSC Art. 140.

has taken root even in the regimes established by industrialized states outside the Convention.[79]

§ 7. Territorial air space

The First World War suddenly made it clear that the legal status of the air was of vital importance; at the same time certain theories on the question were shown to be unpractical. According to one of these theories the analogy of the open sea ought to be applied to the air, and it should therefore be completely free; according to another there should be a lower zone of territorial air analogous to the territorial sea, and above that the air should be free. The experience of the First World War, however, made it certain that states would accept nothing less than full sovereignty over the air space above their territory and territorial sea, and a Convention on Aerial Navigation concluded in Paris in 1919 confirmed this rule as the law. It follows that only by virtue of a treaty can one state enjoy rights in the air space over another state.

Today the key treaty is the Chicago Convention on International Civil Aviation (1944) which reaffirms the complete and exclusive sovereignty rule.[80] There is therefore no right of innocent passage for civil aircraft over the territorial sea in the same way that there is a right of innocent passage through the territorial sea for merchant ships. Furthermore, all rights of overflight (territorial sea and land)

---

79. E.D. Brown, *Sea-Bed Energy and Minerals: The International Legal Regime*, vol. 2 (Dordrecht: Nijhoff, 2001) ch. 7.

80. Arts 1 and 2.

and scheduled landings have to be discerned from the relevant treaties.[81] The Chicago Convention is applicable only to civil aircraft
and each contracting state agrees that all aircraft of the other contracting states which are on a non-scheduled flight have the right to
'make flights into or in transit non-stop across its territory and to
make stops for non-traffic purposes without the necessity of obtaining prior permission'.[82] On the other hand 'No scheduled international air service may be operated over or into the territory of a
contracting State, except with the special permission or other
authorization of that State.'[83] Such scheduled flights therefore have
to be arranged though separate bilateral or multilateral treaties.

Over the years, states have sometimes resorted to force against
foreign planes; such use of force has usually been considered excessive. Following the Soviet Union's downing of the Korean Airways
flight KAL 007 in 1983, the Chicago Convention was amended
through the addition of Article 3bis. This new provision means
that states parties agree to refrain from the use of weapons but
retain their rights to self-defence under the UN Charter.[84] This
rule against the use of weapons was reaffirmed by the Security
Council as a customary rule (even before the entry into force of
the amendment) following the shooting down of two American

---

81. Note there are rights of transit passage over international straits (LOSC Arts 38 and
39) and on designated air routes over archipelagic waters (LOSC Art. 53).

82. Art. 5. See also the International Air Services Transit Agreement (1945).

83. Art. 6.

84. 'The contracting States recognize that every State must refrain from resorting to the
use of weapons against civil aircraft in flight and that, in case of interception, the lives of
persons on board and the safety of aircraft must not be endangered. This provision shall
not be interpreted as modifying in any way the rights and obligations of States set forth
in the Charter of the United Nations.' Art. 3bis (a).

planes by Cuba in 1996.[85] In the wake of the September 11 attacks in the United States, and following an incident in 2003 in Frankfurt, Germany passed a law authorizing the use of weapons against civilian airliners that pose a similar threat. While there are questions as to whether this was compatible with the international rules just outlined,[86] the German Constitutional Court eventually held the law to be invalid as it was, *inter alia*, incompatible with provisions of the German Constitution because innocent passengers would be denied their right to life and would be treated as objects rather than as human beings with dignity and their own value.[87]

§ 8. Outer space, the moon, and other celestial bodies

The point at which territorial airspace becomes outer space is contested among states. At one time it seemed sensible to state that airspace was the area where planes could fly; but it has also been suggested that outer space starts at about 100 kilometres as this is the lowest orbit for a satellite. As it becomes possible for planes to fly at higher and higher altitudes, and as satellite orbits become more and more lucrative, the threshold of this frontier looks likely

---

85. S/RES/1067 (1996) para. 6, see also UN Doc. S/PRST/1996/9, 27 February 1996; see also the discussion by Aust, *Handbook* at 325–6.

86. See R. Geiss, 'Civil Aircraft as Weapons of Large-Scale Destruction: Countermeasures, Article 3bis of the Chicago Convention, and the Newly Adopted German Luftsicherheitsgesetz', 27 *Michigan Journal of International Law* (2005) 227–56.

87. *Bundesverfassungsgericht*, Judgment of 15 February 2006, at para. 124.

to remain uncertain for years to come. Indeed the UK Government 'anticipates that the development of space transportation systems functioning seamlessly between airspace and outer space ... will create uncertainties about the legal regime applicable to them'.[88]

What is clear, however, is that ever since the early days of space flight, states, and in particular those capable of launching satellites and other spacecraft, have agreed a number of prohibitions with regard to outer space, and these prohibitions are considered to have quickly acquired the status of principles of general international law.[89] It is convenient to start from the provisions of the 1967 Treaty on Principles Governing the Activities of States in the Exploration and Use of Outer Space, including the Moon and Other Celestial Bodies. This treaty is ratified by the key states and reflects the consensus resolutions of the UN General Assembly. Article I states that '[t]he exploration and use of outer space, including the Moon and other celestial bodies, shall be carried out for the benefit and in the interests of all countries, irrespective of their degree of economic or scientific development, and shall be the province of all mankind'.[90] Article II states that no sovereignty claims can be made over this area or these bodies, and Article IV prohibits the placing in orbit of nuclear weapons or any other

---

88. Questions on the definition and delimitation of outer space: replies from Member States, UN Doc. A/AC.105/889/Add.6, 4 March 2010; see also the paper prepared by the UN Secretariat A/AC.105/769, 18 January 2002.

89. B. Cheng, *Studies in International Space Law* (Oxford: OUP, 1997).

90. In contrast to the regime for the deep sea bed, the regime for exploitation of the Moon etc. is not spelt out, and the space powers have refrained from ratifying the 1979 Agreement which broadly states that the Moon's natural resources are the common heritage of mankind, and that there should be equitable sharing by states parties of the benefits derived from these resources taking into account the interests and needs of developing

weapons of mass destruction. Astronauts are to be treated as 'envoys of mankind' and states are to render them assistance in the event of an accident on their territory or on the high seas.[91]

The rule against prohibiting appropriation or claims of sovereignty is very clear, and yet a number of equatorial states have made claims to the particular geostationary orbit.[92] This orbit over the equator is especially useful for communication satellites as one only needs three satellites to ensure worldwide coverage, and one satellite can probably remain in constant contact with a whole country. Richard Gardiner considers the argument that such orbits fall within the concept of permanent sovereignty over natural resources of these developing countries, but concludes that this claim is inconsistent with the pre-existing rule prohibiting sovereignty claims in outer space, and points to the regulation of the issue of orbits through the International Telecommunications Union.[93] Gardiner has also pointed out that anyone seeking to acquire private property rights in the Moon (as proposed on the internet) might do well to ask two questions: first, from whom did the vendor get their title? And secondly, which jurisdiction would be able to enforce such a property right? The distinction between private property rights and sovereignty claimed by states is a valid one, but in

---

countries. Agreement Governing the Activities of States on the Moon and Other Celestial Bodies (1979) Art. 11(1)(5)(7)(d). The Agreement does not itself develop the equivalent intergovernmental bodies for exploitation; *The Enterprise* is limited to exploring and exploiting the deep sea bed.

91. Art. V and see Agreement on the Rescue of Astronauts, the Return of Astronauts and the Return of Objects Launched into Outer Space (1968).

92. Declaration of the First Meeting of Equatorial Countries (Adopted on December 3, 1976).

93. R.K. Gardiner, *International Law* (Harlow: Pearson, 2003) at 424–5; see also Constitution of the International Telecommunications Union (1992) Art. 44(2).

this case it makes no sense to see the Moon or any other celestial body as something that can be acquired by corporations or individuals.[94]

More specific rules in the 1967 treaty include an obligation for states parties to inform other states and the UN Secretary-General of 'any phenomena they discover...which could constitute a danger to the life or health of astronauts'.[95] Finally let us mention that, in this field, states are liable for the activities of non-state actors, whether they be private corporations or international organizations.[96] This liability extends to damage done by any object launched from a state party's territory and is owed to other states parties and their natural and legal persons.[97] The Soviet Union paid compensation of 3 million Canadian Dollars to Canada as a result of the disintegration in 1978 of the Soviet satellite Cosmos 954 which deposited radioactive waste over Canada.[98]

---

94. Ibid 426–7 for a discussion of what is understood by the injunction that the 1967 Treaty demands that the Moon and other celestial bodies be used for exclusively peaceful purposes. Note that it is possible to own a piece of Moon rock that has been removed; the terms of the 1979 Treaty only prohibit property rights over natural resources 'in place' on the Moon. Art. 11(3), Gardiner at 426.

95. Art. V 1967 Treaty on Principles Governing the Activities of States in the Exploration and Use of Outer Space, including the Moon and Other Celestial Bodies.

96. Art. VI and see Convention on International Liability for Damage Caused by Space Objects (1972).

97. Art. VII and see the Convention on Registration of Objects Launched into Outer Space (1975) and UNGA RES 59/115, 10 December 2004 on the concept of the 'launching state'; see further M. Forteau, 'Space Law', in J. Crawford, A. Pellet, and S. Olleson (eds), *The Law of International Responsibility* (Oxford: OUP, 2010) 903–14.

98. Protocol between the Government of Canada and the Government of the Union of Soviet Socialist Republics, 2 April 1981; the Canadian claim related in part to the cost of to the clean-up operation, see now UNGA RES 47/68, 14 December 1992, Principles Relevant to the Use of Nuclear Power Sources in Outer Space.

VI | Jurisdiction

IN general, every state has exclusive jurisdiction within its own territory,[1] but this jurisdiction is not absolute, because it is subject to certain limitations imposed by international law. We shall consider here: first the scope of a state's jurisdiction over internal waters, different areas of the seas, and war ships. Second, we will look at the limitations on a state's jurisdiction with regard to

---

1. As we saw at the start of the previous Chapter, a state normally exercises jurisdiction over persons and things to the exclusion of the jurisdiction of other states. Traditionally jurisdiction is seen as being asserted in three ways: legislative, executive, and adjudicative. In each case other states may claim that any such exercise of jurisdiction interferes with their own rights. We will consider the limits that international law may place on such an exercise of jurisdiction in section § 9 below. A state making such a claim often (confusingly) asserts that the other state is exercising 'extraterritorial' jurisdiction. Rather than regarding one state as having exclusive jurisdiction over certain acts it may be more sensible to consider the relative weight that should be accorded to competing 'reasonable' jurisdictional claims: C. Ryngaert, *Jurisdiction in International Law* (Oxford: OUP, 2008). One prohibition is, however, clear: no state may exercise its executive jurisdiction (i.e. its police powers of arrest and detention) in the territory of another state without the consent of that state. English courts may exercise their discretion and *refuse* to exercise their adjudicative jurisdiction where a defendant has been brought before them in violation of the international rule of law: *R v Horseferry Road Magistrates Court, Ex p Bennett* [1994] 1 AC 42; C. Warbrick, 'Judicial Jurisdiction and Abuse of Process', 49 *ICLQ* (2000) 489–96.

human rights, the limits of national criminal jurisdiction, diplomatic protection for foreigners, and immunities.

Before we consider the detailed rules concerning internal waters and the law of the sea, let us examine the popular fiction that some parts of the territory are 'extraterritorial'. There are countless films in which the characters reach their embassy, consulate, or military base and declare that they are now on 'United States territory'. They are not. They remain in the territory of the host state. Even if you are born in an embassy, you are definitely born in the host state. This point was not lost on a recent student who, on hearing this explanation, promptly and successfully applied for a Chilean passport, having been under the mistaken impression that he was ineligible for Chilean nationality because he was born in the Uruguayan Embassy in Santiago Chile during the period of Pinochet.

§ 1. Jurisdiction over internal waters

Rivers. When the whole course of a river and both its banks are within the territory of a single state, that state's control over the river is as great as over any other part of its territory, unless its rights have been limited by treaty. The only rivers which concern international law are those which flow either through, or between, more than one state. Such rivers are conveniently called 'international rivers'; and they raise the question whether each of the riparian states has in law full control of its own part of the river, or whether it is limited by the fact that the river is useful or even necessary to other states. Clearly, one important interest at stake is that of navigation; it may be of vital concern to an up-river state that states nearer the mouth should not cut off its access to the sea. It may also be important to non-riparian states to have access to the upper waters of the river. But we are also increasingly aware of the importance of the economic uses of rivers for such purposes as irrigation, the supply of water to large cities, and the generation of hydro-electric power.[2] It is obviously desirable that all these interests should, so far as possible, be effectively protected.

While treaties between particular states opening particular rivers began to be common from early in the seventeenth century, it was not until the Treaty of Paris in 1814 that a general declaration of freedom of navigation on all international rivers was proclaimed. The declaration was given only a limited effect. Although in the course of the next forty years many rivers were opened to riparian states, there was a tendency to exclude non-riparian states. After the Crimean War, however, the Treaty of Paris, 1856, introduced a new principle. It established a body called the European Danube

---

2. 'Over 40% of the world's population resides in the just under 300 river basins shared by more than one country, which make up almost 50% of the earth's land surface (not including Antarctica). Over 90% of the conventionally calculated water resources of the Middle East cross international borders. Africa alone contains 60 international rivers, 11 of which drain four or more states. The basin of the River Danube is shared by 17 independent states. Across the world, there are 39 states which have over 90% of their territory located within international basins. Global water demand is currently said to double every 21 years, and water scarcity and population growth are becoming major causes of social stress and serious impediments to stability and economic growth in many poorer countries.' L. Boisson de Chazournes and F. Curtin, *National Sovereignty and International Watercourses* (Geneva, Green Cross International, 2000) at 16; S. McCaffrey, *The Law of International Watercourses*, 2nd edn (Oxford: OUP, 2007) chs 1 and 2; L. Boisson de Chazournes, E. Brown Weiss, and N. Bernasconi-Osterwalder (eds), *Freshwater and International Economic Law* (Oxford: OUP, 2005).

Commission, consisting of representatives both of riparian and non-riparian states, to improve the conditions of navigation on the lower Danube. The Commission was intended to be temporary, but its duration was extended and its powers enlarged by successive treaties. When it was instituted, navigation on the Danube was chaotic; the stream was obstructed by shoals, piracy and wrecking were common, and extortionate dues were charged. The Commission altered this, and proved a most successful experiment in international co-operation. It had wide administrative powers to the exclusion of the sovereignty of the territorial state through which the river flows, it controlled and policed navigation, fixed dues, constructed works, and tried offences against its own regulations. The 1948 Belgrade Convention has established a different regime, which creates a more modest supervisory and co-ordinating role for a new Danube Commission, yet still guarantees that '[n]avigation on the Danube shall be free and open for the nationals, vessels of commerce and goods of all States'.[3] The principle of free navigation for all states was extended to the Rhine by the Convention of Mannheim in 1868;[4] and the African Conference of Berlin in 1885 applied it to the Congo and the Niger. Today, independent African states have established their own regimes.[5]

---

3. Convention Regarding the Regime of Navigation on the Danube (1948) Art. 1. See also Convention on Cooperation for the Protection and Sustainable Use of the Danube River (1994) and its International Commission for the Protection of the Danube River.
4. See now the Revised Convention for Rhine Navigation (1963) and the Central Commission for the Navigation of the Rhine.
5. See, e.g. Act regarding Navigation and Economic Cooperation between the States of the Niger Basin (1963); Accord Instituting a Uniform River Regime and Creating the International Commission for the Congo-Oubangui-Sangha Basin (1999); and Southern African Development Community (SADC) Revised Protocol on Shared Watercourse Systems (2000).

Navigation is only one of the uses to which the waters of a river may be put and is not always the most important. Other uses include irrigation, water-supply, and hydro-electric power. The work of the International Law Commission in this area has clarified somewhat the principles which govern such non-navigational uses. The 1997 Convention on the Law of the Non-navigational Uses of International Watercourses (1997) is said to concentrate on three principles: equitable and reasonable utilization, prevention of significant harm, and prior notification of planned measures.[6] The first of these principles was reaffirmed by the International Court of Justice when it found that 'Czechoslovakia, by unilaterally assuming control of a shared resource, and thereby depriving Hungary of its right to an equitable and reasonable share of the natural resources of the Danube—with the continuing effects of the diversion of these waters on the ecology of the riparian area of the Szigetköz—failed to respect the proportionality which is required by international law'.[7]

The 1997 Convention explains that the watercourse state has to apply this principle 'with a view to attaining optimal and sustainable utilization…taking into account the interests of the watercourse States concerned, consistent with adequate protection of the watercourse'.[8] Social and environmental factors are to be taken into account including: the social and economic needs of the watercourse states, the population dependent on the water-

---

6. McCaffrey 'International Watercourses' <mpepil.com>.

7. *Case Concerning the Gabčíkovo-Nagymaros Project (Hungary/Slovakia)*, ICJ Rep. (25 September 1997) at para. 85, see also para. 78.

8. Art. 5(1).

course, and conservation, protection, development, and economy of use of the water resources of the watercourse.[9]

This principle of the 'equitable and reasonable' use of all the benefits of the river system between all the states concerned clearly does not lend itself to the formulation of rules applicable to rivers in general; each river has its own problems and needs a system of rules and administration adapted to meet them.[10]

Canals. In the absence of treaty stipulations, a canal is subject to the sole control of the state in whose territory it lies, and there is no right of passage through it for the ships of other states. But three interoceanic canals: Suez, Panama, and Kiel, have received a special status. They are sometimes, but inaccurately, said to be 'neutralized', or 'internationalized'.

The *Suez Canal* lies in Egyptian territory. It was opened in 1869 under a concession granted to the Universal Suez Ship Canal Company, which was initially majority owned by French investors and in which the British Government afterwards became the largest shareholder. The concession was to run for ninety-nine years and then revert to the Egyptian Government. The international status of the canal was established by the Convention of Constantinople, 1888, but the duration of the Convention was not limited to that of the company's concession.

Under the Convention the Canal is to be open in war and in peace to every vessel of commerce and war, without distinction of

---

9. Art. 6(1). See also Convention on the Protection and Use of Transboundary Watercourses and International Lakes (1992).

10. Consider the work of the Water Governance Facility and the two Water-Co-operation Facilities.

flag. It is never to be blockaded (Art. 1); no act of war is to be committed in the Canal or within three miles of its ports of access (Art. 4); belligerent warships must pass through with the least possible delay and may not stay more than 24 hours at Port Said or Suez; and an interval of 24 hours must elapse between the sailing of two hostile ships from these ports. The defence of the Canal was committed to Turkey and Egypt (Art. 9), but this provision broke down when Turkey attacked the Canal in 1914, and under the Peace Treaties Great Britain was substituted for Turkey. The Anglo-Egyptian Treaty of Alliance of 1936 allowed British forces to be stationed in Egyptian territory for the defence of the Canal, but under an agreement of 1954 these troops were withdrawn while Britain was to retain certain rights.

The arrangements for the operation and defence of the Canal, though not its international status, underwent radical changes in 1956. First, Egypt issued a law nationalizing the Canal Company which led to the widely condemned Anglo-French-Israeli military intervention in Egypt.[11] The Canal and its administration were subsequently vested (and remain) in the Suez Canal Authority, while Egypt responded to the intervention by abrogating its 1954 agreement with Britain. On the other hand, in a 'Declaration on the Suez Canal', registered by Egypt with the UN in 1957,[12] Egypt

---

11. For details of the legal arguments presented at the time see G. Marston, 'Armed Intervention in the 1956 Suez Canal Crisis: The Legal Advice Tendered to the British Government', 37 *ICLQ* (1988) 773–817.

12. This should be considered legally binding as a unilateral declaration, see ch. II §(4)(g) above. Declaration on the Suez Canal and the arrangements for its operation, Cairo, 24 April 1957, UNTS No. 3821; Egypt also accepted the same year jurisdiction of the International Court of Justice with regard to legal disputes for states parties to the 1888 Convention.

solemnly reaffirmed her intention 'to respect the terms and the spirit of the Constantinople Convention of 1888 and the rights and obligations arising therefrom'; and she added that she was 'more particularly determined' 'to afford and maintain free and uninterrupted navigation for all nations within the limits of and in accordance with the provisions' of the Convention. The status of the Canal as an international waterway governed by the provisions of the 1888 Convention therefore remains intact.[13]

The *Panama Canal* runs through a zone of Panamanian territory which was occupied and administered by the United States until 1977 then, pursuant to a transitional agreement, by shared control between the United States and Panama until noon on 31 December 1999, after which it came under the sole control of Panama and the Panama Canal Authority. At the same time, Panama declared 'that the Canal, as an international transit waterway, shall be permanently neutral in accordance with the regime established' in the Treaty.[14] In Article II Panama declared:

the neutrality of the Canal in order that both in time of peace and in time of war it shall remain secure and open to peaceful transit by the vessels of all nations on terms of entire equality, so

13. Note also the 1979 Peace Treaty between Israel and Egypt, Art. V(1) 'Ships of Israel, and cargoes destined for or coming from Israel, shall enjoy the right of free passage through the Suez Canal and its approaches through the Gulf of Suez and the Mediterranean Sea on the basis of the Constantinople Convention of 1888, applying to all nations, Israeli nationals, vessels and cargoes, as well as persons, vessels and cargoes destined for or coming from Israel, shall be accorded non-discriminatory treatment in all matters connected with usage of the canal.'

14. Art. I Treaty Concerning the Permanent Neutrality and Operation of the Panama Canal (1977).

that there will be no discrimination against any nation, or its citizens or subjects, concerning the conditions or charges of transit, or for any other reason, and so that the Canal, and therefore the Isthmus of Panama, shall not be the target of reprisals in any armed conflict between other nations of the world.[15]

The treaty, and hence the international regime, will also cover the third set of locks being built by the Panamanian authorities for 2014.

The *Kiel Canal* was, by the Treaty of Versailles, to be 'free and open to the vessels of commerce and war of all nations at peace with Germany on terms of entire equality'. Germany was bound to maintain it in navigable condition, and to levy only such charges as were necessary for this purpose. The provisions of the Treaty were denounced by Germany in 1936, and subsequent state practice, both in reaction to the denunciation and to the requirement that foreign warships and government ships have to give prior notification, suggests that the Canal is 'again a national waterway under German sovereignty'.[16]

§ 2. Jurisdiction in ports

A private ship in a foreign port is fully subject to the local jurisdiction in civil matters, but there are sometimes said to be two approaches to local jurisdiction in criminal matters. One approach,

---

15. Ibid.
16. Rainer Lagoni 'Kiel Canal' <mpepil.com>. Compare the 6th edn of this book at 236.

followed by Great Britain, asserts the complete subjection of the ship to the local jurisdiction, and regards any derogation from it as a matter of comity (courtesy) in the discretion of the territorial state. Local jurisdiction is regarded as complete, but not exclusive; Great Britain therefore exercises a concurrent jurisdiction over British ships in foreign ports, and is ready to concede it over foreign ships in British ports.

The other approach is founded on an *Avis* of the French *Conseil d'État* in 1806, referring to two American ships in French ports, the *Sally* and the *Newton,* on each of which one member of the crew had assaulted another. Both the American consuls and the French local authorities claimed jurisdiction, and the *Conseil* held that it belonged to the American consuls, on the ground that the offences did not disturb the peace of the port. The *Avis* declared in effect that the ships would be subjected to French jurisdiction in matters touching the interests of the state, and for offences committed, even on board, by members of the crew against strangers; but that in matters of internal discipline, including offences by one member of the crew against another, the local authorities ought not to interfere, unless either their assistance was invoked or the peace of the port compromised. This opinion effected an alteration in French practice, which had previously agreed with the practice of Great Britain. Although the approach in the *Avis* has been followed in many continental countries it cannot be regarded as an authoritative declaration of the international law on the matter. It is, moreover, full of ambiguities. If we are asked, for example, which matters 'touch the interests of a state', we should be inclined to answer that the whole administration of the criminal law does so. Further, the *Avis* says nothing of the position of passengers; it does not indicate the sorts of incidents which ought to be regarded as 'compromising the peace of the port', nor by whom the point is to be decided; nor by whom (e.g. by a consul, by the master, by the accused, or by his victim) the assistance of the port authorities must be invoked in order to justify their interference; it does not even say whether this interference may take the form of assuming jurisdiction.

Indeed, the French courts held in 1859, when a ship's officer on board an American ship, the *Tempest*, had killed a seaman on the same ship, that some crimes are so serious that, without regard to any further consequences, their mere commission compromises the peace of the port, and therefore brings them under the local jurisdiction. Such a decision is sound sense.

These different approaches are, however, perhaps less significant than they appear. The French system does not deny the complete jurisdiction of the state of the port over offences committed on board foreign ships; it merely declares that this jurisdiction will not be exercised in certain cases. The English system likewise does not involve an inevitable exercise of jurisdiction, but it does not declare in advance in what cases the jurisdiction will or will not be exercised. The difference in approach would appear to relate only to the question of jurisdiction over offences committed by members of the crew on board a merchant vessel. There is almost universal agreement that a merchant vessel may not afford asylum to a fugitive from justice, and such a fugitive may, if necessary, be removed from the ship, though as a matter of courtesy it is usual to inform the consul of the state concerned of the intended arrest. Jurisdiction in ports is also limited by the provisions in the 1982 Law of the Sea Convention relating to prompt release of ships and their crews, as well as the provisions limiting imprisonment, prohibiting corporal punishment, and guaranteeing recognized rights in certain proceedings against individuals that might lead to punishment.[17]

Although there is a customary rule that ships in distress have a right to enter a port to save human life,[18] and the right to access a port will often be governed by treaty, states may impose restrictions in other circumstances.[19] Rothwell and Stephens highlight recent bans against certain types of vessels: 'Australia prohibits access by foreign whaling vessels, unless a special permit has been sought or if force majeure conditions apply, whilst New Zealand bars port access to any ship that is partly or wholly nuclear powered.'[20]

§ 3. Jurisdiction over the territorial sea

It is now almost universally accepted that the only limitation on a state's sovereignty in the territorial sea is the existence of a right of 'innocent passage' through those waters for the ships of other states.[21] In time of peace states have allowed this right to be exer-

---

17. See Arts 73(2)(3), 230, 223–33 and 292; see further the multiple cases adjudicated on prompt release by the International Tribunal for the Law of the Sea; and B.H. Oxman, 'Human Rights and the United Nations Convention on the Law of the Sea', 36 *Columbia Journal of Transnational Law* (1997) 339–429 at 421–7.

18. R.R. Churchill and A.V. Lowe, *The Law of the Sea*, 3rd edn (Manchester: MUP, 1999) at 63; *Oppenheim's International Law*, 9th edn at 624; and see IMO Resolution MSC. 167(78), Guidelines on the Treatment of Persons Rescued at Sea, adopted on May 20, 2004, Appendix 'Some Comments on Relevant International Law' para. 6.

19. *Nicaragua v United States*, ICJ Rep. (1986) esp. paras 213, 214, and 125.

20. *The International Law of the Sea* (Oxford: Hart, 2010) at 55–6 (footnotes omitted).

21. Law of the Sea Convention (1982) (LOSC) Arts 17–25.

cised by warships as well as other ships, and the International Court of Justice has held that, in time of peace, warships have a right to pass through straits which are used for international navigation between two parts of the high seas.[22]

The term 'innocent passage' accurately denotes the nature of the right as well as its limitations. In the first place it is a right of 'passage', that is to say, a right to use the waters as a thoroughfare between two points outside them; a ship proceeding through the maritime belt to a port of the coastal state would not be exercising a right of passage. In the second place the passage must be 'innocent'; that is innocent with respect to the coastal state. And according to the 1982 Law of the Sea Convention (the Convention) this means a passage which is not prejudicial to the 'peace, good order or security of the coastal state' and which conforms to the provisions of the Convention and to the rules of international law.[23] The Convention also provides that submarines must navigate on the surface and show their flag, and that foreign ships must comply with the laws and regulations relating to innocent passage and the prevention of infringement of fisheries law.[24]

Clearly, the coastal state is entitled to exercise its jurisdiction over foreign private ships passing through its territorial sea to the extent necessary to enforce applicable local laws and regulations and to ensure the innocence of the passage. The question is how far it may exercise its general jurisdiction over ships in its territorial

---

22. *Corfu Channel Case,* ICJ (1949). For detail concerning the right of innocent passage for warships see Shaw *International Law*, 6th edn (2008) 572–4.

23. LOSC Art. 19(1).

24. Arts 20 and 21.

sea. The Convention makes clear that the coastal state's jurisdiction over its territorial sea is much more limited than its jurisdiction over internal waters. In criminal matters, the Convention provides that the coastal state should not arrest any person or conduct any investigation on board a foreign ship passing through its territorial sea in connection with a crime committed on board during the passage except in the following cases:[25]

(a) if the consequences of the crime extend to the coastal State
(b) if the crime is of a kind to disturb the peace of the country or the good order of the territorial sea;
(c) if the assistance of the local authorities has been requested by the master of the ship or by a diplomatic agent or consular officer of the flag State; or
(d) if such measures are necessary for the suppression of illicit traffic in narcotic drugs or psychotropic substances.

Furthermore the prohibition on arrest or investigation would not apply where the ship is passing through the territorial sea after leaving internal waters.[26] Nevertheless, criminal jurisdiction may not be exercised with regard to 'any crime committed before the ship entered the territorial sea, if the ship, proceeding from a foreign port, is only passing through the territorial sea without entering internal waters.'[27]

As to civil matters, the Convention similarly forbids the coastal state to stop or divert a foreign ship which is merely in passage

---

25. Art. 27.

26. Art. 27(2).

27. Art. 27(5); there are some exceptions relating to Parts XII and V of the Convention.

through the territorial sea, in order to exercise its civil jurisdiction with respect to a person on board. The coastal state is also forbidden to levy execution against, or to arrest, the ship itself, for the purpose of any civil proceedings other than proceedings in respect of liabilities connected with the ship's voyage through the territorial sea; it may do so, however, if the ship is outward bound after having visited internal waters.[28]

§ 4. Jurisdiction in the contiguous zone

Several states have in the past sought to claim for themselves different zones for different purposes, and in such cases it was not always easy to know whether a state was claiming a wide area of territorial waters, that is to say, of waters under its sovereignty for all purposes, or merely certain special rights over an adjacent area. The area over which these special rights were claimed became known as the 'contiguous zone', and the rights were claimed for a variety of purposes. Great Britain initially resisted the doctrine of the contiguous zone, though actually she was probably the first state to introduce it: Great Britain's eighteenth-century 'Hovering Acts', were aimed at ships 'hovering' outside the territorial sea and linked to illegal activities ashore; as such they authorized the seizure of smugglers on the high seas at varying distances from the shore. These Acts were abolished in 1876 as smuggling in the English Channel was brought under control, and the hovering laws were apparently proving embarrassing in contesting Spain's

---

28. Art. 28.

claims to six-mile territorial waters.[29] It is now clear that a state may exercise in a *contiguous zone* the control necessary to prevent and punish infringement of its customs, fiscal, immigration, and sanitary regulations.[30] The contiguous zone may not extend more than 24 nautical miles from the baselines. The wording of the relevant provision in the 1982 Law of the Sea Convention is clear that these rights for the coastal state extend to acts that would take place, or have taken place, within the state's territory or territorial sea and not within the contiguous zone.[31]

§ 5. Jurisdiction with regard to the continental shelf and the exclusive economic zone

As we saw in the previous chapter, the 1982 Law of the Sea Convention recognizes that the coastal state exercises exclusive sovereign rights over the continental shelf 'for the purpose of exploring it and exploiting its natural resources'.[32] Natural resources 'consist

---

29. See the 6th edn of this book at 201–11 for further details on the UK's position on the contiguous zone; see also A.V. Lowe, 'The Development of the Concept of the Contiguous Zone', 52 *BYBIL* (1981) 109–69.

30. Art. 33.

31. Art. 33, see Sir Gerald Fitzmaurice, 'Some Results of the Geneva Conference on the Law of the Sea', 8 *ICLQ* (1959) 73–121, compare S. Oda, 'The Concept of the Contiguous Zone', 11 *ICLQ* (1962) 131–53. The substantive jurisdiction of the coastal state may be interpreted to be greater due to the contiguous zone no longer coming within the scope of the high seas and now being considered part of the exclusive economic zone, see Churchill and Lowe (above) at 139 and Art. 59.

32. Art. 77(1)(2). Note that this is not the same as full territorial sovereignty and the legal status of airspace and superjacent waters remain unaffected; Art. 78(1). For the special

of the mineral and other non-living resources of the seabed and subsoil together with living organisms belonging to sedentary species'.[33] The coastal State has the exclusive right to construct and regulate the use of artificial islands and installations and exclusive jurisdiction over such constructions.[34] It also has the exclusive right to authorize and regulate drilling.[35]

In exercising these rights the coastal state must not unjustifiably interfere with navigation or other rights of states under the Convention.[36] Moreover, the coastal state must respect the rights of other states to lay and maintain cables and pipelines on the continental shelf;[37] exploitation by the coastal state must not result in any unjustifiable interference with navigation; warning must be given of installations constructed on the continental shelf, and installations that are abandoned or disused are to be removed to ensure safety of navigation;[38] and installations may not be put in places where they may interfere with the use of recognized sea lanes essential to international navigation.[39]

The Exclusive Economic Zone (EEZ) extends up to 200 nautical miles from the baselines from which the territorial sea is

---

regime applicable to non-living natural resources in the outer continental shelf see the section on the continental shelf in the previous chapter.

33. Art. 77(4).
34. Arts 80 and 60.
35. Art. 81.
36. Art. 78(2).
37. Art. 79.
38. Arts 80 and 60(3), cf 1958 Convention on the Continental Shelf Art. 5(5) which requires the entire removal of such installations, and see Churchill and Lowe (above) at 155.
39. Arts 80 and 60.

measured.[40] The Convention's 'specific legal regime' governs the rights and jurisdiction of the coastal state and was introduced in order to ensure rights for coastal states over resources in this zone. Most of the world's fish stocks are found in these EEZs and the impetus to create this regime came from developing countries keen to ensure their fair share of these and other resources. Unlike the continental shelf, an EEZ has to be claimed and established by the coastal state. Although most states have done so, the United Kingdom maintains its claim to an Economic Fisheries Zone (EFZ) and has refrained from creating an EEZ, pointing to its existing rights over its continental shelf (which of course also extends 200 nautical miles from the baselines). The jurisdictional rights over the continental shelf apply in the same way in the EEZ; however, there are a number of additional rights and obligations for the coastal state. Article 56(1) of the Convention states that '[i]n the exclusive economic zone, the coastal State has: (a) sovereign rights for the purpose of exploring and exploiting, conserving and managing the natural resources, whether living or non-living, of the waters superjacent to the seabed and of the seabed and its subsoil, and with regard to other activities for the economic exploitation and exploration of the zone, such as the production of energy from the water, currents and winds'. The coastal state has responsibilities for conservation and management of living resources, and may in this context 'take such measures, including boarding, inspection, arrest and judicial proceedings, as may be necessary to ensure compliance with the laws

---

40. Art. 57. The International Court of Justice has stated that the institution of the EEZ has become 'part of customary law'. *Continental Shelf (Libya v Malta)* ICJ Rep. (1985) para. 34.

and regulations adopted by it in conformity with this Convention'.[41] The coastal state also has jurisdiction as provided for in the Convention with regard to not only installations (as seen above) but also marine scientific research and the protection and preservation of the marine environment.[42]

Lastly, we might mention that shipwrecks in the EEZ, or on the continental shelf, are not covered by the Law of the Sea Convention.[43] A UNESCO Convention obliges states parties to 'preserve underwater cultural heritage for the benefit of humanity',[44] sets out reporting and co-operation systems, and states that '[u]nderwater cultural heritage shall not be commercially exploited'.[45]

§ 6. Jurisdiction on the high seas

At the time when international law came into existence, most maritime states claimed sovereignty over certain seas; for example, Venice claimed the Adriatic; England the North Sea, the Channel, and large areas of the Atlantic; Sweden the Baltic; and Denmark-Norway all of the northern seas. Such claims were often disputed,

---

41. Art. 73(1), note 'Arrested vessels and their crews shall be promptly released upon the posting of reasonable bond or other security.' Art. 73(2).

42. Arts 56(1)(b), 60, 246, 220.

43. But see Art. 303(2) on archaeological and historical objects found at sea.

44. The UNESCO Convention on the Protection of the Underwater Cultural Heritage (2001), Art. 2(3). 'Underwater cultural heritage' means all traces of human existence having a cultural, historical or archaeological character which have been partially or totally under water, periodically or continuously, for at least 100 years'; Art. 1(1)(a).

45. Ibid Art. 2(7).

but the principle that sovereignty might exist over the sea was not. Indeed the modern theory that the high seas are free and common to all would have been unsuited to earlier times. The state which claimed the seas often rendered a service to all by policing them against piracy, and in return it claimed proprietary rights over them. It might require ceremonial honours to be paid to its flag; it might reserve the fisheries for itself, or make foreigners take out a licence; it might levy tolls on the ships of other nations; sometimes it might even prohibit navigation to them altogether.

It was the abuse of such rights by Spain and Portugal in the six-teenth century that prepared the ground for a reaction against these claims. Under Bulls of Pope Alexander VI of 1493 these two powers claimed to divide the New World between themselves: Spain claimed the whole Pacific and the Gulf of Mexico; Portugal the Indian Ocean and most of the Atlantic; and both excluded foreigners from these vast areas. The claims of the Portuguese in 1609 provoked the *Mare Liberum* of Grotius, in which he maintained that the sea could not be made the property of any state. His attack met with general oppo-sition, and in England John Selden replied to him with the *Mare Clausum,* published in 1635, maintaining the English claims. As yet there was no general hostility to the existence of sovereignty over the sea; what the nations wanted, and what they gradually succeeded in establishing, was freedom of navigation, which was quite consistent with the existence of sovereignty. Gradually the more extreme claims were dropped, and by the end of the first quarter of the nineteenth century, the freedom of the high seas may be regarded as established. But though the principle of freedom was by then established, it was impossible to leave the high seas, which were used by the ships of all nations, unregulated by any law, and it is necessary therefore to consider the circumstances in which a state may enjoy jurisdiction on the high seas.

The high seas are those parts of the seas that are not included in the territorial waters or an exclusive zone or archipelagic waters of a state.[46] The 1982 Law of the Sea Convention confirms that all states enjoy the freedoms of the high seas,[47] that no state may subject any part of the high seas to its sovereignty,[48] and that the high seas shall be reserved for peaceful purposes.[49] While the freedom to fish may have been conceived with little concern for the fish, today the problems of overfishing and managing the ecosystem are more to the fore, even if the international law is relatively weak. As we have noted, most fish stocks are found within the exclusive economic zones of coastal states. Fishing on the high seas is covered by certain conventions; but many remain concerned that we are doing irreparable harm to the marine environment. Judge Oda (writing non-judicially) has repeatedly suggested that ocean fisheries be considered the 'common heritage of mankind' along with the resources of the deep sea bed.[50]

---

46. LOSC Art. 86.

47. Art. 87 lists '*inter alia*': freedom: of navigation, overflight, laying submarine cables and pipelines, constructing artificial islands and other installations permitted under international law, of fishing, of scientific research. These freedoms are subject to certain conditions under the Convention. It is sometimes suggested that states are also free to conduct weapons testing and military exercises. See also Art. 90.

48. Art. 89.

49. Art. 88; see also Arts 141 and 301, the scope of these provisions is contested; it clearly covers the prohibition of aggression and unlawful use of force (see Ch. IX below); see further Churchill and Lowe (above), ch. 17 and Rothwell and Stephens (above), ch. 12.

50. 'Some Reflections on Recent Developments in the Law of the Sea', 27 *Yale Journal of International Law* (2002) 217–21.

The current regime is less ambitious and leaves considerable discretion to states.[51]

Every state has jurisdiction over ships flying its flag on the high seas; it may apply its law, civil and criminal, to all on board irrespective of their nationality. The justification of this principle is simply that *some* law must prevail on ships, and there is no other law to compete with that of the flag state. One should not try to explain this by regarding ships as floating portions of a state's territory. If pressed, this metaphor would lead to the absurd result that the waters surrounding a ship from time to time would be territorial waters. Ships may only sail under the flag of only one state, and it is that state that normally has exclusive jurisdiction.[52] Each state fixes the conditions for granting this nationality and there must exist a genuine link between the state and the ship.[53]

Collisions at sea between two ships of different nationality are now covered by a specific provision of LOSC 1982 which lays down that no penal or disciplinary proceedings may be instituted in respect of an incident upon the high seas except before the appropriate authorities, either of the flag state, or of the state whose national is accused of being at fault.[54]

---

51. Arts 116–20, 60–8, 297(3)(a); Agreement for the Implementation of the Provisions of the UN Convention on the Law of the Sea relating to the Conservation and Management of Straddling Fish Stocks and Highly Migratory Fish Stocks (1995); see also ITLOS *Southern Bluefin Tuna (Australia v Japan)(provisional measures)* 27 August 1999, paras 70–80.
52. Art. 92(1).
53. Art. 91(1); note the purposeful interpretation of 'genuine link' in this context by the International Tribunal for the Law of the Sea which refused to allow a challenge by Guinea to the genuineness of the link and stressed instead that the purpose of the provision is 'to secure more effective implementation of the duties of the flag State', in *M/V Saiga (No.2) Saint Vincent and the Grenadines v Guinea* (admissibility and merits) 1 July 1999, at para. 83.
54. Art. 97(1).

It follows from the principle that each state has jurisdiction over its own flagged vessels that no state has a general right to police the high seas. But there are certain special cases in which such a right is admissible. We can find numerous cases where states have by treaty accorded to other states certain rights of police or jurisdiction over their ships. Thus the United States, during the era of prohibition, negotiated treaties with many other maritime states, including Great Britain, authorizing U.S authorities to search a private ship within a certain distance outside American territorial waters, and, if there were reasonable cause for doing so, take the ship in for adjudication by the American courts. Rights have been agreed for the suppression of slave-trading and, during the nineteenth century, various conventions were made for the suppression of the trade, e.g. the Congress of Vienna (1815) declared slave-trading illegal; and the Berlin African Conference (1885) and the Brussels Anti-Slavery Conference (1890) adopted measures for suppressing it in Africa. States had always been reluctant to allow their ships to be searched by the ships of other states; but the decline of slavery during the nineteenth century reduced the dimensions of the problem, and these and other treaties eventually gave the armed vessels of one state power to search the suspected ships of another within certain geographical limits. The Law of the Sea Convention now grants a government ship the right to board a ship reasonably suspected of being engaged in the slave trade.[55] The same rights apply where there are reasonable grounds for suspecting a ship is without nationality, or being of the same nationality as the government ship although flying a foreign

---

55. Art. 110(1)(b).

flag or refusing to show its flag.[56] Separate treaties contain specific rules regarding drug trafficking, people trafficking, and the smuggling of migrants at sea.

Any state may seize pirates on the high sea and bring them in for trial by its own courts, on the ground that they are *hostes humani generis* (enemies of all humankind). But this applies only to persons who are pirates under international law. In the present context piracy, briefly stated, consists of any illegal acts of violence or detention, committed for private ends by the crew or the passengers of a private ship on the high seas (or in the EEZ), against another ship or against persons on board such another ship.[57] Note that there need to be two separate vessels involved, and so a takeover launched from within a ship will not constitute piracy under the Convention, and the acts must be committed for 'private ends'.[58]

The present situation off the coast of Somalia is proving that it is not enough to have an international legal framework for repression. In 2011 it was reported that there were 26 ships and 601 individuals being held by pirates in this context;[59] while the average ransom was said to be $4.7m per vessel with a total of $135m being paid in 2011.[60]

---

56. Art. 110(1)(d)(e); there is also a provision on unauthorized broadcasting, so-called 'pirate radio' stations: Arts 110(1)(c) and 109.

57. See Arts 101 and 58(2). Of course states may have national laws on piracy which apply in their territorial sea and which differ in their scope from the international definition, but any exercise of jurisdiction will be authorized as part of their normal territorial jurisdiction.

58. These qualifications were central to the legal imbroglio that surrounded the *Achille Lauro* incident; for a fascinating account see A. Cassese, *Terrorism, Politics, and the Law: The Achille Lauro Affair* (Cambridge: Polity, 1989).

59. UN Doc. S/2011/360 at 27.

60. *Piracy off the coast of Somalia*, HoC Foreign Aff. Cttee, HC 1318 (2012).

Those involved in the acts of piracy are relatively few,[61] but the area of the attacks is vast.[62] Even when pirates are captured it has not proven easy to find states willing to try them in their own courts or to imprison them following a conviction. The situation is further complicated by the difficulties involved in returning convicted pirates to Somalia, especially when they may have co-operated with the prosecution.

Jurisdiction over the perpetrators of similar attacks which do not fall under this definition are regulated by the provisions of the Convention for the Suppression of Unlawful Acts against the Safety of Maritime Navigation of 1988, and a Protocol, adopted in 2005, now adds a whole series of offences related to the use of a ship to further acts of terrorism. The Protocol also includes a series of rules relating to boarding and states 'the use of force shall be avoided except when necessary to ensure the safety of its officials and persons on board, or where the officials are obstructed in the execution of the authorized actions. Any use of force pursuant to this article shall not exceed the minimum degree of force which is necessary and reasonable in the circumstances.'[63] Interestingly, the new amending Protocol is concerned not only with the competing interests of the flag states but also with the treatment of the individuals on board. Where a state party takes measures against a ship it must: 'ensure that all persons on board are treated in a manner

---

61. 'Naval forces estimate that there are about 50 main pirate leaders, around 300 leaders of pirate attack groups, and around 2,500 "foot soldiers". It is believed that financing is provided by around 10 to 20 individuals. In addition, there is a large number of armed individuals guarding captured ships, and numerous ransom negotiators.' S/2011/360 at 27.

62. 2.8m sq. miles.

63. Art. 2 inserting Art. 8*bis*(9) in the 1988 Convention.

which preserves their basic human dignity, and in compliance with the applicable provisions of international law, including international human rights law'.[64] More generally, away from the context of terrorism, the International Tribunal on the Law of the Sea has ruled that the manner of the boarding of a vessel and indiscriminate firing on board violated international law. In the words of the Tribunal: 'Considerations of humanity must apply in the law of the sea, as they do in other areas of international law.'[65]

'Hot pursuit' of a ship on to the high seas and her arrest there are permitted under the Convention when the coastal state has good reason to believe the ship has violated its laws and regulations. This right of the coastal state is subject to the following conditions: (1) the pursuit is begun when the foreign ship or one of its boats is within the internal waters, the archipelagic waters, the territorial sea or the contiguous zone of the pursuing state; (2) a visual or auditory signal to stop has been given at a distance which enables it to be seen or heard by the foreign ship; (3) the pursuit is not interrupted; (4) the foreign ship has not succeeded in reaching the territorial sea of its own state or of a third state; and (5) the pursuit is carried out by a warship (or military aircraft) or an authorized ship (or aircraft) clearly identifiable as being on government service.[66]

---

64. Art. 8*bis*(10)(ii).

65. *M/V Saiga (No. 2) (merits)* (above) at para. 155: 'international law, which is applicable by virtue of article 293 of the Convention, requires that the use of force must be avoided as far as possible and, where force is unavoidable, it must not go beyond what is reasonable and necessary in the circumstances.'

66. LOSC Art. 111; NB 'If the foreign ship is within a contiguous zone, as defined in article 33, the pursuit may only be undertaken if there has been a violation of the rights for the protection of which the zone was established.' Art. 111(1); for violations in the EEZ/continental shelf see Art. 111(2); see further *M/V Saiga*, ibid paras 139–52.

§ 7. Jurisdiction over warships and other state ships

Warships and state ships (as long as the state ship is not engaged in commerce) are wholly exempt from the local jurisdiction; they may not be entered by the port authorities for any purpose without the consent of the commanding officer.[67] This, so far as regards warships, has been generally accepted ever since the judgment of Chief Justice Marshall for the US Supreme Court in the case of *The Schooner Exchange* in 1812.[68] But this does not mean that a state ship or a warship is under no duty to obey the law of the port; on the contrary, she is bound to do so in any matter which has external effects. Thus, while she will observe her own law in a matter of ship's discipline, she must observe the local laws and regulations for example with regard to the environment or pollution;[69] she must not give refuge to fugitive criminals, though at least for some states in the Americas the warship may be a place for political asylum;[70] members of the crew who break the law on shore leave are not

---

67. For more detail see Arts 29–32, 58(2), and 95–6 as well as the Brussels Convention for the Unification of Certain Rules concerning the Immunity of State-owned Vessels (1926) and its Additional Protocol of 1934. See also Art. 16 of the United Nations Convention on Jurisdictional Immunities of States and Their Property (2004).

68. 11 U.S. 116 (1812).

69. See LOSC Arts 21, 30, and 31.

70. See, e.g. the OAS Convention on Diplomatic Asylum (1954) Art. I 'Asylum granted in legations, war vessels, and military camps or aircraft, to persons being sought for political reasons or for political offenses shall be respected by the territorial State in accordance with the provisions of this Convention.' See further P. Shah, 'Asylum, Diplomatic' <mpepil.com>.

protected from the consequences, though the port authorities may, and often do, hand them over to the ship's authorities instead of dealing with the offence.[71] The immunity of a state ship therefore means, not total exemption from the local laws and regulations concerning passage, but her immunity from any kind of legal process. If a state ship violates local law concerning passage or international law more generally, the coastal state 'may require it to leave the territorial sea immediately'.[72] To be clear, the offending state bears international responsibility for any loss or damage to the coastal state as a result of such a breach of the law,[73] and the coastal state can seek to ensure redress through diplomatic action or any applicable dispute settlement procedure.[74]

That a warship is not floating foreign territory but is actually covered by the local law is clear from the decision of the Privy Council in the case of *Chung Chi Chiung v The King*.[75] A British subject had been convicted in a Hong Kong court for murder committed on board a Chinese state ship within the territorial waters

---

71. A distinction is drawn on the one hand between times when the commander and the crew are ashore in an official capacity in the service of the vessel, and on the other hand shore visits for 'pleasure and recreation' (see, e.g. *Oppenheim's International Law* 9th edn at 1169–70). In the former case it has been suggested they remain under the exclusive jurisdiction of the home state even with respect to crimes, while in the latter case they are under the jurisdiction of the port state and may be punished for crimes committed ashore (see further below).

72. Art. 30; Churchill and Lowe (above) at 99 suggest this rule must also apply to state ships and that 'any force necessary' may be used to compel ships to leave the territorial sea.

73. Art. 31.

74. See Ch. VIII below.

75. [1939] AC 160. A British court would have had jurisdiction to try a British subject for murder, even if the crime had been committed abroad, but apparently a Hong Kong court could not do so.

of Hong Kong (at that time under British rule). He had tried to commit suicide, and had been taken to hospital in Hong Kong. On appeal it was argued on his behalf that the Court had had no jurisdiction. If the character of a state ship were truly regarded as being 'exterritorial', that is to say, as foreign territory, this argument would have been sound. The Privy Council, however, took the view that a state ship merely enjoys certain immunities from the local jurisdiction, and that, except to the extent that it is excluded by these immunities, local law applies to her and to everything happening on board. There could therefore be no legal objection to the immunities to which the ship was entitled being waived, and on the facts it was held that China had waived them. The Hong Kong court therefore had jurisdiction to try the case.

The laws and discipline of the ship's state may be enforced on board a state ship by court martial or otherwise, without infringing the sovereignty of the territorial state, and members of the crew are wholly exempt from the local jurisdiction so long as they remain on board. If they go ashore on official business, they have been held to be exempt from the local jurisdiction.[76] While they might be restrained should they commit offences ashore, or in order to prevent further violence, they must be handed over to the ship in order that they be dealt with under the laws of the state ship's state. On the other hand, if they merely go ashore on leave, they are not exempt from local jurisdiction and may be arrested and tried before local courts for breaches of the local

---

76. *Ministère Public v Triandafilou*, 39 *AJIL* (1945) 345–7; Institute of International Law Resolution 'Règlement sur le régime des navires de mer et de leurs équipages dans les ports étrangers en temps de paix' (1928) Art. 20.

law; however, if they regain their ship without having been arrested, the local authorities cannot insist upon their surrender, only that they should be dealt with under the law of the sending state.[77] In many cases, visiting naval forces will be covered under a 'visiting forces agreement' and it will be those detailed provisions that will determine any exclusive or concurrent jurisdiction over the individuals concerned.

§ 8. Limitations on a state's treatment of its own nationals and respect for international human rights

The 1928 edition of this book stated that '[t]he relations between a state and its own nationals are normally a matter of domestic jurisdiction, though like all other matters of domestic jurisdiction they may be brought within the domain of international law by the existence of a treaty'.[78] The last edition, updated by Waldock in 1963, highlighted the role of the Universal Declaration of Human Rights (1948) as having 'authority as a general guide to the content of fundamental rights and freedoms as understood by members of the United Nations, and…as providing a connecting link between different concepts of human rights in different parts of the world'. He lamented, however, that 'over-elaboration and doctrinaire approaches to controversial issues' had deprived the efforts at writing binding covenants of 'any chance of success' and concluded that the United Nations has had to

---

77. *Orfandis v Min Public*, 12 ILR (1943–5) case No. 38, 141–3.
78. 1st edn at 136.

be 'content with completing a few special conventions, such as those on "genocide" and the political rights of women, which contain no machinery for their application'.[79] Over the last 50 years, things have radically changed.[80]

First, the two international human rights Covenants were eventually completed and entered into force in 1976,[81] they are widely ratified and contain machinery for their application, both in terms of independent committees to supervise the reports submitted by states, and through a complaints procedure which allows for individual petitions. In addition, there are now dozens of additional treaties in force covering a range of human rights topics: racial discrimination, discrimination against women, torture, children, migrant workers, persons with disabilities, and disappearances.[82] Each treaty usually has an independent committee to monitor states' compliance and in nearly all cases, to hear complaints. In the case of torture there is a sub-committee which conducts visits to places of detention and issues annual public reports.[83] Taken

79. 6th edn at 294.

80. For a good introduction to the various developments see C. Krause and M. Scheinin (eds), *International Protection of Human Rights: A Textbook* (Turku: Abo Akademi Institute for Human Rights, 2009); S. Shah, S. Sivakumaran, and D. Harris (eds), *International Human Rights Law* (Oxford: OUP, 2010).

81. International Covenant on Economic Social and Cultural Rights, International Covenant on Civil and Political Rights. Each treaty has an optional protocol which allows for complaints against states parties to the protocol.

82. For an overview see W. Kälin and J. Künzli, *The Law of International Human Rights Protection* (Oxford: OUP, 2009).

83. See the Optional Protocol to the Convention against Torture and other Cruel, Inhuman or Degrading Treatment or Punishment (2002); see also the European Convention for the Prevention of Torture and Inhuman or Degrading Treatment or Punishment

together with the almost 200 Conventions of the International Labour Organization, these treaties cover almost all aspects of everyday life. So we now have binding obligations for states as well as machinery for monitoring their application.

Second, the UN Human Rights Commission has been replaced by a UN Human Rights Council in 2006. The new Council has made an effort to avoid the doctrinaire confrontations that characterized the UN debates on human rights. The Council has at its disposal the wide range of 'special procedures' developed by the United Nations over years. The independent experts appointed by the United Nations under such arrangements originally were concentrated on country situations, and were usually established in the face of human rights crises such as the coup in Chile, the disappearances in Argentina, the Soviet occupation of Afghanistan, the Iraqi occupation of Kuwait, the Israeli occupation in the Palestinian Territories, the break-up of Yugoslavia, the genocide in Rwanda, and the human rights violations in Myanmar. Today, complementing such 'country mandates',[84] we find 'thematic mandates' covering a wide range of issues.[85] The work of these

---

(1987); for a revealing insider's account of the working of the latter mechanism see A. Cassese, *Inhuman States: Imprisonment, Detention and Torture in Europe Today* (Cambridge: Polity, 1996).

84. In 2011 these included Cambodia, Côte d'Ivoire, the Democratic People's Republic of Korea, Haiti, Islamic Republic of Iran, Palestinian Territories Occupied since 1967, Somalia, and Sudan.

85. The thematic mechanisms include (in the order of their creation): enforced or involuntary disappearances; extrajudicial, summary or arbitrary executions; torture and other cruel, inhuman or degrading treatment or punishment; freedom of religion or belief; mercenaries; sale of children, child prostitution and child pornography; arbitrary detention; internally displaced persons; racism and xenophobia; freedom of expression; violence

experts cannot be dismissed as interference in matters which are within the exclusive jurisdiction of states. They rely on a normative framework which includes not only the treaties binding on the state concerned but also on the rights found in the Universal Declaration of 1948 and the UN Charter.

Third, in response to heavy criticism of the selective and political way the Commission operated, the new UN Human Rights Council has developed a system of universal periodic review, whereby every state's human rights record is examined at the Council in a public meeting at least every four years.[86] These review sessions are held in public and the webcasts generate considerable interest. Again this probing by individual states into the affairs of other states is no longer challenged on grounds of exclusive jurisdiction. It is agreed that these reviews cover the UN Charter, the Universal Declaration, human rights instruments to which the state is party, voluntary pledges and commitments made by states, and applicable international humanitarian law.[87]

---

against women; independence of judges and lawyers; economic reform policies and foreign debt; toxic and dangerous products and wastes; right to education; extreme poverty; migrants; right to food; adequate housing; human rights defenders; indigenous peoples; right to health; racial discrimination faced by people of African descent; human rights and counter-terrorism; minority issues; international solidarity; human rights and transnational corporations and other business enterprises; trafficking in persons; contemporary forms of slavery; access to safe drinking water and sanitation; cultural rights; freedom of peaceful assembly and of association; and discrimination against women in law and in practice.

86. For an examination of these developments K. Boyle, *New Institutions for Human Rights Protection* (Oxford: OUP, 2009) and B.G. Ramcharan, *The UN Human Rights Council* (London: Routledge, 2011).

87. A/HRC/RES/5/1 Annex, paras 1–2.

Fourth, the United Nations has established a series of commissions of inquiry and field operations to investigate and report on human rights.[88] In some cases the commissions of inquiry were precursors to the establishment of international criminal tribunals (as was the case for the former Yugoslavia and Rwanda). In other cases the commission of inquiry has led to the Security Council triggering the jurisdiction of the International Criminal Court (as in the case of the Darfur inquiry). More recently we have seen detailed reports on Gaza, the Democratic Republic of Congo, Libya, and Syria.

Fifth, parallel developments at the regional level have led to separate treaty monitoring bodies,[89] and in the case of Europe, the Americas and Africa, to regional Human Rights Courts with the power to issue binding judgments against the states parties to the relevant treaties. The case-law from these bodies has provided a rich tapestry of clarifications and interpretations of the international obligations of states, and there is a plethora of publications and courses dedicated to this branch of international law. The last edition of this book, published in 1963, noted that the European Court of Human Rights had delivered its first judgment. Fifty

---

88. P. Alston, 'The Darfur Commission as a Model for Future Responses to Crisis Situations', 3 *JICJ* (2005) 600–7.

89. In addition to the bodies found at the Organization of American States, the Council of Europe and the African Union, we should mention the Committee established under the Arab Charter; see further M. Rishmawi, 'The Arab Charter on Human Rights and the League of Arab States: An Update', 10(1) *Human Rights Law Review* (2010) 169–78; for completeness note the Association of Southeast Asian Nations (ASEAN) Intergovernmental Commission on Human Rights which may in time be supplemented by an independent committee.

years later the Court has delivered 10,000 judgments. These cover extrajudicial killings, torture, the death penalty, forced labour, detention, fair trial, privacy, freedom of expression, the right to a family, freedom of association and assembly, the right to peaceful enjoyment of property and many more topics. In a significant development all the states parties to the European Convention on Human Rights have adopted national legislation allowing for complaints alleging violations of the rights in the Convention to be brought before national courts. It is perhaps in this area that we find the clearest example of a unity between national and international law.[90]

Sixth, as we have already seen, human rights obligations have become part of the international legal framework. The issue of human rights can no longer be addressed as a discrete issue of UN supervision, or a matter exclusively within a state's domestic jurisdiction untouched by international law. International human rights obligations have been used to challenge amnesty laws which prevented the investigation and prosecution of serious human rights violations. And, in a number of cases the Inter-American Court of Human Rights has held such laws to be not only contrary to human rights obligations, but also to lack legal effect.[91] Human rights

---

90. For a detailed look at how these obligations are applied by various courts see R. Clayton and H. Tomlinson, *The Law of Human Rights*, 2nd edn (Oxford: OUP, 2009) and N. Jayawickrama, *The Judicial Application of Human Rights Law: National Regional and International Jurisprudence* (Cambridge: CUP, 2002).

91. See, e.g. *Gomes Lund et al. v Brazil*, 24 November 2010; the Court considers that the 'prohibition of enforced disappearance of persons and its related obligation to investigate and punish those responsible have, for much time now, reached a nature of *ius cogens*' (at para. 137); see also OHCHR *Rule-of-Law Tools for Post-Conflict States: Amnesties* (2009).

norms are now regularly invoked in disputes decided under international law and are shaping how the older rules are interpreted and applied. Examples are given throughout the book as we examine the enforcement action of the Security Council, the creation and recognition of states, the acquisition of territory, the law of immunities, and diplomatic protection. It is this mainstreaming of human rights obligations permeating the international legal system that is transforming the dynamic of international law from a tool for international co-existence and co-operation into a legal system whose purpose is focused on human welfare generally and the dignity of the individual in particular.[92]

Lastly, the focus on the individual has also led to significant developments with regard to individual criminal responsibility for violations of international law. We have already mentioned that individuals may be held directly accountable for violations of international criminal law in international tribunals. There is now a long list of treaties that define offences and call for states parties to prosecute or extradite individuals suspected of such crimes. In addition to treaties on torture there are treaties on hostage taking, child pornography, and disappearances. Senator Pinochet's claim of immunity before the English courts was effectively thwarted by the effects of the UN Convention Against Torture which had been ratified by Chile and the United Kingdom. But in order to understand the exact operation of these treaties, we need to consider the

---

92. See further T. Meron, *International Law in the Age of Human Rights—General Course on Public International Law*, 301 *RCADI* (Leiden: Nijhoff, 2004); M.T. Kamminga and M. Scheinin (eds), *The Impact of Human Rights Law on General International Law* (Oxford: OUP, 2009); P. Capps, *Human Dignity and the Foundations of International Law* (Oxford: Hart, 2009).

scope of a state's criminal jurisdiction more generally, and it is to that topic that we now turn.

§ 9. The limits of national criminal jurisdiction

International practice on the issue of criminal jurisdiction is not uniform. It is agreed that a state is competent to deal with any offence committed within its territory (including the territorial sea and airspace), without regard to the nationality of the offender (territorial jurisdiction). It is also agreed that a state may assume jurisdiction over offences committed by its own nationals abroad (active personality jurisdiction). What is not agreed, however, is when a state may punish foreigners for an act committed outside its territory, and therefore at a time when they were not subject to that state's criminal law.

It is further accepted that in certain circumstances a crime may be committed *within* the territory of a state and therefore be justiciable by its criminal courts, even though the actor may be physically outside the territory. An obvious illustration would be that of a man who fires a gun across a frontier and kills another man in a neighbouring state; in such a case the jurisdiction of the country from which the gun is fired has been called 'subjective', and that of the country in which the shot takes effect 'objective territorial jurisdiction'.[93] The existence of this objective territorial

---

93. Lowe and Staker illustrate this further by explaining that where bombers prepare their explosives in a state and then explode the bomb on an aircraft outside the territory, the state in which the bomb was prepared will have subjective territorial jurisdiction. 'Jurisdiction', in M. Evans (ed.), *International Law*, 3rd edn (Oxford: OUP, 2010) 313–39, at 321–2.

jurisdiction has been recognized frequently by English and American courts. For example, in *Rex v Godfrey*,[94] an English court ordered the extradition to Switzerland for trial there of a man who, although himself in England, was alleged to have procured his partner, who was in Switzerland, to obtain goods there by false pretences. And in *Ford v United States*[95] the US Supreme Court upheld in 1927 the conviction of certain British subjects (whose ship was at the time on the high seas) for conspiracy against the United States' liquor laws. Such cases appear to justify the dictum of Judge Moore in the *Lotus* case, discussed below, that:

> it appears to be now universally admitted that, when a crime is committed in the territorial jurisdiction of one State as the direct result of the act of a person at the time corporeally present in another state, international law, by reason of the principle of constructive presence of the offender at the place where his act took *effect*, does not forbid the prosecution of the offender by the former State, should he come within its territorial jurisdiction.[96]

This recognition that the effects of an act in a territory may be enough to trigger objective territorial jurisdiction has been expanded in ways which test the premises of the theory.[97] There

---

94. [1923] 1 KB 24.

95. 273 US 593.

96. PCIJ Reports, Series A, 10 (1927) at 73 (emphasis added).

97. We might mention here the idea of 'protective jurisdiction' which has been suggested where a crime committed aboard by foreigners threatens the security of the state asserting jurisdiction. See Shaw, *International Law* (above) at 666–8.

have been, for example, attempts to assert jurisdiction when there are simply economic effects (e.g. price rises) rather than physical effects (e.g. a bomb exploding) in the country. Vaughan Lowe explains that such an:

'effects doctrine' has been controversial, for instance when used by US authorities to break up cartels formed lawfully by non-US companies outside the United States. Some such cartels have been organized with the explicit approval and encouragement of the national States of the companies concerned, and the companies have engaged in no actual activity whatever within the United States, but because they affected world prices (which US consumers might have to pay) the cartels have been held to have an impact on the United States and so fall within its jurisdiction.[98]

The European Union has similarly addressed anti-competitive practices of foreign companies and, despite some early protests at the US assertion of jurisdiction, the trend is towards accepting an effects doctrine (albeit adjusted to focus on implementation) so that jurisdiction is extended in some circumstances to the activities of foreign companies operating abroad.[99] But the objective territorial theory does not cover the situation where states claim that

---

98. *International Law* (Oxford: OUP, 2007) at 173.

99. See R. Higgins, *Problems and Process: International Law and How We Use It* (Oxford: Clarendon Press, 1994) at 75–6; for detail B. Sufrin, 'Competition Law in a Globalised Market Place: Beyond Jurisdiction', in P. Capps, M. Evans, and S. Konstadinis (eds), *Asserting Jurisdiction: International and European Legal Perspectives* (Oxford: Hart, 2003) 105–26.

their courts have jurisdiction over a crime committed abroad by a foreigner against one of their own nationals (passive personality jurisdiction). Such an assertion of jurisdiction rests on a false view of the nature of the right of protecting nationals. As we shall see below, international law recognizes that states have a right of diplomatic protection, a right to demand reparation for injuries done to their nationals abroad, but not a right to throw the shield of their own criminal law around their nationals once they have left its shelter.

The Permanent Court considered the law on this matter in the case of the *Lotus,* which arose out of a collision in the Aegean Sea outside Turkish territorial waters, between the French mail steamer *Lotus* and the Turkish collier *Boz-Kourt,* in which the *Boz-Kourt* was sunk with loss of life. The *Lotus* proceeded to Constantinople, where the officers in charge of both ships were tried and convicted of manslaughter. The Turkish court appears to have acted under an article of the Turkish Penal Code, giving jurisdiction, with certain limiting conditions, to Turkish courts to try any foreigner who commits an offence abroad to the prejudice of Turkey or of a Turkish subject. The French Government denied the validity of this article in international law. The majority of the Court, consisting of six of the 12 judges, refrained from expressing an opinion on the international validity of the provision of the Turkish law, but held that no rule of international law forbade the Turkish Court to assume jurisdiction in the specific facts of this case, since the effects of the offence had been produced on the Turkish vessel, although the actor himself was on board the French vessel.

Judge Moore dissented. He agreed with the result reached by the six judges in the majority, but reasoned rather differently. He held that the provision of the Turkish law was 'contrary to well-settled principles of international law'. It meant, he said, that:

> the citizen of one country, when he visits another country, takes with him for his 'protection' the law of his own country, and subjects those with whom he comes into contact to the operation of that law. In this way an inhabitant of a great commercial city, in which foreigners congregate, may in the course of an hour unconsciously fall under the operation of a number of foreign criminal codes.... No one disputes the right of a State to subject its citizens abroad to the operations of its own penal laws, if it sees fit to do so.... But the case is fundamentally different where a country claims either that its penal laws apply to other countries and to what takes place wholly within such countries, or, if it does not claim this, that it may punish foreigners for alleged violation, even in their own country, of laws to which they were not subject.[100]

The five remaining judges also dissented from the judgment of the Court.

It will be observed that the majority of the Court (with the casting vote of the President Judge Huber), by assimilating the Turkish vessel to Turkish territory, brought the case under the principle of 'objective territorial jurisdiction'. That principle, as stated above, is generally accepted, but the idea that in sinking the Turkish ship it was as if the crime had been committed on Turkish territory was described by Lord Finlay in his dissenting judgment

---

100. PCIJ Reports, Series A, 10 (1927) at 92–3.

as 'a new and startling application of a metaphor'.[101] Maritime organizations expressed their concern at the majority judgment. They feared that masters of ships might be exposed to double prosecutions—by the authorities of the foreign port and by the authorities of the flag state—and that ships would be held up by proceedings in foreign courts. The rule which allows the state of the 'injured ship' to prosecute a foreigner from the other foreign ship has now been set aside in a series of treaties. Article 97(1) of the Law of the Sea Convention (1982) is very clear:

> In the event of a collision or any other incident of navigation concerning a ship on the high seas, involving the penal or disciplinary responsibility of the master or of any other person in the service of the ship, no penal or disciplinary proceedings may be instituted against such person except before the judicial or administrative authorities either of the flag State or of the State of which such person is a national.

Where does this leave passive personality jurisdiction in the situation where a national is the victim of crime in another state's territory? With regard to war crimes and other international crimes there would seem to be few objections to a state exercising passive personality jurisdiction,[102] but the issue remains controversial for other crimes. On the one hand, Lowe regards the assertion of such

---

101. Ibid 52.

102. *An Introduction to International Criminal Law and Procedure*, 2nd edn (Cambridge: CUP, 2010); R. Cryer at 49–50.

jurisdiction as 'a form of legal imperialism'.[103] On the other hand, Watson has argued in favour of passive personality jurisdiction suggesting it 'can help ensure that fugitives do not literally get away with murder'.[104] Relatively few problems arise where such jurisdiction is asserted in cases of serious crimes, where the crime is recognized in both jurisdictions. Today, the issue arises most starkly with regard to the victims of torture[105] and terrorist attacks on nationals abroad. In such situations the issue will probably fall to be settled under the relevant treaty. The web of anti-terrorism treaties covers most acts, and arguably those not covered by a specific treaty could now be considered crimes under customary international law.[106]

We should now consider a further claim of jurisdiction. In some situations states have claimed that they have universal jurisdiction over certain crimes. As we saw above, states may seize a pirate ship, arrest the persons, and exercise jurisdiction through their own courts. The recent upsurge in piracy connected to

---

103. *International Law* above at 176.

104. G.R. Watson, 'The Passive Personality Principle', 28(1) *Texas International Law Journal* (1993) 1–46, at 46.

105. The Convention against Torture and Other Cruel, Inhuman or Degrading Treatment or Punishment (1984) states in Article 5(1) that '[e]ach State Party shall take such measures as may be necessary to establish its jurisdiction over the [crime of torture]…(c) When the victim is a national of that State *if that State considers it appropriate*.' Emphasis added. A state party is not obliged to create this jurisdiction but the inclusion in the Treaty suggests that a state is entitled to assert such a jurisdiction.

106. See the lengthy explanation in the Special Tribunal for Lebanon in the Appeal Chamber's Decision in Case STL-11-01/I, 16 February 2011, at paras 83–130 where it is suggested that the proposed customary rule has three elements: '(i) the perpetration of a criminal act (such as murder, kidnapping, hostage-taking, arson, and so on), or threatening such an act; (ii) the intent to spread fear among the population (which would

Somalia has led to Security Council authorization to exercise jurisdiction over this crime in Somali territorial waters and even on land in Somalia. The Security Council has also called on all states to criminalize piracy under their domestic law.[107] The practical problems related to detaining and prosecuting such pirates have presented more obstacles than any jurisdictional problems related to international law. In 2011 there were 20 states prosecuting acts of piracy off the coast of Somalia with over 1,000 persons being detained either as suspects or following conviction for piracy.[108] It can be argued that the theory of universal jurisdiction has been reinforced.[109] But in the case of piracy, such universal jurisdiction is premised on the fact that the crime takes place outside the territory of any state and against the background that the pirate ship may be either flying a false flag—or even a pirate flag such as the skull and cross bones of the 'Jolly Roger'.

But it is the exercise of universal jurisdiction by one state over nationals of another state for international crimes committed *in another state* that has given rise to controversy, including veiled

---

generally entail the creation of public danger) or directly or indirectly coerce a national or international authority to take some action, or to refrain from taking it; (iii) when the act involves a transnational element.' At para. 85; see also A. Cassese, 'Terrorism as an International Crime', in A. Bianchi (ed.), *Enforcing International Law Norms Against Terrorism* (Oxford: Hart Publishing, 2003) 213–25.

107. SC Res. 1950 (2010).
108. See S/2011/360 (above) at 27, the statistics are as follows: Belgium 1; Comoros 6; France 15; Germany 10; India 119; Japan 4; Kenya 119, Madagascar 12; Malaysia 7; Maldives 34; Netherlands 29; Oman 12; Seychelles 64; Somalia 402; Republic of Korea 5; Spain 2; Tanzania 12; United Arab Emirates; United States 28; Yemen 120.
109. For details see 'Piracy Prosecutions' 104 *AJIL* (2010) 397–453.

allegations of neo-colonialism.[110] The issue has arisen with regards to trials for genocide, crimes against humanity, war crimes, and torture.[111] Taken together with the emerging notion that former officials enjoy no immunity before foreign courts when charged with international crimes, this type of jurisdiction has disrupted international relations and caused a degree of outrage in some quarters. Henry Kissinger has famously suggested that there is a risk of 'substituting the tyranny of judges for that of governments; historically, the dictatorship of the virtuous has often led to inquisitions and even witch-hunts'.[112] He further warned that such prosecutions interfere with peace and reconciliation efforts:

> The decision of post-Franco Spain to avoid wholesale criminal trials for the human rights violations of the recent past was designed explicitly to foster a process of national reconciliation that undoubtedly contributed much to the present vigor of Spanish democracy. Why should Chile's attempt at national reconciliation not have been given the same opportunity? Should any outside group dissatisfied with the reconciliation procedures of, say, South Africa be free to challenge them in their own national courts or those of third countries?

---

110. L. Reydams, 'Belgium's First Application of Universal Jurisdiction: the *Butare Four* Case', 1 *JICJ* (2003) 428–36; see also the pleadings before the ICJ in *Case Concerning the Arrest Warrant of 11 April 2000 (Dem. Rep of Congo v Belgium)* 14 February 2002; H. van der Wilt, 'Universal Jurisdiction under Attack', 9(5) *Journal of International Criminal Justice* (2011) 1043–66.

111. Although some states have provided for universal jurisdiction over crimes such as murder, rape, assault, and abduction. See Amnesty International, *Universal Jurisdiction* IOR 53/015/2010.

112. 'The Pitfalls of Universal Jurisdiction' *Foreign Affairs* July/August (2001).

Such disagreements over jurisdiction again expose varying approaches to the purpose of international law and its role in international relations.[113] If we consider that international law is being developed to protect certain universal values, then it reasonably follows that those crimes which shock the conscience of humankind can be tried even when the traditional jurisdictional links of territory or nationality are not met. Sir Frank Berman has suggested that such an approach has echoes of the 'old common lawyer's distinction between *mala prohibita* and *mala in se*, *male in se* being acts of such moral turpitude that the law recognises them to be criminal simply on that account, whereas *mala prohibita* are acts that become criminal only when declared to be so by the legislator'.[114] Guy Goodwin-Gill takes this one step further and argues that 'International crimes, "by their very nature", produce an obligation *erga omnes* to extradite to another competent state, prosecute locally, or surrender the person concerned to the jurisdiction of a competent international tribunal; it is the *jus cogens/erga omnes* combination that makes prosecution (somewhere) unavoidable as a matter of duty'.[115] But for those who consider that international law has to serve states' interests, or even the common interests of states (as defined by states), the exercise of universal jurisdiction, together with any reduced

---

113. See J. d'Aspremont, 'Multilateral Versus Unilateral Exercises of Universal Criminal Jurisdiction', 43 *Israel Law Review* (2010) 301–29.

114. 'Jurisdiction: The State', in P. Capps, M. Evans, and S. Konstadinis (eds), *Asserting Jurisdiction: International and European Legal Perspectives* (Oxford: Hart, 2003) 3–15, at 7.

115. 'Crime in International Law: Obligations *Erga Omnes* and the Duty to Prosecute', in G. Goodwin-Gill and S. Talman (eds), *The Reality of International Law: Essays in Honour of Ian Brownlie* (Oxford: Clarendon Press, 1999) 199–223 at 220.

immunities for state officials, will be considered disruptive and illegitimate.[116]

In practice the legality of the assertion of jurisdiction is not usually subject to question or protest by other states, either because they will implicitly consent to such exercise (as happened for example with regard to the trial of Eichmann by Israel or the trials of Rwandese by Belgium and Switzerland) or because jurisdiction has been addressed in a multilateral treaty.[117] While political scientists and others will continue to complain about national judges and prosecutors illegitimately asserting extraterritorial jurisdiction, a close examination of the relevant treaties shows that the states which would normally exercise jurisdiction have usually in fact consented to the exercise of jurisdiction by another state party. Consider the Afghan warlord Zardad who was tried in London in 2005 with regard to torture and hostage-taking in Afghanistan. Although the trial was conducted with the cooperation of the Afghan authorities, we can consider what would have been the situation had the Afghan Government protested that the UK was exceeding its jurisdiction. The relevant Conventions, to which Afghanistan and the UK are parties, provide that if a person is

---

116. d'Aspremont (above) highlights that the 'value-based discourse' which accompanies the exercise of universal jurisdiction means that the process is '*perceived* as illegitimate', he does not question the *legality* of such an exercise of jurisdiction. Cf A. Cassese, 'Is the Bell Tolling for Universality? A Plea for a Sensible Notion of Universal Jurisdiction', 1 *JICJ* (2003) 589–95.

117. The issues are discussed in the separate opinions of the Judges of the International Court of Justice in the *Arrest Warrant* case (above). The question of universal jurisdiction was not, however, addressed by the Court's judgment but only in some of the separate opinions.

present in the territory of any state party then that state shall take the person into custody, and then, shall either extradite the person, or 'submit the case to its competent authorities for the purpose of prosecution'.[118]

In the context of terrorism there are multiple widely ratified treaties which contain similar provisions but which all differ slightly in their jurisdictional clauses. The most recent developments criminalize using a civilian aircraft for a terrorist attack (such as the attacks of 11 September 2001), discharging weapons of mass destruction from such an aircraft, or using such weapons on board or against such an aircraft. The jurisdictional clauses apply so as to create: (1) an obligation to establish jurisdiction with regards to a first group of offenders with certain nationality and territorial links; (2) a permissive right to establish passive personality jurisdiction; and (3) an obligation to establish jurisdiction where the alleged offender is present in the territory and the state does not extradite to another state party. It is detailed rules such as these that will define the jurisdiction of national courts. The relevant provisions read:

---

118. Convention against Torture (above) Art. 7(1); International Convention Against the Taking of Hostages (1979) Art. 8(1). See also the grave breaches regime of the universally ratified four Geneva Conventions (1949) which states that each state is 'under the obligation to search for persons alleged to have committed, or to have ordered to be committed, such grave breaches, and shall bring such persons, regardless of their nationality, before its own courts. It may also, if it prefers, and in accordance with the provisions of its own legislation, hand such persons over for trial to another High Contracting Party concerned, provided such High Contracting Party has made out a "prima facie" case.' Arts 49. 51, 130, and 147 respectively.

1. Each State Party shall take such measures as may be necessary to establish its jurisdiction over the offences set forth in [the Convention on Suppression of Unlawful Acts Relating to International Civil Aviation] in the following cases:
   (a) when the offence is committed in the territory of that State;
   (b) when the offence is committed against or on board an aircraft registered in that State;
   (c) when the aircraft on board which the offence is committed lands in its territory with the alleged offender still on board;
   (d) when the offence is committed against or on board an aircraft leased without crew to a lessee whose principal place of business or, if the lessee has no such place of business, whose permanent residence is in that State;
   (e) when the offence is committed by a national of that State.
2. Each State Party may also establish its jurisdiction over any such offence in the following cases:
   (a) when the offence is committed against a national of that State;
   (b) when the offence is committed by a stateless person whose habitual residence is in the territory of that State.
3. Each State Party shall likewise take such measures as may be necessary to establish its jurisdiction over the offences set forth in [the Convention] in the case where the alleged offender is present in its territory and it does not extradite that person pursuant to Article 12 to any of the States Parties that have established their jurisdiction in accordance with the

applicable paragraphs of this Article with regard to those offences.[119]

Complaints about excessive assertions of jurisdiction are less about what states are entitled to do under international law, and more about fears that national courts will be used to mount ideological or political attacks on individuals or particular regimes. These fears can be assuaged, in part, by the increasing use of international criminal courts, even though some American commentators continue to raise questions of legitimacy in this context.[120]

§ 10. Limitations on a state's treatment of foreigners

When a state admits foreigners into its territory it must observe a certain standard of decent treatment towards them, and their own state may demand reparation for an injury caused to them by a failure to observe this standard. This is known as 'diplomatic protection'. The legal basis of such a demand, in the words of the Permanent Court, is that:

---

119. Art. 8 Convention on the Suppression of Unlawful Acts Relating to International Civil Aviation (2010) and see the Protocol (2010) Art. VII; these Conventions do not cover the activities of armed forces during an armed conflict: Art. 6 and Art. VI respectively.

120. See generally J.L. Goldsmith and E.A. Posner, *The Limits of International Law* (New York: OUP, 2005); E.A. Posner, *The Perils of Global Legalism* (Chicago: University of Chicago Press, 2009).

in taking up the case of one of its nationals, by resorting to diplomatic action or international judicial proceedings on his behalf, a state is in reality asserting its own right, the right to ensure in the person of its nationals respect for the rules of international law. This right is necessarily limited to the intervention on behalf of its own nationals because, in the absence of a special agreement, it is the bond of nationality between the state and the individual which alone confers upon the state the right of diplomatic protection, and it is as a part of the function of diplomatic protection that the right to take up a claim and to ensure respect for the rules of international law must be envisaged.[121]

There is a certain artificiality in this way of looking at the issue of limitations on a state's treatment of foreigners. No doubt a state has in general an interest in seeing that its nationals are fairly treated in a foreign country, but it is surely an exaggeration to say that whenever a national is injured in a foreign state, their state as a whole is necessarily injured too. In practice, as we shall see, the theory is not consistently adhered to. For instance, the logic of the theory would require that damages should be measured by reference to the injury suffered by the state, which is obviously not the same as the injury suffered by the individual, but in fact the law allows damages to be assessed on the loss to the individual, as though it were the injury to that person which was the cause of action.

The procedure for bringing claims of diplomatic protection is far from satisfactory from the individual's point of view.

---

121. *Panevezys-Saldutiskis Railway Case,* PCIJ Series A/B 76, p. 16.

Individuals often have no remedy of their own, and the state to which they belong may be unwilling to take up their case for reasons which have nothing to do with its merits; and even if the state is willing to take up the case, there may be interminable delays before, if ever, the defendant state can be induced to let the matter go to arbitration or some other settlement.

Claims of diplomatic protection both on behalf of individual nationals and for companies operating abroad have nevertheless been one of the most fertile sources of controversy among states, and legal departments of every foreign office have considerable experience in this domain. Although the original focus was on the mistreatment of foreigners, the principles are now relevant in claims with regard to foreign investment. The attempt, however, to adjust the standards related to the protection of aliens to the protection of corporate foreign investment has been met with resistance by developing states,[122] and is today considered cumbersome.[123] The question of foreign investment is more likely to be covered by bilateral investment treaties, specifying the obligations towards the investor and the forum for settling any dispute. In what follows we will therefore concentrate on the general principles covering

---

122. See M. Sornarajah, *The International Law on Foreign Investment*, 3rd edn (Cambridge: CUP, 2010) 120–34. He also suggests that the distinction between the international and the national standards needs to be re-examined: 'unlike in the past when national treatment was rejected altogether because such treatment was in the case of some countries lower than the minimum standard contended for by the capital exporting states, in modern times national treatment may have its advantages as states reserve many of their economic sectors and privileges to their nationals.' At 202.

123. V. Lowe, *International Law* (Oxford: OUP, 2007) 197–205.

diplomatic protection of individual foreigners rather than the particular developments relating to foreign investment.

In general, people who voluntarily enter the territory of a state
which is not their own must accept the institutions of that state as
they find them. They are not entitled to demand equality of treatment in all respects with the citizens of that state. For example, the
foreigner will often be excluded from running for national office
or voting in national elections; they may be prohibited from engaging in coastal trading (i.e. commercial transportation within the
territorial waters of that one state, also known as cabotage), or
from fishing in territorial waters. These and other restrictions are
not forbidden by international law. However, the rule that a foreigner (traditionally described as an 'alien') must accept the institutions of a foreign state is qualified by the requirement that those
institutions must conform to the standard set by international law;
and if a foreigner (alien) suffers injury in person or property
through the failure of a state to conform to that standard, their
own state may present a diplomatic protection claim for reparation on their behalf.

This international standard cannot be made a matter of precise
rules. It is considered the standard of the 'reasonable state', reasonable, that is to say, according to present day notions. It was described
early on by the US-Mexican Claims Commission as follows:[124]

> the propriety of governmental acts should be put to the test of
> international standards, and…the treatment of an alien, in
> order to constitute an international delinquency, should amount

---

124. Opinions of Commissioners, *Neers* case, at p. 73.

to an outrage, to bad faith, to wilful neglect of duty, or to an insufficiency of governmental action so far short of international standards that every reasonable and impartial man would readily recognize its insufficiency. Whether the insufficiency proceeds from deficient execution of an intelligent law or from the fact that the laws of the country do not empower the authorities to measure up to international standards is immaterial.

The standard does not require a uniform degree of governmental efficiency irrespective of circumstances. For example, measures of police protection which would be reasonable in a capital city cannot fairly be demanded in a sparsely populated territory, and a level of security which is normal in times of tranquillity cannot be expected in a time of temporary disorder. But the standard being an international one, a state cannot relieve itself of responsibility by invoking provisions of its own national law. Thus the central government of a federal or other composite state may be *constitutionally* unable to ensure that justice is rendered to an alien by the authorities of a province; but if the central government is the only government which has relations with other states, that government's *international* responsibility is not affected by any domestic limitation of its own powers.

Today the international standard relating to the safety and security of individuals can be more easily gleaned from international human rights law,[125] and claims will most likely be decided accord-

125. See the *Case Concerning Ahmadou Sadio Diallo (Republic of Guinea v Democratic Republic of the Congo, Preliminary Objections,(Diallo Case)*, ICJ Rep. (2007) at para. 39: 'diplomatic protection, originally limited to alleged violations of the minimum standard of treatment of aliens, has subsequently widened to include, *inter alia*, internationally guaranteed human

ing to the provisions of the human rights treaties.[126] The key provisions apply both to a state's citizens and to foreigners under its jurisdiction. As the focus shifts to these individual international rights and the procedures available to the individual at the international level, one could ask whether diplomatic protection has any continuing relevance.[127] The short answer is yes.

First, while the doctrinal recognition of the individual as a participant with 'personality' on the international stage may be significant, access to effective international human rights remedies is neither universal nor practical for most injured individuals. Second, there are a number of special situations where individuals abroad may be particularly reliant on the possibilities offered by diplomatic protection. For example, individuals seeking to challenge restrictions on their liberty stemming from the Security Council's counter-terrorism measures have had to rely on diplomatic protection through their state of nationality.[128] Furthermore there may be cases where investors are unable to rely on particular

---

rights'. Note that under Article 1 of Protocol 1 to the European Convention on Human Rights a foreigner will be entitled in the context of expropriation to the minimum international standard of compensation, while nationals may enjoy a lower level of protection. See *James v UK*, European Court of Human Rights, 22 January 1986, esp. paras 58–66.

126. See now *Case Concerning Ahmadou Sadio Diallo (Republic of Guinea v Democratic Republic of the Congo*, ICJ Rep. (2010) (merits).

127. See Benounna's report to the ILC, A/CN.4/484 esp. paras 33–41; compare Dugard's report A/CN.4/506 esp. paras 15–32.

128. See the judgment of the EC Ct of First Instance in *Ayadi*, Case T-253/02, esp. paras 148–9 which suggest that EU member states may be required to present such cases to the UN Sanctions Committee as diplomatic protection is the only avenue open to the individuals concerned. See also the judgment of the Grand Chamber of the Court of Justice of the EU, *Kadi* Joined Cases C–402/05P and C–415/05P; and T-85/09.

investment treaties and this could cause real injustice.[129] While there may not be any international law *obligation* for states to take up diplomatic protection claims, some governments will take up claims,[130] and the International Law Commission's draft articles on diplomatic protection propose that a state 'should [g]ive due consideration to the possibility of exercising diplomatic protection, especially when a significant injury has occurred'.[131]

It is normally a condition for an international claim for the redress of an injury suffered by foreigners that the injured foreigner should first have exhausted any remedies available under the local law. A state is not required to guarantee that the person or property of a foreigner will not be injured, and the mere fact that such an injury has been suffered does not of itself give the foreigner's own state a right to demand reparation on their behalf. If the state in which the injury occurs offers the foreigner a proper remedy, it is only reasonable that the foreigner should be required

---

129. See the joint dissenting opinion by Judges Al-Khasawneh and Yusuf in the *Diallo Case* (2010) (above).

130. For the UK Guidelines see C. Warbrick 'Protection of Nationals Abroad' 37 *ICLQ* (1988) 1002–12; see also *Kaunda v President of the Republic of South Africa.* Case CCT 23/04. 2004, 44 *ILM* (2005) 173 and the comment by M. Coombs, 99 *AJIL* (2005) 681–6.

131. Art. 19(a), Recommended Practice, A/61/10, 2006. See also the Court of Appeal's suggestion that the Foreign Office's 'discretion is a very wide one but there is no reason why its decision or inaction should not be reviewable if it can be shown that the same were irrational or contrary to legitimate expectation': *Abbasi v Secretary of State for Foreign and Commonwealth Affairs* [2002] EWCA Civ 1598 at para. 106. Compare *Canada (Prime Minister) v Khadr,* 2010 SCC 3, [2010] 1 SCR 44 (Supreme Court of Canada): 'Consistent with the separation of powers and the well-grounded reluctance of courts to intervene in matters of foreign relations, the proper remedy is to grant Mr Khadr a declaration that his *Charter* rights have been infringed, while leaving the government a measure of discretion in deciding how best to respond.' At para. 2.

to take it. The justification for the rule is obvious; it is right that a state should have a full and proper opportunity of doing justice itself before justice is demanded of it by another state at the international level.

This 'exhaustion of local remedies' rule, however, must be reasonably interpreted. For example, in the remarkable case of *Robert E. Brown*, the South African Chief Justice hearing the case had actually been dismissed by the Government. The Government had then ensured that all the other Justices had 'sworn to abandon all right to test laws and resolutions by reference to the Constitution'.[132] The arbitral Tribunal, referring to the argument that the claimant had not exhausted all the judicial remedies open to him, quoted with approval the statement of US Secretary of State Fish in 1873 that 'a claimant in a foreign state is not required to exhaust justice in such state when there is no justice to exhaust'.[133] Apart from extreme cases such as this one, there are certain wrongs for which it is not unusual to find that the local law provides no remedy. For example, it may be clear that the local courts are bound by their own precedents to deny the claim, or the wrong may have been committed by the legislature itself, or by some high official whose acts are not subject to review.[134] Moreover, the International Court of Justice has explained that remedies have to aim at vindicating rights and 'not at obtaining a favour'. In this sense

---

132. *Robert E. Brown (United States) v Great Britain* (1923) 6 RIAA 120, at 126.

133. Ibid 129.

134. The ILC Draft Articles on Diplomatic Protection set out detailed exceptions to the rule in Article 15. See also *Case concerning Elettronica Sicula SpA (ELSI) (USA v Italy) (Judgment)*, ICJ Rep. (1989) p. 15; *Interhandel Case (Switzerland v United States of America) (Preliminary Objections)*, ICJ Rep. (1959) p. 6.

'submitting a request for reconsideration of the expulsion decision to the administrative authority having taken it—that is to say the Prime Minister—in the hope that he would retract his decision as a matter of grace cannot be deemed a local remedy to be exhausted'.[135]

Another condition is that the injury in respect of which a claim is brought must have been suffered by a national of the claimant state.[136] A further issue concerns determining the nationality of claims with regard to companies. The ILC Draft Articles on Diplomatic Protection clarify that here:

> the State of nationality means the State under whose law the corporation was incorporated. However, when the corporation is controlled by nationals of another State or States and has no substantial business activities in the State of incorporation, and the seat of management and the financial control of the corporation are both located in another State, that State shall be regarded as the State of nationality.[137]

The ILC suggests a further exception, so that the state of nationality of shareholders in a corporation may be entitled to exercise diplomatic protection in respect of such shareholders (in the case of an injury to the corporation) where the corporation had, at the date of injury, the nationality of the state alleged to be responsible for

---

135. *Diallo Case (preliminary measures)* (2007) (above) at para. 47.
136. See ILC Draft Arts 4–8.
137. Draft Art. 9. See also Art. 25(2)(b) of the Washington Convention on the International Settlement of Investment Disputes (1965).

causing the injury, due to the fact that incorporation in that state had been required by the host state as a precondition for doing business there.[138]

A state may incur responsibility by the act or omission of any of its organs, legislative, executive, or judicial, but these cases require separate consideration.[139] As an example of *legislative* action towards a foreigner in violation of international law one may cite the Costa Rican law, already discussed in the context of recognition of governments,[140] nullifying contracts made by the *de facto* government of Tinoco. Difficult questions continue to be raised by legislation in certain states expropriating private property. There is no doubt that such a measure directed against the property of a foreigner as such would violate international law, but, if it is applied for some public purpose without discriminating, either avowedly or in fact between nationals and foreigners, the matter is less clear. According to the distinguished editors of *Oppenheim* 'Perhaps the most clearly established condition is that expropriation must not be arbitrary, and must be based on the application of duly adopted laws'.[141] There is a requirement to pay compensation, but in the

---

138. Draft Art. 11(b) the ICJ rejected a general substitution theory whereby the state of nationality of the shareholders could bring a diplomatic protection claim, but left open whether such a state might be able to bring a claim where incorporation in the host state is a precondition for doing business *Diallo Case (preliminary objections)* (2007) above at paras 86–94; see further the Joint Dissenting Opinion of Judges Al-Khasawneh and Yusuf in *Diallo* (merits) (2010) above.

139. See further Ch. VIII § 2.

140. Above, Ch. IV § 5.

141. *Oppenheim's International Law*, 9th edn at 919–20. Lowe is prepared to go further stating: 'States may not expropriate alien property except on a non-discriminatory basis, for a public purpose, and against proper compensation.... The notion of what is "proper"

words of the same authorities: 'there is much disagreement as to the appropriate standard of compensation'.[142] The so called 'Hull formula' favoured by developed states and corporations states that the compensation must be prompt, adequate, and effective. The idea that this standard is really customary international law would be contested.[143] The standard of 'fair and equitable treatment' along with the Hull formula are now often found in bilateral investment treaties.[144] But the interpretation of 'fair and equitable treatment', or terms such as discrimination, 'full protection and security', and 'due process', involves an appreciation of contemporary expectations of natural justice in judicial proceedings.[145] Zachary Douglas has highlighted the distinction between the agreement over the concept of 'fair and equitable treatment' from the *conception of the concept* that any one arbitrator brings to the

---

compensation has been controversial, but it is now generally accepted that it must reflect the market value of the property taken and be paid at the time of the taking or shortly afterwards and in convertible currency.' *International Law* (above) at 187. See further M. Paparinskis, *The International Minimum Standard and Fair and Equitable Treatment* (Oxford: OUP) forthcoming.

142. *Oppenheim's International Law*, ibid 921.

143. For a detailed analysis see Sornarajah (above) at 210–13 who suggests that the standard of compensation be agreed in the relevant bilateral investment treaty at 412–52.

144. See I. Tudor, *The Fair and Equitable Treatment Standard in the International Law of Foreign Investment* (Oxford: OUP, 2008); S. Ripinsky with K. Williams, *Damages in International Investment Law* (BIICL: London, 2008) esp. 64–100; other references to the Hull formula and the rules concerning expropriation are discussed in M. Shaw, *International Law* (above) 830–43.

145. See further P. Muchlinski, 'Policy Issues', in P. Muchlinski, F. Ortino, and C. Schreuer (eds), *The Oxford Handbook of International Investment Law* (Oxford: OUP, 2008) 3–48 and T.J. Grierson-Weiler and I.A. Laird, 'Standards of Treatment' in the same volume at 259–304.

award. He suggests that the 'most fertile, but underutilised, source of principles for developing coherent conceptions of investment protection standards is general principles of law recognized in municipal legal systems.'[146]

Investment disputes covered by these treaties are usually subject to mandatory arbitration, including through panels established under the International Centre for Investment Disputes, and enforced under the terms of the Convention on the Settlement of Investment Disputes between States and Nationals of Other States (1965).[147]

The wrongful conduct of a *state official* may be attributed to the state so that it is internationally responsible towards the state of an injured alien. The applicable rules of state responsibility originally developed against the practice of diplomatic protection but now have more general application.[148] In the first place, while the state is responsible for the acts and omissions of all of its organs and personnel acting as state organs, the official must have acted in that capacity or with the apparent authority of the state, otherwise their act would be like that of a private individual. Having said this it will be easier to assume the apparent authority of superior officials, and there will be situations where the state is responsible for the acts of persons acting outside their official capacity through the omissions of such superior officials or its

---

146. *The International Law of Investment Claims* (Cambridge: CUP, 2009) at 88; see Ch. II § 4(c) above.

147. See further Ch. VIII § 4(a).

148. See J. Crawford, *The International Law Commission's Articles on State Responsibility: Introduction, Text and Commentaries* (Cambridge: CUP, 2002); see further Ch. VIII § 2 below.

own state organs. Thus in *The Sidra*[149] the Anglo-American Claims Tribunal awarded damages to Great Britain in respect of injury to a British merchant vessel to which the negligent navigation of an American government vessel in Baltimore harbour had contributed; and in the *Zafiro*[150] the same tribunal awarded compensation for British property looted by the Chinese crew of an American supply ship at Manila, on the ground that in the circumstances the American officers were at fault in letting the crew get out of hand; there would have been no liability for the action of the crew as such.

There are many possible ways in which the *judiciary and the courts* may fall below the standard demanded in this context. Such acts cannot be exhaustively enumerated, but some instances are corruption, threats, unwarrantable delay, flagrant abuse of judicial procedure, or a judgment dictated by the executive, or so manifestly unjust that no court which was both competent and honest could have given it. We should also mention certain acts or omissions of organs of government other than courts, but closely connected with the administration of justice, such as execution without trial, inexcusable failure to bring a wrongdoer to trial, long imprisonment before trial, grossly inadequate punishment, or failure to enforce a judgment duly given. A merely erroneous or even unjust judgment of a court will not constitute a 'denial of justice', except where the courts, having occasion to apply some rule of international law, give an incorrect interpretation of that law, or where the judiciary applies, as it may be bound by its municipal

---

149. Nielsen's Report, p. 452.
150. Nielsen's Report, p. 578.

law to do, a rule of domestic law which is itself contrary to international law.[151]

It is apparent from the preceding discussion that a state incurs no responsibility for an injury suffered by an alien unless an act can be attributed to that state, or the state is liable for its omission.[152] The question of omission deserves a little explanation. While the act of a private individual is not attributed to the state,[153] such an act, however, may be an occasion out of which state responsibility arises if it is accompanied by circumstances which can be regarded as a failure to exercise due diligence before the event, or a condonation after the event, making the state itself responsible to the other party for the injurious act of the individual or individuals concerned. It is therefore necessary in such a case to ask first, whether the state ought to have prevented the injurious act, and secondly, whether it has taken the remedial steps which the law requires of it. Thus where the injury in question would not have occurred if the state through its officers had been reasonably diligent, responsibility will be incurred. The standard of due diligence naturally varies with circumstances. For example, the fact that the individual was injured by a mob of rioters or of a body of insurgents might, according to circumstances, indicate either that special precau-

---

151. A distinction has also been drawn between the decision of a lower court and the duty of state to provide a fair and efficient system of justice, see *Loewen v USA* (2003) 42 ILM 811; *Oppenheim's International Law*, 9th edn at 543–5.

152. For the rules with regard to the attribution of acts to a state see the ILC's Articles on the Responsibility of States for Internationally Wrongful Acts (2001) Arts 1–11.

153. Ibid Arts 5, 8, 9, 10, and 11. J. Crawford, A. Pellet, and S. Olleson (eds), *The Law of International Responsibility* (Oxford: OUP, 2010) chs 18 and 19; J. Crawford, *The International Law Commission's Articles on State Responsibility* above.

tions ought to have been taken, or alternatively that the authorities were faced with a situation so difficult that they could not reasonably be expected to do more than they did.[154]

As already mentioned, the theory underlying the law of state responsibility for injuries to foreigners is that the claimant state seeks redress, not directly for an injury to one of its nationals, but for an injury suffered by itself *through* its national. If this principle were consistently applied, we might expect that the measure of damages would be determined by assessing the injury suffered by the state, and so arriving at a figure which would bear no necessary relation to the extent of the loss suffered by the injured individual. This, however, is not the law; for though in practice tribunals exercise a rather wide discretion in fixing the amount of reparation due, they base it primarily on an estimate of the loss caused to the injured individual, or, if they have lost their lives, on the loss caused by the death to the dependants.[155]

---

154. Compare the case *Youmans v Mexico* (1926) U.S.-Mexican Claims Commission Reports, RIAA, vol. IV 110–17 at 115: 'It can not properly be said that adequate protection is afforded to foreigners in a case in which the proper agencies of the law to afford protection participate in murder', with that of the *Home Missionary Society* (1920), before the Anglo-American Claims Tribunal: 'It is a well-established principle of international law that no government can be held responsible for the act of rebellious bodies of men committed in violation of its authority, where it is itself guilty of no breach of good faith, or of no negligence in suppressing insurrection.' RIAA, vol. VI, 42–4 at 44. See also the ICJ judgment in the *Case Concerning US Diplomatic and Consular Staff in Tehran* (1980) where the omissions of Iran were examined with regard to the obligations of Iran under the law of diplomatic relations, esp. paras 56–77.

155. For a discussion of some of the difficulties of applying this principle see Brierly 'The Theory of Implied State Complicity in International Claims', in 9 *BYBIL* (1928) 42–9.

§ 11. Limits to jurisdiction with regard to immunities

(a) *Immunities of Heads of States and other holders of high-ranking office in a state*

We have already considered the immunities enjoyed by foreign state ships, but the immunities of a foreign sovereign are not confined to ships. A foreign sovereign and his or her property were also considered to enjoy complete immunity from jurisdiction. By extension, the rule was applied to foreign states and their property intended for public use.[156] Various justifications for this rule have been put forward. Historically, the expectation that sovereigns be treated with dignity in their persons and as representative of their states played a role.[157] In the case of the *Schooner Exchange* Chief Justice Marshall, delivering the opinion of the US Supreme Court explained the rationale for the rule in the following way:

---

156. See *The Parlement Belge* 'The principle to be deduced from all these cases is that, as a consequence of the absolute independence of every sovereign authority and of the international comity which induces every sovereign state to respect the independence and dignity of every other sovereign state, each and every one declines to exercise by means of its courts any of its territorial jurisdiction over the person of any sovereign or ambassador of any other state, or over the public property of any state which is destined to public use, or over the property of any ambassador, though such sovereign, ambassador, or property be within its territory, and therefore, but for the common agreement, subject to its jurisdiction.' [1874–80] All ER Rep 104 at 114, per Brett LJ.

157. See the previous footnote for the approach of the English Court of Appeal; see also the memorandum by the UN Secretariat prepared for the International Law Commission, 'Immunity of State officials from foreign criminal jurisdiction', UN Doc. A/CN.4/596, 31 March 2008, paras 17–103.

A nation would justly be considered as violating its faith, although that faith might not be expressly plighted, which should suddenly and without previous notice exercise its territorial powers in a manner not consonant to the usages and received obligations of the civilized world.

This full and absolute territorial jurisdiction, being alike the attribute of every sovereign and being incapable of conferring extraterritorial power, would not seem to contemplate foreign sovereigns nor their sovereign rights as its objects. One sovereign being in no respect amenable to another, and being bound by obligations of the highest character not to degrade the dignity of his nation by placing himself or its sovereign rights within the jurisdiction of another, can be supposed to enter a foreign territory only under an express license, or in the confidence that the immunities belonging to his independent sovereign station, though not expressly stipulated, are reserved by implication, and will be extended to him.

This perfect equality and absolute independence of sovereigns, and this common interest impelling them to mutual intercourse, and an interchange of good offices with each other, have given rise to a class of cases in which every sovereign is understood to waive the exercise of a part of that complete exclusive territorial jurisdiction which has been stated to be the attribute of every nation.[158]

---

158. *The Schooner Exchange v McFaddon*, 11 US (1812) 116 at 137.

This passage reveals two further justifications for immunity: first, that no sovereign should have to place themselves under the jurisdiction of another, sometimes seen as an issue of the equality of states, or as falling under the maxim *par in parem non habet imperium* (an equal can have no authority over another equal). Second, that smooth international relations demand that states refrain from exercising jurisdiction over other states and their property. These paragraphs have been cited so often to explain the foundations of sovereign state immunity that it is worth recalling the context a little more carefully.

The case was brought by John McFaddon, claiming to be the owner of the Schooner Exchange. He alleged that the ship had been forcibly taken by people acting under the orders of Emperor Napoleon. The ship was in the port of Philadelphia, on one account due to the need to undertake repairs following a storm. The US Attorney, Mr Dallas suggested to the Court: 'That inasmuch as there exists between the United States of America and Napoleon, Emperor of France and King of Italy, &c., a state of peace and amity, the public vessels of his said Imperial and Royal Majesty, conforming to the law of nations and laws of the said United States, may freely enter the ports and harbors of the said United States and at pleasure depart therefrom without seizure, arrest, detention or molestation.'[159] Relying in part on Vattel's vision of states enjoying complete independence and his statement that he saw it as inconceivable that a prince who sends a minister abroad would accept that such an envoy be subjugated to the authority of another prince, the Supreme Court affirmed that state ships, heads of state, and ambassadors all have absolute immunity.

---

159. Ibid 118.

This rationale for such immunities (and their extension to the state more generally) has been questioned for some time. Some states started to carve out an exception when exercising jurisdiction in cases where other states have engaged in commerce. In 1951 Hersch Lauterpacht asked whether, in the light of the commercial activity of states, together with the abolition of absolute immunity for the Crown before UK courts, a commitment to the rule of law, and the recognition of 'human freedoms' as legal obligations, the idea of absolute immunity for foreign states might not be seen by some as 'artificial, unjust, and archaic'.[160]

Since then, pressure for reducing the scope of immunity continues from at least two principal sources: first those who suffer when states renege on their commercial contracts, and second, victims of human rights violations. Those in the first category question why should those who trade with states be denied a remedy which would be available to them if they were trading with another private actor. Elihu Lauterpacht has suggested: 'There is nothing so inherently special about States that when it comes to a fundamental aspect of the legal system—namely exposure to judicial redress—they should not be treated in the same way as individuals.'[161] Victims of human rights violations have also sought to sue states and prosecute their leaders before foreign courts. As international law has come to concretize these human rights and their

---

160. H. Lauterpacht, 'The Problem of Jurisdictional Immunities of Foreign States', 28 *BYBIL* (1951) 220–72, at 221.

161. *Aspects of the Administration of International Justice* (Cambridge: CUP, 1991) at 24, and see 55–6 where he asks 'What would happen if the immunity of foreign States in national courts were totally abolished?' and concludes that the practical problems are not as great as sometimes imagined.

corresponding international obligations, the argument has developed that there should be no immunity for the state or its agents when they are accused of violating certain fundamental norms. This principle has been accepted by various international criminal tribunals and is included in the Statute of the International Criminal Court.[162] But, when it comes to national jurisdiction, although there are now some clear exceptions to the immunity principle (discussed further below), governments and courts remain wedded to the foundational idea that good international relations depend on granting immunity to foreign sovereign states.

The Institute of International Law, in an effort to dispel uncertainties surrounding the immunity of Heads of States and Government, summarized a number of rules in their 2001 Vancouver Resolution.[163] In brief, they stated that when such persons are present in the territory of a foreign state,[164] they may not be placed

---

162. See Art. 27(1): 'This Statute shall apply equally to all persons without any distinction based on official capacity. In particular, official capacity as a Head of State or Government, a member of a Government or parliament, an elected representative or a government official shall in no case exempt a person from criminal responsibility under this Statute, nor shall it, in and of itself, constitute a ground for reduction of sentence.'

163. Immunities from Jurisdiction and Execution of Heads of State and of Government in International Law, Vancouver 2001/II (IIL Vancouver Resolution).

164. A Head of State or members of their family could not rely on immunity to avoid immigration laws and demand to enter another state. In 2011 the UK Foreign Secretary directed under s. 20(3) that the exemption provided by s. 8(3) of the Immigration Act 1971 did not apply to Col. Qadhafi and named members of his family. See also Security Council Res. 1970 (2011) imposing a world-wide ban on the entry into or transit through the territory of UN member states for Col. Qadhafi, specified members of his family, and others. A state's jurisdiction may however be limited with regard to a high ranking official abroad, for example by issuing an arrest warrant. See ICJ *Case Concerning the Arrest Warrant of 11 April 2000 (Dem. Rep of Congo v Belgium)* discussed at fn 168 below.

under any form of arrest or detention, and that they enjoy immunity from the courts for any crime 'regardless of its gravity'. However, the Resolution states that there is no immunity for civil or administrative matters 'unless that suit relates to acts performed in the exercise of his or her official functions'.

By contrast a *former* Head of State or Head of Government enjoys no inviolability from arrest or detention in the territory of a foreign state, nor does he or she enjoy immunity from jurisdiction from any proceedings, except in respect of acts which were performed in the exercise of official functions and related to the exercise thereof. In an important clarification, the Institute states: 'Nevertheless, he or she may be prosecuted and tried when the acts alleged constitute a crime under international law, or when they are performed exclusively to satisfy a personal interest, or when they constitute a misappropriation of the State's assets and resources.'[165] This last qualification in respect of international crimes stems from the approach of the House of Lords in the *Pinochet* case,[166] but extends the exception to functional immunity beyond the context of torture to other crimes. According to Lady Fox: 'Whether or not strictly in accordance with current State practice, on its face the Resolution offers a workable compromise whereby international communication is facilitated but no lasting impunity afforded to officials who commit grave crimes contrary to international law.'[167]

---

165. Vancouver Resolution Art. 13(2) (above).

166. See *R v Bartle* et al *Ex Parte Pinochet* [1999] UKHL 17.

167. H. Fox, 'The Resolution of the Institute of International Law on the Immunities of Heads of State and Government', 51 *ICLQ* (2002) 119–25, at 125.

Nevertheless, in some quarters it is still asserted that the law of nations demands that former senior ministers, including former Foreign Ministers, retain immunity even from accusations of international crimes such as genocide or crimes against humanity. The argument is that as these acts must have been carried out through the official's functions, the official retains functional immunity.[168] Described as the 'classical viewpoint',[169] there may be

---

168. In the *Case Concerning the Arrest Warrant of 11 April 2000 (Dem. Rep of Congo v Belgium)* 14 February 2002, the International Court of Justice affirmed the absolute personal immunity of 'certain holders of high-ranking office in a State, such as the Head of State, Head of Government and Minister for Foreign Affairs', at para. 51 even in the face of allegations of international crimes. With regard to a former Foreign Minister the Court stated in an *obiter dictum* that the national jurisdiction of another state would be limited to acts committed by a former minister 'in a private capacity', at para. 61. The separate joint opinion of Judges Higgins, Kooijmans, and Buergenthal argues that the immunity of a former foreign minister can only apply to 'official acts' and 'that serious international crimes cannot be regarded as official acts because they are neither normal State functions nor functions that a State alone (in contrast to an individual) can perform', at para. 85, relying in part on A. Bianchi, 'Denying State Immunity to Violators of Human Rights', 46 *Austrian Journal of Public International Law* (1994) 195–229. The ICJ affirmed the immunity of Heads of State in *Certain Questions of Mutual Assistance in Criminal Matters (Djibouti v France)*, 4 June 2008; personal immunity claims for the *procureur général* and the Head of National Security were not upheld, functional immunity was deemed not to be in issue as Djibuti had not claimed such immunity for its agents before the French courts. According to the ICJ, 'Further, the State notifying a foreign court that judicial process should not proceed, for reasons of immunity, against its State organs, is assuming responsibility for any internationally wrongful act in issue committed by such organs' at para. 196.

169. H. Fox, *The Law of State Immunity*, 2nd edn (Oxford: OUP, 2008) at 697. See also R. Jennings, 'The Pinochet Extradition Case in the English Courts', in L. Boisson de Chazournes and V. Gowlland-Debbas (eds), *The International Legal System in Quest of Equity and Universality—Liber Amicorum Georges Abi-Saab* (The Hague: Nijhoff, 2001) 677–98.

some theoretical arguments to back it, and the bulk of state practice may lean in this direction,[170] but such a view no longer sits
easily with our contemporary understanding of the purposes of
the law of nations. It can be argued that a rule of customary law is
forming which precludes any functional immunity being claimed
in the face of accusations of international crimes.[171] Today the
objective of facilitating smooth relations between states has to be
married with the purpose of ensuring respect for international
norms which protect individuals from the excesses of their sovereign rulers. Concern for the dignity of foreign sovereigns is now
tempered by concern for the indignities suffered by their subjects.

(b) *Immunity for the state and its agents*

As mentioned above, absolute state immunity is no longer applied
where the state is engaged in commercial activity rather than acting in its sovereign capacity. Determining the nature of this distinction has not proven a simple matter in those jurisdictions that
apply this sort of restriction on immunity and the case-law is
voluminous.[172] The House of Lords was faced with a claim by the
Chilean owners of two sugar cargoes against the Cuban Government for having ordered two ships (operated by Cuban state

---

170. See the detailed examination by the ILC's Special Rapporteur, R.A. Kolodkin, Second report on immunity of State officials from foreign criminal jurisdiction UN Doc.
A/CN.4/631, 10 June 2010.

171. A. Cassese, *International Criminal Law*, 2nd edn (Oxford: OUP, 2008) at 305–8;
Resolution of the Institute of International Law 'Immunity from Jurisdiction of the State
and of Persons Who Act on Behalf of the State in case of International Crimes' Naples
(2009) Art. III.

172. *The Law of State Immunity* (above) chs 16 and 17.

companies) not to unload sugar in Chile due to General Pinochet's ongoing overthrow of the Allende Government. Lord Wilberforce agreed that the 'restrictive theory' be applied and explained the bases for this limitation on immunity:

> It appears to have two main foundations. (a) It is necessary in the interest of justice to individuals having such transactions with states to allow them to bring such transactions before the courts. (b) To require a state to answer a claim based on such transactions does not involve a challenge to or inquiry into any act of sovereignty or governmental act of that state. It is, in accepted phrases, neither a threat to the dignity of that state nor any interference with its sovereign functions.[173]

He went on to find (along with the majority) that with regard to one ship no immunity should apply to Cuba—as the acts of the Cuban Government in withdrawing the Cuban ship from Chilean waters and denying the cargo to the Chilean owners of the cargo were acts of a nature that any private entity could have taken with regard to its ship and there was no exercise of sovereign powers.[174] He found (in contrast with the majority), however, that the action with regard to the other ship was subject to immunity as it involved a decision at a very high level of the Cuban Government, in accordance with a Cuban law enacted to provide for the freezing and blocking of Chilean assets, to deliver a gift to the people of North

---

173. *I Congresso del Partido* [1981] 2 All ER 1064 at 1070.
174. Ibid 1075.

Vietnam of 10,800 tons of sugar to be discharged at the port of Haiphong.[175] Such differences illustrate how difficult it is to agree on whether acts come 'within the sphere of governmental or sovereign activity'[176] or should alternatively be considered commercial activity, and remind us of the political stakes. Developing countries are said to remain concerned that they retain immunity over political decisions related to emergency food supplies. This has meant that it has proven difficult to codify or develop at the international level a provision containing an exception for commercial activity. The Article in the 2004 UN Convention on Jurisdictional Immunities of States and Their Property seeks to amalgamate different approaches, and this looks set to remain an area where national courts apply the rules on sovereign immunity with some variation.[177]

The other exceptions to state immunity which have developed are now set out in some detail in the 2004 Convention. They relate *inter*

---

175. Ibid 1076.

176. Ibid 1074.

177. For suggested criteria to be taken into account see C.H. Schreuer, *State Immunity: Some Recent Developments* (Cambridge: CUP, 1988) at 42. The 2004 Convention is not in force at the time of writing. The relevant provisions are as follows: '1(c) "commercial transaction" means: (i) any commercial contract or transaction for the sale of goods or supply of services; (ii) any contract for a loan or other transaction of a financial nature, including any obligation of guarantee or of indemnity in respect of any such loan or transaction; (iii) any other contract or transaction of a commercial, industrial, trading or professional nature, but not including a contract of employment of persons. 2. In determining whether a contract or transaction is a "commercial transaction" under paragraph 1 (c), reference should be made primarily to the nature of the contract or transaction, but its purpose should also be taken into account if the parties to the contract or transaction have so agreed, or if, in the practice of the State of the forum, that purpose is relevant to determining the non-commercial character of the contract or transaction.'

alia to contracts of employment, property rights, and proceedings regarding pecuniary compensation for death or injury to the person, or damage to property, where the acts took place in the forum state.[178] It is agreed that the 2004 Convention does not cover criminal proceedings.[179] As we saw above, the question arises whether state agents enjoy functional immunity in the face of criminal proceedings in a foreign court. A cautious approach would suggest that immunity applies, unless there is a relevant applicable treaty such as the UN Torture Convention which makes clear that state officials can be prosecuted abroad for their official acts.[180] Again the Institute of International Law provides a suggestion for progressive development.[181] The 2009 Naples Resolution states that: '[n]o immunity from jurisdiction other than personal immunity in accordance with international law applies with regard to international crimes'.[182] Jurisdiction in this context covers criminal, administrative, and civil jurisdictions. International crimes are defined as including 'serious crimes

---

178. See Arts 10–17. Note also the detailed provisions on execution of judgments in Arts 18–21.

179. UNGA Res. 59/38, 2 December 2004, para. 2.

180. See in particular Lord Bingham in *Jones v Saudi Arabia* [2006] UKHL 26, at para. 19. Lady Fox summarizes her appreciation of the current law as follows: functional immunity enjoyed by officials performing a state function 'bars criminal proceedings for such acts save where they relate to the commission of international crimes, such proceedings being confined to such crimes for which by international convention States are under obligation to make penal offences and prosecute in their national systems'. *The Law of State Immunity* (above) at 699.

181. Lady Fox, Rapporteur for the Commission that prepared the Resolution, has stressed that she sees this restriction on functional immunity as *de lege ferenda*. *The Law of State Immunity* (above) at 141 and 750.

182. Resolution on the Immunity from Jurisdiction of the State and of Persons Who Act on Behalf of the State in case of International Crimes, Naples, 2009. The personal immunity mentioned refers to the absolute immunity that is accepted for incumbent high-ranking

under international law such as genocide, crimes against humanity, torture and war crimes, as reflected in relevant treaties and the statutes and jurisprudence of international courts and tribunals.'[183] This is a useful statement, and as we saw above, some would argue that it represents developing customary international law with regard to criminal prosecutions. However, it fails to address the controversial question of whether states, rather than individuals, can be sued in the domestic courts of other states for acts that amount to violations of international law, especially with regard to acts that amount to international crimes or serious human rights violations.[184]

The House of Lords has recently answered this question in the negative. It held that Saudi Arabia and its agents enjoyed complete immunity before the UK domestic courts with regard to a civil claim of torture. Their Lordships clearly felt constrained by international law and their legitimate role in its development. According to Lord Hoffman:

> As Professor Dworkin demonstrated in *Law's Empire* (1986), the ordering of competing principles according to the importance of the values which they embody is a basic technique of adjudication. But the same approach cannot be adopted in international law, which is based upon the common consent

---

officials such as Heads of State or Government or under the special regime that exists for ambassadors (as we shall see below). Art. III(1).

183. Art. I(1). Immunity with regard to genocide is discussed by P. Gaeta, 'Immunities and Genocide', in P. Gaeta (ed.), *The UN Genocide Convention* (Oxford: OUP, 2009) 310–33 esp. 319–27.

184. A. Bellal, 'The 2009 Resolution of the Institute of International Law on Immunity and International Crimes: A Partial Codification of the Law?' 9 *JICJ* (2011) 227–41.

of nations. It is not for a national court to 'develop' international law by unilaterally adopting a version of that law which, however desirable, forward-looking and reflective of values it may be, is simply not accepted by other states.[185]

But approaches to this question do vary and the United States Congress has passed legislation removing state immunity for claims by US citizens relating to torture and extrajudicial killing, aircraft sabotage, or hostage taking against those states which it has designated as state sponsors of terrorism.[186] Similarly, a US Court denied the immunity to the State of Chile for a car bombing in Washington.[187]

Most recently the International Court Justice upheld the claim of Germany that she was entitled to immunity before the Italian

---

185. *Jones v (Saudi Arabia)* [2006] (above) at para. 63. He later suggests there is no way for judges to fashion exceptions in this area as state immunity 'is imposed by international law without any discrimination between one state and another. It would be invidious in the extreme for the judicial branch of government to have the power to decide that it will allow the investigation of allegations of torture against the officials of one foreign state but not against those of another.' At para. 101.

186. Antiterrorism and Effective Death Penalty Act (1996). Note that the incident referred to in Ch. V § 7 regarding the use of force by Cuba outside its territorial waters against two planes with three US nationals on board resulted in an award against Cuba of $187,627,911 for the extrajudicial killing: *Alejandre v Republic of Cuba* 996 F Supp 1239 (SD Fla 1997); see also the Torture Victim Protection Act 1991; but see *Cicippio-Puelo v Islamic Republic of Iran* 353 F 3d 1024 (DC Cir 2004) with regard to suits against states. The US Supreme Court has held that the US Foreign Sovereign Immunities Act (1976) does not apply to individual defendants in civil cases, their immunity would be covered by Common Law; whether this would include a functional immunity for state officials accused of torture or other international crimes is not clear. *Samantar v Yousef* et al, 560 US ____ (2010).

187. *Letelier v Republic of Chile* (1980) 63 ILR 378.

Courts in relation to claims from the Second World War concerning large scale killings of civilians in occupied territory and deportations from Italy into slave labour in Germany. The Court found that customary international law requires that 'a State be accorded immunity in proceedings for torts allegedly committed on the territory of another State by its armed forces and other organs of State in the course of conducting an armed conflict'.[188]

The differences surrounding this topic mean that we can look forward to further developments and clarifications. Some states have been careful to emphasize that the attempted codification in the 2004 Convention should not preclude progressive developments. The Declaration made by Switzerland on ratification of the 2004 Convention is worth quoting here: 'Switzerland considers that article 12 does not govern the question of pecuniary compensation for serious human rights violations which are alleged to be attributable to a State and are committed outside the State of the forum. Consequently, this Convention is without prejudice to developments in international law in this regard.'[189]

---

188. *Jurisdictional Immunities of the State (Germany v Italy: Greece Intervening)* Judgment of 2 February 2012 at para. 78.

189. 16 April 2010. Interpretive Declaration concerning Article 12. This Article which concerns what is sometimes known as the 'territorial tort exception' reads: 'Unless otherwise agreed between the States concerned, a State cannot invoke immunity from jurisdiction before a court of another State which is otherwise competent in a proceeding which relates to pecuniary compensation for death or injury to the person, or damage to or loss of tangible property, caused by an act or omission which is alleged to be attributable to the State, if the act or omission occurred in whole or in part in the territory of that other State and if the author of the act or omission was present in that territory at the time of the act or omission.'

The divergent views on this issue illustrate the shifting attitudes to international law and how it is formed. Some continue to prioritize smooth inter-state relations and protecting states from vexatious politicized suits; others think these interests should not be at the expense of our contemporary commitment to the rule of law, the end of impunity, and respecting the dignity of the individual.[190] These different attitudes reflect underlying choices about how international law should develop. Should it develop through the slow accretion of state practice essentially reaffirming the interests of states? Or should we look simply to develop a legal order which fulfils the wider stated purposes of international law? At the beginning of this book we suggested that natural law reminds us that law is not simply a set of arbitrary principles to be mechanically applied by courts; law exists for certain ends, and today our aim should be to embody contemporary notions of social justice in law.

---

190. Consider now the dissenting opinions in *Germany v Italy* (above) by Judges Cançado Trindade, Yusuf, and Judge *ad hoc* Gaja. Judge Yusuf's opinion sets out a suggested limited exception to state immunity. 'The assertion of jurisdiction by domestic courts in those exceptional circumstances where there is a failure to make reparations, and where the responsible State has admitted to the commission of serious violations of humanitarian law, without providing a contextual remedy for the victims, does not, in my view, upset the harmonious relations between States, but contributes to a better observance of international human rights and humanitarian law.' The choices are also laid bare in the judgment, separate opinion, and dissenting opinions of the Grand Chamber of the European Court of Human Rights *in Al-Adsani v UK*, 21 November 2001. See also A. Bianchi, '*Ferrini v Federal Republic of Germany*', 99 *AJIL* (2005) 242–8. For a book-length treatment see R. Van Alebeek, *The Immunity of States and Their Officials in International Criminal Law and International Human Rights Law* (Oxford: OUP, 2008).

(c) *Diplomatic, consular, and other immunities*

The early history of the law relating to diplomatic privileges is set out in Adair's valuable study *Extraterritoriality of Ambassadors in the Sixteenth and Seventeenth Centuries*.[191] His historical analysis usefully points to the origins of what was then meant by extraterritoriality. At that time ambassadors were envoys rather than resident:

> theorists were unanimous in recognising the personal immunity of an ambassador and the sacredness of his functions, basing their conclusions on Roman law and on the fact that one of the best-known types of ambassador was the papal legate or nuncio and that the very nature of his office surrounded him with an aura of sanctity—a sanctity which was strengthened by the thunders of canon law.[192] In addition there was the very strong influence of the idea of personal law, the idea that a man carried his own law with him wherever he went and consequently should be tried by that law and not by the law of the country where he happened to be residing. Finally, to the English and French mind at any rate, the liberty, within whose borders the royal writ did not run, had long been only too familiar, and consequently the ambassadorial island in the midst of a sea of national law presented nothing new or unprecedented. Nothing is more fallacious than to imagine a 'rule of law' as universal throughout fifteenth or even sixteenth-century England.[193]

---

191. London: Longmans, 1929.

192. The footnote in the original cites authority to the effect that 'those who maltreated envoys were to be excommunicated'.

193. Adair (above) at 6.

Adair recounts how the status of ambassadors came to be a subject of great practical importance. Ambassadors were often central to plots to overthrow the sovereign, and it was a matter of immense public interest to know the extent of any immunity from criminal prosecution.[194] It was also a matter of popular interest to know whether ambassadors would be able to get away with swindling those they were living amongst by relying on immunity from civil process. As Satow's manual explains: in the sixteenth and seventeenth centuries '[I]t was thought necessary for an ambassador to uphold the prestige of his sovereign by magnificent display. But the sending State did not ordinarily provide allowances for this, and so the ambassador who lacked great private means would often find himself obliged either to go into business or to fall into debt.'[195]

Adair credits the theory of extraterritoriality and the effective immunity that flows from it as instrumental to peace:

The Renaissance and the Reformation brought the reign of the clerical ambassador to an end and at the same time unleashed new international differences that were far more bitter than Europe had ever known before. Yet the need for international relations was greater than ever, for political and economic changes were rapidly binding the nations together—in rivalry if not in friendship. The creation of the doctrine of extraterritoriality was an unconscious, but none

194. For legal opinions in some of the famous early incidents see A.D. McNair, *International Law Opinions* (Cambridge: CUP, 1956) vol. I at 186–224.

195. I. Roberts (ed.), *Satow's Diplomatic Practice*, 6th edn (Oxford: OUP, 2009) at para. 8.1.

the less sure, response to the difficulties of the situation. This doctrine alone made possible the reasonable intercourse of King with Republic, of Protestant state with Catholic state, of Bourbon with Hapsburg. It made possible the smoothing away of difficulties that might have developed into bloody wars, the solving of some few of the many problems of the age; it made possible, in short, all the fruits of sustained diplomatic relations. Disadvantages no doubt came with it. The ambassador sure of his privileged position, proved haughty; his suite, safe in his protection, were lacking in consideration; but this was on the whole a small price to pay for the freedom from patriotic annoyance to which otherwise the foreign minister would have been exposed and which would have made peaceful international relations almost impossible.[196]

Today diplomatic immunities may seem less essential, and the public concerns less relevant, even though incidents concerning diplomatic immunity are still capable of arousing popular sentiments, and landlords and hoteliers may think twice (at least since the scandal surrounding Hannibal Qadhafi in Geneva) before accommodating those covered by diplomatic or other immunities.

In the United Kingdom, the immunities granted to a foreign diplomatic person are governed by the Diplomatic Privileges Act 1964 which incorporates provisions of the Vienna Convention on Diplomatic Relations of 1961 (VCDR). The treaty is almost universally ratified and the provisions on privileges and immunities now consti-

---

196. Ibid 264–5.

tute international law.[197] In brief, a diplomatic agent is wholly exempt from arrest or detention or from criminal proceedings in the country to which he or she is accredited.[198] This does not mean that it is not their duty to obey the criminal law of the country, but if they break the law, the only action that may be taken against them would be a diplomatic complaint to their government (perhaps asking for the diplomat to be withdrawn), or a declaration that the diplomat is *persona non grata* (no reasons need be given), thus obliging the diplomat to leave the country within a reasonable time. Of course the diplomat's sending state can expressly waive the immunity, in which case the police or the courts of the receiving state could exercise their jurisdiction.[199] One can easily imagine cases of serious crimes which could only be halted with the application of restraint by the police. Where such action is necessary, for self-defence or to protect life, it should not be considered a violation of the general immunity.[200]

---

197. *Satow's Diplomatic Practice* (above) at para. 8.6.

198. This personal immunity extends to members of the diplomat's family as well as administrative and technical staff. Whether or not the immunity applies to the particular person is a question of law for the courts, see *Satow's Diplomatic Practice* (above) para. 9.24 and Art. 39 VCDR.

199. Under the Diplomatic Privileges Act, s. 2(3) a waiver by the head of the diplomatic mission will be deemed a waiver in this context. Note that a separate waiver would be required in to order to waive immunity from execution of any judgment. VCDR Art. 32(4).

200. For incidents concerning diplomats with guns in public places, see *Satow's Diplomatic Practice* (above) at paras 9.15 and 9.5. For an account of the legitimate temporary arrest of the French Ambassador's servants involved in a brawl with the people at 'The Feathers' in London see *International Law Opinions* (above) at 191. See also *United States Diplomatic and Consular Staff in Tehran,* ICJ Judgment (1980) at para. 86: the inviolability of a diplomatic agent does not mean that 'a diplomatic agent caught in the act of committing an assault or other offence may not, on occasion, be briefly arrested by the police of the receiving State in order to prevent the commission of the particular crime'.

The diplomatic agent is also generally exempt from civil or administrative proceedings,[201] and even from being required to give evidence in a court of law.[202] There are, however, three exceptions to this rule.[203] Immunity will not apply to: first, claims regarding title or possession of private immovable property situated in the territory of the receiving state;[204] second, matters of succession where the agent is involved not on behalf of the sending state; and third, any professional or commercial activity exercised by the diplomatic agent in the receiving state outside their official functions.[205]

Such diplomatic privilege as does apply is essentially an immunity from the *enforcement* of the local law—and only applies so long as the privilege lasts. Diplomatic agents do not actually enjoy immunity from the *application* of the law. In other words their actions are not outside the law or somehow 'extraterritorial'. This is well illustrated by the following English case. The plaintiff had been injured by the car of the defendant, who was a First Secretary with the Peruvian Legation. The defendant was instructed by his Minister at the Legation not to plead his

---

201. This immunity is only extended to administrative staff to the extent that the acts in question are performed in the course of their duties. VCDR Art. 37(2).

202. This immunity is only extended to administrative staff to the extent that they are not 'acts performed outside the course of their duties'. VCDR Art. 37(2).

203. Execution may be taken in respect of a diplomatic agent in these three cases provided that the measures concerned can be taken without infringing the inviolability of the agent's person or residence. VCDR Art. 31(3).

204. The Convention uses the expression 'real action'; this would exclude actions to recover rent. E. Denza, *Diplomatic Law: Commentary on the Vienna Convention on Diplomatic Relations*, 3rd edn (Oxford: OUP, 2008) at 291.

205. VCDR Art. 31(1)(c).

diplomatic immunity, and served a third-party notice on his insurance company, demanding that they should indemnify him against the claim. The company tried to repudiate liability arguing that the defendant himself was under no legal liability to the injured plaintiff; but the Court held that: '[d]iplomatic agents are not, in virtue of their privileges as such, immune from legal liability for any wrongful acts'.[206] They are merely not liable to be sued unless they submit to the jurisdiction. So the judgment against the defendant therefore created a legal liability—against which the company had agreed to indemnify him. The insurance company's claim failed, they could neither argue that the diplomat had no legal liability, nor that he was obliged by his contract to avoid jurisdiction.[207]

A diplomatic person has some immunity from taxation, but the extent of this varies under different systems of taxation and the Convention contains a long list of exceptions.[208] A diplomatic salary should not be taxed, and customs duties are not usually charged on articles imported for personal use.[209]

The immunities described above continue after the person's functions have come to an end, but only to the extent that immunity is claimed with regard to acts performed by such persons in the exercise of their functions as a member of the

---

206. *Dickinson v Del Solar* [1930] 1 KB 376 at 380.

207. On the subsequent steps taken to ensure that insurance companies would not seek to evade liability through their contracts, the obligation to have third party insurance, and the steps taken to recuperate parking fines in various countries, see Denza (above) at 285–9.

208. VCDR Art. 34.

209. Art. 36.

mission.[210] Even if the diplomat retains immunity for such acts, the state will remain responsible under international law towards the host state, and, as we saw above, the state enjoys no immunity from claims regarding death or personal injury committed in the forum state. For this reason claims are often brought against both the former diplomat and the state in question. It is worth remarking that by asserting functional immunity for its agents acting within their official functions a state may simultaneously assume responsibility for the acts in question.[211]

Diplomatic agents not only have a duty to respect the laws and regulations of the receiving State. 'They also have a duty not to interfere in the internal affairs of that State.'[212] This duty will preclude encouraging a certain outcome for elections or supporting any opposition or rebel groups. Diplomats can nowadays raise issues of human rights, both with regard to their own nationals and others. No longer considered a question of internal affairs, international human rights obligations will be binding on the receiving state and owed to the sending state as a matter of international law.[213]

---

210. According to the German Constitutional Court this immunity only applies vis-à-vis the original receiving state. In the *Case of the former Syrian Ambassador to the German Democratic Republic* it held that the former Ambassador could not claim immunity before the courts of post reunification Germany. The former Ambassador was implicated in a bomb attack in 1983 at an arts centre in West Berlin. He had allegedly failed to prevent the terrorist group 'Carlos' from removing explosives from the Syrian Embassy. 121 ILR 595. Cf Fassbender's note on the case 92 *AJIL* (1998) 72–8.

211. See *Djibuti v France* (above) para. 196 and *Knab v Georgia Civ* 97-CV-03118 (TPH) DDC 29 May 1998. Further, the state notifying a foreign court that judicial process should not proceed, for reasons of immunity, against its state organs, is assuming responsibility for any internationally wrongful act in issue committed by such organs.

212. VCDR Art. 41(1).

213. *Satow's Diplomatic Practice* (above) at para. 9.58.

Consuls are not diplomatic agents; they perform various services for a state or its subjects in another state, without, however, representing the former in the full sense. They may be nationals of either state, and generally they are made subject to the authority of the diplomatic representative of the state for which they act. They watch over commercial interests of the state for which they act, collect information for it, help its nationals with advice, administer their property if they die abroad, and register their births, deaths, and marriages. They authenticate documents for legal purposes, take depositions from witnesses, issue visas, passports, and travel documents. They also have important functions concerned with ships and aircraft registered in the sending state, for instance settling disputes between master and crew.[214] An important rule is that the consular post is to be informed without delay if a national from the sending state is detained or committed to prison.[215] Consular officers have the right to visit such a national. They also have the right to converse and correspond with those so detained and to arrange for legal representation.

Although it is accepted that consular officers will need some immunities in order effectively to fulfil their functions, they do not

---

214. See further Vienna Convention on Consular Relations (1963) (VCCR) Art. 5 and any relevant bilateral agreements setting out a regime for a particular consular district.

215. For cases in which this right, which is also a right of the national concerned, was found by the International Court of Justice to have been violated: *Avena and Other Mexican Nationals (Mexico v USA)* (2004), *LaGrand (Germany v USA)* (2001). Citizens of the EU can call on diplomatic and consular officials from other EU member states where their state of nationality is not represented in a third state. Arts 20(2)(c) and 23 of the Treaty on the Functioning of the European Union, in force 1 December 2009; see also Art. 46 of the Charter of Fundamental Rights of the European Union.

fully represent the sovereign state in the same way as diplomats and their privileges and immunities are not as extensive. For example, the Vienna Convention on Consular Relations states that '[c]onsular officers shall not be liable to arrest or detention pending trial, except in the case of a grave crime and pursuant to a decision by the competent judicial authority'.[216] In other cases 'consular officers shall not be committed to prison or be liable to any other form of restriction on their personal freedom save in execution of a judicial decision of final effect'.[217] And, subject to certain exceptions: 'Consular officers and consular employees shall not be amenable to the jurisdiction of the judicial or administrative authorities of the receiving State in respect of acts performed in the exercise of consular functions.'[218]

Consular functions are defined in the Convention and must be within the limits of international law.[219] In turn the Convention requires that the consular officials not interfere in internal affairs. Such consular functions were held not to include threatening protestors outside the Mexican Consulate in Los Angeles. The US Court of Appeals held that the threatening behaviour was not covered by functional consular immunity:

> Wrongful acts committed by an official or employee of a Mexican consulate within the United States to suppress criticism of Mexico within this country constitute an interference with the

---

216. Art. 41(1). The Consular Relations Act 1968 defines grave crime as any offence punishable (on a first conviction) with imprisonment of five years or more.

217. VCCR Art. 41(2).

218. VCCR Art. 43(1).

219. VCCR Art. 5(1).

United States' internal affairs because these acts impair the citizenry's ability to promote self-government through robust discourse concerning issues of public import. Therefore, the acts of the two consuls general and the vice consul alleged in the complaint are not 'within the limits permitted by international law' and thus are not consular functions as defined in Article 5(a).[220]

Other immunities include those of international organizations, the officials of such organizations, and the special position of visiting armed forces and military bases.[221]

(d) *Diplomatic and consular bags*

The diplomatic bag, which must be visibly marked, 'shall not be opened or detained'.[222] Attempts to formulate rules on scanning, or subjecting the bag to x-rays, have yet to be generally accepted due to the suspicion that modern equipment could permit reading the contents. Sniffer dogs and other methods of detecting explosives and drugs are however employed, and in the event of suspicion the authorities would refuse to allow the diplomatic bag to continue. The consular bag is subject to a slightly weaker level of

---

220. *Gerritsen v De La Madrid* 819 F.2d 1511 (1987) at para. 20.

221. A. Reinisch, *International Organizations before National Courts* (Cambridge: CUP, 2000); A. Reinisch (ed.), *Challenging Acts of International Organizations Before National Courts* (Oxford: OUP, 2010); D. Fleck (ed.), *The Handbook of the Law of Visiting Forces* (Oxford: OUP, 2001) and T. Gill and D. Fleck (eds), *The Handbook of the International Law of Military Operations* (Oxford: OUP, 2010). The English Courts have applied functional immunities to former officials of international organizations. For a case where the previous editor of this book was accorded such immunity as the former President of the European Commission of Human Rights see *Zoernsch v Waldock and anor* [1964] 2 All ER 256.

222. VCDR Art. 27(3).

protection. If the authorities believe that the bag contains something unauthorized, they may request that the bag be opened in
their presence by an authorized representative of the sending state.
If the sending state refuses, the bag is returned to its place of origin.[223] Some well-known incidents of attempts to kidnap and
smuggle people in the diplomatic bag have led to the very reasonable view that the diplomatic or consular bag can be opened in
order to protect a life.[224]

(e) *Diplomatic and consular premises*

The premises of a diplomatic mission and the residences of diplomatic
agents are inviolable and the receiving state has a duty to protect
them.[225] We might see this as encompassing two separate obligations
for the receiving state. First, there is an obligation not to enter the
premises without the consent of the head of the mission.[226] Second,
there is, in the words of the Convention on Diplomatic Relations: 'a

---

223. VCCR Art. 35(3).

224. Denza (above) at 242–3 referring to a kidnapped and drugged Israeli found in 1964
by the Italian authorities in a large diplomatic bag that was 'emitting moans'. The bag was
addressed to the Foreign Ministry in Cairo. She also details the UK opinion that the decision at Stansted airport to break open the crate which smelled of chloroform and contained the kidnapped Nigerian Umaru Dikko (together with an Israeli anaesthetist)
would have been the same had it been a diplomatic bag (it was opened as personal bag-
gage under the conditions stipulated in Art. 36(2) of the VCDR), as there would have
been an 'overriding duty to preserve and protect life'. For full details of the incident see A.
Akinsanya, 'The Dikko Affair and Anglo-Nigerian Relations', 34 *ICLQ* (1985) 602–9.

225. The residence of a consular agent is not protected under the VCCR.

226. With regard to consular premises the VCCR allows that: '[t]he consent of the head
of the consular post may, however, be assumed in case of fire or other disaster requiring
prompt protective action'. Art. 31(2).

special duty to take all appropriate steps to protect the premises of the mission against any intrusion or damage and to prevent any disturbance of the peace of the mission or impairment of its dignity'.[227]

As we saw at the beginning of this chapter, the inviolability of diplomatic premises does not mean they are to be considered as altogether outside the application of the law of the receiving state. Diplomatic premises are not a foreign enclave within the host state's territory. Although diplomatic missions perform certain legal acts for citizens of their home state, such as registration of deaths, births and marriages, issuing passports and so on, these acts are not extraterritorial. A crime committed in the diplomatic premises is still a crime committed within the territory of the receiving state.

In 1896 when Sun Yatsen, then a political refugee from China, had been induced to enter the Chinese Legation in London and was detained there in order to be sent to China. The British Government refused to accept the contention that the Legation was Chinese territory. They stated that the detention was an abuse of diplomatic privilege and peremptorily demanded his release, which was eventually granted. The incident was relayed around the world and it is worth mentioning that Sun Yatsen went on to become the Head of State of China.[228]

Similarly, a crime committed in a foreign embassy in the United Kingdom is a crime committed in the United Kingdom and the offender, if not protected by diplomatic immunity, is liable to prosecution in the UK Courts. In the case of *R v Kent* a cipher clerk

---

227. VCDR Art. 22.2.

228. J.Y. Wong, *The Origins of a Heroic Image: Sun Yatsen in London, 1896–1897* (Hong Kong: OUP, 1986).

working in the US Embassy in London stole copies of top secret documents related to the ongoing Second World War. These included, *inter alia*, communications between Churchill and Roosevelt concerning the future entry of the United States into the War. Ambassador Joseph Kennedy waived Kent's immunity; however, Kent claimed that he was entitled to immunity for a reasonable time before leaving the country, that the acts took place on foreign soil, and that the inviolability of the archives of the Embassy meant he could not be prosecuted for crimes in relation to them.[229] None of these arguments was successful and he was sentenced to seven years in prison.

As already mentioned, some Latin American states recognize certain duties with regard to those who seek diplomatic asylum on warships; this is an extension of the right to grant asylum in legations (embassies).[230] No general rules of international law have developed as regards claims of diplomatic asylum, but in practice temporary asylum for humanitarian purposes has been granted in a number of cases. Eileen Denza suggests that '[t]he sending State may, however—at least where there is an immediate danger to the life or safety of a refugee—claim a limited and temporary right to grant diplomatic asylum on the basis of customary international law'.[231] Furthermore the customary international law rule prohibiting *refoulement* would prohibit

---

229. 10 ILR 365, Case 110.

230. OAS Convention on Diplomatic Asylum (1954); and see the ICJ cases *Colombian-Peruvian asylum case* (1950) and *Haya de la Torre Case* (1951) where the Court found that the Colombian Government was under no obligation to surrender Haya de la Torre to the Peruvian authorities.

231. Above at 142.

surrendering this person where 'substantial grounds can be shown for believing that he or she would face a real risk of being subjected to torture or cruel, inhuman or degrading treatment or punishment'.[232]

The receiving state, in any event, may not enter the premises without permission, and has a set of positive obligations as explained above. These obligations were dramatically violated in the hostage taking in the US diplomatic premises in Tehran. The International Court of Justice ordered as a preliminary measure that Iran restore to the US exclusive control of the Embassy and Consulate and ensure the immediate release of all US hostages.[233] In the final judgment the Court found that Iran had first of all failed to protect the Embassy, and, in a second phase had endorsed the action so that the militants became agents of the Iranian state and the state was internationally responsible for their acts. Ayatollah Khomeini had declared, according to the Court, that the 'premises of the Embassy and the hostages would remain as they were until the United States had handed over the former Shah for trial and returned his property to Iran'.[234] The Court rejected the

232. See E. Lauterpacht and D. Bethlehem, 'The scope and content of the principle of *non-refoulement*: Opinion', in E. Feller, V. Türk, and F. Nicholson, *Refugee Protection in International Law: UNHCR's Global Consultations on International Protection* (Cambridge: CUP, 2003) 87–177, at para. 253, and see para. 114. See further para. 253 and *B v Secretary of State for Foreign and Commonwealth Affairs* [2004] EWCA 1344, concerning Afghan asylum seekers in the British Consulate in Melbourne, Australia; for a full overview of refugee law see G. Goodwin-Gill, *The Refugee in International Law*, 3rd edn (Oxford: OUP, 2007).

233. *Case Concerning United States Diplomatic and Consular Staff in Iran (USA v Iran)* (1979).

234. Ibid para. 73.

argument that there could be any justification for violating the international law protecting diplomatic premises and agents.[235] The Court explained that, even if it had had proper information on alleged crimes and espionage supposed to have been committed by the US against Iran, there are no circumstances which would justify reprisals against diplomatic premises and agents. The Vienna Conventions include provisions which allow a receiving state to declare a diplomat *persona non grata*, to break off diplomatic relations, and to close the mission. The international rules were said to constitute 'a self-contained régime' which applies even in times of armed conflict.[236] The rules are to be respected as a question of treaty law and under 'long-established rules of general international law'.[237]

It remains to discuss the situation where the receiving state is faced with peaceful protests outside the diplomatic premises and the sending state considers this to be a failure by the receiving state to live up to its obligations under the Vienna Conventions to prevent these disturbances and the 'impairment of its dignity'. Here again the traditional concern with smooth international relations and respect for foreign sovereigns has to be married with constitu-

---

235. See also ILC's Articles on Responsibility of States for Internationally Wrongful Acts (2001) Art. 50(2)(b) and the analysis by L. Boisson de Chazournes of which obligations in the realm of diplomatic relations may or may not be the object of reprisals, 'Other Non-Derogable Obligations', in Crawford et al (above) 1205–14, at 1206–8.

236. See *USA v Iran* para. 86 (above); *Armed Activities on the Territory of the Congo (Democratic Republic of the Congo v Uganda)* (2005) paras 323–31; VCDR Arts 45–6.

237. Para. 95 *USA v Iran* (above).

tional and human rights obligations to protect freedom of speech and assembly.[238]

Richard Gardiner has highlighted that one may detect 'a developing shift in the position of diplomats'[239] in the context of the balancing that takes place when judges determine whether demonstrations outside embassies are compatible with the host state's 'special duty to take all appropriate steps to protect the premises of the mission against any intrusion or damage and to prevent any disturbance of the peace of the mission or impairment of its dignity'.[240] He considers the approach of the Australian judiciary, in the context of a protest involving the planting of 124 white crosses next to a footpath on the grass outside the Indonesian Embassy (in response to the 1991 Dili massacre in East Timor), and notes the emphasis the judges gave to domestic traditions of free expression and international human rights obligations with regard to freedom of speech and assembly. In the words of French J:

> It does not seem that a protest or demonstration conducted outside the premises of a diplomatic mission would by reason of its critical content and mere proximity to the mission amount to an impairment of its dignity. On similar reasoning it would not amount to an attack on the dignity of the relevant diplomatic agent. Whether proximity might give rise to

---

238. For a selection of cases decided in the US, Australia, and the UK see Denza above at 169–75.

239. *International Law* (above) at 355.

240. VCDR Art. 22(2).

the possibility of impairment of the dignity of the mission or an attack upon the dignity of the agent is another question. But it is difficult to see how the lawful placement of a reproachful and dignified symbol on public land in the vicinity of a mission would amount to a disturbance of its peace or an impairment of its dignity or an attack upon the dignity of its officers.[241]

241. *Ministry of Foreign Affairs and Trade v Magno* (1992) 101 ILR 202 at 232.

VII | Treaties

CONTRACTUAL engagements between states are called by various names—treaties, conventions, pacts, acts, declarations, protocols, to name just a few. Several of these terms are used in multiple ways. For example 'protocol' is a word with many meanings in diplomacy, denoting the minutes of the proceedings at an international conference, or the formalities used in addressing dignitaries. But a Protocol may also be a supplementary addendum to another treaty, e.g. the Kyoto Protocol of 1997 which is linked to the United Nations Framework Convention on Climate Change, or the Additional Protocols to the 1949 Geneva Conventions for the protection of victims of war. Similarly, a Declaration may be attached to a variety of texts and statements which cannot be seen as encompassing legal rights and obligations, or it may constitute a legally binding engagement, such as the St Petersburg Declaration of 1868, a treaty by which the signatory parties renounced the use of certain exploding bullets in time of war between themselves. In short treaties are given a variety of titles, and the position is sometimes further confused by the deliberate avoidance of the word 'treaty', in order to sidestep certain constitutional requirements before a 'treaty' can enter into force.[1]

§ 1. When is an agreement a treaty?

From the perspective of international law, whatever label a treaty is given, if it is indeed a treaty it will be covered by the law of treaties. The following definition has been suggested to illustrate the main elements of a treaty: 'an *agreement*, of a suitable *formal character*, designed to give rise to *legal rights and obligations*, operating *within the sphere of international law*, and concluded between two or more parties possessing *legal personality under international law*.'[2]

---

1. See the discussion at the ILC of the first report by Brierly as ILC Special Rapporteur of the on the law of treaties, I *Yearbook of the ILC* (1950) at 64–90, and esp. at 70 where UN ASG Kerno explains that the agreement concerning the UN headquarters and the United States was entitled 'agreement' rather than 'treaty' so as to be able to pass by simple majority in the Congress rather than by a two-thirds majority in the Senate. The US nomenclature for binding international agreements is explained by Trimble who succinctly covers the history and implications of the President choosing a particular procedure: submission to the Senate under Article II of the Constitution (a 'treaty'); congressional authorization 'congressional-executive agreements'; executive agreements deriving their authority from an Article II treaty; and 'presidential-executive agreements' based on the President's foreign relations power. *International Law: United States Foreign Relations Law* (New York: Foundation Press, 2002) at 113–40. All four procedures result in international agreements binding on the United States in international law. The effects in internal law will, however, vary: see ibid 132–40 and 152–77.

2. I. Roberts (ed.), *Satow's Diplomatic Practice*, 6th edn, (Oxford: OUP, 2009) ch. 35 (F. Berman) at 535. Cf P. Reuter 'A treaty is an expression of concurring wills attributable to two or more subjects of international law and intended to have legal effects under the rules of international law.' P. Reuter, *Introduction to the Law of Treaties*, J. Mico and P. Haggenmacher (trans.), 2nd edn (London: Kegan Paul, 1995) at 30.

The notion of legal personality here would clearly cover intergov-ernmental organizations entitled to enter into treaty obligations;[3] similarly certain rebel groups have also been considered as having entered into binding international agreements.[4]

British practice stresses that a 'Memorandum of Understand-ing' is a term used for an instrument which is not usually a treaty

---

3. The fascinating topic of the limits to international legal personality highlights the ten-sion between those competing for change and stability in international law. The tempta-tion to embark on an excursus on the 'subjects' of international law will be resisted here. The reader is referred to two book-length treatments of the way in which this debate has evolved: and R. Portmann, *Legal Personality in International Law* (Cambridge: CUP, 2010); J. E. Nijman, *The Concept of International Legal Personality: An Inquiry Into the History and Theory of International Law* (The Hague: T.M.C. Asser Press, 2004). Suffice it to note that Brierly explained that his original proposed articles on the law of treaties prepared for the ILC differed 'from any existing draft in recognizing the capacity of inter-national organizations to be parties to treaties'. Although the Harvard draft considered agreements of international organizations abnormal and *sui generis*, Brierly concluded: 'It is now, however, impossible to ignore this class of agreements or to regard the existence as an abnormal feature of international relations.' II *Yearbook of the ILC* (1950) at 228. The issue was eventually dealt with in a separate treaty concluded in 1986, the Vienna Con-vention on the Law of Treaties between States and International Organizations or Between International Organizations. For an introduction to the other entities entitled to enter into treaties see Reuter (above) at 32–3.

4. Report of the International Commission of Inquiry on Darfur to the UN Secretary-General, 25 January 2005, at paras 76, 168–74. See further A. Cassese, *International Law*, 2nd edn (Oxford: OUP, 2005) at 127–8. Cf O. Corten and P. Klein, 'Are Agree-ments between States and Non-State Entities Rooted in the International Legal Order?' in E. Cannizzaro (ed.), *The Law of Treaties beyond the Vienna Convention* (Oxford: OUP, 2010) 3–24. In the present chapter the parties to treaties are usually referred to as states parties but of course this is simply to keep the prose as clear and unencumbered as possible; it should not be seen as implying that the only parties to treaties are necessarily states.

and does not as such have binding legal effects.[5] States and international organizations resort to such memoranda for multiple reasons: they may wish to avoid being in a situation where a breach of the obligations could be met with a hearing before a court of law or with countermeasures; they may wish to keep the entire arrangement secret; they may consider the issues too fluid or open-ended to be concretized in a treaty; there may be doubts about the international personality of the other party; or they may not want to go through the internal procedures which might be necessary for a treaty to enter into force.[6]

Disputes do arise as to whether a single text or an exchange of notes (sometimes also called an exchange of letters) should be considered an agreement giving rise to binding rights and obligations in international law. Two cases before the International Court of Justice (ICJ) illustrate how the issue has been approached. In the *Aegean Sea Continental Shelf Case* the Court was faced with a claim by Greece that a joint press communiqué by the Prime Ministers of Greece and Turkey was a legally binding agreement which could be used to establish the jurisdiction of the ICJ with regard to a continental shelf dispute between the two states. The Court noted that the Communiqué 'does not bear any signature or ini-

---

5. Again the situation is confusing as some memoranda of understanding (MoUs) are designed as treaties and operate as treaties. For example the UN adopts MoUs with its member states and with other international organizations and considers and registers these as binding agreements.

6. See A. Aust, *Modern Treaty Law and Practice*, 2nd edn (Cambridge: CUP, 2007) ch. 3, and *Satow's Diplomatic Practice* (above) at 538–41. An MoU that is not a treaty may have legal consequences even though it is not legally binding see Aust at 52–7, *contra* J. Klabbers, *The Concept of Treaty in International Law* (The Hague: Kluwer, 1996) at 111–19.

tials', and the Turkish Government claimed that in order to be an international agreement it would have to be 'ratified at least on the part of Turkey'.[7] With regard to the question of form the Court observed that:

> it knows of no rule of international law which might preclude a joint communiqué from constituting an international agreement to submit a dispute to arbitration or judicial settlement... Accordingly, whether the Brussels Communiqué of 31 May 1975 does or does not constitute such an agreement essentially depends on the nature of the act or transaction to which the Communiqué gives expression; and it does not settle the question simply to refer to the form—a communiqué—in which that act or transaction is embodied.[8]

The Court went on to determine the nature of the act embodied in the Communiqué by examining 'its actual terms and... the particular circumstances in which it was drawn up'.[9] The Joint Communiqué stated in part: 'They decided [*ont décidé*] that those problems should be resolved [*doivent être résolus*] peacefully by means of negotiations and as regards the continental shelf of the Aegean Sea by the International Court at The Hague.'[10] The Court found that Turkey, in the run up to the Brussels meeting, 'was ready to consider a *joint* submission of the dispute to the Court by

---

7. *Greece v Turkey* (1978) at para. 95.

8. Ibid para. 96.

9. Ibidem.

10. Ibid para. 97.

means of a *special agreement*.[11] The Court therefore stated that, having regard to the terms and the context of the Communiqué, it 'can only conclude that it was not intended to, and did not, constitute an immediate commitment' by the two governments to submit the dispute to the Court.[12]

In another dispute the Court had to determine the nature of, first, an exchange of letters, and second, Minutes of a meeting between the Foreign Ministers of Qatar and Bahrain in the presence of the Foreign Minister of Saudi Arabia.[13] The parties agreed, and the Court concluded, that the exchange of Notes constituted a binding international agreement. And the Court found that the Minutes of the subsequent meeting: 'enumerate the commitments to which the Parties have consented. They thus create rights and obligations in international law for the Parties. They constitute an international agreement.'[14] The Court then went on to see if these agreements constituted consent to the jurisdiction of the Court and concluded that they did. The Foreign Minister of Bahrain had stated that 'at no time did I consider that in signing the Minutes I was committing Bahrain to a legally binding agreement'.[15] But the Court did not consider the intentions of the Foreign Ministers; it focused on the text and the context in which it was agreed.

For present purposes, the significance of these two cases decided by the ICJ is that an agreement binding in international law

---

11. Ibid para. 105.

12. Ibid 107.

13. Maritime *Delimitation and Territorial Questions between Qatar and Bahrain (Jurisdiction and admissibility)* ICJ Rep. (1994) p. 114.

14. At para. 25.

15. At para. 26.

(treaty) need not necessarily be signed. Such an agreement will contain international rights and obligations, and is capable of being objectively determined to exist—even in the presence of later protestations that one of the parties did not intend the agreement to be legally binding.[16] States are not above the law of treaties; they cannot pick and choose when to be bound by this law.

§ 2. When is an international text not a treaty?

First, an international agreement is not a treaty when it is clear that the agreement is not supposed to be legally binding. As we have just seen, Courts will take into account the context and the content of the agreement. Anthony Aust, a former Deputy Legal Adviser of the British Foreign Office, has experienced various 'misunderstandings' with regard to the status of different texts after they have been finalized. He suggests in his book on treaty law and practice that, in order to avoid any such confusion, the state that intends the instrument to be non-binding write to the other government as follows: 'all the necessary legal requirements having been completed, the instrument will now come into operation on the understanding that it does not constitute a treaty and neither side will publish it as a treaty or register it as a treaty with the United Nations.'[17]

---

16. For a stimulating examination of the minimal role given to intent in determining the existence of a treaty see Klabbers (above) whose examination of the case-law leads him to conclude there is a 'presumption that agreements are intended to be legally binding'. At 257.
17. Aust (above) at 37.

Furthermore, the sort of dispute mechanism built into the agreement may also point to its intended legal effects. Inserting an agreement to submit differences to an international tribunal or arbitrator, and to be bound in international law by the ruling, would obviously suggest that the text is a treaty. Aust's template for a (non-binding) Memorandum of Understanding includes the following paragraph to remove any ambiguity: 'Any dispute about the interpretation or application of this Memorandum will be resolved by consultations between the Participants, and will not be referred to any national or international tribunal or third party for settlement.'[18]

In short, those wishing to avoid the legal effects of any instrument they are negotiating would be best advised to explain this in the text, exclude the procedures normally used for the entry into force for treaties, and be exhaustively clear who has the authority to settle disputes over the text and whether any such ruling is legally binding on the parties.[19]

A second instance where an international agreement will not be a treaty is when the agreement does not take effect under international law—but rather in national law.[20] The representatives of

---

18. Ibid 492.

19. Aust includes a table of comparative treaty and MoU terminology to assist drafters in distinguishing legally binding treaties from other agreements. Ibid 496. On occasion states are quite clear about the type of text they are adopting. Consider the title of the 'Non-Legally Binding Authoritative Statement of Principles for a Global Consensus on the Management, Conservation and Sustainable Development of all Types of Forests' adopted in Rio in 1992 at the UN Conference on Environment and Development; cf the Helsinki Final Act which includes a paragraph stating that the text 'is not eligible for registration under Article 102 of the Charter of the United Nations', see further § 6 below.

20. See the definition of a treaty in the Vienna Convention on the Law of Treaties (1969) Art. 2(1)(a) and the Commentary of the ILC II Yearbook ILC (1966) at 188, para. 6.

two states may sign an agreement to lease some premises, or for the simple purchase of certain goods, and intend any such agreement to be a normal contract generating no international rights or obligations for the parties. Again it may not always be easy to determine whether the parties intend the agreement to be governed by international law or not. By the time this comes to be determined by a judge it means that the parties are in dispute as to what was their intention, and an objective finding will be problematic.[21]

§ 3. Formation of treaties and the issue of coercion

International law has no technical rules for the formation of treaties. In most respects the general principles applicable to private contracts apply; there must be consent and capacity on both sides, and the object must be legal; though naturally, rules peculiar to a special system of municipal law, such as the Common Law rules about consideration, have no application.[22] Previous editions of this book highlighted 'one startling difference' between contract law and trea-

---

21. M. Koskenniemi, *From Apology to Utopia. The Structure of International Legal Argument* (Cambridge: CUP, 2005) at 333–45.

22. In the Common Law a valid contract requires that one side offers something of value and that this is met with consideration by the other side doing something in return. This can be a simple sale of an item for money, or services in return for a fee, or a promise to do something in return for the other side not doing something and so on. A treaty may create an obligation for a state even in the absence of anything of value (a consideration). The origin of this condition for contracts under the Common Law stems from the time when contracts were oral and judges sought a way to distinguish them from gifts. Treaties may be oral but would still not require consideration. Under US law oral international agreements have to be submitted in writing and notified to Congress, Aust (above) at 39–40.

ties. They unambiguously stated: 'Duress does not invalidate consent, as it does in the private law of contract. A dictated treaty is as valid legally as one freely entered into on both sides.' This position is no longer tenable. Indeed already in 1963, the same year as the publication of the last edition of this book, Sir Humphrey Waldock, as the International Law Commission's Special Rapporteur on the law of treaties, included in his second report on the law of treaties two proposed articles on duress and coercion. In the first, Waldock proposed that: '[i]f coercion, actual or threatened, physical or mental, with respect to their persons or to matters of personal concern, has been employed against individual representatives of a State…in order to induce such representative to sign, ratify, accept, approve or accede to a treaty, the State in question shall be entitled' to declare the representative's act to be nullified and the treaty to be void from the beginning.[23]

The second draft Article provided that a state could similarly consider the treaty void if it 'is coerced into entering into a treaty through an act of force, or threat of force, employed against it in violation of the principles of the Charter of the United Nations'.[24] Waldock rejected the idea that states would be able to allege coercion simply to avoid their treaty obligations, stating that as long as coercion was limited to the use of force, rather than economic coercion, there could be an objective determination of whether force had been used or threatened, and the subjective element would be reduced. He also rejected both the argument that such a rule would lead to general uncertainty about the status of peace

---

23. II *Yearbook ILC* (1963) at 50.
24. Ibid 51.

treaties, and the argument that peace should take precedence over 'abstract justice'. Waldock argued that, starting from the time when the use of force became prohibited in international law, and considering that such use of force had been declared to be criminal by the Nuremberg and Tokyo Tribunals, one had to question whether a treaty resulting from such acts could be considered valid. These proposals and arguments were accepted in the International Law Commission (ILC) and the eventual Vienna Convention on the Law of Treaties (1969) adopted two articles along similar lines and confirmed that coercion against a state leads to the invalidity of the treaty in its entirety.[25]

Three important questions arise. First, at what point did the prohibition on the use of force crystallize into a rule of international law so that coercion would render a resulting treaty null and void? Second, to what extent can the use of force be interpreted as covering economic pressure? Third, might there not be situations where an aggressor state ought to be coerced into accepting a peace treaty or agreeing to pay reparations? All these questions were addressed in the context of the process leading to the adoption of the Convention on the Law of Treaties, and we will briefly discuss them here, as they sit on the fault line of a fundamental shift in international law in the twentieth century.

The ILC explained its understanding of the law: 'a peace treaty or other treaty procured by coercion prior to the establishment of the modern law regarding the threat or use of force' would remain valid. However, the Commission considered it would be 'illogical

---

25. Arts 51, 52, and 44(5); note with regard to a multilateral treaty the non-coerced parties will still be bound by a valid treaty: Art. 69(4).

and unacceptable to formulate the rule as one applicable only from the date of the conclusion of a convention on the law of treaties'. The Commission determined:

> whatever differences of opinion there may be about the state of the law prior to the establishment of the United Nations, the great majority of international lawyers to-day unhesitatingly hold that Article 2, paragraph 4, together with other provisions of the Charter, authoritatively declares the modern customary law regarding the threat or use of force. The present article, by its formulation, recognizes by implication that the rule which it lays down is applicable at any rate to all treaties concluded since the entry into force of the Charter.[26]

An amendment, successfully tabled by Czechoslovakia and others at the Vienna Conference,[27] adjusted the wording of what became Article 52 to refer to the 'use of force in *violation of the principles of*

---

26. II *Yearbook of the ILC* (1966) at 247. The rule has been affirmed by the ICJ as part of 'contemporary international law' in *Fisheries Jurisdiction (UK v Iceland) Jurisdiction* (1973) but the Court found that the Exchange of Notes had been 'freely negotiated by the interested parties on the basis of perfect equality and freedom of decision on both sides'. At para. 24.

27. *Official Records of the Vienna* Conference, first session, at 271, 2 May 1968. On the effects of the threats of the use of force on the 1939 treaty signed by the President of Czechoslovakia creating a German protectorate over Bohemia and Moravia and on the 1938 Munich Agreement see *Oppenheim's International Law*, 9th edn at 1290–1, nn1 and 8. It is worth noting that the October 1968 treaty between Czechoslovakia and the USSR allowing for the presence of Soviet forces can also be considered invalid; for details of the events leading up this treaty see N. Stürchler, *The Threat of Force in International Law* (Cambridge: CUP, 2007) at 184–9.

international law embodied in the Charter of the United Nations'. The Delegation of Czechoslovakia explained that it shared the opinion of the ILC that the rule applied retroactively, and the main purpose of their amendment aimed at the time element. They also agreed, however, that the Convention could not 'specify on what precise date an existing general rule in another branch of international law had come to be established'.[28]

Turning to our second question, the ILC's Commentary reveals that '[s]ome members of the Commission expressed the view that any other forms of pressure, such as a threat to strangle the economy of a country, ought to be stated in the article as falling within the concept of coercion'.[29] Yet the Commission eventually preferred to leave the issue to be determined by an interpretation of the concept of the use of force as found in the Charter. Several states sought to have the draft changed before and during the Vienna Diplomatic Conference. An amendment proposed by 19 states at the Conference sought to define force as including economic and political pressure.[30] Economic pressure was argued to be a form of neo-colonialism imposed on the newly independent states.[31] According to negotiators from the United States delegation it was 'clear that if the amendment were put to the vote it

---

28. See at 179.

29. Ibid 246.

30. Afghanistan, Algeria, Bolivia, Congo (Brazzaville), Ecuador, Ghana, India, Iran, Kenya, Kuwait, Mali, Pakistan, Sierra Leone, Syria, Tanzania, United Arab Republic, Yugoslavia, and Zambia.

31. See also M. Craven, 'What Happened to Unequal Treaties? The Continuities of Informal Empire', in M. Craven and M. Fitzmaurice (eds), *Interrogating the Treaty* (Nijmegen: Wolf, 2005) 43–80.

would carry by quite a substantial majority. On the other hand, in private discussions it had been made quite clear to the proponents that adoption could wreck the conference because states concerned with the stability of treaties found the proposal intolerable.'[32] In the end a compromise was reached whereby the attempted amendment of the article would be abandoned in return for the adoption by the Conference of a: 'Declaration on the Prohibition of Military, Political or Economic Coercion in the Conclusion of Treaties', which formed part of the Final Act of the Conference.[33]

Thirdly, Waldock was concerned that invalidating treaties procured through the use of force should not upend the possibility of peace treaties imposed on defeated aggressor states. In his words: 'Clearly, there is all the difference in the world between coercion used by an aggressor to consolidate the fruits of his aggression in a treaty and coercion used to impose a peace settlement upon an aggressor.'[34] In part this problem is met by the prohibition of the

---

32. R.D. Kearney and R.E. Dalton, 'The Treaty on Treaties', 64 AJIL (1970) 495–561, at 534. Sinclair explains the 'intense misgivings' of those 'delegations concerned to preserve the security and sanctity of treaties'. 'Acceptance of the concept that economic pressure could operate to render a treaty null and void would appear, if these sweeping views as to the dominant position of developed countries were accepted, to invite claims which would put at risk any treaty concluded between a developing and a developed country.' *The Vienna Convention on the Law of Treaties*, 2nd edn (Manchester: MUP, 1984) at 178.

33. Para. 1 reads: 'Solemnly condemns the threat or use of pressure in any form, whether military, political, or economic, by any State in order to coerce another State to perform any act relating to the conclusion of a treaty in violation of the principles of the sovereign equality of States and freedom of consent.' For the implications of the Declaration with regard to the interpretation of Article 52 see M.E. Villiger, *Commentary on the 1969 Vienna Convention on the Law of Treaties* (Leiden: Nijhoff, 2009) at 638–57.

34. Second Report on the Law of Treaties, II *Yearbook of the ILC* (1963) at 52.

illegal use of force in the definition of coercion,[35] but there was the additional fear of 'one party unilaterally characterizing another as an aggressor for the purpose of terminating inconvenient treaties'.[36] The concern to preserve the idea that a treaty could impose obligations on an aggressor state was, in the end, met with a savings clause in Article 75 which states that the Vienna Convention is without prejudice to: 'any obligation in relation to a treaty which may arise for an aggressor State in consequence of measures taken in conformity with the Charter of the United Nations with reference to that State's aggression'.[37]

Answering these questions has highlighted how international law can radically change direction, and how such change may sometimes be brought through individuals arguing for one solution over another. Until the articulation of the rule invalidating treaties procured through coercion, it was assumed that priority should be given to peace, stability, and the effectiveness of international law, even if this meant that powerful states could profit from their illegal use of force and historical coercion. In prioritizing justice and the prohibition on the use of force, law is elevated to something which is more than an instrument for states, something

---

35. So a peace settlement could be valid even if coerced, as long as the coercion follows from a peace enforcement operation authorized by the Security Council, or as the result of force used in self-defence. But a transfer of territory would remain invalid; see Ch. V § 2 above.

36. Draft Articles with Commentary by the ILC, II *Yearbook of the ILC* (1966) at 268.

37. The concrete effect of this provision is unclear, perhaps the import lies in the idea that 'an aggressor State should not be able to gain any profit (in this case in the form of the provisions of the Convention) from the aggression it has committed'. Villiger (above) at 918.

over and above a convenient medium for interaction. Moreover in this example, international law's apparent lack of legislative and executive branches is contradicted first by recourse to the UN Charter as universal law, and second by alluding to the role of the Security Council as the entity entitled to authorize the use of force and impose obligations on states that violate the fundamental rule prohibiting aggression.[38]

We have also seen that treaty law is not just contract law applied to states. In contract law any use of force against another party (duress) would nullify the contract. In treaty law it is only the *illegal* use of force that makes the treaty void. So where the Security Council authorizes force to be used against a state, and the state

---

38. Brierly's frustration with this topic may therefore have been partially addressed. In his fifth edition he wrote at this point: 'the change to which we ought to look forward is not the elimination of the use of coercion from the transaction, but the establishment of international machinery to ensure that when coercion is used it shall be in a proper case and by due process of law, and not, as at present it may be, arbitrarily. The problem of treaties imposed by force is therefore in its essence not a problem of treaty law, but a particular aspect of that much wider problem which pervades the whole system, that of subordinating the use of force to law.' At 245. See also his much earlier dissatisfaction: 'It is not within the powers of international lawyers to bring about a change in the law in this respect, but it is within our powers, when we are stating what the law is, to clear our heads of cant; and if we do so we shall surely say that no shred of sanctity attaches to a treaty into which one party has been coerced, nor is good faith in the least engaged in its observance. Such a treaty creates a purely factual relation between the parties, though one which the law must at present uphold, and moral sentiments are singularly out of place in the discussion of it. Let us recognize candidly the existence of a blot upon the system, and admit that here, not as a matter of morality, but for practical utilitarian reasons, *la force prime le droit*.' 'Some Considerations on the Obsolescence of Treaties' paper read before the Grotius Society, 24 March 1925, in *The Basis of Obligation in International Law and Other Papers*, 108–16 at 115.

then enters into a treaty obligation as a result, the state cannot later claim the treaty was void due to coercion or lack of consent.[39]

§ 4. Signature and ratification

Ordinarily there are two stages in the making of a treaty, its signature by 'plenipotentiaries' of the contracting states, and its ratification by or on behalf of the heads of those states.[40] There are good reasons why this second stage should be necessary before a treaty, at any rate an important treaty, becomes actually binding. In some states, constitutional law vests the treaty-making power in some organ which cannot delegate it to plenipotentiaries, and yet that organ cannot itself carry on negotiations with other states. For

---

39. Aust (above) offers an illustration: 'The Agreement concerning the restoration of the Government of President Aristide, signed in Port au Prince on 18 September 1994 by the provisional President of Haiti and ex-US President Jimmy Carter on behalf of US President Bill Clinton, might at first sight appear to have been obtained by the threat of unlawful force, since at the time US bombers were in the air on their way to Haiti. However, the Security Council had adopted on 16 October 1993 Resolution 875 which authorized the use of force to restore the legitimate government of Haiti.' At 318. Compare the discussion of the use of force by the United States against Haitian representatives in 1905, and against Cuba in 1903, in the Harvard Research Draft Convention on the Law of Treaties *AJIL Special Supplement* (1935) 'Duress', at 1148–61, esp. 1157–9. See also I. Sinclair (above) at 180 who points out that 'the sanction of nullity will not apply to a treaty imposed by the United Nations, in the course of enforcement action, upon a State guilty of an act of aggression'.

40. A plenipotentiary is literally someone with full powers. The 1969 VCLT defines full powers in Art. 2(1)(c) as the document from the competent authority authorizing the relevant acts. Today it is assumed that the Foreign Minister, the Head of Government, and the Head of State all have full powers to adopt, sign, or consent to be bound by, a treaty: see Art. 7(2), Art. 46 (discussed in § 8 below).

example, in the United States the treaty-making power is vested in the President, but subject to the advice and consent of the Senate for certain treaties.[41]

But apart from such cases where national law demands that a political body approve the treaty, it may be that the interests with which a treaty deals are so complicated and important that it is reasonable that there should be a further opportunity for considering the treaty as a whole.[42] A democratic state must consult public opinion, and this can hardly take shape while the negotiations, which may be largely confidential, are going on.

Ratification is not, however, a legal requisite for all treaties. There are many agreements of minor importance in which ratification would be an unreasonable formality, and normally the treaty itself states, either expressly or by implication, whether it is to become binding on signature or only when it has been ratified.

States which have not taken part in the negotiation of a treaty, and so were not in a position to sign the treaty following its adoption, are sometimes invited by the negotiating states to become parties by 'acceding' to the treaty.[43] This expression is employed

---

41. For an explanation as to which procedure is appropriate in the United States see Trimble (above). For speculation as to why the parties to an agreement might prefer that it be subject to the advice and consent of the Senate see J.L. Goldsmith and E.A. Posner, *The Limits of International Law* (New York: OUP, 2005) at 91–5.

42. For the UK constitutional practice see Aust (above) at 189–94. See now section 20 of the Constitutional Reform and Governance Act 2010; J. Barrett, 'The United Kingdom and Parliamentary Scrutiny of Treaties: Recent Reforms', 60 *ICLQ* (2011) 225–45.

43. Although accession may be used simply to denote the way in which parties become bound where the treaty does not provide for signature and ratification. E.g. the Convention on Privileges and Immunities of the United Nations (1946).

because they are not engaged in ratifying their signature, but simply becoming parties to the treaty in a one-step process. Other expressions which are used to denote the equivalent step are adhesion, acceptance, and approval.[44]

The treaty should specify when it is to enter into force. For a treaty merely requiring signature this could be immediately. In the case of a complex multilateral treaty it may be specified that the treaty enters into force for the parties once a fixed number of states have become parties. For example the Genocide Convention entered into force on the 90th day following the 20th state becoming a party.

§ 5. Reservations

In accepting a treaty, a state sometimes formulates a 'reservation', that is to say, it proposes a new term which limits or varies the application of the treaty.[45] When a treaty has only two parties, the matter is simple; if the other party does not accept the tendered reservation the treaty will fall. If the other party accepts the

---

44. See further *Satow's Diplomatic Practice* (above) at 583–9.

45. It may be convenient here to reproduce the composite definition of a reservation included in the ILC's Guide to Practice on Reservations to Treaties (2011) (ILC Guide) reproduced in UN Doc. A/66/10: 1.1 ' "Reservation" means a unilateral statement, however phrased or named, made by a State or an international organization when signing, ratifying, formally confirming, accepting, approving or acceding to a treaty, or by a State when making a notification of succession to a treaty, whereby the State or organization purports to exclude or to modify the legal effect of certain provisions of the treaty in their application to that State or to that international organization.' For 'interpretive declarations' see paras 1.3, and 2.4 and the Commentaries thereto.

reservation, we are in the presence of an amended text, and for this reason it is more usual to speak of amendments, or offers to rene-gotiate, in the context of bilateral treaties.[46] But when there are numerous parties the matter becomes more complicated, for some of these other parties may be willing to accept the reservation and others may not. And some may be willing to see the reserving state become a party to the treaty and others may not.

With regard to reservations to such multilateral treaties there is an underlying policy factor at play: is it better to have a maximum number of states join the treaty, albeit with reservations which adjust their obligations and the rights and obligations of all the other parties? Or is it preferable to see the treaty regime in terms of uniform rights and obligations, even at the expense of excluding those states who wish to join with reservations? We can see here the need to bear in mind two principles. First, we have 'the desirabil-ity of maintaining the integrity of international multilateral con-ventions'. And here the desire is not merely to maintain integrity for integrity's sake, but due to the role played by multilateral con-ventions: 'It is to be preferred that some degree of uniformity in the obligations of all parties to a multilateral instrument should be maintained. One of the ways in which international law is devel-oped is by a consistent rule of general application being laid down in multilateral…conventions.' 'Frequent or numerous reservations by States to multilateral conventions of international concern hinder the development of international law by preventing the

---

46. See further the ILC Guide Commentary to 1.6.1 'Reservations' to bilateral treaties. The United States practice is to communicate 'reservations' to its bilateral partners; these are then usually incorporated into a fresh text and agreed.

growth of a consistent rule of general application.' 'Secondly, and on the other hand, there is the desirability of the widest possible application of multilateral conventions. It may be assumed, from the very fact that they are multilateral, that the subjects with which they deal are of international concern, i.e., matters which are not only susceptible of international regulation but regarding which it is desirable to reform or amend existing law. If they are to be effective, multilateral conventions must be as widely in force or as generally accepted as possible.'[47]

These competing desires came to be described as a choice between integrity and universality.[48] The answer to this dilemma must be that it depends on the type of treaty regime being established.[49] The Law of the Sea Convention and the Statute of the International Criminal Court state that no reservations are permitted. For such treaties it makes sense that states cannot pick and choose obligations and undermine the integrity of the regime. On the other hand, a treaty for judicial co-operation may restrict the

---

47. All quotes from Brierly, Special Rapporteur on the law of treaties, 'Report on Reservations to Multilateral Conventions' UN Doc. A/CN.4/41, II *ILC Yearbook* (1951) 1–17 at paras 11–12.

48. See Joint Dissenting Opinion by Judges Guerrero, McNair, Read, and Hsu Mo, Advisory Opinion on *Reservations to the Convention on Genocide* ICJ Rep. (1951) p. 15, at 46–7.

49. Note the VCLT includes the following provisions: Article 20(3) 'When a treaty is a constituent instrument of an international organization and unless it otherwise provides, a reservation requires the acceptance of the competent organ of that organization.' For certain plurilateral treaties a reservation will have to be accepted unanimously. 'When it appears from the limited number of the negotiating States and the object and purpose of a treaty that the application of the treaty in its entirety between all the parties is an essential condition of the consent of each one to be bound by the treaty, a reservation requires acceptance by all the parties.' Art. 20(2).

topics on which states parties are prepared to co-operate, and may have to be adjusted to fit the different domestic legal orders. In this way certain reservations may actually facilitate greater participation and ultimately a wider range of possibilities for co-operation.[50] States which might otherwise feel obliged to remain outside the regime may feel comfortable joining with reservations and other states may be ready to accept this situation.

Where a treaty is silent on the issue of reservations, or only allows for specified reservations, a problem arises where some states object to the proposed reservation. Is the state attempting to make the reservation to be considered a party to the treaty? This question was put to the International Court of Justice in connection with reservations to the Genocide Convention. At that time it had been assumed that the rule in the law of treaties was that reservations had to be accepted by all parties to the treaty in order for the reserving state to be considered a party to the treaty.[51] Reservations had been made, in particular by eight states excluding the jurisdiction of the Court for inter-state disputes, and some states had objected to some of these reservations. The question originally had a practical dimension. The UN Secretary-General, as depositary of the treaty, needed to know whether the requisite number of parties had been reached for the treaty to enter into force. Although this point was moot by the time the Court delivered its opinion, the question still remained whether the reserving states could be considered parties to the treaty.

---

50. Consider the European Convention on Mutual Assistance in Criminal Matters (1959) and its multiple reservations.
51. *Reservations to the Convention on Genocide*, ICJ Rep. (1951) p. 15, at 31.

The Court took into consideration the nature of the Genocide Convention as something concluded under the auspices of the United Nations, an organization of universal character envisaging a wide degree of participation in the Convention. Furthermore, the Court pointed out: 'that although the Genocide Convention was finally approved unanimously, it is nevertheless the result of a series of majority votes. The majority principle, while facilitating the conclusion of multilateral conventions, may also make it necessary for certain States to make reservations.'[52] The Court concluded that even though the Convention was silent on the issue of reservations, taking into consideration the character, purpose, provisions, mode of preparation and adoption of the Convention, reservations were permitted. It then addressed the questions: what kinds of reservations were permitted? What kind of objections can be made to them? And what are the effects of such objections?

The Court recalled the intention to create a Convention which would be universal in scope, and went on to state that in this type of Convention: 'the contracting States do not have any interests of their own; they merely have, one and all a common interest, namely, the accomplishment of those high purposes which are the *raison d'être* of the convention.'[53] This represented a radical departure from the traditional idea that treaties were founded on state consent; the Court prioritized a common interest over individual interests. The implication was that reservations would be valid not according to the unanimous consent of the states parties, but according to the compatibility of the reservations with the *raison*

---

52. Advisory Opinion, ibid 22.

53. Ibid 23.

d'être of the Convention. The Court (by a majority of seven to five) prioritized universality over integrity:

> The object and purpose of the Genocide Convention imply that it was the intention of the General Assembly and of the States which adopted it that as many States as possible should participate. The complete exclusion from the Convention of one or more States would not only restrict the scope of its application, but would detract from the authority of the moral and humanitarian principles which are its basis. It is inconceivable that the contracting parties readily contemplated that an objection to a minor reservation should produce such a result. But even less could the contracting parties have intended to sacrifice the very object of the Convention in favour of a vain desire to secure as many participants as possible. The object and purpose of the Convention thus limit both the freedom of making reservations and that of objecting to them. It follows that it is the compatibility of a reservation with the object and purpose of the Convention that must furnish the criterion for the attitude of a State in making the reservation on accession...
>
> It has nevertheless been argued that any State entitled to become a party to the Genocide Convention may do so while making any reservation it chooses by virtue of its sovereignty. The Court cannot share this view. It is obvious that so extreme an application of the idea of State sovereignty could lead to a complete disregard of the object and purpose of the Convention.[54]

---

54. Ibid 24.

The Court held that, in the case before it, a state making a reservation to which some, but not all the parties, objected would become a party, if its reservation should be 'compatible with the object and purpose of the convention', but not otherwise. The problem is that in many situations the decision on compatibility is left entirely to the other states.

The Vienna Convention follows this logic in the main but, as predicted at the time, such a system has led to confusion and uncertainty. The eventual rule included in the Vienna Convention works as follows: the reservation formulated (at the appropriate time[55]) by the reserving state is circulated to all the parties to the treaty, as well as to all those entitled to become parties to the treaty. These addressees then have a fourfold choice:

- to remain *silent* (S);
- to *accept* the reservation (A);
- to formulate an *objection* to the reservation—but accept that the treaty will enter into force between itself and the reserving state (O);
- to *object* to the reservation and *oppose* the entry into force of the treaty between itself and the reserving state (OO).

Each course of action gives rise to different legal results. In order to assist the reader in understanding the consequences of choosing

---

55. When signing, ratifying, formally confirming, accepting, approving, or acceding to a treaty, or when a state is making a notification of succession to a treaty. Note that although the VCLT states that a reserving state becomes a party once at least one state has accepted the reservation, the practice of the UN Secretary-General is to consider the state that has formulated the reservation to be a party to the treaty as of the date of its instrument joining the treaty. See ILC Guide, Guideline 2.6.12 Commentary para. 6.

one or another response, we here work through the different options, taking an actual reservation as an example, in order to demonstrate how this arrangement is supposed to take effect in practice.

We saw in the previous chapter that there is disagreement over whether the diplomatic pouch can be subject to x-ray or search. On acceding to the Diplomatic Relations Convention in 1977, Libya formulated a reservation to Article 27(3) stating that it 'reserves its right to request the opening of such pouch in the presence of an official representative of the diplomatic mission concerned. If such request is denied by the authorities of the sending state, the diplomatic pouch shall be returned to its place of origin.'[56]

State S which stays *silent* has 12 months to consider whether to object or not.[57] After that time it is considered to have accepted the reservation and will be in the same position as State A which has explicitly *accepted* the reservation. For State A the treaty is in force between it and the reserving state and modified to the extent of the reservation. This may work in a reciprocal fashion.[58] So, in our exam-

---

56. Art. 27(3) states: 'The diplomatic bag shall not be opened or detained.' A number of other Arab states made similar reservations.

57. More precisely, we should say that the state is deemed to have accepted the reservation 'if it shall have raised no objection to the reservation by the end of a period of twelve months after it was notified of the reservation or by the date on which it expressed its consent to be bound by the treaty, whichever is later'. VCLT Art. 20(5). Of course a treaty may specify a different timeline.

58. Note that reciprocity will not apply if this is not appropriate in view of 'nature of the obligations or the object and purpose of the treaty' or where 'reciprocal application is not possible because of the content of the reservation'. ILC Guideline 4.2.5. So for example where France had formulated a reservation to the European Convention on Human

ple, the United Kingdom, having remained silent for 12 months in the face of the Libyan reservation, would be deemed to have accepted it, and the Convention would be in force between the two states. Should the Libyan authorities suspect the content of the British diplomatic bag arriving at Tripoli airport from the Embassy, they would be entitled under the treaty to demand that a UK official be present while the bag is opened. If the United Kingdom refused, and the bag were sent back to the British Embassy in Tripoli, the UK could not complain as the treaty has been modified between these two states. The reciprocal effect of the reservation is as follows: if the British authorities at Heathrow suspect the Libyan diplomatic bag en route to Tripoli they can ask to open it in the presence of a Libyan official. If this is refused the bag can be sent back to the Libyan Embassy in London. Libya could not complain of a violation of the Convention.[59]

For the *objecting* State O the treaty is in force but the relevant provision does not apply to the extent of the reservation. This would mean that neither state would be legally obliged to allow the bag to be opened in the way foreseen in the reservation. Neither the rule forbidding the opening of the bag nor the modified

---

Rights with regard to the threshold for a state of emergency in France, Turkey could not rely on that reservation when France brought a complaint against Turkey for human rights violations in Turkey. The European Commission stressed that the Convention created 'objective obligations' and that complaints about a breach of the Convention were not actions to enforce a state's own rights but rather 'an alleged violation of the public order of Europe'. *France v Turkey* 35 D&R 143, at paras 37–43.

59. The UK authorities chose for political reasons not to challenge the Libyan bags leaving the Libyan Embassy in St James's Square following the shooting of WPC Fletcher outside the Embassy. According to Denza they 'almost certainly contained the murder weapon'. E. Denza, *Diplomatic Law: Commentary on the Vienna Convention on Diplomatic Relations*, 3rd edn (Oxford: OUP, 2008) at 236.

rule allowing for the opening of the bag in certain conditions would apply between the two states.[60] The rest of the provision that states that the bag may not be detained would continue to apply. And indeed the rest of the treaty would apply so that diplomatic agents would remain immune and embassies would remain inviolable and so on.

For State OO that both *objects* to the reservation and *opposes* the entry into force of the treaty between itself and the reserving state, there are no treaty rights and obligations between the two states. Neither state can complain about a violation of any of the provisions of the whole treaty by the other state, nor are they able to use any mechanisms that provide for the settlement of a dispute with regard to the treaty because the treaty is not in force between them.[61]

For all four types of non-reserving state the treaty will apply in its entirety between themselves. Unfortunately the permutations do not end here. We have still not considered the effect of invalid reservations. In making their objections states often claim that the reservation is invalid.[62] While multiple claims of this sort may be evidence that the reservation is indeed contrary to the object and purpose of the treaty, such a claim may be merely subjective, and validity is a separate issue from acceptability. Validity depends first, on whether such reservations are foreseen in the treaty, and

60. The issue would fall to be determined by customary international law. See further Denza (above) 236–7 who discussed some of the similar reservations and objections.

61. Consider for example the Optional Protocol to the Vienna Convention on Diplomatic Relations, concerning the Compulsory Settlement of Disputes (1961).

62. For example Canada responded to Libya's reservation by stating that she did not regard it as valid.

second, on whether the reservation is compatible with the object and purpose of the treaty.[63]

This problem has come to a head in the context of human rights treaties. Human rights treaties are not generally enforced by other states; nor is their object primarily to provide reciprocal benefits for other states. The beneficiaries of a state accepting a human rights treaty are the individual human beings who find themselves under that state's jurisdiction. Supervision of a state's respect for its treaty obligations is usually left to an international human rights court or a treaty monitoring body. Other states can of course object and deny that the treaty enters into force between them and the reserving state—but this can hardly help those the treaty is intended to protect.

Human rights bodies have been faced with seemingly invalid reservations when adjudicating individual petitions. In some cases they have decided to 'sever' invalid reservations, even where a state argues that the reservation was a condition for its accepting to be bound by the treaty in the first place. In these cases the state may have a choice: to leave the relevant treaty regime (where this is possible under the treaty), or decide to remain in the regime without the benefit of the reservation.

The first scenario took place against the background of a reservation formulated by Trinidad and Tobago stating: 'the Human Rights Committee shall not be competent to receive and consider communications relating to any prisoner who is under sentence of death in respect of any matter relating to his prosecution, his detention, his trial, his conviction, his sentence or the carrying out

---

63. VCLT Art. 19.

of the death sentence on him and any matter connected therewith.' The Committee (by a majority) decided that it 'cannot accept a reservation which singles out a certain group of individuals for lesser procedural protection than that which is enjoyed by the rest of the population'. In their view 'this constitutes a discrimination which runs counter to some of the basic principles embodied in the Covenant and its Protocols, and for this reason the reservation cannot be deemed compatible with the object and purpose of the Optional Protocol.'[64] Trinidad and Tobago then denounced the Optional Protocol allowing for individual complaints, and left that treaty regime. This meant that complaints could no longer be brought with regard to alleged violations of any of the provisions of the Covenant on Civil and Political Rights.

The second scenario arose in cases brought against Switzerland and Turkey. In the first case the European Court of Human Rights held that Switzerland's interpretive declaration sought to limit Switzerland's obligations with regard to fair trial and found that the interpretation was invalid as incompatible with the conditions for reservations.[65] The Court went on to apply the provision on fair trial against Switzerland. The Court determined that 'it is beyond doubt that Switzerland is, and regards itself as, bound by the Convention irrespective of the validity of the declaration'.[66] The Turkish declaration conditioning its acceptance of the Court's

---

64. *Rawle Kennedy v Trinidad and Tobago*, Communication 845/1999, Decision of 2 November 1999.

65. For a detailed analysis of the implications of this case see S. Marks, 'Reservations Unhinged: The *Belilos* Case before the European Court of Human Rights', 39 *ICLQ* (1990) 300–27.

66. *Belilos v Switzerland* (1988) para. 60.

jurisdiction sought to restrict the territorial protection of the Convention. It was also considered invalid, and the restrictions were 'severed' from the declaration accepting the jurisdiction of the Court.[67] Both Turkey and Switzerland chose to remain parties to the Convention and to continue to recognize the jurisdiction of the Court.

There are a number of contextual differences relating to these two scenarios which continue to influence the ILC in its work on reservations to treaties. First, the judgments of a regional Court of Human Rights are binding on the states parties. By contrast some states have resisted the idea that a treaty monitoring body which is not empowered to deliver binding judgments should be able to determine the validity of reservations. These states insist on the overriding idea that a treaty only takes effect if the state consents to be bound. For these states a formulated reservation should be seen as a pre-condition of acceptance to be bound by the treaty, and so the consequence of discounting a reservation as invalid is that the reserving state cannot be considered a party to the treaty.[68]

The ILC has struggled with this problem for a number of years, and its Special Rapporteur, Alain Pellet, has now considered the issue in some detail. The ILC Guide to practice includes the following guidelines, which supplement the relevant provisions of the Vienna Convention on the Law of Treaties.[69]

---

67. *Loizidou v Turkey (preliminary objections)* (1995) paras 95–97.
68. See the separate Observations by the United Kingdom, the United States, and France to General Comment 24 of the UN Human Rights Committee, 3 IHRR (1996) at 261–9, and 4 IHRR (1997) at 6–9.
69. See Arts 19–23.

1. The status of the author of an invalid reservation in relation to a treaty depends on the intention expressed by the reserving State or international organization on whether it intends to be bound by the treaty without the benefit of the reservation or whether it considers that it is not bound by the treaty.

2. Unless the author of the invalid reservation has expressed a contrary intention or such an intention is otherwise established, it is considered a contracting State or a contracting organization without the benefit of the reservation.

3. Notwithstanding paragraphs 1 and 2, the author of the invalid reservation may express at any time its intention not to be bound by the treaty without the benefit of the reservation.

4. If a treaty monitoring body expresses the view that a reservation is invalid and the reserving State or international organization intends not to be bound by the treaty without the benefit of the reservation, it should express its intention to that effect within a period of twelve months from the date at which the treaty monitoring body made its assessment.[70]

The solution includes what can be described as a rebuttable 'presumption that the author of the reservation is bound by the treaty without being able to claim the benefit of the reservation, unless the author has expressed the opposite intention'.[71]

The ILC Guidelines also articulate the factors to be taken into account in determining the validity of a reservation. First, the treaty may prohibit certain types of reservation; second, the reservation

---

70. Guideline 4.5.3.

71. Commentary to Guideline 4.5.3 at para. 1.

must not be incompatible with the object and purpose of the treaty. It will be incompatible if 'it affects an essential element of the treaty that is necessary to its general tenour, in such a way that the reservation impairs the *raison d'être* of the treaty'.[72] Third, reservations may not be formulated 'concerning rights from which no derogation is permissible under any circumstances, unless the reservation in question is compatible with the essential rights and obligations arising out of that treaty. In assessing that compatibility, account shall be taken of the importance which the parties have conferred upon the rights at issue by making them non-derogable.'[73] Fourth, a reservation which 'purports to exclude or to modify the legal effect of certain provisions of a treaty or of the treaty as a whole in order to preserve the integrity of specific rules of the internal law of that State ... may be formulated only insofar as it does not affect an essential element of the treaty nor its general tenour'.[74] Fifth, in order to assess compatibility with the object and purpose of a treaty containing numerous interdependent rights and obligations, 'account shall be taken of that interdependence as well as the importance that the provision to which the reservation relates has within the general tenour of the treaty, and the extent of the impact that the reservation has on the treaty.'[75]

If we return to our diplomatic bag example the guidelines would apply as follows. The terms of this reservation do not suggest that its acceptance is a condition for becoming a party to the treaty. The third party adjudicator would probably apply the presump-

72. Guideline 3.1.5.
73. Guideline 3.1.5.4.
74. Guideline 3.1.5.5.
75. Guideline 3.1.5.6.

tion that Libya intended to be bound by the Convention (whether or not the reservation be considered invalid) and move on to decide whether the reservation was invalid as contrary to the object and purpose of the treaty. The questions then are whether the reservation affects the general *raison d'être* of the treaty and what is the relationship of the obligations concerning the diplomatic bag to the general thrust of the treaty. Should the adjudicator determine the reservation to be invalid, the reservation would be severed, and the treaty provision stating that the diplomatic bag may not be opened or delayed would apply to Libya with no adjustments.

The issues are often seen as more complex in the context of human rights treaties: the advantages for the reserving state to remain in the regime will be reputational rather than related to the rights acquired by the reserving state; the other states may not see an interest in challenging the validity of a reservation; and designated monitoring bodies will be caught between a desire to reinforce the values embodied in the treaty and the risk of the reserving state exiting the regime on the grounds that the reservation was wrapped up in its consent to be bound by the treaty in the first place. But should it be necessary to decide on the validity or acceptability of such a reservation, a human rights body will be able to apply similar reasoning. It will take into account, however, that the object and purpose of human rights treaties are different from those regulating diplomatic relations, and that certain human rights, such as the right not to be tortured, allow for no derogation under any circumstances whatsoever.[76]

---

76. See further I. Boerefijn, 'Impact on the Law on Treaty Reservations', and M. Scheinin, 'Impact on the Law of Treaties', both in M.T. Kamminga and M. Scheinin (eds),

A key controversy has concerned the authority of UN human rights treaty bodies when considering the validity of reservations. The ILC Guidelines call for states to 'give consideration' to a treaty body's 'assessment of the permissibility of the reservations'.[77] But the Guidelines carefully limit the right to come to a legally binding decision on the validity of a reservation to those dispute settlement bodies that are empowered to adopt decisions that are binding on the parties.[78]

By now the reader may be bemused by the complexity of the issue of the validity of reservations, but the tension at the heart of the relevant ILC Guidance is really the tension we have been exploring now for some pages. Who is authorized to determine objectively the subjective intentions of sovereign states? Leaving this merely to other states seems to deny the idea that international law exists over and above the consent of states. Allowing this to be determined by someone else seems to surrender sovereignty.

§ 6. The role of the depositary and the requirement to register

As we have seen, the role of the depositary is crucial when determining whether there exists the requisite number of states parties

---

The Impact of Human Rights Law on General International Law (Oxford: OUP, 2009) at 63–97, and 23–36; see also the Report of the UN Human Rights Treaty Body Working Group on Reservations, HRI/MC/2007/5, 9 February 2007; for further examples of peremptory norms that allow for no derogation see § 7 below.

77. Guideline 3.2.3.

78. Guidelines 3.2.1.–3.2.5.

for a treaty to enter into force. Depositaries can be single states, two or more states, the United Nations, or another international organization. Some of the formal duties of depositaries are laid out in the VCLT.[79] The emphasis has been on the need for the depositary to be neutral and impartial.[80] Indeed when faced with demands from entities which are not yet members of the UN, the UN Secretary-General follows the practice and advice of the UN General Assembly.[81] In the context of liberation movements, that guidance is clear: 'The Secretary-General has no authority to grant recognition to a Government', and authority to join a treaty is dependent on action taken by a UN political body or UN specialized agency.[82]

The practice of the Secretary-General will be of particular interest where an entity has been recognized as a state by part of the international community. The situation is explained by the UN Office of Legal Affairs as follows:

But when a treaty is open to 'States', how is the Secretary-General to determine which entities are States? If they are Members of the United Nations or Parties to the Statute of the International Court of Justice, there is no ambiguity. However, a difficulty has occurred as to possible participation in treaties when entities which appeared otherwise to be States could not be admitted to the United Nations, nor

---

79. VCLT Arts 76–9.

80. For more detail see Aust (above) ch. 18.

81. Summary of Practice of the Secretary-General as Depositary of Multilateral Treaties, ST/LEG/7/Rev. 1, at paras 79–100.

82. Ibid para. 100.

become parties to the Statute of the International Court of Justice owing to the opposition of a permanent member of the Security Council. Since that difficulty did not arise as concerns membership in the specialized agencies, where there is no 'veto' procedure, a number of those States became members of specialized agencies, and as such were in essence recognized as States by the international community.[83]

The practice with regard to the Cook Islands is worth noting:

[A]n application by the Cook Islands for membership in the World Health organization was approved by the World Health Assembly in accordance with its article 6, and the Cook Islands, in accordance with article 79, became a member upon deposit of an instrument of acceptance with the Secretary-General. In the circumstances, the Secretary-General felt that the question of the status, as a State, of the Cook Islands, had been duly decided in the affirmative by the World Health Assembly, whose membership was fully representative of the international community.[84]

Article 102 of the Charter of the United Nations requires that 'every treaty and every international agreement entered into by

---

83. Ibid para. 79 (footnote omitted).

84. Para. 86 reference omitted. Palestine was admitted to UNESCO by a vote of 107 votes in favour of admission and 14 votes against, with 52 abstentions. Admission to UNESCO for states that are not members of the UN requires a recommendation by the Executive Board, as well as a two-thirds majority in favour by the General Conference of Member States present and voting (those abstaining are not considered as voting).

any member of the United Nations after the present Charter comes into force shall as soon as possible be registered with the Secretariat and published by it'. This requirement stems from the aim of preventing secret treaties.[85] Treaties and international agreements (including unilateral declarations that are binding in international law) are registered by the UN only when they have entered into force, and most are published *in extenso* (online and in hard copy) in the UN Treaty Series in their authentic languages followed by English and French translations.[86]

§ 7. The issue of *jus cogens*

Previous editions of this book again highlighted a supposed difference between the national and international legal orders. It was stated that, on the one hand, 'in our national law we have long ceased to regard absolute freedom of contract as either possible or socially desirable', and as a result 'our courts will not enforce contracts…whose object is contrary to public policy'. On the other hand, 'no such process has yet been possible in international law;

---

85. Although Article 102(2) states that parties to unregistered treaties may not invoke such treaties before UN organs, in practice this rule has not been applied. A somewhat similar article in the Covenant of the League of Nations had left in some doubt the effect of a failure to register on a treaty. The discovery of secret treaties during and after the First World War caused some public outrage and President Wilson addressed the question by including a demand for open covenants of peace in his Fourteen Points. See A.D. McNair, *The Law of Treaties* (Oxford: Clarendon, 1961) at 179ff.

86. See UN *Treaty Handbook* (New York, UN Publications, 2006) paras 5.6 and 5.7.4. and see the website <treaties.un.org>.

no doctrine of international public policy exists as yet to restrict the freedom of states to insert in their treaties such provisions as they think fit.'[87] This has now changed; and the Vienna Convention on the Law of Treaties (VCLT) foresees that a treaty can be found to be void if it conflicts with a peremptory norm of general international law (also known as *jus cogens*).[88] Sir Hersch Lauterpacht, as Special Rapporteur on the law of treaties, had first sought to articulate this idea when dealing with the 'legality of the object of the treaty':

> It would thus appear that the test whether the object of the treaty is illegal and whether the treaty is void for that reason is not inconsistency with customary international law pure and simple, but inconsistency with such overriding principles of international law which may be regarded as constituting principles of international public policy (*ordre international public*). These principles need not necessarily have crystallized in a clearly accepted rule of law such as prohibition of piracy or of aggressive war. They may be expressive of rules of international morality so cogent that an international tribunal would consider them as forming part of those principles of law generally recognized by civilized nations which the International Court of Justice is bound to apply by virtue of Article 38 [1(c)] of its Statute.[89]

---

87. See, e.g. 6th edn at 332.

88. VCLT Art. 53.

89. II *Yearbook ILC* (1953) at 155.

The issue proved extremely divisive at the Vienna Conference. Again the two sides are depicted as reflecting a separation between those concerned about the stability and certainty that should attach to treaty obligations, and those who were keen to emphasize the moral high ground and the unacceptability of *inter alia* slavery, genocide, and aggressive war.[90] Sinclair memorably explained his apprehension: '*Jus cogens* is neither Dr Jekyll nor Mr Hyde; but it has the potentialities of both. If it is invoked indiscriminately and to serve short term political purposes, it could rapidly be destructive of confidence in the security of treaties; if it is developed with wisdom and restraint in the overall interest of the international community it could constitute a useful check upon the unbridled will of individual states.'[91]

As with the question of coercion, the idea of invalidating treaties having an object contrary to public policy is relatively radical. But the final version of the VCLT adopted in Vienna built in a number of safeguards. First, retroactive effect was explicitly ruled out. 'A treaty is void if, *at the time of its conclusion*, it conflicts with a peremptory norm of general international law.'[92] Second, the final 'package deal' adopted in Vienna on the last day of the Conference resolves the problem of who has the authority to divine the existence of such a rule and thereby determine that the treaty in question is void.[93] The VCLT provides that, in a situation where the parties have been unable to resolve their dispute, one party can

---

90. Sinclair (above) ch. 7.

91. Ibid 223.

92. VCLT Art. 53 (emphasis added) see also Art. 64 discussed below.

93. See T.O. Elias, 'Problems Concerning the Validity of Treaties', III *RCADI* (1971) 341–416, at 397–404.

bring the question of the validity of the treaty to the International Court of Justice.[94]

Again the conceptual point is perhaps more important than the practical application of the rule. No treaties have been invalidated as a result of this rule. No attempts have been made to draft new treaties to engage in aggression, the slave trade, or genocide. But the idea that there are principles of international public policy that can invalidate a treaty and override the consent of states is a powerful one. It remains for us to try to pin down what principles constitute *jus cogens* today.

The final provision described a *jus cogens* norm for the purposes of the VCLT as follows: 'a peremptory norm of general international law is a norm accepted and recognized by the international community of States as a whole as a norm from which no derogation is permitted and which can be modified only by a subsequent norm of general international law having the same character.'[95] During the Vienna Conference, Ambassador Yasseen, the Chair of the Drafting Committee, explained two relevant points concerning this description of *jus cogens*. First the word 'accepted' was added to reflect wording in Article 38(1) of the ICJ Statute, and secondly the reference to the community of states *as a whole* was to reflect the apparent agreement that 'no individual State should have the right of veto'.[96] But the source and content of these norms

---

94. Art. 66(1)(a). Note that for the Court to have jurisdiction both parties to the dispute need to be parties to the VCLT.

95. Art. 53.

96. Official Records, 21 May 1968, p. 471, paras 4 and 7; see also the explanation at 472 para. 12.

remains rather mysterious.[97] As we saw in Chapter II § 4(b), the ILC has most recently limited itself to stating that the concept includes the rules on aggression, genocide, apartheid, slavery, the slave trade, racial discrimination, crimes against humanity, torture, self-determination, as well as the basic rules of international humanitarian law applicable in armed conflict. The UN Human Rights Committee has described as peremptory norms Articles 6 and 7 of the International Covenant on Civil and Political Rights (prohibitions on arbitrary deprivation of life and torture or cruel, inhuman or degrading treatment or punishment). They also refer to further examples such as 'taking hostages, by imposing collective punishments, through arbitrary deprivations of liberty or by deviating from fundamental principles of fair trial, including the presumption of innocence'.[98]

The most striking thing about the introduction of *jus cogens* into the law of treaties is that its actual impact has been almost entirely outside the context of the validity of treaties.[99] A significant development has been the approach taken in the ILC's Articles on State Responsibility. These make clear that all states have

97. See A. Bianchi, 'Human Rights and the Magic of *Jus Cogens*', 3 *EJIL* (2008) 491–508; For a detailed examination see A. Orakhelashvili, *Peremptory Norms in International Law* (Oxford: OUP, 2008) ch. 5.

98. General Comment 29, adopted 24 July 2001, para. 11.

99. *Jus cogens* is regularly invoked as an argument against immunity, or in order to ground a case for universal jurisdiction. See, e.g. the dissenting opinions in *Al-Adsani v UK*, European Court of Human Rights, 21 November 2001; see also *R v Bartle* et al *Ex Parte Pinochet* [1999] UKHL 17. It has also been argued (without success) that a reservation excluding the jurisdiction of the International Court in the context of the Genocide Convention should be disregarded due to the *jus cogens* nature of the prohibition of genocide. *Armed Activities on the Territory of the Congo (New Application: 2002)* (*DRC v Rwanda*),

duties when faced with a serious breach of a *jus cogens* norm by another state. First, to co-operate to bring to an end through lawful means such a serious breach; second not to recognize as lawful a situation created by the serious breach; and third not to render aid or assistance in maintaining that situation.[100] These injunctions were applied by the International Court of Justice when it delivered its Opinion on the *Legal Consequences of the Construction of a Wall in the Occupied Palestinian Territory*.[101] More recently, Lord

---

ICJ Rep. (2006). See also A. Cassese, *International Law*, 2nd edn (Oxford: OUP, 2005) at 201–12; the Swiss Constitution includes a provision that popular initiatives to revise the Constitution may not violate 'les règles impératives du droit international', for details on how this provision may or may not be applicable see L. Langer, 'Panacea or Pathetic Fallacy? The Swiss Ban on Minarets', 43(4) *Vanderbilt Journal of Transnational Law* (2010) 863–951. A recent official report explains in its summary that this concept encompasses '*le jus cogens, les principes fondamentaux du droit international humanitaire et les garanties du droit international qui ne souffrent aucune dérogation même en état de nécessité*'. See *Rapport additionnel du Conseil fédéral au rapport du 5 mars 2010 sur la relation entre droit international et droit interne* of 30 March 2011. For more detail of what this includes see para. 2.4.1. The proposal in the report is that the Constitution be amended so that popular initiatives should not only respect peremptory rules of international law, but also the essence of fundamental constitutional rights (at para. 4.3).

100. See Arts 40 and 41 of the ILC's Articles on Responsibility of States for Internationally Wrongful Acts (2001); cf VCLT Art. 71. The argument that the *jus cogens* nature of the violations by Germany should alter the scope of any obligations on Italy to grant Germany immunity was rejected by the ICJ in *Jurisdictional Immunities of the State (Germany v Italy: Greece Intervening)* Judgment of 2 February 2012; cf the dissenting opinions Judge *ad hoc* Gaja and Judge Cançado Trindade. See also C. Tams, *Enforcing Obligations* Erga Omnes *in International Law* (Cambridge: CUP, 2005) at 310 who concludes that '*jus cogens* rules are by necessity valid *erga omnes*.' (*Erga omnes* obligations are dealt with in the next Chapter), and L. Yarwood, *State Accountability under International Law: Holding states accountable for a breach of* jus cogens *norms* (Abingdon: Routledge, 2011).

101. ICJ Rep. (2004) at para. 159.

Bingham's reference, in *A v Secretary of State for Home Depart-ment*, to both the ILC's Article 41 as requiring 'states to cooperate to bring to an end through lawful means any serious breach of an obligation under a peremptory norm of general international law' and the International Court's Opinion, may be seen to indicate that a state has a duty to reject the fruits of torture committed by another state.[102] In this case the House of Lords rejected arguments that evidence obtained from detainees in Guantánamo Bay should be admitted in hearings concerning the detention in the United Kingdom of suspected terrorists. The House of Lords ruled that evidence procured by torture was not admissible before the British courts even where the allegations related to torture by for-eign officials.[103]

Finally, we should note that under the VCLT: 'If a new per-emptory norm of general international law emerges, any existing treaty which is in conflict with that norm becomes void and termi-nates.'[104] Again any dispute over the application of this provision can be eventually submitted to the International Court of Justice. There are however two key differences with regard to the effects of such a supervening norm of *jus cogens*. First, the treaty becomes invalid at the time the new norm appears—it is not void from its

---

102. *A v Secretary of State for the Home Department* [2005] UKHL 71 at para. 34.

103. Per Lord Bingham 'The issue is one of constitutional principle, whether evidence obtained by torturing another human being may lawfully be admitted against a party to proceedings in a British court, irrespective of where, or by whom, or on whose authority the torture was inflicted. To that question I would give a very clear negative answer.' At para. 51.

104. VCLT Art. 64. For an application of this principle see *Case of Aloeboetoe* et al *v Suriname,* Judgment of the Inter-American Court of Human Rights, 10 September 1993 at para. 57.

adoption. This is sometimes expressed as the difference between a treaty being voidable or void *ab initio*; the supervening norm renders the treaty voidable but up until that point the treaty was valid and the parties had to abide by their obligations. Second, in the case of a supervening norm it is possible to sever the offending clause and leave the rest of the treaty in force.[105]

While the practical effects of the inclusion of these provisions on *jus cogens* have yet to be explored, their adoption is better seen in historical perspective. The inclusion of these provisions was symbolic of a new law displacing the traditional law, of the developed countries accepting that concerns regarding justice, voiced by developing and socialist countries, may have a place in the law of treaties. T.O. Elias, Head of the Nigerian Delegation and Chairman of the Committee of the Whole in Vienna, wrote that the *jus cogens* rule is 'a form of international public policy or *ordre public* for the community of States. There has thus been recognised a transition from the concept of an international *society* to that of an international *community*, ever more closely integrated and inter-dependent.'[106]

§ 8. Other grounds of invalidity

The other grounds of invalidity included in the VCLT relate to error, fraud, corruption, and defects in capacity. In each case the treaty will be voidable rather than *void ab initio*. And in each case

---

105. Art. 44(3).

106. Above fn 93 at 410. Elias was later President of the International Law Commission and of the International Court of Justice.

it is the victim state that has to raise the invalidity.[107] This is some-times known as 'relative nullity' in contrast to 'absolute nullity'.[108] We will simply examine here the issue of defects in capacity as it highlights some doctrinal differences related to the relationship between international law and national law.

The VCLT provides in Article 46:

1. A State may not invoke the fact that its consent to be bound by a treaty has been expressed in violation of a provision of its internal law regarding competence to conclude treaties as inval-idating its consent unless that violation was manifest and con-cerned a rule of its internal law of fundamental importance.
2. A violation is manifest if it would be objectively evident to any State conducting itself in the matter in accordance with normal practice and in good faith.

Today this may seem fairly self-explanatory, but the text represents a compromise between those who saw constitutional law as essen-tial to the state's right to enter into treaty obligations (constitu-tionalists), and those who saw international law taking effect irrespective of what a state's constitution might or might not say about international law (internationalists).[109] As we have already

---

107. Note also the provision on acquiescence with regard to these grounds of invalidity: Art. 45. In the case of fraud or corruption the victim state may invoke invalidity with respect to particular clauses: Art. 44(4).

108. See further Cassese (above) at 177–8.

109. Brierly's first report is sometimes characterized as constitutionalist, but at that time his draft included treaties with international organizations, and although he could foresee a clause stating that one could assume the capacity of a Head of State to enter into treaties,

seen, different countries have different methods for absorbing international law in their domestic legal orders. These rules stem from the ways in which treaties have to be approved. If the Senate or Parliament has to approve a treaty, one can consider that the treaty in this way may *democratically* pass into law. In other systems, where for example a Head of State may bind a state without parliamentary approval, absorption may be delayed until the legislature has had a chance to address the issues.

The eventual compromise in the VCLT is that one may presume that a state is complying with its internal law, but there will be an exception when the other state should have realized that there was a manifest violation of a fundamental rule. In a case concerning the Maroua Declaration, signed by the Heads of State of Nigeria and Cameroon, Nigeria claimed that it was not bound by the Declaration as its Constitution required the ratification of treaties by the Nigerian Supreme Military Council. The International Court of Justice rejected Nigeria's claim. The Court confirmed that the 'rules concerning the authority to sign treaties for a State are constitutional rules of fundamental importance'. But they found that 'a limitation of a Head of State's capacity in this respect is not manifest in the sense of Article 46, paragraph 2,

---

the situation would be more complicated with regard to any assumed authority of international organizations; for example, the UN Security Council and the Economic and Social Council have different capacities in this context. II *Yearbook of the ILC* (1950) at 231. For examples where the European Union or a member state was held not entitled under EU law to enter into a treaty, see Aust (above) at 314. He explains that an EU member state would not be able to invoke Art. 46 of the VCLT as 'a non-Member State cannot be expected to know all the intricacies of [EU] law, the violation would not seem to be manifest'.

unless at least properly publicized'.[110] Heads of State, by virtue of their function, do not have to produce 'full powers' and are considered as representing their state for the purposes of expressing the consent of the state to be bound by a treaty.[111]

§ 9. Interpretation

The object of interpretation is to give effect to the intention of the parties as fully and fairly as possible. We should, however, consider the real nature of the process that a court goes through when it interprets a document, whether it be a municipal court interpreting a statute or contract, or an international court interpreting a treaty. We speak of the process as interpretation because we do not care to admit that the court puts something into the document which was not there before; practically no document needs interpretation when the case which has arisen was foreseen by its framers. The difficulty arises precisely because they did not foresee or provide for it; and what a court really does when we say that it interprets, is that,

---

110. *Land and Maritime Boundary between Cameroon and Nigeria* ICJ Rep. (2002) p. 303, at para. 265.

111. VCLT Art. 7(1) and (2)(a), see § 4 above. It has been suggested that treaties that cede territory or move boundaries represent a special category and so the burden of establishing the notoriety of the rule should be adjusted, see M. Fitzmaurice and O. Elias, *Contemporary Issues in the Law of Treaties* (Utrecht: Eleven, 2005) ch. 11. See also the Declaration of Judge Rezec who did not consider that Cameroon could be considered to be unaware of the internal Nigerian rule: 'I know of no legal order which authorizes a representative of a Government alone definitively to conclude and put into effect, on the basis of his sole authority, a treaty concerning a boundary, whether on land or at sea—and *ergo* the territory—of the State.' At pp. 191–2.

by employing well-known methods of judicial reasoning, it says what it thinks the framers of the document must have intended to say. But they did not intend to say that; they probably had no intention at all in the matter that has arisen, almost certainly no common intention. The act of the court is a creative act, in spite of our conspiracy to represent it as something less. Moreover, although it is not an arbitrary or capricious act, interpretation is an act in which different minds, equally competent, may, and often do, arrive at different and equally reasonable results.[112]

We should bear in mind that while Acts of Parliament may lend themselves to strict methods of interpretation, treaties do not, as a rule, invite those same very strict methods of interpretation as applied in the English courts. Those who draft treaties are not used to drafting national legislation; and the international context, and the circumstances of the negotiations, are different from those of a national legislature. Westlake made the point in the following way:

[T]he nature of the matters dealt with by [the eminent diplomats and ministers from other countries], and the peculiar conditions under which they work, must be considered. A style of drafting accommodated to the expectation of a very literal interpretation would necessitate the suggestion and discussion of so many possible contingencies, as would be likely to cause needless friction between the representatives of countries not always very amicable. It seems best in the interest of peace that,

112. This paragraph is adapted and transposed from Brierly 'The Judicial Settlement of International Disputes' in *The Basis of Obligation in International Law,* 93–107 at 98.

when an agreement on broad lines has been reached, it should be expressed in language not striving to hide a felt doubt, but on the other hand not meticulously seeking occasions for doubt; and to such a style of drafting, which we believe to be that most common in treaties, a large and liberal spirit of interpretation will reasonably correspond.[113]

We might also suggest two further reasons which explain why treaties are interpreted differently from national law. First, although treaties are interpreted every day by foreign offices and their legal advisers, the art of treaty interpretation is most exposed when the text is interpreted by an international court. As should by now be clear, international courts depend on states choosing to submit to their jurisdiction. Governments will be ready to withdraw their custom should they feel that treaties are being interpreted in ways that they did not intend. At the national level we have mostly no choice but to submit to the jurisdiction of our national courts and the national judge's interpretation of the law. Moreover the national legislature can if necessary intervene to correct deviations from their intentions.[114] By contrast international courts may have

---

113. Westlake, *International Law,* 2nd edn (Cambridge: CUP, 1910), Part I, p. 293–4.

114. See Reuter (above) 'The primacy of the text, especially in international law, is the cardinal rule of any interpretation. It may be that in other legal systems, where the legislative and judicial processes are fully regulated by the authority of the State and not by the free consent of the parties, the courts are deemed competent to make a text say what it does not say or even the opposite of what it ways. But such interpretations, which are sometimes described as teleological, are indissociable from the fact that recourse to the courts is mandatory, that the court is obliged to hand down a decision, and that it is moreover controlled by an effective legislature whose action may if necessary check its bolder undertakings. When an international judge or arbitrator departs from a text, it is because he is satisfied that another text or practice, ie another source of law, should prevail.' At 96.

to be mindful of losing the confidence of states as potential litigants or having their jurisdiction restricted by those they are seeking to judge.

Second, whether the interpretation is done by legal advisors or an international court, the parties disputing the interpretation of a treaty are often the same entities that negotiated the treaty. As Richard Gardiner explains: 'those in dispute internationally over a treaty are commonly representatives of the actual originators of the treaty terms in issue, or at least later parties to the treaty. Hence their interpretation has a special value.'[115]

Previous editions of this book were able at this point to state boldly that '[t]here are no technical rules in international law for the interpretation of treaties'. This is no longer really true, and, as we shall see, the eventual rules included in the 1969 Vienna Convention are quite detailed and are now applied to all treaties. Sinclair explains the doctrinal divisions over treaty interpretation in the prelude to the Vienna Conference.

> There have been three distinct schools of thought reflecting respectively (a) the 'textual' approach, (b) the 'intentions' approach and (c) the 'teleological' approach. Those favouring the 'textual' approach place particular emphasis on the text of the treaty as incorporating the authentic expression of the intentions of the parties. Those favouring the 'intentions' approach insist that the prime goal of treaty interpretation is to endeavour to ascertain the intentions of the parties. And

---

115. *Treaty Interpretation* (Oxford: OUP, 2010) at 11; and see the rules on subsequent practice and authentic interpretation by the parties referred to below.

those favouring the more dynamic 'teleological' approach maintain that the task of the decision-maker is to ascertain the object and purpose of the treaty and then to interpret the treaty so as to give effect to that object and purpose. As between the 'textual' approach and the intentions approach, the main difference lies in the extent to which and the circumstances in which recourse to preparatory work should be admitted as an aid in the process of interpretation.[116]

The eventual rule adopted in the Vienna Convention combines these approaches in Article 31. The Article also explains what material is relevant in the interpretative process. In order not to distort the provision it seems appropriate here to reproduce the whole Article.

Article 31
General rule of interpretation

1. A treaty shall be interpreted in good faith in accordance with the ordinary meaning to be given to the terms of the treaty in their context and in the light of its object and purpose.
2. The context for the purpose of the interpretation of a treaty shall comprise, in addition to the text, including its preamble and annexes:
    (a) any agreement relating to the treaty which was made between all the parties in connection with the conclusion of the treaty;

---

116. I.M. Sinclair, 'Vienna Conference on the Law of Treaties', 19 *ICLQ* (1970) 47–69, at 61.

(b) any instrument which was made by one or more parties in connection with the conclusion of the treaty and accepted by the other parties as an instrument related to the treaty.

3. There shall be taken into account, together with the context:
   (a) any subsequent agreement between the parties regarding the interpretation of the treaty or the application of its provisions;
   (b) any subsequent practice in the application of the treaty which establishes the agreement of the parties regarding its interpretation;
   (c) any relevant rules of international law applicable in the relations between the parties.

4. A special meaning shall be given to a term if it is established that the parties so intended.

Most of the terms in this Article in turn lend themselves to interpretation,[117] and here we will only sketch the essential details.

Emphasis has been placed on the labelling of Article 31 as a single rule, thereby reminding us that the provision is to be applied in its entirety. There is no suggestion that some elements are to be given priority over others in applying the rule. The opening reference to good faith has been understood as encompassing the principle of *effectiveness*. In turn this has two dimensions: first, that *effect* must be given to *all* the terms of the treaty; and second that the interpretation should enable the treaty to have appropriate *effects*.[118]

---

117. See Gardiner (above) chs 5–7.

118. We will consider below the application of these principles in the *Georgia v Russia (preliminary objections)* 2011 judgment of the ICJ.

Ordinary meaning is to be determined in the light of the object and purpose of the treaty, and in the context of the treaty. What constitutes context in this regard includes the preamble and annexes as well as agreements and instruments accepted as relating to the conclusion of the treaty. These agreements could take the form of understandings agreed at the final Conference but not included in the text of the treaty,[119] or paragraphs included in the Final Act of the Conference or in a General Assembly Resolution to which the text of the treaty is annexed. Instruments may be unilateral, and where interpretative declarations are accepted by the other parties they may constitute an *agreement* regarding the interpretation of the treaty.[120] While reservations modify the terms of the treaty, an instrument in this case is part of the context which the interpreter considers in determining the meaning of the actual text.

The inevitable importance of context when determining the meaning of terms is nicely illustrated by McNair:

A man, having a wife and children, made a will of conspicuous brevity consisting merely of the words 'All for mother'. No term could be 'plainer' than 'mother', for a man can only

---

119. See for example the Understandings on the amendments concerning the crime of aggression in the International Criminal Court Statute contained in Annex III of Resolution 6 adopted 11 June 2010 (discussed in Ch. IX below);

120. This could fall under any of the following paras of Art. 31(2)(a)(b)(3)(a)(b), see ILC Guidelines (above) 4.7.3 at para. 3 to the Commentary. Where the other parties have not acquiesced, a unilateral declaration is simply evidence that may or may not be taken into account under the general rule. See Guideline 4.7.1 and the Commentary thereto which explains that such a declaration is not autonomous but may confirm an interpretation based on the objective factors listed in Arts 31 and 32. At paras 26 and 31.

have one mother. His widow claimed the estate. The court, having admitted oral evidence which proved that in the family circle the deceased's wife was always referred to as 'mother', as is common in England, held that she was entitled to apply for administration…and she took the whole estate. 'Mother' is, speaking abstractly, a 'plain term' but, taken in relation to the circumstances surrounding the testator at the time when the will was made, it was anything but a 'plain term'.[121]

Subsequent practice in the application of the treaty relates to acts attributable to a state. Not *all* states need engage in the practice, but there should be 'manifested or imputable agreement' from the other parties.[122] In some cases a court will impute an intention to be bound by an evolving interpretation of the terms of a treaty. The International Court of Justice explained the approach in the context of the need to decide whether the word 'commerce' should be interpreted to cover solely goods—or rather be seen as including services such as passenger transport.

On the one hand, the subsequent practice of the parties, within the meaning of Article 31(3)(b) of the Vienna Con-

---

121. McNair (above) at 367. For a situation where the International Court of Justice interpreted a text by focusing on context rather than the literal meaning of the words see *Anglo-Iranian Oil Co. case (jurisdiction)*, ICJ Rep. (1952) p. 93. McNair's Separate Opinion explained as follows: 'there is a real ambiguity in the text, and, for that reason, it is both justifiable and necessary to go outside the text and see whether any light is shed by the surrounding circumstances.' At 117–18.

122. Gardiner (above) 225–49 at 236.

vention, can result in a departure from the original intent on the basis of a tacit agreement between the parties. On the other hand, there are situations in which the parties' intent upon conclusion of the treaty was, or may be presumed to have been, to give the terms used—or some of them—a meaning or content capable of evolving, not one fixed once and for all, so as to make allowance for, among other things, developments in international law. In such instances it is indeed in order to respect the parties' common intention at the time the treaty was concluded, not to depart from it, that account should be taken of the meaning acquired by the terms in question upon each occasion on which the treaty is to be applied...

The Court concludes from the foregoing that the terms by which the extent of Costa Rica's right of free navigation has been defined, including in particular the term 'comercio', must be understood to have the meaning they bear on each occasion on which the Treaty is to be applied, and not necessarily their original meaning.

Thus, even assuming that the notion of 'commerce' does not have the same meaning today as it did in the mid-nineteenth century, it is the present meaning which must be accepted for purposes of applying the Treaty.[123]

---

123. *Case Concerning the Dispute Regarding Navigational and Related Rights (Costa Rica v Nicaragua)* judgment 13 July 2009, at paras 64 and 70. See also *Kasikili/Sedudu Island (Botswana v Namibia)* judgment 13 December 1999 at paras 47–80 for a rejection of claims by both sides that certain subsequent practice was not relevant for the purposes of Art. 31(3)(b). In the *Arbitration concerning Heathrow Airport User Charges*

The obligation to take into account 'relevant rules of international law' under Article 31(3)(c) seems to cover the need to interpret the terms of the treaty in the light of the international law applicable at the time of the conclusion of the treaty, as well as the evolving law applicable to the terms.[124] The presumption must be that the drafters would have accepted that certain terms will evolve under international law. This rule of interpretation has, however, in some circumstances been regarded as a fulcrum for weighing international obligations in competing regimes.[125] What weight is to

(USA v UK), 30 November 1992, XXIV RIAA, 3, the Tribunal considered that a Memorandum of Understanding constituted 'consensual subsequent practice of the Parties' and therefore an aid to interpretation of the relevant treaty. At para. 6.7. For a full review of these and related questions see the Report being prepared in the context of the ILC by Professor Nolte's 'study group on treaties over time'. Amendment of a treaty by practice can occur outside the rules in the VCLT; see for example the question of the death penalty under the European Convention on Human Rights (1950). Article 2 on the right to life had an exception allowing for 'execution of a sentence of a court following his conviction of a crime for which this penalty is provided by law'. In a case concerning the transfer by the United Kingdom of two individuals from its jurisdiction into the jurisdiction of the Iraqi authorities, the European Court of Human Rights found a violation of the prohibition of inhuman or degrading treatment (due to the psychological effect of the possible death penalty). With regard to Article 2 the Court stated: 'All but two of the Member States have now signed Protocol No. 13 and all but three of the States which have signed have ratified it. These figures, together with consistent State practice in observing the moratorium on capital punishment, are strongly indicative that Article 2 has been amended so as to prohibit the death penalty in all circumstances.'

124. On these two aspects of intertemporal law see the discussion related to the effects of discovery and the question of title over territory in the award of Judge Huber discussed in Ch. V § 2 above. See also the ICJ Judgments in *Certain Questions of Mutual Assistance in Criminal Matters (Djibouti v France)*, 4 June 2008, at paras 113–14; *Case Concerning Pulp Mills on The River Uruguay (Argentina v Uruguay)*, 20 April 2010, at paras 55–66.
125. For the separate issue of successive treaties on the same subject matter see VCLT Arts 30 and 59.

be given to the rules on sovereign immunity when interpreting access to court under a human rights treaty?[126] What weight to be given to freedom of expression when interpreting the obligation to protect the dignity of an embassy?[127] What weight to be given to the prohibition on the use of force when interpreting a friendship treaty?[128] How to include human rights and environmental obligations when interpreting trade[129] or investment agreements?[130] At one level, resolving the tension between these competing obligations through the technique of interpretation is very satisfying and allows us to see international law as a coherent system.[131] At

126. See ECtHR *Al-Adsani v UK*, 21 November 2001, at para. 55ff.

127. See Ch. VI § 11(e) above.

128. See *Oil Platforms (Iran v USA)* ICJ Rep. (2003) p. 161 at para. 41ff. Compare the Separate Opinion of Judge Higgins paras 44–52.

129. J. Pauwelyn, *Conflict of Norms in Public International Law: How WTO Law Relates to other Rules of International Law* (Cambridge: CUP, 2003);G. Marceau, 'WTO Dispute Settlement and Human Rights', 13 *EJIL* (2002) 753–814;T. Cottier, J. Pauwelyn, and E. Bürgi (eds), *Human Rights and International Trade* (Oxford: OUP, 2005); M. Andenas and S. Zleptning, 'Proportionality: WTO Law in Comparative Perspective', 42 *Texas International Law Journal* (2007) 371–427.

130. P. Sands, 'Treaty, Custom and the Cross-fertilization of International Law', 1 *Yale Human Rights and Development Law Journal* (1998) 85–105; P.-M. Dupuy, 'Unification Rather than Fragmentation of International Law? The Case of International Investment Law and Human Rights Law', in P.-M. Dupuy, E.-U. Petersmann, and F. Francioni (eds), *Human Rights in International Investment Law and Arbitration* (Oxford: OUP, 2009) 45–62, esp. at 55ff; A.S. Sweet, 'Investor-State Arbitration: Proportionality's New Frontier', 4 *Law Ethics and Human Rights* (2010) 47–76; B. Simma, 'Foreign Investment Arbitration: A Place for Human Rights?' 60 *ICLQ* (2011) 573–96.

131. See the ILC Report 'Conclusions of the work of the Study Group on the Fragmentation of International Law: Difficulties arising from the Diversification and Expansion of International Law' (2006) at paras 17–23; UN Doc. A/61/10, para. 251; C. McLachlan, 'The Principle of Systemic Integration and Article 31(3)(c) of the Vienna Convention', 54 *ICLQ* (2005) 279–320.

another level it obscures the fact that states may have actually taken on competing obligations reflecting different values to be protected, and, in most cases, the international court or panel will have its jurisdiction restricted to only one of the competing treaties.[132] While the national judge may be entitled to weigh multiple competing values, rights, and obligations to arrive at a judicious result, international judges may ultimately be restricted in their jurisdiction to the treaty before them.[133]

Nevertheless there will be cases where judges do indeed have to choose between competing values. In such a situation the late Judge Antonio Cassese suggested that 'an interpreter will necessarily have to rely upon his or her personal ideological or political leanings. What matters, however, is that he or she should make it explicit and clear that the choice between two conflicting values is grounded in a personal slant or bias, and not in any "objective" legal precedence of one value over the other.'[134]

---

132. Klabbers concludes in this context that 'where values clash, the law offers little solace, and can only offer what has become known as the "principle of political decision": in case of such unavoidable treaty conflict, the responsible party will eventually have to choose which commitment to honour, and make sure that it compensates the other partner or partners.' 'Beyond the Vienna Convention: Conflicting Treaty Provisions', in E. Cannizzaro (ed.), *The Law of Treaties beyond the Vienna Convention* (Oxford: OUP, 2010) 192–205, at 195. He also makes the following important point: 'it is by no means clear that the marketing of genetically modified organisms should be regarded as a trade issue rather than, say, a health issue, an environmental issue, a security issue, or a human rights issue. How to constitute the proper field (or system) is itself a political question, something the mechanics of a system approach have a hard time accommodating.' J. Klabbers, *Treaty Conflict and the European Union* (Cambridge: CUP, 2009) at 39.

133. R. Higgins, 'A Babel of Judicial Voices: Ruminations from the Bench', 55 *ICLQ* (2006) 791–804.

134. *Five Masters of International Law: Conversations with R-J. Dupuy, E. Jiménez de Aréchaga, R. Jennings, L. Henkin and O. Schachter* (Oxford: Hart, 2011) at 259.

Attitudes to *travaux préparatoires* (preparatory work) have in the past reflected different legal traditions. The confrontation prepared by Professor Myres McDougal, as a member of the US delegation to the Vienna Conference, is perhaps emblematic of a more general historical division over interpretative method and the application of international law. In short, McDougal argued that preparatory work should be considered alongside the elements contained in Article 31. He stressed that '[i]n reality, words had no fixed or natural meaning which the parties to an agreement could not alter. The "plain and ordinary" meanings of words were multiple and ambiguous and could be made particular and clear only by reference to the factual circumstances of their use.'[135] He emphasized that '[i]t was essential to respect the free choice of the States parties regarding their agreements, and not to impose upon them the choices of others'.[136]

Sinclair, from the UK delegation, summarized the position of those who preferred to concentrate on the text rather than the original common intention of the parties:

As a matter of experience it often occurred that the difference between the parties to the treaties arose out of something which the parties had never thought of when the treaty was concluded and that, therefore, they had had absolutely no common intention with regard to it. In other cases the parties might all along have had divergent intentions with regard to

---

135. Official Records, 1st Session, Meeting of the Committee of the Whole, 19 April 1968 at p.167, para. 44.
136. Ibid p. 168, para. 46.

the actual question which was in dispute; each party had
deliberately refrained from raising the matter, possibly hop-
ing that that point would not arise in practice, or possibly
expecting that if it did, the text which was agreed would
produce the result which it desired.[137]

He went on to argue that in practice, reliance on preparatory work
was inevitably selective and would disadvantage both small delegations and new states.

In the first place, preparatory work was almost invariably
confusing, unequal and partial: confusing because it commonly consisted of the summary records of statements made
during the process of negotiation, and early statements on the
positions of delegations might express the intention of the
delegation at that stage, but bear no relation to the ultimate
text of the treaty; unequal, because not all delegations spoke
on any particular issue; and partial because it excluded the
informal meetings between heads of delegations at which
final compromises were reached and which were often the
most significant feature of any negotiation. If preparatory
work were to be placed on equal footing with the text of the
treaty, there would be no end to debate at international
conferences....

Finally, if greater significance were attributed to preparatory work than in the Commission's text of article [31], a
greater degree of risk would be created for new States wishing

---

137. 22 April 1968, p. 177 para. 4.

to accede to treaties in the drafting of which they had taken no part. The text of the treaty was what those new States had before them when deciding whether or not to accede; if more weight were attached to preparatory work in the rules of treaty interpretation, new States would be obliged to undertake a thorough analysis of the preparatory work before acceding to treaties, and even a thorough analysis was likely to give them limited enlightenment on the intentions of the parties.[138]

The United States' proposal was rejected by a vote at the Vienna Conference, and the VCLT only allows for recourse to supplementary material including preparatory work when application of the Article 31 rule leads to an absurd result, or leaves the meaning ambiguous or obscure.[139]

In sum, the rule contained in Article 31 is carefully constructed and comprehensive, and yet, as suggested at the outset, there is still plenty of room for different judges to come to different conclusions. The point is starkly illustrated by the recent judgment of the International Court of Justice in the case brought by Georgia against Russia. The Court had to decide as a preliminary matter whether Article 22 of the UN Racial Discrimination Convention could provide the necessary jurisdiction for the Court. Article 22 reads:

---

138. Ibid p. 178, paras 8 and 10.

139. See Art. 32. In practice parties and judges will often refer to the preparatory work in order to reinforce their arguments. For example in the *Georgia v Russia* case considered below, the Court's judgment and the dissenting opinions examine the preparatory work and each finds that that work reinforces their divergent interpretations. For a full examination of what constitutes supplementary means and preparatory work see Gardiner (above) at 99–108 and 301–50.

Any dispute between two or more States Parties with respect to the interpretation or application of this Convention, which is not settled by negotiation or by the procedures expressly provided for in this Convention, shall, at the request of any of the parties to the dispute, be referred to the International Court of Justice for decision, unless the disputants agree to another mode of settlement.

The Court explains the differences in interpretation:

There is much in this compromissory clause on which the two Parties hold different interpretations. First they disagree on the meaning of the phrase '[a]ny dispute...which is not settled by negotiation or by the procedures expressly provided for'. The Russian Federation maintains that the phrase imposes a precondition to the jurisdiction of the Court, in that it requires that an attempt must have been made to resolve the dispute by the means specified in Article 22 and that that attempt must have failed before the dispute can be referred to the Court. Georgia on the other hand interprets the phrase as imposing no affirmative obligation for the Parties to have attempted to resolve the dispute through negotiation or through the procedures established by CERD. According to Georgia, all that is required is that, as a matter of fact, the dispute has not been so resolved.[140]

---

140. At para. 118.

The Court explains a further difference:

> assuming that negotiations are a precondition for the seisin of the Court, the two Parties disagree as to what constitutes negotiations including the extent to which they must be pursued before it can be concluded that the precondition under Article 22 of CERD has been fulfilled. Additionally, they disagree as to the format of negotiations and the extent to which they should refer to the substantive obligations under CERD.[141]

The Court (by a majority of ten votes to six) upheld the Russian argument that the words 'which is not settled by negotiation' must be given effect. This is an application of the rule regarding effectiveness or *effet utile* (referred to above). The Court considered that the Georgian argument that it was sufficient that the dispute had not been resolved by negotiation would lead to a result whereby 'a key phrase of this provision would become devoid of any effect'.[142]

The dissenting judges considered that the Court had relied solely on this one aspect of the effectiveness rule. They argued that the Court should have considered that the literal meaning of the words '*is not settled by negotiation*' is clearly different from the

---

141. At para. 120.

142. At para. 133. For an the explanation of the effectiveness principle, sometimes referred to as *ut res magis valeat quam pereat* (roughly translated as: words are to be given value rather than ignored), see the Third Report by Waldock on the law of treaties, II *Yearbook of the ILC* (1964) at 52–61.

alternative clause found in other treaties '*which cannot be settled by negotiation*'.[143] Second, they emphasized that 'while diplomatic negotiations concerning a dispute may be helpful before judicial proceedings are brought, particularly in clarifying the terms of the dispute and delimiting its subject-matter, they as a general rule are not a mandatory precondition to be satisfied in order for the Court to be able to exercise jurisdiction'.[144] The dissenting Judges concluded therefore that the Georgian interpretation of the expression 'is not settled by negotiation' should have been preferred.

The Judges of the Court were also divided on the meaning of the word 'negotiation' in this context. The Court's judgment held that the negotiation must go beyond protest, and relate specifically to the dispute over the treaty in question. The dissenting judges argued 'a firmly realistic, rather than formalistic, approach should be taken to the question of negotiations', and they concluded that 'there was no reasonable possibility of a negotiated settlement of the dispute as it was presented to the Court, and the condition in Article 22, if one exists, had been met'.[145]

In closing this section on interpretation we can conclude that while it is no longer correct to claim that there are no technical rules for treaty interpretation, when applying the rules on interpretation, different judges can still arrive at different interpretations of the same provision of a treaty.

---

143. Joint dissenting opinion of President Owada, Judges Simma, Abraham, and Donoghue, and Judge *ad hoc* Gaja at paras 21–3. See also the dissenting opinion by Judge Cançado Trindade.

144. Joint dissenting opinion at para. 24.

145. Joint dissenting opinion at paras 55 and 84.

§ 10.   Third party rights and obligations

The general rule is that a 'treaty does not create either obligations or rights for a third State without its consent'.[146] However, if it is shown that the parties clearly intended to confer a *right* on one or several states not a party to the treaty in question, there is nothing in international law to prevent effect being given to this intention, and it can be assumed that the third state has assented to benefiting from such a conferred right.[147] According to the VCLT where states intend to impose an *obligation* on a third state, that state will need to accept that obligation in writing.[148]

The question of when a treaty between states may create rights or obligations for *individuals* and *other non-state actors* is a complex one.[149] As the ILC's Special Rapporteur on the law of treaties,

146. VCLT Art. 34. For a detailed examination of the this area see C. Chinkin, *Third Parties in International Law* (Oxford: Clarendon Press, 1983) 25–119.

147. See PCIJ *Free Zones of Upper Savoy and the District of Gex,* Series A/B, No. 46, at p. 147. '[I]t must be ascertained whether the States which have stipulated in favour of a third State meant to create for that State an actual right which the latter has accepted as such.' VCLT Arts 36 and 37(2).

148. VCLT Arts 35 and 37(1).

149. For an early examination of the individual as a potential subject of international treaty rights see H. Lauterpacht, 'General Rules of the Law of Peace' at 279–94 in E. Lauterpacht (ed.), *International Law: Collected Papers*, vol. 1 (Cambridge: CUP, 1970). (English version of the Cours Général 62 *RCADI* (1937)); see also C. Chinkin, *Third Parties in International Law* (above) chs 1, 4, 5, and 16. C. Tomuschat, 'The Responsibility of Other Entities: Private Individuals', in J. Crawford, A. Pellet, and S. Olleson (eds), *The Law of International Responsibility* (Oxford: OUP, 2010) 317–29. M. Milanović, 'Is the Rome Statute Binding on Individuals? (And Why We Should Care)', 9 *JICJ* (2011) 21–52.

Waldock had proposed an article for the Vienna Convention which referred to the situation where 'a treaty provides for obligations or rights which are to be performed or enjoyed by individuals, juristic persons, or groups of individuals in question'. The draft article set out how such rights and obligations take effect at the national and international levels: '(a) through the contracting States by their national systems of law; (b) through such international organs and procedures as may be specially provided for in the treaty or in any other treaties or instruments in force.'[150]

The debate in the Commission in 1964 was very divisive; some members were not convinced that any treaties at that time provided for such individual rights, and regarded the idea of giving an individual access to an international court to be an unnecessary prolongation of the legal process at the national level, arguing that it 'would be extremely dangerous to attack the jurisdiction of the State on the pretext of providing international protection for the individual citizen'. Others, however, considered that the idea that individuals could have subjective rights against their own state was 'gradually gaining ground' in the context of the drafting of the UN Human Rights Covenants. Waldock eventually agreed to withdraw the provision, but recorded his view that individuals already had access to international bodies, and that he regretted the deletion of this reference as 'it would not accord with the high importance attached by the Charter and by modern international law generally to human rights and freedoms'.[151]

---

150. Third Report on the Law of Treaties, II *Yearbook ILC* (1964) at 45–8.
151. 9 June 1964, I *Yearbook ILC* (1964) at 114–19, esp. at paras 30–1, 40, 43, 46–7, 53, 54, and 61.

The doctrinal debate that dominated the Commission's discussion in 1964 has now been overtaken by writers citing modern examples of treaties which do indeed create rights and obligations for entities that are not parties to the treaties. Many accept that certain treaties, such as the 1948 Genocide Convention or the 1949 Geneva Conventions setting out war crimes (labelled grave breaches) create international obligations for individuals.[152] Similarly, armed groups are said to be bound by the laws of armed conflict contained in, *inter alia*, Common Article 3 to the 1949 Geneva Conventions.[153] Theodor Meron has given examples of provisions in human rights treaties as intended by the parties to create obligations for individuals;[154] Harold Hongju Koh has pointed to oil spill treaties and hazardous waste conventions as creating liability for corporations.[155] And European Union law has been interpreted by the European Court of Justice as creating rights and obligations for individuals which flow from the treaties and take direct effect in the member states.[156]

---

152. For an early finding that international criminal law such as the Genocide Convention 'creates duties for the individual directly' see Waldock 'General Course on Public International Law'. 106 *RCADI* II (1962) 1–251 at 229. For the conditions under which the International Criminal Court has jurisdiction over such individual international crimes see Ch. III § 4 above. Cf M. Milanović, 'Is the Rome Statute Binding on Individuals? (And Why We Should Care)', 9(1) *JICJ* (2011) 25–52.

153. See also A. Cassese, 'The Status of Rebels under the 1977 Geneva Protocol on Non-International Armed Conflicts', 30 *ICLQ* (1981) 416–39. Chinkin (above) at 132–3; S. Sivakumaran, 'Binding Armed Opposition Groups', 55 *ICLQ* (2006) 369–94.

154. T. Meron, *Human Rights in Internal Strife: Their International Protection* (Cambridge: Grotius, 1987) at 33–40.

155. H.H. Koh, 'Separating Myth from Reality about Corporate Responsibility Litigation', 7(2) *Journal of International Economic Law* (2004) 263–74.

156. See, e.g. *Van Gend & Loos v Netherlands Fiscal Administration* [1963] ECR 1 at 12: 'Independently of the legislation of Member States, Community law therefore not

The International Court of Justice itself has considered that the Vienna Convention on Consular Relations creates individual rights for those detained individuals entitled to consular assistance.[157] While the individuals are to assert those rights in the domestic legal system of the state where they are detained; the state of nationality of the detained person can invoke those rights, and its own rights, before the International Court of Justice (where the jurisdiction does not extend to individuals). Some international courts, such as the European Court of Human Rights, do however have jurisdiction beyond inter-state cases and can hear complaints brought by individuals and other non-state entities. In these cases it again makes sense to see the treaties as creating international rights for such third parties.[158]

---

only imposes obligations on individuals but is also intended to confer upon them rights which become part of their legal heritage. These rights arise not only where they are expressly granted by the Treaty, but also by reason of obligations which the Treaty imposes in a clearly defined way upon individuals as well as upon the Member States and upon the institutions of the Community.'

157. *Avena and Other Mexican Nationals (Mexico v USA)* (2004) at para. 40, *LaGrand (Germany v USA)* (2001) at para. 77. See Ch. VI § 11(c) above and VCCR Art. 36(1). See further B. Sepúlveda-Amor, 'Diplomatic and Consular Protection: The Rights of the State and the Rights of the Individual in the *LaGrand* and *Avena* Cases', in U. Fastenrath et al (eds), *From Bilateralism to Community Interest: Essays in Honour of Judge Bruno Simma* (Oxford: OUP, 2011) 1097–117.

158. Indeed already in the 1964 ILC debate (above) Waldock complained that 'he could hardly conceive of the European Commission of Human Rights as a municipal tribunal, and it applied a Convention through international machinery; he believed the view expressed by the Chairman [Ago] on that point to be in contradiction with the existing practice'. At para. 60. A similar argument has been made by Gaeta who has recently suggested that the protected persons under the Geneva Conventions of 1949 are the holders of rights under those treaties. P. Gaeta, 'Are Victims of Serious Violations of International Humanitarian Law Entitled to Compensation?', in O. Ben-Naftali (ed.), *International*

The extent to which an international right or obligation for an individual or corporation can be vindicated in a national legal order depends on the ways in which international law is received in that order.[159] But there is no reason to equate the existence of an international right or obligation with access to a national remedy or an international jurisdiction. Even where no national or international court has jurisdiction over the case, the rights and obligations exist and could be addressed through negotiation or the creation of a new remedy or jurisdiction.

In sum, in the words of Yoram Dinstein: 'It is a commonplace today that treaties can directly impose obligations on—and accord rights to—individual human beings.'[160] The more problematic issue is usually how to vindicate those rights and enforce such obligations. The presumption is that states are responsible for ensuring that such rights and obligations may take effect in national law. Today this may happen in some countries even in the absence of specific implementing legislation. Moreover, international human rights courts apply these rights and obligations on a daily basis,

Humanitarian Law and International Human Rights Law (Oxford: OUP, 2011) 305–27, at 319; see further the Basic Principles and Guidelines on the Right to a Remedy and Reparation for Victims of Gross Violations of International Human Rights Law and Serious Violations of International Humanitarian Law, GA Res. 60/147 of 16 December 2005.

159. See Ch. II § 8 above. See D. Shelton *International Law and Domestic Legal Systems: Incorporation, Transformation, and Persuasion* (Oxford: OUP, 2011); see also H. Lauterpacht, 'General Rules of the Law of Peace' at 279–94 in E. Lauterpacht (ed.), *International Law: Collected Papers*, vol. 1 (Cambridge: CUP, 1970). (English version of the Cours Général) 62 *RCADI* (1937)).

160. Y. Dinstein, *The Interaction Between Customary International Law and Treaties*, 322 *RCADI* (2006) 243–427, at 339.

awarding compensation to individuals, non-governmental organizations, and corporations; while international criminal tribunals hear cases alleging the commission of international crimes—and imprison those who are found guilty.[161] The rights and obligations of these third parties to the relevant treaties are therefore no longer merely topics of doctrinal debate—they are given very concrete effect.

§ 11. Breach, suspension, and termination of treaties

(a) *Material breach*

A treaty may be simply terminated through mutual consent, performance of the relevant obligations, or the expiration of a time-limit.[162] But there are more difficult cases. From the time of

---

161. In addition to the European Court of Human Rights, the ECOWAS Community Court of Justice and the African Court of Human and Peoples' Rights both have jurisdiction over cases brought by individuals. In the sphere of international criminal obligations imposed on individuals international treaties may often be inadequate on their own to detail all the elements of a crime, and international tribunals will in practice rely heavily on customary international law. This does not apparently mean, however, that treaties on their own may not provide for individual obligations. An appeal complaining that the Trial Chamber of the International Criminal Tribunal for the former Yugoslavia had relied on treaty law rather than customary law was rejected in the *Galić* case. The Appeal Chamber noted: 'However, while binding conventional law that prohibits conduct and provides for individual criminal responsibility could provide the basis for the International Tribunal's jurisdiction, in practice the International Tribunal always ascertains that the treaty provision in question is also declaratory of custom.' IT-98-29-A, 30 November 2006, at para. 85.

162. For background see McNair, 'La Terminaison et la dissolution des traités', in *Hague Recueil,* 1928, xxii, 463.

Grotius,[163] many writers propounded the view that the breach of *any* term of a treaty by one party will release the other from all obligations of the treaty. But such a doctrine, applied to any of the more important treaties, would lead to results so startling that it has never been adopted in international practice, and ought equally to be rejected by legal theory.[164]

The Vienna Convention developed provisions to address the situation where one party is said to be in *material breach* of a treaty. For a bilateral treaty the rule is apparently quite simple: a material breach entitles the other party 'to invoke the breach as a ground for terminating the treaty or suspending its operation in whole or in part'.[165] What then constitutes a 'material breach'? The VCLT defines this as '(*a*) a repudiation of the treaty not sanctioned by the present Convention; or (*b*) the violation of a provision essential to the accomplishment of the object or purpose of the treaty.'[166] Scholars have criticized the 'inherent vagueness' of this provision,[167] and in practice, states may choose to label certain provisions as 'essential' in order to avoid any

---

163. *De jure belli* (1625), book ii, 15, 12.

164. For an examination of a proposed principle that performance of an obligation may be withheld if the other party has itself failed to perform the same or a related obligation (*exceptio inadimpleti contractus*) see J. Crawford and S. Olleson, 'The Exception of Non-performance: Links between the Law of Treaties and the Law of State Responsibility', 21 *Australian Year Book of International Law* (2001) 55–74.

165. Art. 60(1).

166. VCLT Art. 60(3).

167. Simma and Tams (above) at 1361.

argument as to whether suspension or termination is justified.[168]

The provisions for multilateral treaties reflect the fact that even if a specially affected state may suspend the treaty towards the state which is in material breach, that injured state will still owe obligations to the other parties.[169] We can also see that the aggrieved party cannot simply terminate the treaty; it merely has a right to *invoke* the breach and follow the Convention's procedures.[170]

---

168. See for example the EU Cotonou Agreement with African, Caribbean and Pacific States (2010), which stipulates in Article 9 (2) that '[r]espect for human rights, democratic principles and the rule of law, which underpin the ACP-EU Partnership, shall underpin the domestic and international policies of the Parties and constitute the essential elements of this Agreement'. Article 96 sets out the procedure to be followed for suspension. Of course the rationale for suspension will be dependent on political factors and the chances of improving rather than worsening the situation, the law of treaties simply gives the parties the option. For a discussion of the policy issues see E. Paasivirta, 'Human Rights, Diplomacy and Sanctions: Aspects to "Human Rights Clauses" in the External Agreements of the European Union', in J. Petman and J. Klabbers (eds), *Nordic Cosmopolitanism: Essays in International Law for Martti Koskenniemi* (Leiden: Nijhoff, 2003) 155–80; see also E. Riedel and M. Will, 'Human Rights Clauses in External Agreements of the EC', in P. Alston (ed.), *The EU and Human Rights* (Oxford: OUP, 1999) 723–54.

169. VCLT Art. 60(2). 'A material breach of a multilateral treaty by one of the parties entitles: (*a*) the other parties by unanimous agreement to suspend the operation of the treaty in whole or in part or to terminate it either: (i) in the relations between themselves and the defaulting State; or (ii) as between all the parties; (*b*) a party specially affected by the breach to invoke it as a ground for suspending the operation of the treaty in whole or in part in the relations between itself and the defaulting State; (*c*) any party other than the defaulting State to invoke the breach as a ground for suspending the operation of the treaty in whole or in part with respect to itself if the treaty is of such a character that a material breach of its provisions by one party radically changes the position of every party with respect to the further performance of its obligations under the treaty.'

170. See Arts 65–8.

Klabbers reminds us that these procedures are 'famously underutilized', and in any event, 'suspension or termination may be the last thing the aggrieved party desires and may simply be counterproductive'.[171]

The question for us then, is what else can a state do in the face of a breach (material or otherwise) of a treaty by another state? This issue falls to be dealt with under the general law of state responsibility and applies to all breaches of treaties.[172] Although there may be diplomatic reasons for avoiding references to 'breaches' or 'violations' of a treaty, a breach can be defined as a state's acts or omissions which are 'incompatible with an obligation grounded in that treaty'.[173] The other state may demand reparation for the breach of the obligation. An injured state may also wish to engage in countermeasures.[174]

(b) *Countermeasures in response to breach of treaty*

The conditions for such *countermeasures* to be lawful can be summarized as follows: they must be proportionate, allow for the

---

171. J. Klabbers, 'Side-stepping Article 60: Material Breach of Treaty and Responses Thereto', in M. Tupamäki (ed.), *Finnish Branch of International Law Association 1946–1996: Essays on International Law* (Helsinki: Finnish ILA Branch, 1998), 20–42 at 22.

172. For a detailed look at this issue see the very incisive piece by Simma 'Reflections on Article 60 of the Vienna Convention on the Law of Treaties and Its Background in General International Law', 20 *Österreichische Zeitschrift für öffentliches Recht* (1970) 5–83.

173. S. Rosenne, *Breach of Treaty* (Cambridge: Grotius, 1985) at 123.

174. Here we only sketch the principles as applied to a state responding to a breach of a treaty; we examine further the detailed general rules relating to countermeasures as elaborated by the ILC in the context of the draft articles on state responsibility in Ch. VIII § 3.

resumption of performance of the obligation that has been violated, and finish as soon as the violating state has complied with its obligations.[175] Countermeasures are not permitted if they affect obligations to protect fundamental human rights or those persons and objects protected from reprisal under the laws of war.[176] Furthermore, as we have seen, countermeasures cannot be used with regard to obligations owed in the context of respecting the inviolability of ambassadors, embassies and so on. They will not be possible where the state in breach can claim that the act or omission can be justified by self-defence, *force majeure*, distress, or necessity.[177]

It has been noted that a countermeasure 'must be provisional'.[178] Furthermore, as Simma and Tams explain: 'a countermeasure constitutes the (justified) violation of the binding norm; it has no

---

175. See Arts 49–54 of the ILC's Articles on Responsibility of States for Internationally Wrongful Acts (2001) (hereafter ARSIWA); and J. Crawford, A. Pellet, and S. Olleson (eds), *The Law of International Responsibility* (Oxford: OUP, 2010) chs 79–86.

176. Compare Art. 60(5) VCLT which states that the provisions on suspension or termination do not apply to treaties of a humanitarian character. This exclusion in Art. 60(5) is now considered to cover human rights treaties as well as those related to humanitarian law, Simma and Tams (above) at 1366–8; Aust (above) at 295. See further Ch. VIII § 3 for prohibited reprisals in times of armed conflict.

177. See ARSIWA Arts 21, 23, 24, 25, 26, and 27; one should note that self-defence cannot be argued as precluding the wrongfulness of breaches of humanitarian law or human rights obligations, and necessity may be a factor within primary obligations in times of conflict rather than a defence to a breach of the obligations; on distress and necessity in the context of the application of treaties see further *Rainbow Warrior (NZ v France)* 82 ILR 499 at para. 75ff.; *Case Concerning the Gabčíkovo-Nagymaros Project (Hungary/Slovakia)* ICJ Rep. (25 September 1997) at paras 47–8.

178. J. Verhoeven, 'The Law of Responsibility and the Law of Treaties', in J. Crawford et al (above) 105–13 at 111; and see ARSIWA Art. 49.

effect on the continued existence of the norm as such'.[179] The risk for any state engaging in countermeasures is that the alleged original breach may not have been a breach after all, and the countermeasures thereby become themselves a breach of the treaty which continues in force. This point can perhaps best be illustrated by the well-known *Air-Services Agreement* award.

Under a treaty between the United States and France certain airlines were authorized to operate services between the West Coast of the United States and France (via London). The airline Pan Am notified the French authorities that it planned to arrange its flights on this route with a change of 'gauge' in London, replacing the Boeing 747 with a Boeing 727 for the shorter Paris–London leg. The French authorities refused to approve this plan on the grounds that the treaty only allowed for a change of gauge in the territory of either the United States or France. The United States Government failed to get the French Government to change its mind and Pan Am started operating its service with the change of planes in London. The French Government considered that these were unlawful flights and, when the second flight landed at Orly Airport, the plane was surrounded by French police. The Captain of the Pan Am flight was instructed to return to London with all

---

179. B. Simma and C.J. Tams, 'Article 60', in O. Corten and P. Klein (eds), *The Vienna Conventions on the Law of Treaties: A Commentary* (Oxford: OUP, 2011) 1351–78, at 1354. Iain Cameron suggests that states have invoked suspension of a treaty as a countermeasure and that '[t]he preponderant view is that the substantive conditions, as well as the procedural requirements, laid down by the VCLT do not apply to such provisional suspension or non-performance. Instead, the lawfulness of this, being a countermeasure, falls to be judged under the law of State responsibility.' 'Treaties, Suspension' <mpepil. com> at para. 12; see also Verhoeven (previous fn) esp. at 112–13.

the passengers and cargo and Pan Am's future flights were suspended.

The United States Civil Aeronautics Board reacted by issuing an order to prevent Air France from operating its flights to and from Los Angeles via Montreal, for the period during which Pan Am was prevented from operating its service with a change of gauge in London. The two states submitted the dispute to arbitration, and the arbitral Tribunal confirmed that certain countermeasures could be a legitimate response to a breach of a treaty. The Tribunal's assessment of the meaning of proportionality in the context of countermeasures was that:

> [t]heir aim is to restore equality between the Parties and to encourage them to continue negotiations with mutual desire to reach an acceptable solution.... It goes without saying that recourse to counter-measures involves the great risk of giving rise, in turn, to a further reaction, thereby causing an escalation which will lead to a worsening of the conflict. Counter-measures therefore should be a wager on the wisdom, not on the weakness of the other Party. They should be used with a spirit of great moderation and be accompanied by a genuine effort at resolving the dispute.[180]

In this case the change of gauge by Pan Am was found to be legal under the treaty. The French action was therefore a breach of the treaty (and not a legitimate countermeasure) and the proposed

---

180. *Air Service Agreement of 27 March 1946 between the United States of America and France,* 9 December 1978, vol. 18 RIAA 417–93 at paras 90–1.

countermeasures by the United States were seen as a proportionate response to the French breach (and so legal and not a further breach of the treaty). There is no reason, however, to believe that countermeasures need relate to a similar provision or even the same treaty.

(c) *The position of non-injured states parties*

According to the ILC Articles a non-injured state party is entitled to invoke the responsibility of the party in breach where the treaty 'is established for the protection of a collective interest of the group'.[181] Such obligations have sometimes been known as 'obligations *erga omnes partes*'. The ILC suggests such treaties would address, for example, the environment, regional security and human rights.[182] Whether or not such a non-injured state would be entitled to engage in actual countermeasures is debatable.[183]

The idea that a *non-injured state* can react to protect community interests, rather than a bilateral interest, is obviously an important development, for it alters our conception of the international legal system;[184] but, in practice, states are rarely held to account in this way by non-injured states. In many situations there will be no interested non-injured state to hold another state to its treaty obligations. The key examples are environmental pollution and human rights violations against a state's own citizens. In such cases treaty violations are often monitored by specialist treaty bodies and other states play little role. Compliance will be carefully scrutinized by

---

181. ARSIWA Art. 48(1)(a).

182. UN Doc. A/56/10 at 126–7 para. 7.

183. See ARSIWA Art. 54 (discussed in Ch. VIII § 4 below).

184. C.J. Tams, 'Individual States as Guardians of Community Interests', in Fastenrath et al, *From Bilateralism to Community Interest* (above) 379–405.

non-governmental organizations but they may fail to interest governments from other states in taking any action. UN bodies and civil society engage with states every day in an effort to ensure enhanced compliance with their treaty obligations without necessarily cataloguing 'breaches'. The 'constructive dialogue' refrains from accusations of breach, violations, or non-compliance. One is more likely to find possible breaches met with expressions of 'concern' and 'regret' by the relevant international monitoring bodies.[185] In part this is due to the fact that many such multilateral treaties set out broad obligations which need to be monitored through indicators and focused recommendations, rather than a crude binary finding of compliance/breach.

(d) *The impact of war and armed conflict on treaties*

The outbreak of war is another event which may bring a treaty to an end, but the modern view is that it does not necessarily do so. The approach of Justice Cardozo was to suggest that international law deals with this problem pragmatically so that 'provisions compatible with a state of hostilities, unless expressly terminated, will be enforced, and those incompatible rejected'.[186] Sir Cecil Hurst suggested a rather different approach to the question: that the fate of a treaty depends on the intention of the parties.[187] In some cases

---

185. See, e.g. the concluding observations by the UN Human Rights Committee on the United Kingdom UN Doc. CCPR/C/GBR/CO/6, 30 July 2008. The International Committee on Economic, Social and Cultural Rights employs similar terms and one can also find instances where this Committee is: very concerned, deeply concerned, gravely concerned, or profoundly dissatisfied.

186. *Techt v Hughes* [1920] 229 NY 222.

187. 'The Effect of War on Treaties', 2 *BYBIL* (1921–2) 37–47.

their intention is clear; for instance, a treaty which regulates the conduct of war is clearly intended to retain its force if war breaks out. But more often the minds of the parties have not been addressed to the possibility that they may some day be at war with one another, and they cannot be said to have had any real intention as to what should happen to their treaty in that unforeseen event. Such a difficulty as this, however, is in no way peculiar to the interpretation of treaties, and law often does not hesitate to attribute an intention to parties who have never thought of the situation with which in the event the law has to deal. In such a case the so-called intention is a 'presumed' intention; it is what the law thinks it reasonable to suppose that the parties *would* have intended if the situation had been present in their minds.

We have therefore to examine the particular treaty with which we are concerned in the light, both of its subject-matter, and of all the relevant surrounding circumstances. Certain presumptions have been applied in the past. Bilateral treaties dealing with political matters or with commercial relations may be assumed to have been made with reference to the relations existing between the parties at the time, and we might find that the provisions of such treaties may be incompatible with a state of war or armed conflict. Or, if we prefer to put it the other way, that the parties must have intended that war should abrogate those provisions. On the other hand, a multilateral treaty, such as a postal convention, though its operation may have to be suspended between the belligerents while the war lasts, will, by the same reasoning, generally revive and recover its force when the war is over. Although the VCLT does not cover the effect of hostilities on treaties,[188] it does clearly state that breaking off diplomatic relations

---

188. VCLT Art. 73.

does not in itself affect treaty relations 'except insofar as the existence of diplomatic or consular relations is indispensable for the application of the treaty'.[189]

The ILC has recently considered the issue of the 'effects of armed conflicts on treaties',[190] and its work proceeds from the acceptance of the 'basic idea that the outbreak of an armed conflict involving one or more States parties to a treaty does not, in itself, entail termination or suspension'.[191] The overarching principle is that in order to determine the susceptibility of the treaty to termination, withdrawal, or suspension one looks at the nature of the treaty together with the effects of the particular armed conflict on the treaty.[192] The draft articles cover both inter-state conflicts and those where a government is fighting an armed group. The definition of armed conflict is therefore narrower than that used by international criminal tribunals as it does not cover protracted fighting between armed groups. The Commission has provided an indicative list of treaties where the subject-matter implies that such

---

189. VCLT Art. 63, and see also Art. 74.

190. The legal concept of war is too problematic and has now been overtaken in this context by the concept of armed conflict, see further C. Greenwood, 'The Concept of War in Modern International Law', 36 *ICLQ* (1987) 283–306.

191. L. Caflisch, First report on the effects of armed conflicts on treaties, UN Doc. A/CN.4/627, 22 March 2010, at para. 33.

192. See 'Draft articles on the effect of armed conflicts on treaties' (2011) Art. 6: 'In order to ascertain whether a treaty is susceptible to termination, withdrawal or suspension in the event of an armed conflict, regard shall be had to all relevant factors, including: (a) the nature of the treaty, in particular its subject-matter, its object and purpose, its content and the number of parties to the treaty; and (b) the characteristics of the armed conflict, such as its territorial extent, its scale and intensity, its duration and, in the case of non-international armed conflict, also the degree of outside involvement.'

treaties continue in whole or in part during such armed conflicts.[193]

(e) *Other grounds for termination*

One of the most difficult and practically important questions of the law of treaties relates to the termination of treaties which contain no express provision for withdrawal or termination. Such treaties raise two questions which require discussion: first, whether one party may in any circumstances give notice to terminate the treaty without the consent of the other, and second, whether the treaty is liable to be terminated by the operation of any rule of law.

The answer to the first of these questions is probably that we must again inquire into the intention of the parties. The VCLT explains that where a treaty is silent on these issues and there is no

---

193. See ibid Art. 2(b) for the purposes of the draft articles: '"armed conflict" means a situation in which there is resort to armed force between States or protracted resort to armed force between governmental authorities and organized armed groups.' The indicative list of treaties is as follows: '(a) Treaties on the law of armed conflict, including treaties on international humanitarian law; (b) Treaties declaring, creating or regulating a permanent regime or status or related permanent rights, including treaties establishing or modifying land and maritime boundaries; (c) Multilateral law-making treaties; (d) Treaties on international criminal justice; (e) Treaties of friendship, commerce and navigation and agreements concerning private rights; (f) Treaties for the international protection of human rights; (g) Treaties relating to the international protection of the environment; (h) Treaties relating to international watercourses and related installations and facilities; (i) Treaties relating to aquifers and related installations and facilities; (j) Treaties which are constituent instruments of international organizations; (k) Treaties relating to the international settlement of disputes by peaceful means, including resort to conciliation, mediation, arbitration and judicial settlement; (l) Treaties relating to diplomatic and consular relations.'

consent from all the other parties there can be no withdrawal unless: (*a*) it is established that the parties intended to admit the possibility of denunciation or withdrawal; or (*b*) a right of denunciation or withdrawal may be implied by the nature of the treaty.[194] These rules have been applied by the UN Secretary-General as depositary in the context of the attempt by North Korea to withdraw from the International Covenant on Civil and Political Rights. It was held that North Korea could not withdraw and so it remains a party.[195]

The second question brings us to the doctrine which was once known as *clausula rebus sic stantibus*. In every treaty, it was said, there is implied a clause which provides that the treaty is to be binding only 'so long as things stand as they are'; the expressed terms may be absolute, but a treaty is never more than conditional, and when a 'vital change of circumstances' has occurred, the condition of the treaty's validity has failed, and it ceases to be binding. Such a doctrine, without careful definition, is capable of being used, and often has been used, merely to excuse the breach of a treaty obligation that a state finds it inconvenient to fulfil.[196]

---

194. VCLT Arts 56 and 54.

195. The Human Rights Committee's General Comment 26 explains 'the Covenant is not the type of treaty which, by its nature, implies a right of denunciation. Together with the simultaneously prepared and adopted International Covenant on Economic, Social and Cultural Rights, the Covenant codifies in treaty form the universal human rights enshrined in the Universal Declaration of Human Rights, the three instruments together often being referred to as the "International Bill of Human Rights". As such, the Covenant does not have a temporary character typical of treaties where a right of denunciation is deemed to be admitted, notwithstanding the absence of a specific provision to that effect.'

196. For a full history see A. Vamvoukos, *Termination of Treaties in International Law: The Doctrines of* Rebus Sic Stantibus *and Desuetude* (Oxford: Clarendon, 1985).

Not every important change of circumstances will put an end to the obligations of a treaty. The principle will not relieve a state from treaty obligations merely because new and unforeseen circumstances have made obligations unexpectedly burdensome to the state party, or because some consideration of equity suggests that it would be fair and reasonable to give such relief. The rule concerning change of circumstances bears no analogy to a principle such as that of *laesio enormis* in the Roman law.[197] What puts an end to the treaty is the disappearance of the foundation upon which it rests.[198] The familiar fiction of a presumed intention, or implied clause, was eventually rejected by the ILC in the drafting of the Vienna Convention.[199] The ILC wanted to stress an objective rather than a subjective test, and decided to avoid the use of the expression *rebus sic stantibus* altogether.[200] Moreover the rule is expressed as a presumption that a change of circumstances may *not* be invoked unless very specific conditions are fulfilled. Article 62 reads:

1. A fundamental change of circumstances which has occurred with regard to those existing at the time of the conclusion of a

---

197. Literally 'enormous loss'; allowing a vendor to resile from a sale of land where the land was sold for less than half the market value.

198. Note the separate rule which allows a party to invoke the impossibility of performance of a treaty where this arises from the 'permanent disappearance or destruction of an object indispensable for the execution of the treaty'. VCLT Art. 61.

199. Compare the previous edition of this book at 336–8; N. Kontou, *The Termination and Revision of Treaties in the Light of New Customary International Law* (Oxford: Clarendon, 1994) at 35.

200. II *Yearbook ILC* (1966) at 258.

treaty, and which was not foreseen by the parties, may not be invoked as a ground for terminating or withdrawing from the treaty unless:

(a) the existence of those circumstances constituted an essential basis of the consent of the parties to be bound by the treaty; and

(b) the effect of the change is radically to transform the extent of obligations still to be performed under the treaty.

2. A fundamental change of circumstances may not be invoked as a ground for terminating or withdrawing from a treaty:

(a) if the treaty establishes a boundary; or

(b) if the fundamental change is the result of a breach by the party invoking it either of an obligation under the treaty or of any other international obligation owed to any other party to the treaty.

The exclusion of boundary treaties in Article 62(2) was aimed at the preservation of stability and to reassure states at a time when the third party dispute settlement was being reinforced though the new law of treaties. Concerns were raised during the drafting as to the effect such a provision might have on the principle of self-determination in cases where a boundary treaty had been imposed on a people in the context of decolonization. The ILC Commentary explained that the principle of self-determination would remain unaffected.

> Some members of the Commission suggested that the total exclusion of these [boundary] treaties from the rule might go too far, and might be inconsistent with the principle of self-

determination recognized in the Charter. The Commission, however, concluded that treaties establishing a boundary should be recognized to be an exception to the rule, because otherwise the rule, instead of being an instrument of peaceful change, might become a source of dangerous frictions. It also took the view that 'self-determination', as envisaged in the Charter was an independent principle and that it might lead to confusion if, in the context of the law of treaties, it were presented as an application of the rule contained in the present article. By excepting treaties establishing a boundary from its scope the present article would not exclude the operation of the principle of self-determination in any case where the conditions for its legitimate operation existed.[201]

The International Court of Justice later explained that, once established, the boundary exists independently of the treaty. 'Once agreed, the boundary stands, for any other approach would vitiate the fundamental principle of the stability of boundaries, the importance of which has been repeatedly emphasized by the Court... A boundary established by treaty thus achieves a permanence which the treaty itself does not necessarily enjoy. The treaty can cease to be in force without in any way affecting the continuance of the boundary.'[202]

Returning to the general rule on fundamental change of circumstances, the International Court of Justice has had to deal with

---

201. II *Yearbook ILC* (1966) at 259 para. 11.
202. *Territorial Dispute (Libyan Arab Jamahiriya/Chad)*, ICJ Rep. (1994) p. 6 at paras 72–3.

a set of arguments by Hungary claiming that due to a fundamental change of circumstances it was no longer bound under a treaty with Czechoslovakia to work on a particular hydro-electric project involving dams on the River Danube.

> Hungary identified a number of 'substantive elements' present at the conclusion of the 1977 Treaty which it said had changed fundamentally by the date of notification of termination. These included the notion of 'socialist integration', for which the Treaty had originally been a 'vehicle', but which subsequently disappeared; the 'single and indivisible operational system', which was to be replaced by a unilateral scheme; the fact that the basis of the planned joint investment had been overturned by the sudden emergence of both States into a market economy; the attitude of Czechoslovakia which had turned the 'framework treaty' into an 'immutable norm'; and, finally, the transformation of a treaty consistent with environmental protection into 'a prescription for environmental disaster'.[203]

The Court stated that such arguments failed to fulfil the conditions set out in Article 62, and that the plea of fundamental change of circumstances will only apply in exceptional cases:

> In the Court's view, the prevalent political conditions were thus not so closely linked to the object and purpose of the Treaty that they constituted an essential basis of the consent

---

203. *Case Concerning the Gabčíkovo-Nagymaros Project* (above) at para. 95.

of the parties and, in changing, radically altered the extent of the obligations still to be performed. The same holds good for the economic system in force at the time of the conclusion of the 1977 Treaty. Besides, even though the estimated profitability of the Project might have appeared less in 1992 than in 1977, it does not appear from the record before the Court that it was bound to diminish to such an extent that the treaty obligations of the parties would have been radically transformed as a result. The Court does not consider that new developments in the state of environmental knowledge and of environmental law can be said to have been completely unforeseen.[204]

This confirms that there is a heavy burden on a state raising the plea of fundamental change of circumstances.[205]

The rule on fundamental change of circumstances has little to do with the problem of obsolete or oppressive treaties, for which *rebus sic stantibus* was too often supposed to be the solution. The problem of oppressive or obsolete treaty obligations is, in fact, only

---

204. Ibid para. 104.

205. See also *Fisheries Jurisdiction (UK v Iceland) jurisdiction*, ICJ Rep. (1973) at paras 32–40. The ILC Commentary suggests the rule offers a safety valve rather than an escape clause: 'there may remain a residue of cases in which, failing any agreement, one party may be left powerless under the treaty to obtain any legal relief from outmoded and burdensome provisions. It is in these cases that the *rebus sic stantibus* doctrine could serve a purpose as a lever to induce a spirit of compromise in the other party. Moreover, despite the strong reservations often expressed with regard to it, the evidence of the acceptance of the doctrine in international law is so considerable that it seems to indicate a recognition of a need for this safety-valve in the law of treaties.' II *Yearbook ILC* (1966) at 258 at para. 6.

one aspect, and not the most important aspect, of a much wider problem of international relations; for the danger to international order comes more often from oppressive *conditions*, and especially frontier conditions, than from the obligations of a treaty. Whether these conditions were, or were not, originally created by a treaty, and whether they have, or have not, been brought into existence by some change of circumstances, are from a practical point of view irrelevant considerations. Dissatisfaction, unrealized national ambitions, inequalities between states, are all relevant grievances but they do not usually have their source in oppressive treaties; many are created by geography, or climate, or the distribution of nature's resources, or by historical events which happened centuries ago. When these things can be remedied or alleviated by changes in the law, it is right and necessary that those changes should be made, and that is why peaceful change through law deserves our serious consideration.[206] It is perhaps a mistake to think that by some ingenious manipulation of existing legal doctrines we can always find a solution for the problems of a changing

---

206. For a fuller version of Brierly's concern with peaceful change, understood as adjusting treaty obligations in order to prevent war, see the previous edition of this book at pp. 331–45 and more fully J.L. Brierly, *The Outlook for International Law* (Oxford: Clarendon, 1944) at 124–42; see also Craven (above) at 65–71. The expression 'peaceful change' had multiple meanings in the inter-War years; some went so far as to build on Article 19 of the League of Nations Covenant to propose a world legislature with the power to rewrite treaties (see, e.g. H. Lauterpacht, 'The Legal Aspect' in C.A.W. Manning (ed.), *Peaceful Change: An International Problem* (London: MacMillan, 1937) 135–65. The expression has been retained here as it is emblematic of Brierly's articulation of his seemingly contradictory dual concern that international law provide both stability and justice. For the use of this expression in contemporary international relations see H. Miall, *Emergent Conflict and Peaceful Change* (Basingstoke: Palgrave, 2007).

international world. That is not so; for many of these problems—
and oppressive treaties are one of them—the only remedy is that
states should be willing to take measures to bring the legal situation into accord with new needs, and if states are not reasonable
enough to do that, we must not expect the existing law to relieve
them of the consequences. Law is bound to uphold the principle
that treaties are to be observed; it cannot be made an instrument
for revising them, and if political motives sometimes lead to a
treaty being treated as 'a scrap of paper' we must not invent a
pseudo-legal principle to justify such action. The remedy has to be
sought elsewhere, in political, not in juridical action.

VIII | International Disputes and the Maintenance of International Peace and Security

§ 1. Dispute settlement

THE PROBLEM of effecting the peaceful settlement of a dispute is addressed through two methods; we may either induce the disputing parties to accept terms of settlement dictated to them by some third party, or we may persuade them to come together and agree on terms of settlement for themselves. In the international field, the former method takes the form either of arbitration or of judicial settlement; the latter method takes the form of negotiation, good offices, mediation, or conciliation.

As we saw in the previous chapter, the methods of peaceful settlement arise against a background of the possibility of counter-measures. In the past, and in previous editions of this book, these countermeasures were referred to under the headings reprisals and retorsion; and these topics were included in the chapter on the use of force. Today, war and the use of force are not permitted as responses to violations of international law.[1]

---

1. The exceptions are when a state is the object of an armed attack and acts in self-defence or when states are authorized to use force by the Security Council, see Ch. IX below.

We have also seen how countermeasures, in the form of a peaceful reprisal, may be used in response to the breach of a treaty in order to bring the other party back into compliance with its international obligations.[2] It was explained that the legality of such countermeasures demands that they be proportionate, and not affect particular obligations such as those which protect fundamental human rights or certain categories of persons under humanitarian law. The regime of state responsibility for internationally wrongful acts, and the rights of other states to respond to such wrongful acts, covers not just violations of treaties but also all violations of customary international law. It is bound up with questions of dispute settlement and so we will consider these issues here. Let us examine first the rules for attribution of conduct to a state, and then look at reprisals, retorsion, and countermeasures before considering dispute settlement more generally.

§ 2. Attribution of conduct to a state

We have already seen, in the context of the treatment of foreigners, that a state will be internationally responsible for the conduct of any of its organs, executive, legislative, or judicial.[3] We now look at questions of *attribution* in more detail. It is clear that the conduct of any organ acting in exercise of governmental authority is attrib-

---

2. For a detailed review of the law and practice in this area see the seminal article by B. Simma 'Reflections on Article 60 of the Vienna Convention on the Law of Treaties and Its Background in General International Law', 20 *Österreichische Zeitschrift für öffentliches Recht* (1970) 5–83.

3. See above Ch. VI § 10 on a state's treatment of foreigners.

utable to the state: 'even if it exceeds its authority or contravenes instructions'.[4] So, where two officers unsuccessfully tried to extort money from a French citizen, took him to a military barracks, and then later drove him to a village and shot him, the state of Mexico was held responsible, since: 'the murderers had acted in their capacity of military officers and had taken advantage of the power and compulsory means at their disposal by reason of that very capacity'.[5] In times of armed conflict all the actions of the persons forming part of the armed forces of a state party to the conflict will be attributed to the state.[6]

The conduct of persons or entities that are not organs of the state may nevertheless be considered an act of the state where the law of that state has empowered them 'to exercise elements of governmental authority'.[7] Brigitte Stern suggests that 'any institution which fulfils one of the traditional functions of the State, even if such functions have been privatized, should be considered as an organ of the State from the point of view of international law and for the purposes of the law of responsibility'.[8] This idea is reflected in the ILC's commentaries, a distinction being drawn between governmental activity and commercial activity: 'Thus, for example,

---

4. Art. 7. International Law Commission's Articles on Responsibility of States for Internationally Wrongful Acts (2001) (hereafter ARSIWA).

5. *Caire Case (France v United Mexican States)* Case No. 91 5 ILR 146, at 149; for the full original award see 5 RIAA (1929) 516–34.

6. See *Armed Activities on the Territory of the Congo (Democratic Republic of the Congo v Uganda)*, ICJ Rep. (2005) paras 213–14.

7. ARSIWA Art. 5.

8. B. Stern, 'The Elements of an Internationally Wrongful Act', in J. Crawford, A. Pellet, and S. Olleson (eds), *The Law of International Responsibility* (Oxford: OUP, 2010) 193–220, at 204.

the conduct of a railway company to which certain police powers have been granted will be regarded as an act of the State under international law if it concerns the exercise of those powers, but not if it concerns other activities (e.g. the sale of tickets or the purchase of rolling stock).'[9] Stern offers us the following contemporary explanation: 'the mere fact that a State confers management of its prisons or control of immigration in its airports, or even certain police functions to private entities, does not mean that the State can absolve itself from all international responsibility when those entities commit acts contrary to the State's international obligations.'[10]

Conduct can also be attributed to a state where the persons or group are 'acting on the instructions, or under the direction or control, of the State in carrying out the conduct'.[11] Disputes before international tribunals will often centre on whether particular acts can be attributed to a state in this way. The International Court of Justice examined this question in some detail when it found that the acts of the *contras* in Nicaragua could not be attributed to the United States in the 1980s.[12] It held 'that United States participation, even if preponderant or decisive, in the financing, organizing, training, supplying and equipping of the *contras*, the selection of its military or paramilitary targets, and the planning of the whole of its operation, is still insufficient in itself'.[13] The Court

---

9. ILC Commentary, UN Doc. A/56/10, at p. 43 para. 5.

10. 'The Elements of an Internationally Wrongful Act' (above) at 204.

11. Art. 8 ARSIWA.

12. *Military and Paramilitary Activities in and against Nicaragua (Nicaragua v USA)*, ICJ Rep. (1986) at para. 109ff.

13. Ibid para. 115.

concluded on this point: 'For this conduct to give rise to legal responsibility of the United States, it would in principle have to be proved that that State had effective control of the military or paramilitary operations in the course of which the alleged violations were committed.'[14]

More recently, in the context of claims by Bosnia and Herzegovina that the acts of the 'Scorpions', with regard to Srebrenica, be attributed to the Federal Republic of Yugoslavia, the Court reinforced its approach stating that it would have to be shown that: '"effective control" was exercised, or that the State's instructions were given, in respect of *each operation* in which the alleged violations occurred, not generally in respect of the overall actions taken by the persons or groups of persons having committed the violations'.[15]

Other situations where the conduct of non-state actors will be attributed to the state include: the situation where non-state actors are in fact exercising elements of governmental authority (for example in times of natural catastrophe or some other break-down in normal government), the situation where insurgents become the new government (or establish a new state)—at this point their conduct as insurgents is attributed to the state they newly govern—and lastly, situations where the state adopts the conduct in question as its own.[16]

---

14. Ibidem.

15. *Case Concerning the Application of the Convention on the Prevention and Punishment of the Crime of Genocide (Bosnia and Herzegovina v Serbia and Montenegro)* judgment of 26 February 2007, at para. 400 (emphasis added).

16. ARSIWA Arts 9, 10, 11. For a full discussion of the theory and practice of attribution (or imputation) see Crawford et al (above) at 187–315.

§ 3. Retorsion, reprisals, and countermeasures

Retorsion is a measure of self-help taken in response to an illegal or unfriendly act, where the self-help measure itself is within the law. It differs therefore from the reprisals (countermeasures) we have already considered in the previous chapter;[17] those measures would be illegal *but for* the fact that they fall within the conditions for a legitimate countermeasure as a response to an internationally wrongful act committed by a state. The following examples of retorsion are familiar: breaking off diplomatic relations; imposing visa restrictions on nationals from the other state; withdrawing aid; and downgrading diplomatic relations. These actions are legal as such but taken in response to illegal acts committed by states. This form of self-help is not covered by the rules relating to state responsibility for internationally wrongful acts, but it is sometimes suggested that such retaliation should be proportionate and should be discontinued as soon as the other state's behaviour ceases.[18]

Reprisal is a word with a long history. Literally and historically it denotes the seizing of property or persons by way of 'retaking', and formerly it was not uncommon for a state to issue 'letters of reprisal' to their subjects, who may have met with a denial of justice in another state, authorizing them to redress the wrong for themselves by forcible action (retaliation), such as the seizure of the property of subjects of the delinquent state. The practice was called 'special' or 'private' reprisals, but it has long been obsolete.[19]

---

17. § 11(b).

18. See A. Cassese, *International Law*, 2nd edn (Oxford: OUP, 2005) at 310.

19. For a detailed examination of the history and the law of private and public reprisals as well as retaliation in war see E.S. Colbert, *Retaliation in International Law* (New York: King's Crown Press, 1948).

We might also note the practice of issuing 'letters of marque' which authorized a 'privateer' in time of war to seize enemy public and private ships. In these cases there was no issue of the privateer having suffered any previous wrong; the letters of marque authorized privateers to use force thereby distinguishing them from pirates.[20]

Reprisals when they are taken today are taken by a state as such. Nowadays the preference is to refer to reprisals as *countermeasures*, reserving the expression reprisals for particular countermeasures taken in times of armed conflict.[21]

Countermeasures, as we have seen in the context of responses to breach of treaty, are a form of legitimate non-forcible self-help, to which states may resort in order to bring another state back into compliance with its international obligations. As long as the international legal system does not provide an organized machinery for coercing a delinquent state to conform to all its international obligations,[22] self-help remains an option for states, albeit, as we shall see, in quite circumscribed circumstances.

---

20. The practice, which operated from the thirteenth century through to the nineteenth century, was applied by several naval and other powers. In French the equivalent was a *lettre de course* generating the term *corsair* for those engaging in such reprisals. The practice was abolished by the Paris Déclaration réglant divers points de droit maritime (1856) Art. 1': 'La course est et demeure abolie'. The US Constitution still states in Art. I(8) that Congress has the power '[t]o declare War, grant Letters of Marque and Reprisal, and make Rules concerning Captures on Land and Water'. For an interesting set of studies see D.J. Starkey, E.S. van Eyck van Heslinga, and J.A. de Moor (eds), *Pirates and Privateers: New Perspectives on the War on Trade in the Eighteenth and Nineteenth Centuries* (Exeter: University of Exeter Press, 1997).

21. On the lexicon of terms used in this context and their etymology see D. Alland, 'The Definition of Countermeasures', in J. Crawford et al (above) 1127–36.

22. The term sanctions is increasingly reserved for collective action determined by the relevant organ of an international organization. Whether or not such sanctions can relieve

The conditions of a legal resort to reprisals were discussed in the *Naulilaa* arbitral award in 1928, and certain principles, which had previously depended for their authority on academic writing, were accepted and applied by the tribunal.[23] In 1915, while Portugal was still neutral in the First World War, an incident took place at Naulilaa, a Portuguese post on the frontier between Angola and what was then German South-West Africa. Three Germans were killed. On the evidence it was clearly established that the incident arose out of a pure misunderstanding.[24] The Germans, however, as a measure of reprisals, had sent an expedition into Portuguese territory, attacked several frontier posts, and drove out the garrison from Naulilaa. A local uprising took place which was then suppressed by the Portuguese.

states of their obligations to the targeted state depends on the constituent treaty of the organization and the relationship between the state and the organizations and its members. See for a full account V. Gowlland-Debbas (ed.), *United Nations Sanctions and International Law* (The Hague: Kluwer, 2001).

23. *Portugal v Germany (The Naulilaa case)*, vol. 2 RIAA (1928) 1011–33; summary 4 ILR 526.

24. The incident is nicely captured by Julia Pfeil: 'On 19 October 1914, the German governor, who was accompanied by 20 soldiers and an interpreter, approached the border at the Portuguese fort of Naulilaa. Negotiations were difficult, however, because the Germans did not speak or understand any Portuguese and the Portuguese did not speak or understand any German. Due to several misunderstandings caused by the German interpreter's manifest ignorance of Portuguese, the Portuguese were led to believe that the German governor had the secret intent of commencing an invasion into Angola. The German side, however, believed that the Portuguese lieutenant and captain had entrapped the German governor and his officers in an ambush. When the Germans decided to leave Fort Naulilaa and mounted their horses, the Portuguese tried to keep them from leaving. The Germans then drew their firearms; at that moment, the Portuguese fired several shots and killed the German governor and two of his officers. The interpreter and a soldier were interned.' *Naulilaa Arbitration (Portugal v Germany)*, <mpepil.com>.

The arbitrators laid down three conditions for the legitimacy of reprisals: (*a*) there must have been an illegal act on the part of the other state; (*b*) reprisals must be preceded by a request for redress of the wrong, for the necessity of resorting to force cannot be established if the possibility of obtaining redress by other means is not even explored; and (*c*) the measures adopted must not be excessive, in the sense of being out of all proportion to the provocation received; they are limited by: 'les expériences de l'humanité et les règles de la bonne foi'.[25] In this case Portugal had committed no illegal act; Germany had made no request for redress; and the disproportion between the German action and its provocation was evident. The award was therefore given in favour of Portugal.

The principles remain relevant, even if today reprisals involving the use of force are forbidden and the preferred terminology is countermeasures. Several treaties played a role in limiting reprisals and we might briefly refer here to the so-called *Drago doctrine*. In 1902, when Great Britain and Germany were conducting a pacific blockade of Venezuela in the interests of her British and German creditors, Luis María Drago, then the Argentinean Foreign Minister, put forward the contention that the failure of a state to pay its debts does not justify the use of force against it. There may have been good reasons even at that date from a domestic point of view against employing the British fleet as a debt-collecting agency on behalf of British subjects who had made risky investments abroad, but there was then little authority in international law for Drago's contention. It led, however, in 1907 to a Hague Convention (No. II) 'respecting the limitation of the employment of force for the

---

25. *Naulilaa* (above) at 1026 (requirements of humanity and rules of good faith).

recovery of contract debts', whereby the signatory states agreed not to use force for that purpose unless, in effect, the debtor state had refused to submit to arbitration, or having agreed to do so, had failed to obey the award.

At least since 1928, the date of the Pact of Paris (or General Treaty for the Renunciation of War), it has been clear that reprisals which involve the use of force are no longer legal. By Article 2 the 'High Contracting Powers' agreed 'that the settlement or solution of all disputes or conflicts, of whatever nature or of whatever origin they may be, which may arise between them, shall never be sought except by pacific means'. This prohibition is reaffirmed in the UN Charter of 1945.[26]

The modern conditions for peaceful countermeasures build on the principles outlined in the *Naulilaa* case and have been elaborated by the International Law Commission.[27] They can be summarized as follows. First, countermeasures must be aimed at the state that has violated its obligations towards the injured state.[28] Second, they are limited to the temporary non-performance of the obligations of the injured state and should as far as possible be reversible so as to allow for the resumption of the performance of the original obligation.[29] Third, they have to be terminated when the wrongdo-

---

26. See Art. 2(3) 'All Members shall settle their international disputes by peaceful means in such a manner that international peace and security, and justice, are not endangered. (4) All Members shall refrain in their international relations from the threat or use of force against the territorial integrity or political independence of any state, or in any other manner inconsistent with the Purposes of the United Nations.' See also Arts 33 and 37, and the Manila Declaration on the Peaceful Settlement of International Disputes annexed to the GA Resolution of 15 November 1982, A/RES/37/10.

27. For a full discussion see Crawford et al (above) at 1127–214.

28. See ARSIWA Art. 49(1).

29. Ibid Art. 49(2)(3).

ing state has complied with its obligations (including the obligation to provide reparation).[30] Fourth, they should be commensurate with the injury suffered and have as their purpose to induce the wrongdoing state to comply with its obligations under international law.[31] Fifth, they cannot involve the use of force or affect peremptory norms (*jus cogens*), fundamental human rights obligations,[32] humanitarian obligations prohibiting reprisals,[33] or obligations to respect the inviolability of diplomatic and consular agents, premises,

---

30. Ibid Arts 53, 28–41, 52(3).

31. Ibid Art. 51, *Case Concerning the Gabčíkovo-Nagymaros Project (Hungary/Slovakia)*, ICJ Rep. (25 September 1997) at paras 85–7; Thomas Franck suggests: 'In assessing the acceptability of a response, the principle of proportionality allows those affronted by unlawful conduct to respond by taking into account the level of response necessary to prevent recurrences.' 'On Proportionality of Countermeasures in International Law', 102 *AJIL* (2008) 715–67, at 765–6; in the same vein see Omer Yusif Elagab: 'the motivation for resorting to counter-measures, namely self-protection, reciprocity, and a desire to achieve a speedy settlement may be used as the main criteria for determining proportionality. Thus, in cases of unusual danger such as when the nationals of the aggrieved State are seized as hostages, that State will be entitled on the ground of self-protection to employ countermeasures of extreme severity in order to secure their release.' *The Legality of Non-Forcible Counter-measures in International Law* (Oxford: Clarendon Press, 1988) at 216. See also Cassese (above) at 305–7.

32. Ibid Art. 50(1)(b); see further S. Borelli and S. Olleson, 'Obligations Relating to Human Rights and Humanitarian Law', in J. Crawford et al (above) 1177–96; R. Provost, *International Human Rights and Humanitarian Law* (Cambridge: CUP, 2002) at 182–227.

33. Ibid Art. 50(1)(c). The prohibition refers to humanitarian obligations forbidding reprisals in armed conflict; these obligations are dealt with in the relevant treaties: reprisals against protected persons under the 1949 Geneva Conventions are forbidden (the wounded, shipwrecked, prisoners of war, and certain internees). So, for example mistreatment of prisoners of war cannot be met with mistreatment of the other side's prisoners of war. Protocol I of 1977 to the Conventions expands these protections from reprisal, covering *inter alia* the sick, wounded, shipwrecked, hospital ships, medical vehicles (Art. 20); civilians, the civilian population, and civilian objects; cultural objects and places of worship; objects indispensable to the civilian population; the natural environment;

archives, and documents. Lastly, the state resorting to countermeasures may have to comply with certain dispute settlement procedures and other preliminary procedural requirements.

Certain treaties provide that states parties will be obliged to take their dispute to a dispute settlement body rather than engaging in unilateral countermeasures.[34] For example there are provisions to this effect for members of the European Union, the World Trade Organization, and the North Atlantic Free Trade Association.[35] The preliminary procedural conditions, according to the ILC Articles on State Responsibility (ILC Articles), are that, before taking countermeasures, the injured state shall: call on the responsible state to fulfil its obligations, notify any decision to take countermeasures, and offer to negotiate.[36]

---

and installations containing dangerous forces (Arts 51–6). The customary law prohibiting belligerent reprisals is outlined in J.-M. Henckaerts and L. Doswald-Beck, *Customary International Humanitarian Law—Volume 1: Rules* (Cambridge: CUP, 2005) at 513–29. See also the prohibition on reprisals in Protocol II on Restrictions on the Use of Mines to the UN Conventional Weapons Convention (1980). For a detailed discussion of the controversy surrounding reprisals against the civilian population see F. Kalshoven 'Reprisals and the Protection of Civilians: Two Recent Decisions of the Yugoslavia Tribunal' in L.C. Vohrah et al (eds), *Man's Inhumanity to Man: Essays on International Law in Honour of Antonio Cassese* (The Hague: Kluwer, 2003) 481–509.

34. These are sometimes referred to as 'self-contained regimes'. In addition the state taking countermeasures has to comply with any obligations which flow from an applicable dispute settlement procedure, ARSIWA Art. 50(2)(a); see also Art. 52(3)(4).

35. See further D.W. Bowett, 'Economic Coercion and Reprisals by States', 13 *Virginia Journal of International Law* (1972) 1–12.

36. ARSIWA Arts 52(1) and 43. The obligations to notify the responsible state and offer to negotiate may not apply where urgent countermeasures are necessary to preserve the injured state's rights. The example given by the ILC is the temporary freezing of assets without notice in order to prevent a state from withdrawing its assets from the banks in the injured state. ILC Commentary A/56/10 at 136 para. 6.

This framework does not necessarily capture all restrictions on countermeasures. It remains rather state-centric, and Laurence Boisson de Chazournes asks whether we should not also consider, first, the effects of economic and political coercion, and secondly, the effects on the environment and community interests more generally. She suggests that: 'economic and political countermeasures may be illegal if they are aimed at coercing a State to subordinate the exercise of its sovereign rights or its independence'.[37] Her point is that fairness, the non-abuse of rights, and good faith should all be taken into account in evaluating economic countermeasures that might have long-term consequences for the population.[38] With regard to the environment she states:

> Scientific uncertainty in environmental matters makes it necessary to rethink the criteria of validity or legality of countermeasures according to different paradigms. One is led to the conclusion that the uncertainty which might surround the risk and effects of a countermeasure on the environment could be a factor in assessing the inadmissibility of a countermeasure. In this context the precautionary principle could act as a framework norm which would oblige all States to refrain from adopting in any significant way countermeasures which would threaten the environment and human health.[39]

---

37. 'Other Non-derogable Obligations', in J. Crawford et al (above) 1205–14, at 1211.

38. The example of Cuba is given to illustrate how temporary measures can be renewed exacerbating the gap between unequal partners. Eadem 'Economic Countermeasures in an Interdependent World' *ASIL Proceedings* (1995) 337–40.

39. 'Other Non-Derogable Obligations' (above) at 1212 (footnotes omitted); see further L. Boisson de Chazournes, 'New Technologies, the Precautionary Principle and Public Participation', in T. Murphy (ed.), *New Technologies and Human Rights* (Oxford: OUP, 2009) 161–94.

So far we have only dealt with countermeasures undertaken by an *injured* state. Controversy remains with regard to other *non-injured* states, and whether such states may take such countermeasures against a state that has violated an obligation owed to the international community as a whole (*erga omnes*). It is clear that collective measures taken through an international organization against a member (sanctions) will be governed by the constituent instrument of that organization. In this case the Charters of the United Nations, the Organization of American States, the African Union, or the Arab League will provide the legal framework.[40] But what is less clear is the right of states (individually or collectively) to apply countermeasures under the general rules of international law outlined above. This can in particular arise in the context of responses to grave violations of human rights where those immediately affected are individuals rather than other states.

The ILC concluded that there did not appear to be a 'clearly recognized entitlement' for non-injured states to take countermeasures in the collective interest, leaving the matter 'to the further development of international law'.[41] Article 54 of the ILC Articles simply refers to the right of a non-injured state to take 'lawful measures' against the state in breach of these community obligations. The Commission's hesitation on this point has been criticized by scholars,[42] although those who propose that non-

---

40. See further Gowlland *United Nations Sanctions* (above).

41. ILC Commentary (above) at 139, para. 6.

42. C. Tams, *Enforcing Obligations* Erga Omnes *in International Law* (Cambridge: CUP, 2005) who after a study of state practice concludes that Art. 54 'is unduly restrictive and unfortunate' at 311; 'Obligations *erga omnes*' J.A. Frowein <mpepil.com>; Cassese (above) at 262–77, 306–7.

injured states should be able to take countermeasures usually present this as a last option, to be used after there have been failed attempts to achieve sanctions or collective action through the United Nations and other international organizations.[43] The Institute of International Law has contributed to the debate by adopting a Resolution stating that those states that are owed *erga omnes* obligations are entitled to take countermeasures where there was a '*widely acknowledged grave* violation of an *erga omnes* obligation.'[44]

Views are divided over whether non-injured third parties should be entitled to ensure respect for international law through countermeasures. It might be tempting to see this division as the distinction between those scholars who see international law as a series of bilateral (contractual) relationships between states, and those who see international law as something aimed at protecting community interests. But this would be to miss the particular underlying concern. The issue is only partly about larger states coming to the rescue of helpless smaller states or peoples faced

---

43. L.-A. Sicilianos, 'Countermeasures in Response to Grave Violations of Obligations Owed to the International Community', in Crawford et al (above) 1137–48; Cassese (above) at 310–13. N. White and A. Abass, 'Countermeasures and Sanctions', in M. Evans (ed.), *International Law*, 3rd edn (Oxford: OUP, 2010) 531–58.

44. 'Obligations and rights *erga omnes* in international law', Resolution of the Fifth Commission (2005), Art. 5 (Rapporteur Gaja), (emphasis added). Although the Resolution does not detail which specific obligations should be considered in this context, its preamble includes the following two paragraphs: '*Considering* that under international law, certain obligations bind all subjects of international law for the purposes of maintaining the fundamental values of the international community; *Considering* that a wide consensus exists to the effect that the prohibition of acts of aggression, the prohibition of genocide, obligations concerning the protection of basic human rights, obligations relating to self-determination and obligations relating to the environment of common spaces are examples of obligations reflecting those fundamental values.'

with violations of international law. The fear of those resisting this development is that powerful states will engage in countermeasures to the detriment of smaller states (and their population) with little outside control over the legality of such countermeasures. Michael Akehurst explored this paradox in depth and concluded in part:

> In international disputes of a legal character, *both* sides usually accuse each other of breaking international law; if third States were able to intervene, there is a serious danger that they would be biased and that they would tend to support their allies, rather than the side which was objectively in the right. The result would be more likely to weaken international law than to strengthen it; and it would certainly cause a very disturbing increase in international tension.[45]

It is suggested that the real significance of the ILC's conclusions with regard to the rights of non-injured states facing violations of such *erga omnes* obligations lies in the ILC's stated principles that the non-injured state has a legal interest in such violations and can invoke the violation of international law before an international tribunal.[46] It is to this type of dispute settlement that we now turn.

---

45. M. Akehurst, 'Reprisals by Third States', 44 *BYBIL* (1970) 1–18, at 15–16; although he finally concludes that the rules on the use of force, war crimes, and crimes against humanity are so important that they could justify every state in taking countermeasures.
46. J. Crawford, 'Responsibility for Breaches of Communitarian Norms: An Appraisal of Article 48 of the ILC Articles of Responsibility of States for Internationally Wrongful Acts', in U. Fastenrath, R. Geiger, D.-E. Khan, A. Paulus, S. Von Schorlemer, and

§ 4. Arbitration and judicial settlement

(a) *Arbitration*

Arbitration and judicial settlement are closely allied; indeed the former is only a species of the latter. For arbitrators are judges, although they differ from the judges of a standing court of justice in two respects. First, they are chosen by the parties,[47] and second, their judicial functions end when the particular case for which they were appointed has been decided. The distinction is important, because a standing court is able to build up a judicial tradition, and so develop the law from case-to-case. A standing court with a body of judges is therefore, not only a means of settling disputes, but to some extent a means of preventing them from arising.[48]

C. Vedder (eds), *From Bilateralism to Community Interest: Essays in Honour of Judge Bruno Simma* (Oxford: OUP, 2011) 224–40. See also the 2005 Resolution of the *Institut de droit international* (above) Arts 3 and 4. See also the argument that non-injured states should be able to claim reparation, including restitution on behalf of individuals where there have been violations of *erga omnes* obligations, P. Gaeta, 'Are Victims of Serious Violations of International Humanitarian Law Entitled to Compensation?', in O. Ben-Naftali (ed), *International Humanitarian Law and International Human Rights Law* (Oxford: OUP, 2011) 305–27, at 317–18.

47. The International Court of Justice has since 1972 offered the parties the chance to have their dispute settled by a Chamber rather than the full Court. In effect, this has meant that states can now choose from among the Judges on the Court, see the explanation by J.G. Merrills, *International Dispute Settlement*, 5th edn (Cambridge: CUP, 2011) at 137–41.

48. For an examination of the work of the different international courts and tribunals that operate at the international level see R. Mackenzie, C. Romano, and Y. Shany, with P. Sands (eds), *Manual on International Courts and Tribunals*, 2nd edn (Oxford: OUP, 2010). In this chapter we will only examine the jurisdiction of the International Court of Justice.

But so far as the parties are concerned, they are as likely to get a satisfactory decision from a court of arbitration as from a court of justice, and there may even be special circumstances which make the former a preferable tribunal.[49] For example, some special technical skill in the members of the court of arbitration may be more important than a profound knowledge of law possessed by the judges in a standing court of justice; or arbitration may offer a more private way to settle the dispute as, unlike the International Court of Justice, the proceedings will not necessarily be public; or the special subject-matter may warrant a whole new arrangement—as was provided for in the Iran-US Claims Tribunal arising out of the US Teheran Embassy Hostages Crisis and the freezing of Iranian assets in the United States.[50]

Arbitrators and judges alike are bound to decide according to rules of law; neither possess a discretionary power to disregard the law and to decide according to their own ideas of what is fair and just. Of course the parties, if they so choose, may confer such a power on an arbitrator, or they may agree on special rules which are to be applied to the exclusion of the ordinary rules of law, but they may also confer such a special power of this kind on judges, as is expressly provided in Article 38(2) of the Statute of the International Court of Justice and Article 293(2) of the Law of the Sea Convention.

---

49. The UN Convention on the Law of the Sea 1982 offers states parties a choice between judicial settlement (by the Law of the Sea Tribunal or the ICJ) or arbitration; where no choice is made the state is deemed to have accepted arbitration (Art. 287).

50. For details see D. Müller, 'The Iran-US Claims Tribunal', in J. Crawford et al (above) 843–8.

This purely judicial character of an arbitrator's function was not always recognized. This is because arbitrators in the past sometimes claimed and exercised a discretionary power to give what they regarded as a just, rather than a strictly legal, decision; and courts of arbitration have not always given the reasons for their decisions. Indeed, arbitration was a fairly frequent method of settling international disputes in medieval times, but with the rise of the modern state system it fell into disuse until its revival in the nineteenth century, largely through the example of Great Britain and the United States in submitting the *Alabama* Claims to arbitration in 1871.[51]

This dispute concerned complaints by the United States that Great Britain had violated international law on neutrality by allowing ships to be built and sold to the Confederate States during the American Civil War. The Confederate Government had announced in April 1861 that 'letters of marque and reprisal' would be issued to privateers to enable them to seize goods from Federal merchant ships. In turn President Lincoln announced a blockade of Confederate ports. In May 1861, the British Government recognized the Confederates as belligerents and declared that Great Britain was neutral. Lord Bingham's very engaging account sets the scene:

> The Northern blockade was a real threat to the Confederacy, which had no navy, no merchant marine and no private ship-

---

51. For a detailed look at the background see T. Bingham, 'The *Alabama* Claims Arbitration', 54 *ICLQ* (2005) 1–25. The synopsis which follows relies heavily on this account.

building capacity to speak of. The problem was not, to begin with, to export its cotton, since the 1860 crop had been largely exported and it was believed that denial of cotton would force Britain and France to recognize the Confederacy. But there was an urgent need to obtain military armaments and supplies, which required ships to break (the admittedly not very effective) Northern blockade, and there was a strategic need, if possible, to cripple Northern commerce. To this end Confederate agents were sent to Europe, particularly Britain and France, to buy or procure ships to prey on Northern merchant vessels.[52]

The *Alabama* was built in Birkenhead. It was known in the Laird shipyard as '290', as it was the 290th ship they had built, and later renamed *Enrica* as it set sail. It was re-equipped with coal, guns, ammunition, uniforms and supplies in the Azores by a ship (the *Aggrapina*) that had sailed from London Docks. Captain Raphael Semmes of the Confederate Navy boarded in the Azores with Confederate officers and crew. The Confederate Flag was run up, and the *Alabama* 'embarked on her voyage of destruction during which she preyed on US merchantmen wherever she could find them: in the Atlantic, off Newfoundland and the New England coast, the West Indies, Brazil, South Africa, Singapore, Capetown, and back to Europe. During this period she burned or sank 64 US vessels'.[53] She sank only one warship. She was eventually sunk, hav-

---

52. Ibid 3–4 (footnotes omitted).

53. Ibid 6–7.

ing been challenged to a battle by the USS *Kaersage* in 1864 near Cherbourg.[54]

Attempts by US diplomats to prevent the *Alabama* (or '290' as she was then known) leaving Britain had failed, in part, due to the inadequacy of the national law which prohibited the fitting out of ships for war, but did not explicitly cover the situation where a ship could be adapted for war outside the jurisdiction.[55] The *Alabama* claims by the United States remained a point of friction and the negotiation of the Treaty of Washington (1871) finally allowed for an arbitration to 'provide for the speedy settlement of such claims'.[56] The Arbitrators met in the Geneva Town Hall, in what is now known as the *Salle Alabama*, and determined the liability of Great Britain under three rules that had been agreed to, but which the British Government did not consider to represent principles of international law at the time the claims arose. The Arbitrators were to be governed by these three rules and 'such principles of international law not inconsistent therewith as the Arbitrators shall determine to have been applicable to the case'.[57] This then was the *applicable law* for the arbitration. The first rule stated in part that a neutral government is bound 'to use due diligence to prevent the fitting out, arming, or equipping, within its jurisdiction, of any vessel which it has reasonable ground to believe is intended to cruise or to carry on war against a Power with which it is at peace'. The rules also contained obligations for states related to prevent-

---

54. Manet's famous painting of the battle is part of the collection of the Philadelphia Museum of Art.

55. Foreign Enlistment Act 1819, s. 7; cf the 1870 Act s. 8.

56. Art. I.

57. Ibid Art. VI.

ing such vessels leaving their jurisdiction and prohibiting belligerents to use their ports for the renewal of military supplies.

The arbitrators' award with regard to the *Alabama* found that Great Britain had failed in her obligations, as she had omitted to take timely effective measures of prevention, and the measures she took after the escape of the *Alabama* were insufficient to release Great Britain from the responsibility already incurred. The Tribunal explicitly stated that 'the government of Her Britannic Majesty cannot justify itself for a failure in due diligence on the plea of insufficiency of the legal means of action which it possessed'.[58] Compensation of $15.5m was awarded and later paid to the United States. *The New York Times* reported the London *Times* as saying 'willingly we consent to pay this sum to improve the law of nations'.[59]

The significance of the arbitration has often been noted as it spawned an enthusiasm for the peaceful settlement of disputes as well as treaties providing for such arbitration. Although states continue to resort to arbitration, the major development has in recent times been the use of arbitration between states and companies in international investment disputes. And in such cases, treaties now facilitate enforcement of such awards.[60] For present purposes we

58. J.B. Moore (ed.), vol. 1, *History and Digest of the International Arbitrations to which the United States has been a Party* (Washington: Govt Printing Office, 1898) at 657.
59. 15 September 1872.
60. See below Art. 54 of the Washington Convention on the International Settlement of Investment Disputes (1965); see also the New York Convention on the Recognition and Enforcement of Foreign Arbitral Awards (1958); and at the regional level: the Geneva Convention on the Execution of Foreign Arbitral Awards (1927); the Amman Arab Convention on Commercial Arbitration (1987); the Inter-American Convention on International Commercial Arbitration (1975); and the European Convention on International Commercial Arbitration (1961).

will simply consider those basic issues that distinguish all sorts of arbitration from judicial settlement. First, the parties choose the arbitrators or how they are to be appointed; second, the parties choose the applicable law; third enforcement may depend on resort to a regular national legal order and forms of judicial settlement.

(i) Choosing the arbitrators

In the *Alabama* claims the Treaty provided that five arbitrators were to be chosen by the President of the United States, the British Government, the King of Italy, the President of Switzerland, and the Emperor of Brazil.[61] Many different ways of constituting the arbitral court or finding an 'umpire' have been used. Sometimes the head of some foreign state has been appointed, and the award is given in their name, though they are not expected to act personally; sometimes the arbitrators have consisted of representatives of the disputing states, with or without the addition of other members.

The Permanent Court of Arbitration was created by the Hague Convention for the Pacific Settlement of International Disputes, adopted in 1899, and revised in 1907. But the name 'Permanent Court' is a misnomer. There is a *permanent panel of arbitrators,* but the Court itself has to be constituted anew for each case. An arbitral award is final unless the parties have otherwise agreed. Since 1962 the Court has allowed for arbitrations between states and non-state entities, and it has since then also developed rules for such arbitrations as well as for those involving international organ-

---

61. Treaty of Washington 1871 Art. I.

izations and private parties.[62] Despite a period of relative inactivity in the second half of the twentieth century, the Court is now attracting important disputes and has a full docket. An award in 2009 was decided under the rules for arbitrations between states and non-state entities and concerned a dispute over the borders of the Abyei Area submitted by Sudan and the Sudan People's Liberation Movement/Army.[63]

Where there is more than one arbitrator it is normal for each side to agree to one or two arbitrators each, and then, either agree on an 'umpire' or further 'neutral' arbitrators. Where they cannot agree, the arbitral agreement may provide for a third party to appoint the necessary arbitrator.[64] Under different regimes for international commercial arbitration this may be done by the institutional authority designated under the arbitration rules agreed to by the parties or by an 'appointing authority' designated by the Secretary-General of the Permanent Court of Arbitration.[65] In the case of disputes brought to the International Centre for the Settlement of Investment Disputes this deadlock can be broken by the President of the World Bank.[66]

---

62. Optional Rules for Arbitrating Disputes Between Two Parties of Which Only One is a State; Optional Rules for Arbitration Involving International Organizations and States; and Optional Rules for Arbitration between International Organizations and Private Parties.

63. *Abyei Arbitration*, 22 July 2009, <http://www.pca-cpa.org>.

64. See, e.g. European Convention for The Peaceful Settlement of Disputes (1957) Art. 21; American Treaty on Pacific Settlement 'Pact of Bogotá' (1948) Art. XL; Revised General Act for the Pacific Settlement of International Disputes (1949).

65. ICC Rules for Arbitration (1998) Rule 8; UNCITRAL Arbitration Rules (2010) Art. 6.

66. Convention on the Settlement of Investment Disputes Between States and Nationals of Other States (1965) Arts 5, 37–40.

(ii) Choosing the applicable law

The law the arbitrator is to apply is chosen by the parties. As we saw in the *Alabama* claims states may choose rules which are not necessarily binding rules of international law. In some cases, such as that submitted to the UN Secretary-General with regard to the sinking of the Greenpeace Ship *Rainbow Warrior*, the terms may be rather vague. It has been suggested that in that case the parties were 'more concerned with finding an acceptable solution to the dispute than with justifying their past actions'.[67] The Secretary-General explained that he sought to give a ruling that was both 'equitable and principled',[68] and ruled *inter alia* that: France should convey to New Zealand a formal and unqualified apology for the attack which was contrary to international law; that France should pay New Zealand $7m compensation; and that the French agents (who had been sentenced by a New Zealand Court for manslaughter) be transferred to the French military authorities and then 'to a French military facility on an isolated island outside of Europe for a period of three years'.[69] The Secretary-General also built in a provision for further binding arbitration should a dispute arise with regard to any agreements arising from his ruling. When France evacuated her agents without the consent of the New Zealand

---

67. Merrills (above) at 91.

68. *New Zealand v France* 74 ILR 256, at 271.

69. Ibid 272. In a separate arbitration between France and Greenpeace an arbitral tribunal in Geneva awarded Greenpeace $5 million for the loss of the Rainbow Warrior, $1.2 million aggravated damages, plus expenses, interest and legal fees. English law was used as the Rainbow Warrior was a British-flagged ship. Philip Shabecoff, *New York Times*, 3 October 1987.

authorities the arbitral tribunal was established and ruled on the dispute.[70]

The Washington Convention on the Settlement of Investment Disputes between States and Nationals of Other States (1965) provides that: 'The Tribunal shall decide a dispute in accordance with such rules of law as may be agreed by the parties. In the absence of such agreement, the Tribunal shall apply the law of the Contracting State party to the dispute (including its rules on the conflict of laws) and such rules of international law as may be applicable.'[71]

(iii) Enforcement of arbitral awards

The Washington Convention also addresses the problem of enforcement. States parties to the Convention are obliged 'to recognize an award rendered pursuant to this Convention as binding and enforce the pecuniary obligations imposed by that award within its territories as if it were a final judgment of a court in that State'.[72]

---

70. *Rainbow Warrior* (*New Zealand v France*) 82 ILR 499; the award was referred to in Ch. VII § 11 above as an example of a state invoking distress and necessity in the face of accusations of breach of treaty (one agent was ill and the other pregnant); the Tribunal found that breaches had occurred with regard to the removal of both agents and recommended a friendship fund be established with France paying an initial instalment of $2m. The Fund continues to distribute small grants totalling about €200,000 per year.

71. Art. 42(1) for detail on this regime and commercial arbitrations more generally J. Collier and V. Lowe, *The Settlement of Disputes in International Law: Institutions and Procedures* (Oxford: OUP, 1999) chs 3, 4, and 8.

72. Art. 54(1) for more detail on this regime and the suggestion that the investor/state regime be considered a 'sub-system' of state responsibility; see Z. Douglas, 'Investment Treaty Arbitration and ICSID', in J. Crawford et al (above) 815–42.

The enforcement of awards against foreign states will of course be more problematic as we could run into questions of state immunity. But this is to miss the point; once states have decided to submit their dispute to arbitration they are likely to be prepared to abide by the award; and this is what generally happens. The basis of obligation for states to abide by the award is the original will of the states to submit to arbitration.[73]

An arbitral award is final unless the parties have otherwise agreed. But arbitrators have only such powers as the parties have conferred upon them in the *compromis,* the document by which the dispute is referred to the arbitral court, and if the arbitrators should depart from the *compromis,* for example, by purporting to decide some question which was not submitted to them, or by not applying the rules of decision agreed to by the parties, it follows that the award is a nullity without binding force. It is, in fact, not an award at all. After the award has been given, one of the parties might allege that it is null and void on this ground, for *excès de pouvoir* as it is commonly called. In international commercial arbitrations there may be national legislation giving jurisdiction to the national courts over these and other questions. This is known as the *lex arbitri.*[74] Occasionally the departure from the terms of the *compromis* has been so evident that the states parties have agreed to

---

73. See further Waldock, *General Course on Public International Law,* 106 *RCADI* II (1962) 1–251, at 88–90; see also *Case concerning the Arbitral Award made by the King of Spain on 23 December 1906,* ICJ Rep. (1960) p. 192.

74. See the UNCITRAL Model Law on International Commercial Arbitration (2006); see also the Arbitration Act 1996 and the Arbitration (Scotland) Act (2010). Note under the ICSID Convention Arts 50–2 include international procedures for interpretation, revision and annulment of the Award.

regard the award as null,[75] and sometimes they have agreed to refer the question of nullity itself to a further arbitration,[76] or even for judicial settlement before the International Court of Justice.[77] Let us now consider the work of this Court.

(b) *Judicial settlement and the International Court of Justice*

The Permanent Court of International Justice was created by a treaty, generally called the 'Statute' of the Court, in 1921. Under the Charter of the United Nations it is now replaced by the International Court of Justice, but the Statute of the new Court, which forms part of the Charter, is identical with that of the old, except for a very few and not very important changes. Both Courts have been referred to as the 'World Court'; this expression, according to Georges Abi-Saab, suggests that the International Court of Justice: 'is expected to be universalist in its composition, outlook and vocation, truly representing and at the service of the international community in its entirety, and not dominated by the legal or social culture of special interests of any segments thereof'.[78] Vera Gowlland-Debbas consid-

---

75. E.g. the award of the King of Holland in the *Maine Boundary* dispute between Britain and the United States in 1831.

76. E.g. in the *Orinoco Steamship Co. Case (United States v Venezuela)* xi RIAA (1910) 227–41.

77. *Case concerning the Arbitral Award made by the King of Spain on 23 December 1906, Judgment* ICJ Rep. (1960) p. 192; *Arbitral Award of 31 July 1989, Judgment*, ICJ Rep. (1991) p. 53.

78. 'The International Court as a world court', in V. Lowe and M. Fitzmaurice (eds), *Fifty Years of the International Court of Justice: Essays in honour of Sir Robert Jennings* (Cambridge: CUP, 1996) 3–16, at 3. Note the Statute demands that at every election for the judges the electors bear in mind 'that in the body as a whole the representation of the main forms of civilization and of the principal legal systems of the world should be assured'. Art. 9.

ers that the specificity of the International Court of Justice 'lies in the fact that it does not merely offer States another choice of means of settlement, but that it is an international judicial body of general competence open to all States and as a court of the United Nations, it is conceived to be a world court serving the international community'.[79]

The judges of the World Court are appointed by the following procedure: each of the national groups of members of the Permanent Court of Arbitration nominates not more than four persons.[80] From these lists the Security Council and the General Assembly each separately choose 15 judges. Any person who is chosen by a majority vote in both bodies is elected (the veto does not apply), except that, if two persons of the same nationality are chosen, only the elder becomes a member of the Court.

A judge of the same nationality as one of the parties to a dispute before the Court retains the right to sit, but if a party has no judge of its nationality on the Court, it may nominate one for the particular case. This provision for *ad hoc* 'national' judges is explained by the fact that cases before the Court may raise complex questions of national law, and in this way the *ad hoc* judge can not only explain the law to the other judges, but in some sense

---

79. 'Article 7 UN Charter', in A. Zimmermann, C. Tomuschat, and K. Oellers-Frahm (eds), *The Statute of the International Court of Justice: A Commentary* (Oxford: OUP, 2006) 79–105, at 101.

80. For a detailed look at the background, selection and approach of judges in this Court and a dozen other international Courts and Tribunals see D. Terris, C.P.R. Romano, and L. Swigart, *The International Judge: An Introduction to the Men and Women Who Decide the World's Cases* (Oxford: OUP, 2008).

'represent' the relevant party during the judges' private deliberations.[81]

The Court is open to all the states which are parties to its Statute (this automatically includes all UN member states), and to others on conditions laid down by the Security Council.[82] Its jurisdiction covers 'all cases which the parties refer to it'.[83] Jurisdiction arises therefore when the parties have agreed to submit a particular dispute to it through what is called a *compromis* (or special agreement); but the Court also possesses a quasi-compulsory jurisdiction which applies in two ways. First, a large number of treaties (over 300) have included a compromissory clause allowing states to submit to the Court disputes arising under these treaties.[84] Secondly, Article 36(2) of the Statute contains an 'Optional Clause', whereby states may declare that they recognize as compulsory the jurisdiction of the Court in all legal disputes in relation to any other state accepting the same obligation. But neither the treaties providing for jurisdiction through such a compromissory clause,

---

81. See further P. Kooijmans, 'Article 31', in A. Zimmermann et al (above) 495–506; see also the American Convention on Human Rights Art. 55 which has a similar rule; compare Art. 19 of the Regulations of the Inter-American Commission on Human Rights which precludes a Commissioner who is a national from the state involved from taking part in the discussion, investigation, deliberation or decision. The practice for UN human rights treaty bodies is for a national to recuse themselves from the public discussion or decision making in the case of individual complaints. The situation in the WTO is dealt with below.

82. See Art. 93 UN Charter, Art. 35(2) Statute of the Court.

83. Art. 36(1) of the Statute.

84. The ICJ's jurisdiction covers these disputes by virtue of the reference in Art. 36(1) to 'all matters…in treaties and conventions in force'. Such a compromissory clause was the basis of the *Georgia v Russia* case before the ICJ discussed above in Ch. VII § 9.

nor the 'Optional Clause', affects the voluntary basis of the Court's jurisdiction; they merely make it possible for states to accept the Court's jurisdiction in anticipation of their being involved in a dispute.

The 'Optional Clause' has been accepted by only about a third of states, and many have attached reservations to their acceptances. The British acceptance of the clause, which was first given in 1929, now applies only to disputes arising after 1 January 1974, and further excludes, *inter alia* 'any dispute with the government of any other country which is or has been a Member of the Commonwealth'. The acceptance by Switzerland contains no reservations and took effect from 1948. Australia's 2002 Declaration excludes *inter alia*: 'any dispute concerning or relating to the delimitation of maritime zones, including the territorial sea, the exclusive economic zone and the continental shelf, or arising out of, concerning, or relating to the exploitation of any disputed area of or adjacent to any such maritime zone pending its delimitation'. Pakistan's Declaration of 1960 excludes *inter alia* '[d]isputes relating to questions which by international law fall exclusively within the domestic jurisdiction of Pakistan'.

This last type of reservation can be found in multiple declarations and is worth reflecting on. This concept of a domain which is exclusive and protected from international dispute settlement mechanisms dates to the time of the League of Nations.[85] At the time it seemed fair to refer to domestic jurisdiction as a 'new fetish,

---

85. 'If the dispute between the parties is claimed by one of them, and is found by the Council, to arise out of a matter which by international law is solely within the domestic jurisdiction of that party, the Council shall so report, and shall make no recommendation as to its settlement.' Art. 15 para. 8 of the Covenant of the League of Nations (1919); see also Art. 5 from the defunct Geneva Protocol on the Peaceful Settlement of

about which, however, little seems to be known except its extreme sanctity'.[86] States may continue to wish to prevent interference in their domestic affairs by other states and international organizations,[87] but if a dispute is to be settled according to international law then what is a matter of exclusive domestic jurisdiction is the same as a matter that is outside the scope of international law. What was said in 1925 remains true today: 'international law can adopt only one of two alternative attitudes towards any action by a state out of which an international dispute has arisen; it may say that the action in question falls under some rule of law by which its legitimacy ought to be tested; or it may say that no rule of law is applicable, and this, it is submitted, is equivalent to saying that the matter is one which it leaves solely within the domestic jurisdiction of the state concerned'.[88] In any event, Article 36(6) of the Statute goes on to provide that 'in the event of a dispute as to whether the Court has jurisdiction, the matter shall be settled by the decision of the Court'.[89]

The limiting effect of these reservations is multiplied by the fact that acceptance of the optional clause is on a reciprocal basis,

International Disputes (1924) which read in part: 'If in the course of an arbitration ... one of the parties claims that the dispute, or part thereof, arises out of a matter which by international law is solely within the domestic jurisdiction of that party, the arbitrators shall on this point take the advice of the Permanent Court of International Justice through the medium of the Council.'

86. Brierly, 'Matters of Domestic Jurisdiction', 6 *BYBIL* (1925) 8–19, at 8.

87. See further M. Jamnejad and M. Wood, 'The Principle of Non-intervention', 22 *Leiden Journal of International Law* (2009) 345–81.

88. Brierly, 'Domestic Jurisdiction' (above) at 10–11.

89. The situation becomes more complex where a reservation states that jurisdiction is excluded for matters within domestic jurisdiction as 'understood' by the relevant government. See *Case of Certain Norwegian Loans,* ICJ Rep. (1957) p. 9 esp. the separate and dissenting opinions. On the effect of reservations to the compromissory clause in

each state only accepting compulsory jurisdiction vis-à-vis another state to the extent that the obligations undertaken in their mutual declarations mutually correspond. This means that for the Court to have compulsory jurisdiction over any given dispute, both states, plaintiff and defendant, must have made declarations which comprise that dispute within its scope.[90] It also means that a defendant state, even when its own declaration includes the dispute within its scope, is always entitled to invoke a reservation in its opponent's declaration for the purpose of seeking to exclude the Court's jurisdiction in the case.[91] In other words, a reservation may have a boomerang effect on the state which makes it, defeating its own attempt to bring another state before the Court. To illustrate the point: if the United Kingdom were to bring a claim against Switzerland with regard to a hypothetical dispute which arose in 1970, Switzerland would be able to point to the British reservation (which, as we saw, excludes disputes which arose before 1974) and successfully claim that the Court had no jurisdiction. The wider the scope of the reservation, the more difficult it will be for the reserving state to ever use the World Court to settle its disputes.[92]

---

the Genocide Convention see *Armed Activities on the Territory of the Congo (New Application: 2002)(DRC v Rwanda)*, ICJ Rep. (2006) p. 6, compare the Joint Separate Opinion of Judges Higgins, Kooijmans, Elaraby, Owada, and Simma which suggests the validity of reservations to the jurisdiction of the Court under the compromissory clause in the Genocide Convention may have to be revisited (at para. 29).

90. *Anglo-Iranian Oil Co. case (jurisdiction)*, ICJ Rep. (1952) p. 93.
91. See *Norwegian Loans* (above).
92. See C. Tomuschat, 'Article 36', in A. Zimmermann, C. Tomuschat, and K. Oellers-Frahm (eds), *The Statute of the International Court of Justice: A Commentary* (Oxford: OUP, 2006) 589–657, esp. 632–40.

We have mentioned three ways to ground jurisdiction (1) a *compromis* agreed between the parties, (2) a compromissory clause in a treaty, (3) overlapping declarations under the optional clause. For completeness we should now include a fourth possibility (4) *forum prorogatum*. In this last instance one state unilaterally applies to the Court and the other respondent state accepts jurisdiction explicitly or through its actions. So when the Republic of Congo filed a case against France in 2002 it was enough that France simply informed the Court that it consented to the jurisdiction of the Court.[93]

The law that the Court is to apply is, as already explained in chapter II, laid down as follows: (1) international conventions, (2) international custom as evidence of a general practice accepted as law, (3) the general principles of law recognized by civilized nations, (4) judicial decisions and teachings of publicists as subsidiary means for the determination of the law, and (5) if the parties agree, the Court may decide *ex aequo et bono* (finding a just and equitable solution irrespective of the applicable law).[94]

Besides the Court's contentious jurisdiction over disputes referred to it by states, the Court, under Article 96 of the UN Charter, may be requested by the UN General Assembly or the Security Council 'to give an advisory opinion on any legal

---

93. Letter of 3 April 2003 from the Minister of Foreign Affairs accepting jurisdiction according to Art. 38(5) of the Rules of Court. See also *Corfu Channel case*, ICJ Rep. (1949) p. 4; C.H.M. Waldock, '*Forum Prorogatum* or Acceptance of a Unilateral Summons to Appear before the International Court', 2 *ILQ* (1948) 377–91.

94. For a detailed study of the Court's use of these sources see A. Pellet, 'Article 38', in A. Zimmermann et al (above) 677–792.

question'.[95] Other UN organs and Specialized Agencies may also request advisory opinions 'on legal questions arising within the scope of their activities', if authorized to do so by the General Assembly.[96] The Court has consistently treated this advisory jurisdiction as a judicial function, and it has assimilated the proceedings in most respects to those used in the contentious jurisdiction.[97]

Indeed in certain cases the advisory opinion may actually resolve a dispute by decisively applying the law.[98] So, in the context of a dispute between the United Nations and a member state over the immunity of its officials, the opinion of the Court can be decisive for the UN and the state in question. The dispute between the UN and Malaysia was settled in this way by the Court's Advisory Opinion, which declared that Malaysia must respect the immunity of the UN Special Rapporteur on the Independence of Judges and Lawyers

---

95. Recent Advisory Opinions have generated considerable interest; see the *Legality of the Threat or Use of Nuclear Weapons*, ICJ Rep. (1996), p. 226; the *Legal Consequences of the Construction of a Wall in Occupied Palestinian Territory*, ICJ Rep. (2004) p. 136; and *Accordance with International Law of the Unilateral Declaration of Independence in Respect of Kosovo*, 22 July 2010.

96. ECOSOC and the International Atomic Energy Agency are also authorized to request advisory opinions, as are the following specialized agencies: ILO, FAO, UNESCO, WHO, IBRD, IFC, IDA, IMF, ICAO, ITU, IFAD, WMO, IMO, WIPO, and UNIDO. The ICJ held that the question of the legality of nuclear weapons was outside the scope of the World Health Organization's activities in *Legality of the Use by a State of Nuclear Weapons in Armed Conflict, Advisory Opinion*, ICJ Rep. (1996) p. 66.

97. *Applicability of Article VI, Section 22, of the Convention on the Privileges and Immunities of the United Nations, Advisory Opinion*, ICJ Rep. (1989) p. 177.

98. Although the Opinion as such has no binding force, a treaty between the parties may state that the Opinion is decisive for the parties; see, e.g. Convention on Privileges and Immunities of the United Nations (1946) Art. VIII Section 30.

(Param Cumaraswamy, a Malaysian lawyer).[99] The Malaysian Courts had accepted jurisdiction over defamation suits demanding a total of $112m in response to an interview the Rapporteur had given to the magazine *International Commercial Litigation*. The UN Secretary-General considered that the interview had been given in the Rapporteur's official function as a UN expert appointed by the UN Human Rights Commission. The World Court held that the Rapporteur had immunity from legal process for the words spoken by him in the published interview, that the Malaysian courts were under an obligation to deal expeditiously with the immunity issue as a preliminary question, and that no costs should be imposed on the Rapporteur.[100] The issue was henceforth settled.

Other points of interest in the Statute of the Court include: that cases must be heard in public unless the Court decides otherwise or the parties demand a private hearing; that reasons for the decision are to be stated, and dissenting judgments may be given; that the official languages are French and English, but the Court may authorize other languages; that the Court may order binding interim measures;[101] that third states may apply

---

99. *Difference Relating to Immunity from Legal Process of a Special Rapporteur of the Commission on Human Rights, Advisory Opinion,* ICJ Rep. (1999) p. 62.

100. For detailed examination of the Opinion see H. Fox, 'The Advisory Opinion on the Difference Relating to Immunity From Legal Process of a Special Rapporteur of the Commission of Human Rights: Who Has the Last Word?' 12 *Leiden Journal of International Law* (1999) 889–918.

101. Art. 41 of the Statute, and see *LaGrand (Germany v USA)* (2001) for the conclusion that such Orders are binding. Orders can be quite simple, e.g. 'The United States of America should take all measures at its disposal to ensure that Walter LaGrand is not executed pending the final decision in these proceedings' (*LaGrand*, Order of 3 March

to intervene;[102] that there is no appeal but states can request an interpretation or revision of the judgment;[103] and that decisions are only binding between the parties and for the particular case.[104] This last provision merely means that the binding authority which Anglo-American law attaches to precedents does not apply to the decisions of the Court; it does not mean that the decisions may not be quoted as precedents, or that the Court will not strongly incline to follow them, for no court can be indifferent to its own previous decisions.[105]

1999); or more complex: 'Each Party shall refrain from sending to, or maintaining in the disputed territory, including the *caño*, any personnel, whether civilian, police or security…Notwithstanding point (1) above, Costa Rica may dispatch civilian personnel charged with the protection of the environment to the disputed territory, including the *caño*, but only in so far as it is necessary to avoid irreparable prejudice being caused to the part of the wetland where that territory is situated; Costa Rica shall consult with the Secretariat of the Ramsar Convention in regard to these actions, give Nicaragua prior notice of them and use its best endeavours to find common solutions with Nicaragua in this respect.' *Certain Activities Carried Out by Nicaragua in the Border Area (Costa Rica v Nicaragua) Order* 8 March 2011.

102. See Arts 62 and 63 of the Statute; see, e.g. *Territorial and Maritime Dispute (Nicaragua v Colombia) Application by Costa Rica for Permission to Intervene*, Judgment 4 May 2011; note that where a third state's legal interests constitute the very subject-matter of the dispute, the Court will decline jurisdiction over the whole case on the grounds that the consent of the third state is indispensable. See C. Chinkin, *Third Parties in International Law* (Oxford: Clarendon Press, 1983) 198–212; *East Timor (Portugal v Australia)*, ICJ Rep. (1995) p. 90; Collier and Lowe (above) 158–68.

103. Arts 60 and 61 of the Statute.

104. Art. 59 of the Statute.

105. We have only considered the work of the ICJ, for an introduction to the work of Courts such as the International Tribunal on the Law of the Sea, the European Court of Justice, and the regional human rights courts see Mackenzie et al (above).

§ 5. The limits of arbitration and judicial settlement

It has been a common assumption among international lawyers that not all disputes between states are 'justiciable', that is to say, susceptible of decision by the application, in an arbitral or judicial process, of rules of law. This is a mere truism in one sense—no dispute is 'justiciable' unless the parties have made it so by undertaking an obligation to treat it as such. But the distinction between 'justiciable' and 'non-justiciable' disputes usually implies more than this; it implies the belief that international disputes are of two distinct kinds, one of which, the justiciable or legal, is inherently susceptible of being decided on the basis of law, while the other, the non-justiciable or political, is not.

International lawyers have generally agreed that this distinction exists, but they have not always agreed on its content. One commonly held view has been that a justiciable dispute is one where there exists a rule of law applicable to the dispute. This implies that for other disputes, the non-justiciable disputes, no applicable rules exist in the law, and accordingly that a court of law called upon to deal with such a dispute would find itself unable to pronounce a decision. We have seen that this difficulty may be imaginary.[106] It is a corollary of the extreme positivist view of the nature of international law, according to which, since nothing is law except the rules that states have consented to, the number of legal rules is necessarily finite. It overlooks the dynamic element,

---

106. Above, Ch. II § 4(e).

which international law, like every other system of law, reveals as soon as it ceases to be a merely academic study, and begins to be applied to factual situations by the accepted processes of judicial reasoning.

International law, then, is never formally or intrinsically incapable of giving a decision, on the basis of law, on the respective rights of the parties to any dispute, and if that is so, we must look for the difference between justiciable and non-justiciable disputes elsewhere than in some assumed specific quality which distinguishes international law from other legal orders. Probably today all we can say is that it depends upon the attitude of the parties: if, whatever the subject-matter of the dispute may be, what the parties seek is their legal rights, the dispute is justiciable.[107]

It is certain that many serious disputes between states are demands for satisfaction of some interest—rather than a demand based on existing legal rights, and we should bear this in mind. But this fact does not mean that we can predict, merely from knowledge of the subject-matter of a dispute, that it will be justiciable or that it will be non-justiciable; it merely reminds us that states do sometimes regard a decision on the basis of law as a satisfactory method of disposing of their disputes, and that sometimes, for whatever reason, good or bad, at least one of the states concerned does not.[108]

---

107. Cf H. Lauterpacht, *The Function of Law in the International Community* (Oxford: Clarendon Press, 1933) 'the only decisive test of the justiciability of the dispute is the willingness of the disputants to submit the conflict to the arbitrament of law.' At 164.
108. See further Collier and Lowe (above) at 10–16.

Most lawyers would agree that it would be better if states were more willing to accept the settlement of their disputes on the basis of law. The present freedom of states to reject that method of settlement is entirely indefensible; it makes possible the grossest injustices, and it is a standing danger to the peace of the world by encouraging the habit of states regarding themselves each as a law unto itself. But the solution is not as easy as it looks, and we cannot simply pretend that existing law is the applicable basis for the settlement of all disputes.[109] A declaration of their legal rights, when states are quarrelling about something other than their legal rights, is not in any true sense a 'settlement' of their dispute.[110] It may occasionally facilitate a settlement by subsequent agreement, but it may have exactly the opposite effect—by making a compromise seem unnecessary to the party that is satisfied with the declaration of its rights.

The dissatisfaction of a state with the *status quo* raises a question which is not always a juridical one, and cannot be turned into

---

109. This was the aim of the General Act of Geneva (Pacific Settlement of International Disputes) (1928); see further Brierly 'The General Act of Geneva, 1928', 11 *BYBIL* (1930) 119–33 and 'British Reservations to the General Act', 12 *BYBIL* (1931) 132–5. See also the discussion in the first edition of this book of the abortive Geneva Protocol of 1924 'which professed, in the words of the official General Report, to create "a system of arbitration from which no international dispute, whether juridical or political, could escape"'. At 187.

110. Alan Boyle emphasizes how environmental disputes maybe better tackled through non-compliance committees in a multilateral forum more appropriate to the protection of common interests. Moreover traditional dispute settlement mechanisms may not allow for technical or third party input. 'Environmental Dispute Settlement' <mpepil.com>. For an analysis of the vast array of environmental treaties see P. Sands, *Principles of International Environmental Law*, 2nd edn (Cambridge: CUP, 2003).

a juridical question by adopting judicial methods of procedure. The state's dissatisfaction may raise a question which is essentially *political,* susceptible of amicable settlement no doubt, but only by appropriate *political* methods, by negotiation, by compromise, by mediation, or conciliation.[111] It is to some of these political methods of dispute settlement that we now turn.

§ 6. Good offices, mediation, commissions of inquiry, conciliation

In these modes of dispute settlement, the intervention of a third party aims, not at *deciding* the quarrel *for* the disputing parties, but at inducing them to *decide it for themselves*. The difference between *good offices* and *mediation* is not so important. Strictly speaking, a third party is said to offer 'good offices' when it tries to induce the parties to negotiate between themselves, and it 'mediates' when it *takes a part* in the negotiations itself; but clearly the one process merges into the other. Both, moreover, are political processes, rather than judicial settlements, which are only based on international law to the extent that the parties so choose, and these political processes may be chosen precisely because there is no agreement to settle the dispute according to the legal rights and obligations of the parties.[112] The Hague Con-

---

111. For a detailed consideration see Office of Legal Affairs—Codification Division, *Handbook on the Peaceful Settlement of Disputes* (New York: UN, 1992) (*UN Handbook*).

112. Consider the mediations by the Pope Jean Paul II and Vatican Secretary of State Cardinal Agostino Casaroli in the 1980s for the dispute between Argentina and Chile concerning the Beagle Channel, which came in the wake of the rejection by Argentina of an arbitral award based on law.

ventions for the Pacific Settlement of International Disputes recommend that states that are strangers to a dispute offer their good offices and mediation (even during the course of hostilities), and state that such an offer can never be regarded as an unfriendly act. A number of treaties now provide for good offices and mediation, and, while it is 'generally understood that the proposals made by the mediator for a peaceful solution of a dispute are not binding on the parties', the final results could be 'embodied in such instruments as an agreement, a protocol, a declaration, a communiqué, an exchange of letters or a "gentleman's agreement" signed or certified by a mediator'.[113]

The same Conventions also introduced a new device for the promotion of peaceful settlements: *Commissions of Inquiry*, whose function was simply to investigate the facts of a dispute and to make a report stating them. This report would not have the character of an award, and the parties were free to decide what effect, if any, they would give it. The Commission would be constituted for each occasion by agreement between the parties.[114] This machinery was used with good effect in the Dogger Bank dispute between Great Britain and Russia in 1904.[115] The Russian navy had fired on

---

113. *UN Handbook* (above) para. 138, for the treaties which refer to good offices and mediation see paras 123–37.

114. Such Commissions are rather different from the Commissions of Inquiry presently established by the UN and other international organizations in the context of allegations of war crimes and human rights violations (see Ch. VI § 8 above) as the latter Commissions would not normally include a national from the relevant state, see also Art. 90(3) of the 1977 Protocol I to the 1949 Geneva Conventions which foresees that none of the members of the Commission of Inquiry should be a national of the states concerned (unless the states agree otherwise).

115. For detailed examination see N. Bar-Yaacov, *The Handling of International Disputes by Means of Inquiry* (London: OUP, 1974).

a fishing fleet from Hull, sinking one vessel and killing two persons. Tensions were running high, in the context of the war between Russia and Japan, and the Russian explanation that the fishing boats must have been considered Japanese torpedo boats did not defuse the situation. The establishment of the International Commission of Inquiry, based on the mechanism in the Hague Convention, was seen at the time as 'appeasing the conflicting national susceptibilities' and ensuring that the 'acute character of crisis would disappear'.[116]

The idea underlying these Commissions, that if resort to war can only be postponed and the facts clarified and published, war will probably be averted altogether, inspired the so-called 'Bryan treaties', the first of which was concluded between Great Britain and the United States in 1914. Under these treaties the parties agreed to refer 'all disputes of every nature whatsoever' which cannot be otherwise settled to a standing 'Peace Commission' for investigation and report, and not to go to war until the report was received, which had to be within a year. The Commission consisted of one national and one non-national chosen by each party, and a fifth, not a national of either party, chosen by agreement. No disputes whatsoever were excluded from the operation of these treaties.

This arrangement was used much later in 1990 to settle the dispute over the compensation to be paid by Chile concerning the 1976 car bomb that exploded in Washington DC killing Orlando Letelier, the Chilean former foreign Minister, and Mrs Moffitt (a

---

116. Ibid 87. The report did not suggest any discredit on the Russian side and £65,000 damages were paid by Russia to Britain.

US national). Although the US courts had awarded the claimants approximately $5m in damages, this was unenforceable against Chile due to the rules of sovereign state immunity, and the United States relied on the 1914 Agreement to Settle Disputes that May Occur Between the United States and Chile (Bryan-Suárez Mujica Treaty) to 'determine the amount of the payment to be made by the Government of Chile in accordance with applicable principles of international law, as though liability were established'. The five-member Commission of Inquiry established under the terms of the treaty used legal methods and fixed the sum for the *ex gratia* payment at $2,611,892.[117]

The methods first suggested in the 'Bryan treaties' have been adapted to what is now known as *conciliation*. Conciliation involves an individual or commission proposing the settlement of the dispute in a report which is not binding on the parties. Conciliation, therefore, differs from arbitration; the terms of the settlement are merely proposed and not dictated to the disputing states. The conciliator 'attempts to define the terms of a settlement susceptible of being accepted' by the parties.[118]

In the period between the two World Wars conciliation machinery was set up by multiple treaties between particular states. It was usual to set up a conciliation commission of five persons, consisting of one national of each of the signatory states and three non-nationals. But these treaties setting up conciliation commis-

---

117. 31 ILM 1, at para. 4 of the *compromis* and para. 43 of the Decision; see further Merrills (above) at 51–3.

118. See the definition of conciliation proposed by the Institute of International Law, Regulations on the Procedure of International Conciliation (1961) Art. 1.

sions hardly fulfilled the hopes that were placed in them, and very few of the commissions ever had occasion to meet.[119] Conciliation is now more likely to be used in international commercial disputes, but certain key multilateral treaties have also made conciliation an essential step for dispute settlement.[120] Again, it is clear that the parties are not bound by the result, but under these treaties they may be bound to submit to conciliation before resorting to judicial settlement or countermeasures. So far these and other conciliation mechanisms remain rather underutilized.[121] The friendly settlement procedure found in human rights treaties such as the European Convention on Human Rights means that the Court automatically places itself at the disposal of the parties in order to secure a settlement on the basis of respect for human rights. In this

---

119. The OSCE Stockholm Convention on Conciliation and Arbitration (1992) provides for a Court of Conciliation and Arbitration (which is based in Geneva). It has yet to be used; <http://www.osce.org/cca>. The Geneva General Act (revised 1949), the European Convention for the Peaceful Settlement of Disputes 1957; the Pact of Bogotá (1948); and the Protocol on the Commission of Mediation, Conciliation and Arbitration (1964) (African Union) all include provisions for conciliation. The Treaty Establishing the Organisation of Eastern Caribbean States (1981) establishes a conciliation procedure whose decisions and recommendations are binding on the parties.

120. See, e.g. Vienna Convention on the Law of Treaties (1969) regarding claims for invalidity, termination, withdrawal from or suspension of the operation of a treaty Arts 65–6 and Annex; Vienna Convention on Succession of States in Respect of Treaties (1978); UN Convention on the Law of the Sea (1982); Vienna Convention on the Protection of the Ozone Layer (1985). For a full discussion see Merrills (above) ch. 4; *UN Handbook* (above) paras 14–67.

121. Some UN human rights treaties allow for inter-state disputes to be settled through conciliation. These mechanisms have never been triggered. See Convention on the Elimination of All Forms of Racial Discrimination (1965) Arts 11–13; International Covenant on Civil and Political Rights Arts 41–42.

case the complaining party might be a state but in the vast majority of cases it is an individual or a non-state legal entity. Hundreds of cases are settled this way and these can be seen as a form of conciliation.[122]

§ 7. Dispute settlement at the World Trade Organization

The World Trade Organization (WTO) has over 153 members from all regions.[123] The WTO provides an institutional framework for the settlement of disputes among its members relating to specific agreements annexed to the WTO Agreement (referred to as the 'covered agreements').[124] The Organization's dispute settlement mechanism contains elements of all forms of dispute settlement discussed above. The starting point includes non-judicial

---

122. See Art. 39 European Convention on Human Rights (1950); for a recent study see H. Keller, M. Forowicz, and L. Engi, *Friendly Settlement before the European Court of Human Rights* (Oxford: OUP, 2010); similar arrangements exist in the American Convention on Human Rights (1969) and the African Charter of Human and Peoples' Rights (1981).

123. Note some members such as the EU and Hong Kong (China) are not states, but are admitted as customs unions or customs territories.

124. We should also note that the complaint need not necessarily allege a violation of international law contained in the treaties covered by the WTO; 'non-violation complaints' may allege that benefits that a member could reasonably have expected to accrue to it under particular covered agreements are being 'nullified or impaired' or the attainment of an objective of such an agreement is being impeded by conduct of a member or existence of a situation, even if there is no conflict with provisions of the agreement. See Art. 26 of the Understanding on Rules and Procedures Governing the Settlement of Disputes (DSU), and Art. XXIII GATT (1994).

forms of dispute settlement such as consultations, as well as optional good offices, mediation, and conciliation.[125] Arbitration and judicial settlement are available through recourse to a kind of arbitration panel, with the possibility of appeal on points of law to the Appellate Body. The mechanism also includes multilateral supervision of the implementation of recommendations, and should implementation not occur in a timely manner, the mechanism sets a level and form of compensation for the successful party. All these steps are supervised by the WTO membership acting as the 'Dispute Settlement Body' (DSB). Let us look at the process more closely.

The Dispute Settlement Understanding (DSU) sets out in detail how each phase should operate according to a strict timetable. A WTO member is under an obligation to enter into consultations with another member requesting such consultations pursuant to one or more of the WTO 'covered agreements'. Consultations are a compulsory preliminary step before resorting to other forms of dispute settlement under the Understanding. If consultations are unsuccessful the complaining party has the right to demand the establishment of a panel by the DSB. In the same way: 'Good offices, conciliation or mediation may be requested at any time by any party to a dispute. They may begin at any time and be terminated at any time. Once procedures for good offices, conciliation or mediation are terminated, a complaining party may then proceed with a request for the establishment of a panel.'[126]

---

125. DSU Arts 4 and 5.

126. Art. 5(3) DSU; Art. 5(6) states that the Director General of the WTO may offer these types of dispute settlement in an *ex officio* capacity.

A panel of three (or exceptionally five) experts is established by the DSB. They must be 'well-qualified governmental and/or non-governmental individuals', and should not be citizens of the parties or third parties to the dispute, unless the parties to the dispute agree otherwise. Where customs unions or common markets are parties to a dispute, this rule applies to citizens of all member countries of the customs union or common market. So, for example, an EU national cannot serve on a panel involving a dispute between the EU and another member of the WTO (unless the parties agree otherwise). Even where panellists are government officials, they have to serve in a personal capacity and do not represent their government. Should the parties fail to agree on the membership of a panel, there is a provision for the WTO Director-General to appoint appropriate panellists.

In proceedings before both the panel and the Appellate Body, the parties make their submissions orally and in writing as they would in the context of any arbitration. Other WTO members with a substantial interest in the matter before the panel have the right to be heard and make submissions. A panel's report is produced in three steps. The parties are first asked to comment on a draft which contains only a description of the facts and the arguments of the parties. In the second phase the parties receive, not only this description (revised as appropriate), but also a confidential interim version of the panel's findings and conclusions, on which again the parties may comment. Eventually the final report is issued to the parties and, after translation into the WTO official languages, the WTO membership and the public.[127]

---

127. By contrast, there is no interim review stage with respect to the issuance of reports of the Appellate Body.

This final panel report is then considered by the membership of the WTO. All members have an opportunity to comment on the report, but it will be automatically adopted unless one of the parties to the dispute decides to appeal on a point of law (rather than a finding of fact) to the Appellate Body, or if there should be, what is confusingly called, 'reverse consensus' in the DSB.[128] Reverse consensus requires that every WTO member agree that a panel report should *not* be adopted. This is unlikely in practice as the 'winning' party would not normally want to reject the report; but it is at least theoretically possible that the implications of a report are so unacceptable that all WTO members would all vote in the DSB *not* to adopt a report.

Recommendations and rulings of panels, as modified by the Appellate Body, have to be implemented within a tight timeframe, and the party concerned has to inform the DSB what it intends to do in this regard. The DSB monitors this implementation and may take into account the effects on the economy of developing countries. If there is no implementation within a reasonable time, negotiations have to start with regard to mutually acceptable compensation. If there is no agreement on compensation, the complaining party can ask the DSB for authorization to suspend trade concessions to the non-implementing party (i.e. to engage in certain countermeasures).

The level of suspension of concessions that may be authorized should be equivalent to the disadvantage suffered by the complaining party due to the non-implementing party's failure to implement the recommendations and rulings of the DSB. Such

---

128. Also called 'negative consensus'.

countermeasures, sometimes referred to as retaliation, should first aim at obligations or trade concessions in the same industrial sector.[129] So a failure by the United States to bring cotton subsidies into compliance with its obligations under WTO rules could lead to Brazilian retaliation including 100 per cent tariffs on imports of cotton trousers and shorts from the United States.[130] If suspension of concessions or obligations with respect to the same sector is not practicable or effective, the complaining party may be authorized to suspend concessions or obligations in other sectors under the same WTO Agreement or under a different WTO Agreement.[131] Where retaliation was authorized against the European Communities for discrimination with regard to banana imports, the United States chose to impose 100 per cent tariffs on a list of luxury items from Europe, targeted for the most part at European states that the US considered supported the European banana regime. 100 per cent tariffs were thus proposed on items such as bath preparations produced by the United Kingdom and France, pecorino cheese from Italy, and cashmere from Scotland.[132]

---

129. Art. 22(3) DSU.

130. In 2010, Brazil and the United States entered into a bilateral agreement under which the United States would pay an annual sum to the Brazil Cotton Institute (a technical fund to assist Brazilian farmers) in exchange for Brazil delaying its planned retaliation until 2012.

131. Art. 22(3) DSU. Authorization for cross-agreement retaliation was first granted to Ecuador in the long-running *Bananas* dispute against the European Communities.

132. In 1999, the US Congress implemented the 'carousel' provision which required the US Trade Representative to revise its retaliation list every 180 days; section 407 of Public Law 106–200. The intent behind this provision was to exert additional pressure on a non-implementing party to comply with WTO rulings by changing the domestic industries of the non-implementing party that would be adversely affected by the retaliation. This provision was controversial, both within the United States and among WTO members. As it turned out, the United States did not change the products on the final retaliation list.

Opinion is divided over whether the purpose of WTO trade retaliation is to redress the imbalance in benefits arising from the non-implementing party's breach, or to induce compliance. Parties have sought to design retaliation measures that maximize the domestic political pressure on the non-implementing party to comply with its WTO obligations. The potential effects of such retaliatory trade measures on third parties can be dramatic; the proposed US tariffs on luxury goods apparently threatened the existence of particular small cashmere enterprises in Scotland, generating a series of bilateral discussions aimed at reversing retaliation in this area.[133] Countermeasures against a state will nearly always affect the population of the state in some concrete way and in this way they must be seen as a rather crude form of law enforcement. It is worth noting, however, that although Ecuador, Brazil, Antigua, and Barbuda have been authorized to engage in certain retaliations, none of them have gone ahead.

For smaller partners however, trade retaliation may not be particularly effective in inducing a larger trading partner to comply. Where the smaller trading partner's imports represent only a small percentage of the non-implementing parties' trade, then suspension might have little impact on the larger party, and inflict potentially significant costs on the smaller partner.[134] As a group of developing

---

133. Some of the politics surrounding such choices and the impact in Scotland are recounted in C. Meyer, *DC Confidential* (London: Weidenfeld and Nicolson, 2005) ch. 15 'The Great Banana War'.

134. This was the case in relation to Antigua and Barbuda's threatened retaliation against the United States, where the arbitrators agreed with Antigua that if it were to suspend concessions to the United States in respect of its most important service sectors (travel, transportation, and insurance), such suspension would have little impact on

country members explained: 'The economic cost of withdrawal of concessions in the goods sector would have a greater adverse impact on the complaining developing-country Member than on the defaulting developed-country Member and would only further deepen the imbalance in their trade relations already seriously injured by the nullification and impairment of benefits.'[135]

Trade disputes now benefit from this multifaceted dispute settlement mechanism. Unlike many of the regimes we have considered, the WTO system provides for compulsory settlement through an enforceable binding award. The prospect of being subjected to these compulsory procedures may induce members to comply with their international obligations. However, as we have seen, problems of access to justice remain. These problems are due to: the prospective nature of the remedies, the complexity of the proceedings, and the limited possibilities for small developing states to deploy effective retaliatory measures against larger states.

§ 8. Settlement under the UN Charter

The good offices and mediation functions outlined above have been fulfilled by the UN Secretary-General in contexts such as

US service providers while forcing Antiguan consumers to find replacement services at an uncertain cost; Decision by the Arbitrator, *United States—Measures Affecting the Cross-Border Supply of Gambling and Betting Services—Recourse to Arbitration by the United States under Article 22.6 of the DSU*, WT/DS285/ARB, 21 December 2007, DSR 2007:X, 4163, para. 4.59.

135. 'Special and Differential Treatment for Developing Countries', proposals on DSU by Cuba, Honduras, India, Indonesia, Malaysia, Pakistan, Sri Lanka, Tanzania and Zimbabwe, TN/DS/W/19, 9 October 2002, at 1.

the Congo in the 1960s, Afghanistan in the 1980s, the Iran–Iraq war in the 1980s, the peace accords finalized in the 1990s for Guatemala and El Salvador, and Cyprus to the present day.[136] The General Assembly is given a role under the Charter to recommend measures for the peaceful adjustment of situations impairing friendly relations, and may discuss any questions relating to the maintenance of international peace and security brought before it by any member state.[137] Furthermore, in addition to these good offices roles, the UN Declaration on Fact-finding has reinforced this role for the UN stating: 'Fact-finding missions may be undertaken by the Security Council, the General Assembly and the Secretary-General, in the context of their respective responsibilities for the maintenance of international peace and security in accordance with the Charter.'[138]

The Security Council is given particular responsibilities under the Charter. Articles 24 and 25 of the UN Charter (reproduced in Chapter III § 5) confer on the Security Council primary responsibility for the maintenance of international peace and security, and bind member states to accept and carry out the Security Council's

---

136. For a review of the Good Offices function exercised by the UN Secretary-General see T. Whitfield, 'Good offices and "groups of friends"', in S. Chesterman (ed.), *Secretary or General? The UN Secretary-General in World Politics* (Cambridge: CUP, 2007) 86–101; T.M. Franck and G. Nolte, 'The Good Offices Function of the UN Secretary-General' in A. Roberts and B. Kingsbury (eds), *United Nations, Divided World*, 2nd edn (New York: OUP, 1993) 143–82; see also *UN Handbook on the Peaceful Settlement of Disputes* (above) at paras 367–81.

137. For details as this relates to the settlement of disputes see *UN Handbook* ibid at paras 352–62.

138. Declaration on Fact-finding by the United Nations in the Field of the Maintenance of International Peace and Security, A/RES/46/59, 9 December 1991, para. 7.

decisions. Later articles of the Charter refer to certain 'specific powers' which are granted to the Security Council 'for the discharge of these duties'.

The Charter contains no specific programme for the exercise of the powers of the Security Council, and the Council has established good offices missions, commissions of inquiry, criminal tribunals, and in the case of Iraq, a Compensation Claims Commission.[139] But the Charter makes an important distinction between powers relating to the Security Council's function of promoting pacific settlement of disputes (Chapter VI) and those relating to enforcement action (Chapter VII). In relation to the former it may call upon the parties to any dispute 'the continuance of which is likely to endanger the maintenance of international peace and security' to settle it by some peaceful method of their own choice.[140] It may 'investigate any dispute, or any situation which might lead to international friction or give rise to a dispute' in order to determine whether its continuance is likely to endanger peace and security.[141] And, at any stage of such a dispute or situation, it may 'recommend appropriate procedures or methods of settlement'.[142] In an underused provision, the Charter also states that: '[i]n making recommendations under this Article the Security Council should also take into consideration that legal disputes should as a general rule be referred by the parties to the Interna-

---

139. For an overview see D. Petrović, 'The UN Compensation Commission', in J. Crawford et al (above) 849–59.

140. Art. 33.

141. Art. 34.

142. Art. 36(1).

tional Court of Justice in accordance with the provisions of the Statute of the Court'.[143] If the Council should decide that the continuance of the dispute is, in fact, likely to endanger peace and security, it may go farther than this and 'recommend such terms of settlement as it may consider appropriate'.[144] But it cannot dictate such terms.

When, however, the decisions of the Security Council involve action for the maintenance of peace, they may be more than recommendations; they may be directions which the members of the United Nations are bound to carry out.[145] The Council must determine 'the existence of any threat to the peace, breach of the peace, or act of aggression', and 'make recommendations, *or decide* what measures shall be taken' to maintain or restore international peace and security.[146] Before making such a recommendation or decision it may call upon the parties, in order to prevent an aggravation of the situation, to comply with any necessary provisional measures

---

143. Article 36(3) was applied by the Security Council in the dispute between the UK and Albania when in Resolution 22 (1947) it recommended that the two governments immediately refer the dispute to the ICJ. The Court later considered the two states had themselves accepted the jurisdiction of the Court. With regard to the argument that the Security Council may be able to generate the conditions for compulsory jurisdiction see *Corfu Channel case, Judgment on Preliminary Objection*, ICJ Rep. (1948) p. 15 at 31, Separate Opinion by Judges Basdevant, Alvarez, Winiarski, Zoričić, De Visscher, Badawi Pasha, and Krylov; see further T. Stein and S. Richter, 'Article 36', in B. Simma (ed.), *The Charter of the United Nations: A Commentary* (1995) 534–46.

144. Art. 37(2).

145. It has been suggested that there may be limited cases where a binding decision may be taken under Chapter VI: R. Higgins, 'The Advisory Opinion on Namibia: Which UN Resolutions are Binding under Article 25 of the Charter?' 21 *ICLQ* (1972) 270–86.

146. Art. 39 (emphasis added).

without prejudice to their rights or claims, and it 'shall duly take account of failure to comply with such provisional measures'.[147] When it has decided that action is called for, the Security Council may direct measures not involving the use of armed force, such as sanctions,[148] and if it considers such measures inadequate, 'it may take such action by air, sea, and land forces' as may be necessary to maintain or restore the peace.[149]

All the members of the United Nations have bound themselves under the Charter to make available to the UN for this purpose 'on its call and in accordance with a special agreement or agreements' armed forces and other forms of assistance and facilities, and these agreements are to specify the numbers and types of forces, their degree of readiness and general location, and the nature of the facilities and assistance to be provided;[150] and in order to enable 'urgent military measures' to be taken, the members are to 'hold immediately available national air force contingents for combined international enforcement action'.[151] Although the UN has around 100,000 peacekeeping personnel deployed on peace operations around the world at the time of writing, the major problem is that the so-called additional 'standby' troops are not really at the disposal of the UN. A decision by the Security Council to create a new peace-keeping operation requires the consent of each individual troop contributing state before those troops

---

147. Art. 40.
148. For some of the other measures see Ch. III § 5.
149. Art. 42.
150. Art. 43.
151. Art. 45.

can be deployed.[152] As we know, with regard to the tragic case of Rwanda in 1994, and more recently with regard to Darfur in Sudan, such consent may not be immediately forthcoming when it is most needed.

This rather elaborate schema for UN enforcement action remained rather underutilized until the end of the cold war. The 1991 Security Council authorization of the use of force by a coalition (albeit outside UN command and control) to liberate Kuwait from the Iraqi invasion radically changed how the Security Council was seen. These forces were not fighting under a UN flag, but were authorized by the Security Council to use force to restore the peace and the international rule of law. The Security Council, acting under Chapter VII, subsequently authorized member states, their coalitions, and regional organizations,[153] to use force (outside a UN command and control) on a number of occasions including with regard to Somalia, Bosnia and Herzegovina, Haiti, Rwanda, Sierra Leone, Côte d'Ivoire, Liberia, East Timor, Kosovo, Afghanistan, the Democratic Republic of Congo, Iraq, Central African Republic, and Libya.

The ability of the Security Council to authorize such a variety of operations is clearly linked to the end of the cold war antagonism which had paralysed the Council. Action is still dependent

---

152. The *United Nations Standby Arrangements System Military Handbook* (2003) reinforces the point in explaining the concept: 'One of the most important conditions is that the final decision whether to actually deploy the resources or not remains a national decision.' At 4.

153. For an analysis of Security Council authorization of regional peacekeeping operations see C. Gray, *International Law and the Use of Force*, 3rd edn (Oxford: OUP, 2008) ch. 9.

on the absence of disapproval of any of the permanent members, but the threshold for action may have been adjusted now, as the focus is less on breaches of the peace and acts of aggression and more on general threats to international peace and security. In its landmark 1992 Summit the Council stated:

> The absence of war and military conflicts amongst States does not in itself ensure international peace and security. The non-military sources of instability in the economic, social, humanitarian and ecological fields have become threats to peace and security. The United Nations membership as a whole, working through the appropriate bodies, needs to give the highest priority to the solution of these matters.[154]

---

154. UN Doc. S/23500, 31 January 1992.

IX | Resort to Force

§ 1. Intervention and the prohibition on the use of force

THE word intervention is often used quite generally to denote almost any act of interference by one state in the affairs of another; but in a more special sense it means dictatorial interference in the domestic or foreign affairs of another state which impairs that state's independence. A mere tender of advice by one state to another about some matter on which the latter is entitled to decide for itself would not be an intervention in this sense, although it might be popularly so described. For the interference to be illegal intervention it must involve coercion.[1]

---

1. See *Military and Paramilitary Activities in and against Nicaragua (Nicaragua v USA)*, ICJ Rep. (1986) at para. 205; see also GA Res. 2131 Declaration on the Inadmissibility of Intervention in the Domestic Affairs of States and the Protection of Their Independence and Sovereignty (1965) and GA Res. 2625 Declaration on Principles of International Law concerning Friendly Relations and Cooperation among States in accordance with the Charter of the United Nations (1970). See further P. Kunig, 'Intervention, Prohibition of', <mpepil.com>.

State practice on this matter has in the past been determined more often by political motives than by legal principles. Moreover, the most extreme form of intervention was always war, and for some time international law made no attempt to distinguish between legal and illegal occasions of making war. As long as this was the attitude of the law to war, it is not surprising that there should have been little agreement on the principles which regulated the less extreme measures of coercion by which one state might assume to dictate a certain course of action to another. For there was a certain unreality in attempting to formulate a law of intervention and at the same time admitting that a state might go to war for any cause, or for no cause at all, without any breach of international law.

How easily international law could be circumvented was shown by Great Britain and Germany in 1901. These two governments were in dispute with Venezuela over its failure to pay compensation claims due to damage done to their nationals during civil strife in Venezuela, and for failure to repay a contractual debt following a loan to build the Venezuelan railway. When the United States objected to certain measures which these states proposed to take against Venezuela under the guise of a 'pacific blockade', Great Britain and Germany then regularized the matter by acknowledging a state of war to exist,[2] sinking Venezuelan ships and bombarding Puerto Cabello.

Today, all such use of force is prohibited under customary international law and the Charter of the United Nations. Article 2(4), which is the corner-stone of the Charter system, reads as fol-

---

2. See Moore, *International Law Digest,* vol. vii, at 140–1.

lows: 'All Members shall refrain in their international relations from the threat or use of force against the territorial integrity or political independence of any state, or in any other manner inconsistent with the Purposes of the United Nations.'[3] Because states can no longer circumvent the rules on intervention by notifying others of a state of war, the contours of any non-interference (or non-intervention) rule have therefore become more significant. The International Court of Justice has found, for example, that providing training and military support to rebels in another state constitutes a violation of the non-interference rule.[4]

Operations to rescue nationals abroad have been seen in the past as exceptions to the rule on non-intervention and the prohibition on the use of force. Waldock's edition of the present book explained: 'Whether the landing of a detachment of troops to save the lives of nationals under imminent threat of death or serious injury owing to the breakdown of law and order may be justifiable is a delicate question. Cases of this form of intervention have not been infrequent in the past and, when not attended by suspicion of being a pretext for political pressure, have generally been regarded as justified by the sheer necessity of instant action to save the lives of innocent nationals, whom the local government is unable or unwilling to protect. Clearly every effort must be made to get the local government to intervene effectively and, failing that, to obtain its permission

---

3. As we saw in Ch. VIII § 8 one exception to this rule is where states are authorized by the Security Council to use force, the second exception relates to self-defence; both are dealt with below.

4. See *Armed Activities on the Territory of the Congo (Democratic Republic of the Congo v Uganda)*, ICJ Rep. (2005) at paras 161–5; *Nicaragua v USA* (1986) (above) at para. 246.

for independent action; equally clearly every effort must be made to get the United Nations to act. But, if the United Nations is not in a position to move in time and the need for instant action is manifest, it would be difficult to deny the legitimacy of action in defence of nationals which every responsible government would feel bound to take, if it had the means to do so; this is of course, on the basis that the action was strictly limited to securing the safe removal of the threatened nationals.'[5]

John Dugard, Special Rapporteur on Diplomatic Protection for the International Law Commission, proposed a draft article which would have set down the conditions for a lawful intervention in this context. Modelled on the circumstances surrounding the 1976 Israeli rescue raid in Entebbe airport in Uganda, it read as follows:

The threat or use of force is prohibited as a means of diplomatic protection, except in the case of rescue of nationals where:

(a) The protecting State has failed to secure the safety of its nationals by peaceful means;
(b) The injuring State is unwilling or unable to secure the safety of the nationals of the protecting State;
(c) The nationals of the protecting State are exposed to immediate danger to their persons;

---

5. 6th edn at 427–8; Waldock goes on to consider the reaction of states to the sending of Belgian troops to the Congo but considered 'no clear conclusions can be drawn as to their attitude on the general legal question'. Subsequent rescue missions and the reactions of states have not really clarified the situation.

(d) The use of force is proportionate in the circumstances of the situation;

(e) The use of force is terminated, and the protecting State withdraws its forces, as soon as the nationals are rescued.[6]

Dugard considered that any right to use of force in the protection of nationals abroad had to be narrowly formulated, bearing in mind how states had abused this concept in the past. Dugard had suggested in his commentary: 'From a policy perspective it is wiser to recognize the existence of such a right, but to prescribe severe limits, than to ignore its existence, which will permit States to invoke the traditional arguments in support of a broad right of intervention and lead to further abuse.'[7] The draft article found no support and was deleted. The issue will now most likely be considered an aspect of the law of self-defence (considered below).

Another question concerning intervention arises from the contemporary focus on the protection of human beings as forming part of the purpose of international law. The independence of states clearly obliges us to consider carefully any exceptions to a general rule of non-intervention. But it will be difficult to limit interventions in practice to those for which a legal justification can be pleaded, unless international law also restrains some of the excesses in which states indulge with regard to their own population. At present, an intervention, which we may be forced to stigmatize as illegal, may even deserve moral approval, as did possibly some of the collective humanitarian interventions which took

6. A/CN.4/506, 7 March 2000, at 16.

7. Ibid para. 59.

place in the nineteenth century in affairs of the former Turkish Empire.[8] It is probably the realization of this possible contradiction between law and morality that leads some to regard humanitarian reasons as a legal justification for intervention. This tension was evident in the debate surrounding the 1999 NATO intervention over Kosovo, where the Security Council refused to authorize the use of force, and NATO used force anyway.[9] The United Kingdom stated in its *Manual on the Law of Armed Conflict* that:

cases have arisen (as in Northern Iraq in 1991 and Kosovo in 1999) when, in the light of all the circumstances, a limited use of force was justifiable in support of purposes laid down by the Security Council but without the Council's express authorization when that was the only means to avert an immediate and overwhelming humanitarian catastrophe. Such cases are in the nature of things exceptional and depend on an objective assessment of the factual circumstances at the

8. D. Rodongo, *Against Massacre: Humanitarian Interventions in the Ottoman Empire* (Princeton: Princeton University Press, 2011); for the legality of humanitarian intervention in this context see P.H. Winfield, 'The Grounds of Intervention in International Law', vol. v *BYBIL* (1924) 149–62; I. Brownlie, *International Law and the Use of Force by States* (Oxford: OUP, 1963); see further J.L. Holzgrefe, 'The humanitarian intervention debate', in J.L. Holzgrefe and R.O. Keohane (eds), *Humanitarian Intervention: Ethical, Legal, and Political Dilemmas* (Cambridge: CUP, 2003) 15–52.

9. See in particular the exchange between B. Simma, 'NATO, the UN and the Use of Force: Legal Aspects', 10 *EJIL* (1999) 1–22 and A. Cassese, '*Ex iniuria ius oritur: Are We Moving towards International Legitimation of Forcible Humanitarian Countermeasures in the World Community*', ibid 23–30, and 'A Follow-Up: Forcible Humanitarian Countermeasures and *Opinio Necessitatis*', ibid 791–9.

time and on the terms of the relevant decisions of the Security Council bearing on the situation in question.[10]

But, for many, any such justification would be political, humanitarian, or moral, rather than legal. Scholars are divided on whether
developments since 1945 have left room for a right for states to use
force in a humanitarian intervention without explicit authorization from the Security Council. Olivier Corten has incisively
revealed how these differences reflect different methodological
approaches to international law more generally. The 'restrictive
approach', which he favours, focuses on the customary and treaty
rules and strictly applies the International Court of Justice's

---

10. *UK Manual on the Law of Armed Conflict* (Oxford: OUP, 2004) at para. 1.6, pp. 2–3;
see also to the same effect Baroness Symons of Vernham Dean, Parliamentary Under-
Secretary of State, FCO, written answer, Hansard, 16 November 1998, WA col 140; UK
Foreign Secretary Robin Cook in a speech on 28 January 2000 at Chatham House,
explained that the UK had submitted to the UN Secretary-General: 'a set of ideas to help
the international community decide when it is right to act: first, any intervention is by
definition a failure of prevention. Force should always be the last resort; second, the
immediate responsibility for halting violence rests with the state in which it occurs; but,
third, when faced with an overwhelming humanitarian catastrophe and a government
that has demonstrated itself unwilling or unable to halt or prevent it, the international
community should act; and finally, any use of force in this context should be collective,
proportionate, likely to achieve its objective, and carried out in accordance with international law.' In 2007 Lord Malloch Brown (Minister of State, FCO) offered a 'set of criteria
against which one might want to assess such interventions: first, that they are rule-based;
secondly, that we are willing to sustain them over many decades; thirdly, that they are
adequately burden-shared with others to allow us to sustain them; and, fourthly—this is
what I think Mr Blair had in mind—that they are doable and achievable and that we will
not end doing more harm than good and causing more loss of life.' Vol. 696 *Hansard* HL,
15 November 2007, cols 626–30 at 627.

approach to understanding the evolution of those rules. So, 'first, a State must invoke a new right, in other words claim that a modification of the rule occurred; second, this claim must be accepted by other States.'[11] If these conditions are fulfilled there is both an evolution of the customary rule and the necessary subsequent practice relevant to prove agreement on an interpretation of the UN Charter. Of course in reality states use a number of arguments and do not articulate their reliance on a particular emerging international law. Nor do other states express their explicit approval using legal vocabulary. Corten highlights this possibility that a state might 'approve an action in the name of a particular moral or political philosophy, while reserving its position in strictly legal terms.'[12] But he then explains that under the restrictive approach, such conduct does not enable one to conclude that the customary rule has evolved; the practice has to be accepted 'as law'.[13]

An 'extensive' approach is said by Corten to be taken by those who begin from the position that: '[p]ositive law can only correspond to objective law, that is, rules considered as necessary in a given social context and at a given historical period'.[14] In this way humanitarian intervention 'is acceptable in the light of the progress of the humanistic values at the heart of the international commu-

---

11. *The Law Against War: The Prohibition on the Use of Force in Contemporary International Law* (Oxford: Hart, 2010) at 29.

12. Ibid 38–9.

13. At 39 referring to the ICJ Statute Art. 38(1)(b) see Ch. II § 4(b) above. Corten examines with great care what states say with regard to humanitarian intervention and concludes that in almost all cases states rely on self-defence or Security Council authorization and not on any new humanitarian exception *The Law Against War* (above) at 495–549.

14. Ibid 10.

nity. It is objectively necessary to allow certain unilateral actions in cases in which the collective security mechanisms have not functioned.'[15] This last approach reflects the argument made above with regard to the rescue of nationals abroad. Waldock saw the interpretation of the rules on the use of force as inextricably linked to the capacity of the United Nations to act in any one context. The last page of the previous 1963 edition of the present book contained the following passage: 'The "cold war" has imposed severe limits on the possibilities of United Nations action to enforce peace, but the Organization, as we have seen, has developed certain techniques for bringing about a cease-fire and even for providing a limited form of international policing of critically dangerous areas. The more effective the executive arm of the United Nations is made, the stricter, we may be sure, will become the attitude of members to the use of force and their insistence that, except in case of urgent self-defence, lawful use of force is a monopoly of the United Nations itself.'[16]

It is suggested that this difference in methodology is the key to understanding the arguments as to the legitimacy of humanitarian intervention. The difference reflects not only separate understandings about *how law is formed*, but also a difference in emphasis with regard to including the *purpose* for which the law exists in a particular context. As the Rwandan genocide unfolded the UN Security Council was paralysed, and even when the Council approved a UN force, the UN Secretary-General was unable to find states willing to contribute troops in time. In such cases it is unlikely that, with the pros-

---

15. Ibid 11.

16. At 432 of the 6th edn. Cf ICJ judgment in *Nicaragua* (above) at para. 188.

pect of imminent massive loss of life, a state engaging in humanitarian intervention in Rwanda would suffer widespread condemnation for breaching the UN Charter. Almost everyone would accept that a better solution than unilateral intervention is approval through the United Nations,[17] and yet the scenario of political stalemate in the Security Council remains a real one. Were a state to engage in a humanitarian rescue mission as just described, whether or not one sees this as a breach of the UN Charter, some, such as Tom Franck, have envisaged a lack of a response from other states as part of a sort of 'international law of mitigation'[18] so that few consequences accrue for the transgressor, even though the law remains unaltered and there may be a formal situation of illegality. Although national analogies are always dangerous, we might allude to the idea that a fire-engine rushing to a fire may run a red light in violation of the law, but should the circumstances have required this there would unlikely be any sanctions. Of course the problem with developing a right of humanitarian intervention is the fear that it will be abused for neo-colonial or other extraneous reasons, but the stakes are too high for us to shut

17. Cf Brierly *The Outlook for International Law*, who writing in 1944 saw that breach of a future human rights treaty could permit intervention where a state treats its own subjects 'with gross inhumanity' but concluded nevertheless: 'The exercise of a right of intervention in such cases should probably be safeguarded against abuse by requiring the authorization of whatever international authority may be set up after the war.' At 117, see also 108.

18. T.M. Franck, *Recourse to Force: State Action Against Threats and Armed Attacks* (Cambridge: CUP, 2002) at 139; Franck also points out that the sentences handed down in the lifeboat cases recounted in the next section of this chapter took into account the pleas of mitigation and were reduced to six months, 'What, eat the cabin boy? Uses of force that are illegal but justifiable' ibid ch. 10.

the door on any emerging right to use force as a last resort to prevent imminent loss of life.[19]

The concept of humanitarian intervention, however, is not the sole focus in this context. In 1996, the Sudanese scholar Francis Deng and his co-authors had already started to reconceptualize sovereignty as an issue of responsibility.[20] The parameters of the debate concerning the right of humanitarian intervention were altered by questioning assumptions about sovereignty, and refocusing the discussion on what is now termed the 'responsibility to protect', 'R2P', or 'RtoP'. Before considering the significance of this emerging *responsibility to protect* (as subsequently enshrined in UN texts), we should briefly consider the background to these developments.

The 1994 Rwandan genocide shocked the world.[21] Crucially, there was a degree of soul-searching as to why the UN and the international community had failed to intervene to stop the killing

19. For a small sample of writing on this topic see P. Alston and E. Macdonald (eds), *Human Rights, Intervention and the Use of Force* (Oxford: OUP, 2008); G.P. Fletcher and J.D. Ohlin, *Defending Humanity: When Force Is Justified and Why* (New York: OUP, 2008) ch. 7; T.G. Weiss, *Humanitarian Intervention* (Cambridge: Polity, 2007); F.R. Tesón, *Humanitarian Intervention: An Inquiry into Law and Morality*, 3rd edn (Ardsley, NY: Transnational, 2005); Holzgrefe and Keohane (above); S. Chesterman, *Just War or Just Peace? Humanitarian Intervention and International Law* (Oxford: OUP, 2001); N.J. Wheeler, *Saving Strangers: Humanitarian Intervention in International Society* (Oxford: OUP, 2000); O. Ramsbotham and T. Woodhouse, *Humanitarian Intervention in Contemporary Conflict* (Cambridge: Polity, 1996); for a critical look at humanitarianism more generally see D. Kennedy, *The Dark Sides of Virtue: Reassessing International Humanitarianism* (Princeton NJ: Princeton University Press, 2004) D. Rieff, *A Bed for the Night: Humanitarianism in Crisis* (London: Vintage, 2002).

20. F.M. Deng, S. Kimaro, T. Lyons, D. Rothchild, and I.W. Zartman, *Sovereignty as Responsibility: Conflict Management in Africa* (Washington DC: Brookings Inst. Press, 1996).

21. P. Gourevitch, *We wish to inform you that tomorrow we will be killed with our families* (London: Picador, 2000).

and defend the defenceless.[22] The reasons for this spectacular failure are multifaceted, but it is important to understand the political context. Relevant factors certainly included: the 1993 humiliation of US troops operating as part of a UN peace operation in Somalia, the subsequent development of a more restrictive US policy with regard to the approval of UN peace enforcement operations (Presidential Decision Directive 25), and a feeling that the UN was ill-equipped to cope with the demands already being made with regard to the humanitarian situation in the former Yugoslavia.[23] Nevertheless, attention focused on the legal framework and some sought to blame the UN Charter's provisions on non-intervention.

The unauthorized NATO intervention over Kosovo in 1999 rekindled the sense that the UN Charter was part of the problem rather than a framework for maintaining international peace and security. In the run up to the 60th anniversary of the UN in 2005, the scene was set for the UN Secretary-General to question whether the concept of sovereignty was not getting in the way of the protection of individuals at risk.[24]

---

22. S. Power, 'A Problem from Hell' America and the Age of Genocide (New York: Harper Collins, 2003).

23. See further M. Barnett, Eyewitness to a Genocide: the United Nations and Rwanda (Ithaca: Cornell University Press, 2002); D. Scheffer All the Missing Souls: A Personal History of the War Crimes Tribunals (Oxford: Princeton University Press, 2012) 45–68.

24. See, e.g. K. Annan, 'Two concepts of sovereignty', The Economist, 18 September 1999; 'The legitimacy to intervene: international action to uphold human rights requires a new understanding of state and individual sovereignty', Financial Times, 10 January 2000; In Larger Freedom A/59/2005, 21 March 2005, 'experience has led us to grapple with the fact that no legal principle—not even sovereignty—should ever be allowed to shield genocide, crimes against humanity and mass human suffering'. At para. 129. For detailed examination of the divisions these speeches caused within the UN Secretariat and within the UN member states see R. Zacklin, The United Nations and the Use of Force in a Unipolar World: Power v. Principle (Cambridge: CUP, 2010).

The International Commission on Intervention and State Sovereignty, established by the Canadian Government in 2000, entered the debate and sought to provide a set of principles to ensure better protection for civilians whose lives were at risk. The members of the Commission sought to reorient the debate. They eschewed the term humanitarian intervention, in part to avoid a perceived militarization of humanitarian work, and in part due to the mounting opposition among states to the development of any such exception to the prohibition on the use of force. The Commission instead called for recognition of a 'responsibility to protect'. It stressed two principles: first, that sovereignty implies a responsibility of a state towards its people, and second, that the principle of non-intervention yields to the international responsibility to protect where a population is suffering serious harm as a result of internal armed conflict, repression, or state failure, and the state in question is unwilling or unable to stop this.[25] Reiterating the rules on the use of force, the Commission went on to leave the humanitarian intervention door slightly ajar, admitting the use of force, even in the absence of a Security Council authorization, in exceptional cases involving large-scale killing or ethnic cleansing. But the Commission set out only two alternative options in this context: consideration of the matter by the General Assembly in Emergency Special Session under the 'Uniting for Peace' procedure; or action by regional organizations acting within their jurisdiction, subject to their seeking subsequent authorization from the Security Council.[26]

---

25. *The Responsibility to Protect: Report of the International Commission on Intervention and State Sovereignty* (Ottawa: International Development Research Centre, 2001) Basic Principles (1)A and B, at xi.

26. Ibid. Principles for Military Intervention (3)E., at xiii. On 'Uniting for Peace' see Ch. III § 5 fn 56.

This move towards to a right (or duty) to intervene in the context of humanitarian catastrophe might have been consolidated more widely in the run up to the 60th anniversary of the United Nations. World events took a dramatic turn. The terrorist attacks of 11 September 2001, the subsequent invasion of Afghanistan, and the bombing and occupation of Iraq in 2003 all changed the context. These events, and the accompanying climate, led the majority of states to continue to question the wisdom of opening up a new exception to the established prohibition on the use of force outside the accepted justifications: Security Council authorization and self-defence (both dealt with below). The eventual key paragraphs in the 2005 Summit Outcome, adopted by all UN member states, warrant close reading as they carefully retain the Charter framework for the use of force and recall the role of the Security Council as the entity entitled to authorize force to protect populations from serious harm.[27]

The significance of the responsibility to protect framework lies therefore not so much in any development in the law on the use of force, but rather in the recalibration of the rule on non-forcible intervention and the generation of an expectation that the international community must act to protect those in danger. In the case of Libya such a concept of the responsibility to protect set the scene for the Security Council authorization of the use of force to protect civilians. What is therefore now clear is that it can no longer

---

27. 'Each individual State has the responsibility to protect its populations from genocide, war crimes, ethnic cleansing and crimes against humanity. This responsibility entails the prevention of such crimes, including their incitement, through appropriate and necessary means. We accept that responsibility and will act in accordance with it. The international community should, as appropriate, encourage and help States to exercise this responsibility and support the United Nations in establishing an early warning capability.

be claimed that the UN has no business interfering in a situation of civil war or crimes against humanity. Such a situation is not to be considered a matter of exclusive domestic jurisdiction, and gives rise to responsibilities: first on the part of state concerned, and then on the part of all other states, and, most crucially, on the UN itself, to prevent such crimes and to protect the population from serious harm.[28]

The international community, through the United Nations, also has the responsibility to use appropriate diplomatic, humanitarian and other peaceful means, in accordance with Chapters VI and VIII of the Charter, to help to protect populations from genocide, war crimes, ethnic cleansing and crimes against humanity. In this context, we are prepared to take collective action, in a timely and decisive manner, through the Security Council, in accordance with the Charter, including Chapter VII, on a case-by-case basis and in cooperation with relevant regional organizations as appropriate, should peaceful means be inadequate and national authorities are manifestly failing to protect their populations from genocide, war crimes, ethnic cleansing and crimes against humanity. We stress the need for the General Assembly to continue consideration of the responsibility to protect populations from genocide, war crimes, ethnic cleansing and crimes against humanity and its implications, bearing in mind the principles of the Charter and international law. We also intend to commit ourselves, as necessary and appropriate, to helping States build capacity to protect their populations from genocide, war crimes, ethnic cleansing and crimes against humanity and to assisting those which are under stress before crises and conflicts break out.' At paras 138–9, A/RES/60/1, 24 October 2005. See also paras 5, 6, and 69–80. Reaffirmed by the Security Council in S/RES/1674 (2006), 28 April 2006; see also G. Evans, *The Responsibility to Protect: Ending Mass Atrocity Crimes Once and for All* (Washington DC: Brookings Inst., 2008).

28. See further, for the subtle shifts between the UN and its member states, A. Orford, *International Authority and the Responsibility to Protect* (Cambridge: CUP, 2011); Boisson de Chazournes has suggested that R2P helps us to think about the 'collectivisation' of the responsibility to react to grave human rights violations and in turn that this is an expression of 'solidarity'. L. Boisson de Chazournes, 'Responsibility to Protect: Reflecting Solidarity?' in R. Wolfrum and C. Kojima (eds), *Solidarity: A Structural Principle of International Law* (Heidelberg: Springer, 2010) 93–122, at 114.

§ 2. Self-defence

(a) *Self-preservation and the* Caroline *incident*

A state, like an individual, may protect itself against an attack, actual or threatened. In the nineteenth century, however, there was a tendency, by widening the principle to cover 'self-preservation', to give the principle of self-defence a scope which is quite inadmissible.[29] Even Hall (a writer generally moderate in his views) went so far as to say: 'In the last resort almost the whole of the duties of states are subordinated to the right of self-preservation.'[30] Such a doctrine would destroy the imperative character of any system of law in which it applied, for it makes all obligation to obey the law merely conditional; and there is hardly any act of international lawlessness which, taken literally, it would not excuse. Self-preservation was, for example, one of the pretexts advanced by Germany in 1914 to justify her attack on Belgian neutrality, although she herself was under no apparent threat or attack either from Belgium or any other state. Nor does the analogy with

---

29. More recently it has been suggested that the inherent right to self-defence means that any state has the ability to use military force to 'defend what we define to be in our national interests'. J.R. Bolton, 'Is there Really "Law" in International Affairs?', 10 *Transnational Law and Contemporary Problems* (2000) 1–48, at 38; for a similar argument defending the sovereignty of independent states more generally see J.A. Rabkin, *Law Without Nations? Why Constitutional Government Requires Sovereign States* (Princeton: Princeton University Press, 2005).

30. *International Law* (Oxford: Clarendon Press, 1880), at 226. For further examples see P. Haggenmacher, 'Self-Defence as a General Principle of Law and Its Relation to War', in A. Eyffinger, A. Stephens, and S. Muller (eds), *Self-Defence as a Fundamental Principle* (Hague: Hague Academic Press, 2009) 3–49, esp. at 10–13.

national law, which influenced Hall,[31] in any way support this extensive view of the principle of self-defence.

In English law, for example, a plea of self-preservation will not justify an otherwise criminal use of violence against another person. Thus in *R v Dudley and Stephens*,[32] when two men and a boy were cast away at sea in an open boat, and the men, after their food and water had been exhausted for many days, killed and ate the boy, they were actually convicted of murder, although the jury found that in all probability all three would have died unless one had been killed for the others to eat. An American case is to the same effect.[33] The ship *William Brown* struck an iceberg, and some of the crew and passengers took to the boats. The boat was leaking and overloaded, and, in order to lighten it, the accused helped to throw some of the passengers overboard. He was convicted of murder. In both these cases a right of self-preservation, if any such right were known to the law, would have justified the acts committed, but it is equally clear that in neither were the acts truly defensive, for they were directed against persons from whom danger was not even apprehended. The truth is that self-preservation is not a legal right but an instinct, and no doubt when this instinct comes

---

31. 'Even with individuals living in well ordered communities the right of self-preservation is absolute in the last resort. *A fortiori* it is so with states, which have to protect themselves.' But Hall himself went on to set out conditions for what we now call self-defence which would apply: 'If the safety of a state is gravely and immediately threatened either by occurrences in another state, or aggression prepared there, which the government of the latter is unable, or professes itself to be unable to prevent, or when there is an imminent certainty that such occurrences or aggression will take place if measures are not taken to forestall them.' At 46.

32. *R v Dudley and Stephens* (1884) 14 QBD 273.

33. *U.S. v Holmes* (1842) 26 F Cas 360; (1842) I Wallace Junior, 1.

into conflict with legal duty, either in a state or an individual, it often happens that the instinct prevails over the duty. It may sometimes even be morally right that it should do so. But we ought not to argue that because states or individuals are likely to behave in a certain way in certain circumstances, therefore they have a right to behave in that way. Strong temptation may affect our judgment of the moral blame which attaches to a breach of the law, but no self-respecting system can admit that it makes breaches of the law legal; and the credit of international law has more to gain by the candid admission of breaches when they occur, than by attempting to throw a cloak of legality over them.[34]

Self-defence, properly understood, is a legal right, and as with other legal rights the question whether a specific state of facts warrants its exercise is a legal question. It is not a question on which a state is entitled, in any special sense, to be a judge in its own cause. In one sense a state in international law may always be a judge in its own cause, for, in the absence of a treaty obligation, it is not compulsory for a state to submit its conduct to the judgment of any international tribunal. But this is a loose way of speaking. A state which refuses to submit its case does not become a 'judge'; it merely blocks the channels of due process of law, as, owing to the defective organization of international justice, it is still able to do. This is a defect of general application in international law, which

---

34. The reference by the International Court of Justice to the use of nuclear weapons in self-defence when the 'very survival of a state would be at stake' cannot be seen as a resurrection of the notion of self-preservation. See further M. Kohen, 'The Notion of "State Survival" in International Law', in L. Boisson de Chazournes and P. Sands (eds), *International Law, The International Court of Justice and Nuclear Weapons* (Cambridge: CUP, 1999) 293–314.

applies, but not in any special sense, to a disputed case of self-defence. There is, however, another circumstance which gives a certain plausibility to the common claim that every state is competent to decide for itself whether a necessity for self-defence has arisen. It is, or may be, of the nature of the emergency which seems to justify defensive action, that action, if it is to be effective, must be immediate. This is equally true of defensive action by an individual. To wait for authority to act from any outside body may mean disaster, either for a state or an individual, and either may have to decide *in the first instance* whether or in what measure the occasion calls for defensive action. With the individual, under any civilized system of law, this initial decision is not final; it may be reviewed later by the law in the light of all the relevant circumstances. There is no reason to believe that the case is different with a state, apart from the procedural difficulty of procuring the submission of the question to judicial review; and fortunately this conclusion does not depend on *a priori* argument. For the practice of states decisively rejects the view that a state need only declare its own action to be defensive for that action to become defensive as a matter of law. It is clear that the defensive or non-defensive character of any state's action is universally regarded as a question capable of determination by an objective examination of the relevant facts.

The principle of self-defence is clear, though its application to specific facts may often be a matter of difficulty. But a particularly well-known example of an intervention justified on grounds of self-defence is afforded by the incident of the steamer *Caroline* in 1837. During an insurrection in Canada the *Caroline* was used to transport men and materials for the Canadian rebels from American territory into

Canada across the Niagara River. The American Government had shown itself unable or unwilling to prevent this traffic, and in these circumstances a body of Canadian militia commanded by the British Royal Navy crossed the Niagara, and, after a scuffle, sent the *Caroline* adrift over the Niagara Falls. Two American citizens were killed including the cabin boy known as 'little Billy'.

In the controversy that followed, the United States did not deny such action by Great Britain could be justified under certain circumstances, and Great Britain for her part admitted that in order to justify such action there needed to be circumstances of extreme urgency. The two states differed only on the question whether the facts brought the case within the exceptional principle.[35]

The formulation of the principle of self-defence in this case by the American Secretary of State, Daniel Webster, continues to be cited as encapsulating the self-defence exception to the prohibition on the use of the force.[36] There must be shown, he said, 'a

---

35. For a fascinating examination of the facts see R.Y. Jennings, 'The *Caroline* and McLeod Cases', 32 *AJIL* (1938) 82–99; note Jennings highlights how the assumption at the time was that the British action was justified by self-preservation and that was the term generally used in the doctrine at the time rather than the concept of self-defence. 'Yet, there is a considerable difference between the two conceptions, for whereas self-defence presupposes an attack, self-preservation has no such limitation, and broadly applied, would serve to cloak with an appearance of legality almost any unwarranted act of violence on the part of a state.' At 91.

36. See, however, Brownlie's point that using this exchange from 1838–42 'as the critical date for the customary law said to lie behind the United Nations Charter, drafted in 1945, is anachronistic and indefensible'. *Principles of Public International Law*, 7th edn (Oxford: OUP, 2008) at 734. He explains that: '[t]he statesmen of the period used self preservation, self-defence, necessity, and necessity of self-defence as more or less interchangeable terms, and the diplomatic correspondence was not intended to restrict the right of self-preservation which was in fact reaffirmed'. Ibidem.

necessity of self-defence, instant, overwhelming, leaving no choice of means and no moment for deliberation'; and, further, the action taken must involve 'nothing unreasonable or excessive, since the act justified by the necessity of self-defence must be limited by that necessity and kept clearly within it'. The second of these propositions is as important as the first and more likely to be overlooked, for there is a natural temptation, when force has been resorted to, to continue its use after the needs of defence have been fairly met.

The trials before the Military Tribunals at the end of the Second World War demonstrated the need to keep self-defence within strict limits, for nearly every aggressive act has been portrayed as an act of self-defence. The right of self-defence was pleaded at Nuremberg and Tokyo on behalf of the German and Japanese major war criminals and rejected by the International Tribunals. The Nuremberg Tribunal expressly endorsed the statement of Secretary Webster in the *Caroline* exchange as to the proper limits of the right:

> it is clear that as early as October 1939, the question of invading Norway was under consideration. The defence that has been made here is that Germany was compelled to attack Norway to forestall an Allied invasion, and her action was therefore preventive. It must be remembered that preventive action in foreign territory is justified only in case of 'an instant and overwhelming necessity for self-defence, leaving no choice of means, and no moment of deliberation.' (The *Caroline* Case)[37]

---

37. *Trial of German Major War Criminals* (1946) Cmd 6964 (London: HMSO) at 28–9.

As we saw above, a state cannot be the sole judge of the need to have recourse to self-defence. But if it must necessarily be left to every state to decide in the first instance whether or in what measure an occasion calls for defensive action, it does not follow that the decision may not afterwards be reviewed by the law in the light of all the circumstances. Here again we might refer to the judgment of the Nuremberg Tribunal, in dealing with the same charge of German aggression against Norway:

> It was further argued that Germany alone could decide, in accordance with the reservations made by many of the Signatory Powers at the time of the conclusion of the Briand-Kellogg Pact, whether preventive action was a necessity, and that in making her decision her judgment was conclusive. But whether action taken under the claim of self-defence was in fact aggressive or defensive must ultimately be subject to investigation and adjudication if international law is ever to be enforced.[38]

We will consider the potential jurisdiction of the International Criminal Court over the international crime of aggression in § 4 below. In order to really understand the contemporary prohibition on the use of force (and whether such a use of force could amount to a manifest violation of the Charter amounting to the individual crime of aggression) we have to examine more closely the two justifications for the use of force accepted under the UN Charter: self-defence and authorization by the Security Council. We now examine these in some detail.

---

38. Ibid 30.

(b) *Contemporary law of self-defence*

The right to self-defence is expressly affirmed in the Charter of the United Nations, Article 51 of which provides that: '[n]othing in the present Charter shall impair the inherent right of individual or collective self-defence if an armed attack occurs against a Member of the United Nations, until the Security Council has taken the measures necessary to maintain international peace and security'. The Article then goes on to provide that any measures of self-defence must be immediately reported to the Security Council, whose general responsibility and authority for taking action remain unaffected. Thus, any exercise of the right of self-defence is expressly made subject to the judgment and control of the Council; and if the veto is used to prevent the Council from intervening, the power of judgment and control can be transferred to the General Assembly under the Uniting for Peace Resolution. While the principle of self-defence is clearly accepted, several controversies surround its application.[39]

(i) Anticipatory self-defence

Most observers would agree that the victim state does not have to wait until the actual attack on its territory has started (notwith-

---

39. Sometimes these controversies have been expressed as being about whether a party considers that the right of self-defence is an inherent continuing right under customary international law, or whether the right is completely circumscribed by the UN Charter, which in turn now defines customary international law. See the previous edition of the present book at 416–21. These controversies are today more likely to be simply expressed as policy arguments rather than issues that can be resolved by an interpretation of the UN Charter which allows for a parallel customary pre-existing right of self-defence based on *inter alia* the exchange following the *Caroline* incident.

standing that the English text of the Charter says 'if an armed attack occurs').[40] The problems arise when determining how imminent the attack needs to be before one can resort to force in self-defence. We saw above that the International Military Tribunal rejected the argument advanced by the German defendants in Nuremberg of the need to forestall an Allied attack from Norway, citing the *Caroline* formula, which suggests a degree of imminence. We might recall, however, that in the *Caroline* incident self-defence was not really purely anticipatory as attacks had already been launched on Canada.

More recently in 1981, when Israel used force against the Osirak nuclear reactor in Iraq she was strongly condemned by the UN Security Council for a military attack in 'clear violation of the Charter of the United Nations and the norms of international conduct'.[41] Israel claimed that she had 'performed an elementary act of self-preservation, both morally and legally. In so doing, Israel was exercising its inherent right of self-defence as understood in general international law and as preserved in Article 51 of the UN Charter'.[42] In his summary of the debate the President of the Security Council stated that it was 'inadmissible to invoke the right to self-defence when no armed attack has taken place. The concept of preventive war, which for many years served as a justification for the abuses of powerful States, since it left to their discretion to

---

40. Compare the French 'dans le cas où un Membre des Nations Unies est l'objet d'une agression armée'.

41. SC Res. 487 (1981).

42. Debate in the Security Council, S/PV.2280, 12 June 1981, 16–51; ILM (1981) 965 at 970.

define what constituted a threat to them, was definitively abolished by the Charter of the United Nations.'[43]

In debates over the last 30 years states have referred to their readiness to use pre-emptive strikes, particularly in the context of a threat from nuclear weapons, and threats from terrorist organizations in the wake of the September 11 attacks on the United States. In a study of these statements Tom Ruys concludes that while the 'circle of States accepting anticipatory self-defence has expanded since 2002', even those states that argued for an expansive interpretation allowing for anticipatory self-defence have continued to focus on actual or *imminent* attacks.[44] Nevertheless, a large number of states, including China and India, would reject any interpretation which allows for pre-emptive self-defence.[45]

Although the International Court of Justice has refrained from expressing its view on the 'lawfulness of a response to an imminent threat of armed attack',[46] it did observe in 2005 that the position of the Ugandan High Command had been that the presence of the Ugandan army in the Democratic Republic of Congo was necessary 'to secure Uganda's legitimate security interests'. The Court considered that these security needs were 'essentially preventive', and focused instead exclusively on the question of whether the

---

43. Ibid 991.

44. T. Ruys, *'Armed Attack' and Article 51 of the UN Charter: Evolutions in Customary Law and Practice* (Cambridge: CUP, 2010) ch 4 at 336ff; Corten (above) 406–43; C. Gray, *International Law and the Use of Force*, 3rd edn (Oxford: OUP, 2008) at 160–6.

45. Ibid 338–42. See also Y. Dinstein, *War, Aggression and Self-Defence*, 5th edn (Cambridge: CUP, 2012) ch 7. Compare M.W. Doyle, *Striking First: Preemption and Prevention in International Conflict* (Princeton: Princeton University Press, 2008).

46. See *Nicaragua* (above) at para. 194, and *Armed Activities on the Territory of the Congo (Democratic Republic of the Congo v Uganda)*, ICJ Rep. (2005) at para. 143.

attacks that had actually occurred constituted 'armed attacks' such as would entitle Uganda to use self-defence.[47]

(ii) Armed attack

Next there is the question of an 'armed attack'. The first question is the nature of the attack. States have claimed the right to self-defence not only when there is an attack on their territory, but also when their embassies, nationals, and ships are attacked abroad. In determining what constitutes an armed attack much depends on the context. In the *Oil Platforms Case* the International Court of Justice separated out incidents of the use of force from the 'most grave' form of the use of force amounting to an armed attack. It found that an attack on a merchant ship with a US flag in Kuwaiti waters, which could not be shown to have targeted that ship as opposed to other ships in the area, and the mining of a US flagged ship in an international shipping channel, which again could not be shown to have been aimed in particular at US shipping, did not constitute an armed attack (assuming that the acts could have been shown to be attributable to Iran). Similar problems arose with regard to the evidence needed to attribute to Iran the mining of the warship the USS *Samuel B. Roberts*. The Court, however, did not 'exclude the possibility that the mining of a single military vessel might be sufficient to bring into play the "inherent right of self-defence"'.[48]

In the *Nicaragua v United States* case the International Court of Justice had insisted on this separation between a state's unlawful

---

47. Ibid paras 143–7.
48. *Oil Platforms (Iran v USA)*, ICJ Rep. (2003) at para. 72.

use of force or intervention and the 'most grave' forms of the use of force that amount to an 'armed attack'. This distinction was drawn in the context of one state supporting rebels in another state, and the Court concluded that the concept of armed attack did not include: 'assistance to rebels in the form of the provision of weapons or logistical or other support. Such assistance may be regarded as a threat or use of force, or amount to intervention in the internal or external affairs of other States.'[49] The essential difference between this situation and that of armed attack is the distinction between a state *supporting* armed bands and a state *sending* armed bands into another state.

There is, as we have just seen, a separate second question of *who* carries out the attack. While it is fair to say that the drafters of the UN Charter may have had in mind an attack by one state on another, today states have asserted the right to self-defence when attacked by terrorist groups, rebels or insurgents. As we shall see below, the definition of aggression includes in paragraph (g) the situation where a state sends armed bands or irregulars to carry out certain acts which attain a degree of gravity to put them on a par with aggression as defined for state forces. The International Court of Justice considered, not only that such state action is a violation of the Charter by the sending state, but also that these acts could be considered 'armed attacks': 'if such an operation, because of its scale and effects, would have been classified as an armed attack rather than a mere frontier incident had it been carried out by regular armed forces.'[50] In this case the victim state would be entitled to act in self-defence.

---

49. Above at para. 195, see also paras 191 and 227–31.

50. *Nicaragua* (above) at para. 195.

Today the controversy now centres on a situation where the armed non-state actor mounts an attack and no state is found to have sent or financed such attackers. Is an attack by such a non-state entity in such circumstances to be considered 'an armed attack' entitling a state to use force in self-defence? Put like this, in the wake of terrorist attacks resulting in hundreds, if not thousands of deaths, many would respond in the affirmative. Few states openly questioned the right of the United States to use self-defence to respond to the attacks of 11 September 2001.[51] In that case Afghanistan was seen as harbouring Al Qaeda, or at least seen as unwilling to cooperate, and there were Security Council resolutions which evoked the right of self-defence. But what of the situation where a government is simply unable to tackle a rebel group launching attacks from its state into another state? Opinion here is divided on the contours of a right to self-defence in international law.[52] As we shall see, the International Court of Justice has yet to address the issue head on; although the judges have left clues as to considerable differences in approach.[53]

---

51. For an interesting analysis of why this was so see S.B. Ratner, '*Jus ad Bellum* and *Jus in Bello* After September 11', 96 *AJIL* (2002) 905–21.

52. See T.M. Franck, 'Terrorism and the Right of Self-Defense', 95 *AJIL* (2001) 839–43, A. Cassese, *International Law*, 2nd edn (Oxford: OUP, 2005) 354–5, N. Lubell, *Extra-territorial Use of Force Against Non-State Actors* (Oxford: OUP, 2010), Gray (above) ch 6; Corten (above) ch 3; and Ruys (above) at 447–72 who provides a detailed analysis of states reactions in particular with regard to the following post-September 11 incidents of states claiming self-defence in response to non-state actor attacks, Israel–Syria 2003, Rwanda–Congo 2004, Ethiopia–Somalia 2006, Israel–Lebanon 2006, Turkey–Iraq 2007–8, Colombia–Ecuador 2008.

53. In *Nicaragua* (above) we saw that the Court did not consider that an 'armed attack' had occurred such as to entitle the US claim to be entitled to use collective self-defence

In the case brought before the ICJ by the Democratic Republic of Congo against Uganda it was claimed that Uganda had the right to act in self-defence in response to attacks by the Alliance of Democratic Forces for the Liberation of the Congo. The Court found in its 2005 judgment that there was no direct or indirect involvement of the Democratic Republic of Congo in these attacks, and therefore 'the legal and factual circumstances for the exercise of a right of self-defence by Uganda against the DRC were not present'.[54] The Court said it was declining to answer the question 'whether and under what conditions contemporary international law provides for a right of self-defence against large-scale attacks by irregular forces'.[55] Judge Simma's Separate Opinion complains that the 'unnecessarily cautious way the Court handle[d] this matter ... creates the impression that it somehow feels uncom-

---

on behalf of El Salvador (due to the alleged Nicaraguan support for armed rebels in El Salvador), the judgment concluded: 'As stated above, the Court is unable to consider that, in customary international law, the provision of arms to the opposition in another State constitutes an armed attack on that State. Even at a time when the arms flow was at its peak, and again assuming the participation of the Nicaraguan Government, that would not constitute such armed attack.' At para. 230. But see the dissenting opinions on this point by Judges Jennings and Schwebel who considered that, although the provision of arms on its own would not constitute an armed attack, there could be situations where the substantial involvement of a state with such non-state actor attacks would rise to the level of armed attacks that entitle the victim state to engage in self-defence. In the *Legal Consequences of the Construction of a Wall in Occupied Palestinian Territory*, ICJ Rep. (2004) p. 136 the Court excluded self-defence where the threat emanates from occupied territory at para. 139, but see the Separate Opinions of Judges Higgins and Kooijmans and the Declaration by Judge Buergenthal.

54. *Armed Activities on the Territory of the Congo (Democratic Republic of the Congo v Uganda)*, ICJ Rep. (2005) at paras 146–7.
55. Ibid para. 147.

fortable being confronted with certain questions of utmost importance in contemporary international relations'.[56] The Court therefore can be seen as having left for another day a judgment on the conditions for self-defence against large-scale attacks by non-state actors.[57] For present purposes it is suggested that rather than concentrating on whether self-defence can be used in response to an attack by a non-state actor, the more important interrelated issues will be: against what may the force be directed? Whether the force was necessary? And whether the force was proportionate? We now turn to these questions.

(iii) Appropriate military targets

The use of force in self-defence must obviously respect the laws of armed conflict and international human rights law (considered below). In addition, the targets must relate to the self-defence action. Targeting a military objective must therefore be related to the aim of ending the attack or preventing the next imminent attack. The right to self-defence is not a right to engage in armed retaliation or retribution. The International Court in the *Oil Platforms Case* suggested that the state relying on the right to self-defence will have to show that its use of force against a particular target was necessary to deal with the attacks to which it had been subjected:

> In the case both of the attack on the *Sea Isle City* and the mining of the USS *Samuel B. Roberts*, the Court is not satisfied

---

56. At para. 15. See also the Separate Opinion by Judge Kooijmans.
57. See further Gray (above) at 132–6 and 198–202; Moir (above) 135–9; Ruys (above) 479–85; Lubell (above) at 30–6.

that the attacks on the platforms were necessary to respond to these incidents. In this connection, the Court notes that there is no evidence that the United States complained to Iran of the military activities of the platforms, in the same way as it complained repeatedly of minelaying and attacks on neutral shipping, which does not suggest that the targeting of the platforms was seen as a necessary act. The Court would also observe that in the case of the attack of 19 October 1987, the United States forces attacked the R-4 platform as a 'target of opportunity', not one previously identified as an appropriate military target.[58]

(iv) Necessity

Necessity is a principle of international law which limits the right to use self-defence. The right to self-defence only extends to those measures that are necessary to respond to the armed attack. Although not mentioned in Article 51, the International Court of Justice states that this rule is 'well established in customary international law'.[59] The question of necessity is not something to be evaluated by the state concerned according to its own perceptions of the danger being faced. The Court explained in the context of the self-defence claim by Uganda that 'Article 51 of the Charter may justify a use of force in self-defence only within the strict confines there laid down. It does not allow the use of force by a State to protect perceived security interests beyond these parameters.

---

58. *Oil Platforms* (above) at para. 76. Corten (above) helpfully labels this aspect a question of *effectiveness* (above) at 488–93.

59. *Nicaragua* (above) at para. 176.

Other means are available to a concerned State, including, in particular, recourse to the Security Council.'[60]

There is no reason to believe that self-defence must be instantaneous in order to be legal (notwithstanding the *Caroline* formula). The coalition that was assembled to come to the self-defence of Kuwait in 1990 chose not to react instantaneously. Judith Gardam points out that, in fact 'States regard themselves under a continuing obligation to endeavour to settle their differences by peaceful means. Depending on the circumstances, the failure to acknowledge peaceful overtures could transform a legitimate response in self-defence into an aggressive use of force.'[61]

(v) Proportionality

The facts of the *Oil Platforms Case* afforded the World Court the opportunity to explain how it would apply the proportionality rule in the event that a state be entitled to use self-defence.[62] With regard to one particular incident of the use of force by the United States, the Court said: 'As a response to the mining, by an unidentified agency, of a single United States warship, which was severely damaged but not sunk, and without loss of life, neither "Operation Praying Mantis" as a whole, nor even that part of it that destroyed the Salman and Nasr platforms, can be regarded, in the circumstances of this case, as a proportionate use of force in self-

---

60. *DRC v Uganda* (above) at para. 148.

61. J. Gardam, *Necessity, Proportionality and the Use of Force by States* (Cambridge: CUP, 2004) at 155.

62. The Court has also affirmed that the proportionality rule is a rule of customary international law. *Nicaragua* (above) at para. 176.

defence.'[63] Similarly, with regard to the claims of Uganda, the Court observed that 'the taking of airports and towns many hundreds of kilometres from Uganda's border would not seem proportionate to the series of transborder attacks it claimed had given rise to the right of self-defence, nor to be necessary to that end'.[64]

Proportionality means evaluating the force used in self-defence against the threat posed. Proportionality is not limited to evaluating what has happened but rather focuses on what needs to happen. Elizabeth Wilmshurst's introduction to the Chatham House Principles on the Use of Force explains: 'because the right of self-defence does not allow the use of force to punish an aggressor, proportionality should not be thought to refer to parity between a response and the harm already suffered from an attack, as this could either turn the concept of self-defence into a justification for retributive force, or limit the use of force to less than what is necessary to repel the attack'.[65]

---

63. *Oil Platforms* (*above*) at para. 76.

64. *DRC v Uganda* (*above*) at para. 147.

65. E. Wilmshurst, 'The Chatham House Principles of International Law on the Use of Force in Self-Defence', 55 *ICLQ* (2006) 963–72 at 968. The Principles also state that '[t]he physical and economic consequences of the force used must not be excessive in relation to the harm expected from the attack'. See also the helpful conclusion by Franck referred to in Ch. VIII in the context of trade, but which he applied in the present context too: 'An aggrieved party is not required to respond only in kind, whether the subject is trade, the use of force, or human rights. In assessing the acceptability of a response, the principle of proportionality allows those affronted by unlawful conduct to respond by taking into account the level of response necessary to prevent recurrences. This latitude may turn on the severity, frequency, and duration of the unlawful behavior. It potentially also invokes a version of the "precautionary approach" so well known from its deployment in environmental law.' 'On Proportionality of Countermeasures in International Law', 102 *AJIL* (2008) 715–67, at 765–6; and with regard in particular to Afghanistan (2001) see Moir (above) at 68–71.

There is a second proportionality rule which has to be respected by all sides whenever there is resort to force. We include it here because it represents a separate rule which needs to be considered in conjunction with the rule just explained. This rule derives from the law of armed conflict and the principle of distinction between combatants and civilians. Once one has identified an appropriate military target and the proposed use of force is both necessary and proportionate under the tests outlined above, one then must determine whether the expected civilian loss of life or damage is proportionate to the anticipated military advantage.

Whether something is a military objective is context-specific. As explained in Protocol I to the Geneva Conventions: 'military objectives are limited to those objects which by their nature, location, purpose or use make an effective contribution to military action and whose total or partial destruction, capture or neutralization, in the circumstances ruling at the time, offers a definite military advantage'.[66] Again one needs to examine carefully the context. A bridge or a power station may be purely civilian objects, or may be making an effective contribution to military action. Even where it is suggested that such objects represent military objectives, the use of force will only be legal where the proportionality test is satisfied. Whether such objects represent an appropriate target therefore depends on the direct and indirect effects of their destruction as well as the anticipated advantage. Article 51(5)(b) of the Protocol prohibits 'an attack which may be expected to cause incidental loss of civilian life, injury to civilians, damage to civilian objects, or a combination thereof, which would be excessive in relation to the concrete and direct military advantage

---

66. Art. 52(2).

anticipated'.[67] This is the rule that prohibits disproportionate collateral damage. We will examine some of the other laws of armed conflict towards the end of this chapter.

§ 3. Authorization by the Security Council

Having outlined the contours of a state's right to self-defence, we now turn to a second exception to the prohibition on the use of force. It is clearly established that the Security Council can authorize states to use force. We saw in the previous chapter how, in the context of a threat to the peace, breach of the peace, or act of aggression, the Charter foresaw that the Security Council 'may take such action by air, sea, and land forces' as may be necessary to maintain or restore international peace and security.[68] This was to be done with UN forces placed at the Security Council's disposal. As already mentioned, the current standby arrangements only partially fulfil this idea. In practice the use of force has been either authorized for UN peace-keeping operations assembled on an *ad hoc* basis with personnel from troop contributing countries, or for coalitions of member states acting outside UN command and control.

---

67. This rule is included in the ICRC Study on Customary International Humanitarian Law as applicable in both international and non-international armed conflicts, Rule 14; J.-M. Henckaerts and L. Doswald-Beck, *Customary International Humanitarian Law—Volume 1: Rules* (Cambridge: CUP, 2005). See also the Statute of the International Criminal Court for a war crime based on this rule, Art. 8(2)(b)(iv).
68. See Chapter VII of the UN Charter, Arts 39–50.

There is no need for the Security Council first to find that there has been an illegal use of force by a particular state. For enforcement action to be authorized it is enough that there should be a breach or threat to the peace. The formula used by the Security Council today, when it authorizes the use of force for states acting outside UN command and control, will be along the lines that it determines that the situation constitutes a threat to international peace and security, that it is acting under Chapter VII of the Charter, and that it authorizes certain member states to 'use all necessary means' or 'take all necessary measures'.[69]

The Security Council's authorization for member states to use force acting outside UN command and control has attracted considerable controversy. First, there has been concern that states (whether acting individually, through regional organizations, or in coalition) may use such authorizations simply to pursue their own interests.

Second, Security Council resolutions have been relied on as a justification for using force even where there had been no explicit authorization of the use of force with respect to the military action being undertaken. In this way the 1999 NATO bombing of the Federal Republic of Yugoslavia in the Kosovo conflict was justified by some participating states as authorized by previous Chapter VII resolutions which had authorized force with regard to the earlier conflicts in the former Yugoslavia. Similarly, the United Kingdom and the United States relied on a Security Council resolution authorizing the use of force in response to Iraq's 1990 invasion of Kuwait to justify the use of force in 2003 involving the bombing, invasion, and occupation of Iraq.

---

69. See, e.g. Resolutions 678 (1990) (Kuwait) and 1973 (2011) (Libya).

Third, disagreements can quickly develop over whether the limitations in the authorization are being respected. This was most recently the case with regard to the authorization of the use of force with respect to Libya in 2011, which was limited to the protection of civilians. All these developments have led to greater caution in the Security Council, this caution being manifested in extra conditions being imposed on the authorized states, the setting of time limits on mandates, and a reluctance to include references to 'Chapter VII' or the need to use 'all necessary means'.[70]

The reader may be understandably frustrated that, even if individual states remain free to find that other states have violated the UN Charter,[71] UN organs such as the Security Council and the General Assembly have failed to condemn the illegal use of force by big powers, while the International Court of Justice only enjoys jurisdiction in those disputes where states have consented to its jurisdiction. Moreover the controversy over the 2003 Iraq war[72]

70. See the detailed discussion in Gray (above) ch. 8 and Moir (above) 107–17.

71. The resort to force against the Federal Republic of Yugoslavia and Iraq was widely condemned (see the details in Corten (above) ch. 6 and Gray ibid at 354–69). Where a state concludes that such action is not authorized by the Security Council it may be obliged under its law to refuse to allow overflight or other forms of co-operation. In the context of the US/UK armed conflict with Iraq in 2003, Switzerland by law fulfilled its obligations by ensuring that 'conflicting parties were not allowed to fly over Swiss territory before and during this conflict. Moreover the Confederation was forbidden to export arms and services to states involved in the conflict.' 'Neutrality Under Scrutiny in the Iraq Conflict: Summary of Switzerland's neutrality policy during the Iraq conflict' Federal Department of Foreign Affairs, 5 December 2005, at 2.

72. The term 'war' in this section is used in the non-technical sense, in *Amin v Brown* [2005] EWHC 1670 (Ch) the High Court held that there was no war between the UK and Iraq (there was of course an international armed conflict). Mrs Amin, as an Iraqi national, was therefore not prevented under the national law on enemy aliens from

has led to disillusion in some quarters at the impotence of international law to rein in those resorting to force in the absence of a clear mandate from the Security Council. While these sentiments are understandable, there is, however, a real danger that by unduly focusing on the adoption of certain resolutions, we too easily satisfy ourselves of the wisdom or otherwise of the use of force. For many commentators the appropriateness or otherwise of the use of force with regard to Kosovo or Iraq seems to turn on the voting outcome in the Security Council. If nine votes can be found, and there is no veto, then the use of force is seemingly legal, legitimate, and to be supported. But such a limited focus is very dangerous; the appropriateness of any use of force should be debated with regard to the multiple dimensions of the issue.

In the run up to the 2003 Iraq war, Sir Adam Roberts asked us to consider, in addition to the legal dimension, the following questions: 'Has deterrence of Iraq failed so clearly that action must now be taken? Is it wise to start this war when there is so much unfinished business in Afghanistan? Should action be taken against Iraq before there is a further effort to address the Israel-Palestine problem? Is there any viable plan for the future of Iraq?'[73] While the question of the legality of any resort to force remains important, we must not forget to question the wisdom of war, and we must remain alert to the prospect that, even if a Security Coun-

---

bringing a case concerning a house in London before the UK courts. When the term 'war' is used in commercial or insurance contracts courts may take a more pragmatic approach depending on the context and there will be no need for a formal declaration of war. On the uncertain status of the concept of war in international law see C. Greenwood, 'The Concept of War in Modern International Law', 36 *ICLQ* (1987) 283–306.

73. 'The Case for War', *The Guardian*, 17 September 2002.

cil resolution legalizes an attack that would otherwise be an act of aggression, such resort to force may still be very unwise.

As regards UN peace operations, a distinction is often drawn between UN operations established under Chapter VI and those under Chapter VII. But this can be misleading. All UN peace operations have been seen as having the right to use force in self-defence or defence of their mandate. This right is exercised in a state under Chapter VI because that host state has consented to such an operation. Just because an operation is established under Chapter VII does not mean that the UN operation is necessarily entitled to use a greater degree of force. A Chapter VII operation implies international obligations for all UN member states, but any authorization of the use of force will usually be separately addressed in the Security Council resolution in the context of spelling out the mandate. So for example, in 2007 in its Chapter VII resolution on the United Nations Assistance Mission in Darfur (UNAMID) the Security Council *decided*

> that UNAMID is authorised to take the necessary action, in the areas of deployment of its forces and as it deems within its capabilities in order to:
>
> (i) protect its personnel, facilities, installations and equipment, and to ensure the security and freedom of movement of its own personnel and humanitarian workers,
>
> (ii) support early and effective implementation of the Darfur Peace Agreement, prevent the disruption of its implementation and armed attacks, and protect civilians, without prejudice to the responsibility of the Government of Sudan....

This wider recourse to force by UN troops is not without controversy, and appeals for a 'robust doctrine' for peace-keeping have so far failed to attract support across the member states of the UN.[74] In turn the UN Secretariat has been frustrated by the Council's ability to craft ambitious mandates which are then matched with miserly resources and inadequate troop contributions from member states.

> The presence of a peacekeeping mission generates high expectations among host populations and international opinion to protect individuals and communities in conflict. Yet, the ability of small numbers of under-equipped peacekeepers to protect civilian populations, often numbering several millions over vast distances, is finite. UN missions are regularly assigned a broad range of tasks that go well beyond providing physical security, including support for the voluntary return of refugees and displaced persons, and protection of civilians from sexual violence. These tasks require the engagement of all parts of the mission, whether military, police or civilian. The mismatch between expectations and capacity to provide comprehensive protection creates a significant credibility challenge for UN peacekeeping.[75]

At present, it would appear that there is little hope that UN peacekeeping operations can play the world-wide role of maintaining

---

74. Report of the Panel on United Nations Peace Operations (Brahimi Report), A/55/305–S/2000/809, 21 August 2000.

75. Department of Peacekeeping Operations and Department of Field Support, *A New Partnership Agenda: Charting a New Horizon for Peace-Keeping* (2009) at 20.

the peace and protecting those at risk from violence. States have failed to give the UN the means to carry out this function adequately. Although the cold war divisions that prevented the creation of such operations are no longer with us, the world has failed to create the sort of capacity that would enable the UN to react on the ground in an effective way. The Secretariat's perspective again reveals the problems. 'Each new operation is built voluntarily and from scratch on the assumption that adequate resources can be found and is run on individual budget, support and administrative lines. Peacekeeping in its current form requires more predictable, professional and adaptable capacities. It needs a global system to match the global enterprise it has become.'[76] The momentum for such a system will depend on whether states (and the individuals who represent them) feel a sense of sensibility to everyone in the global community.

§ 4. Aggression in the Statute of the International Criminal Court

As mentioned in Chapter III it is likely that the International Criminal Court (ICC) will have jurisdiction over the crime of aggression from 2017.[77] The amended Statute excludes jurisdic-

---

76. *A New Partnership Agenda: Charting a New Horizon for Peace-Keeping* (2009) (above) at iii.

77. Under the amendment to the Statute the new Art. 15*bis*(3) reads: 'The Court shall exercise jurisdiction over the crime of aggression in accordance with this article, subject to a decision to be taken after 1 January 2017 by the same majority of States Parties as is required for the adoption of an amendment to the Statute.' For a full discussion see volume 10(1) of the *Journal of International Criminal Justice* (2012).

tion over nationals from states which have not ratified the Statute, unless the situation has been referred by the Security Council.[78] The crime is defined for the purposes of the Statute of the ICC as 'the planning, preparation, initiation or execution, by a person in a position effectively to exercise control over or to direct the political or military action of a State, of an act of aggression which, by its character, gravity and scale, constitutes a manifest violation of the Charter of the United Nations'.[79] The crime can therefore be described as a 'leadership crime' and the Statute limits the scope of complicity in this crime to those who can control or direct the armed forces of a state.[80]

In turn an 'act of aggression' is defined as 'the use of armed force by a State against the sovereignty, territorial integrity or political independence of another State, or in any other manner inconsistent with the Charter of the United Nations'.[81] There then follows a list of acts that may qualify as an act of aggression:

Any of the following acts, regardless of a declaration of war, shall, in accordance with United Nations General Assembly resolution 3314 (XXIX) of 14 December 1974, qualify as an act of aggression:

(a) The invasion or attack by the armed forces of a State of the territory of another State, or any military occupation, how-

---

78. Arts 15*bis*(5), and 15*ter*. See also the additional procedural steps under Arts 15*bis*(6) (7)(8) and Ch. III § 4 (above).

79. Art. 8*bis*(1) ICC Statute.

80. Art. 25*bis*(3).

81. Art. 8*bis*(2) ICC Statute.

ever temporary, resulting from such invasion or attack, or
any annexation by the use of force of the territory of
another State or part thereof;

(b) Bombardment by the armed forces of a State against the
territory of another State or the use of any weapons by a
State against the territory of another State;

(c) The blockade of the ports or coasts of a State by the armed
forces of another State;

(d) An attack by the armed forces of a State on the land, sea or
air forces, or marine and air fleets of another State;

(e) The use of armed forces of one State which are within the
territory of another State with the agreement of the receiving State, in contravention of the conditions provided for
in the agreement or any extension of their presence in such
territory beyond the termination of the agreement;

(f) The action of a State in allowing its territory, which it has
placed at the disposal of another State, to be used by that
other State for perpetrating an act of aggression against a
third State;

(g) The sending by or on behalf of a State of armed bands,
groups, irregulars or mercenaries, which carry out acts of
armed force against another State of such gravity as to
amount to the acts listed above, or its substantial involvement therein.[82]

There will be no crime of aggression where the use of force was
legal as an exercise of self-defence or because it had been author-

---

82. Resolution RC/Res.6, adopted 11 June 2010, Annex I, Art. 8*bis* paras 1 and 2.

ized by the Security Council. In such cases there will have been no 'manifest violation of the Charter of the United Nations'.

In 1946 the International Military Tribunal in Nuremberg stated that 'to initiate a war of aggression ... is the supreme international crime'.[83] The Tribunal found 12 of the defendants guilty on counts related to aggression. The Tokyo Tribunal found 24 of the defendants guilty on similar counts. Since that time there has been little appetite for the prosecution of the international crime of aggression; the Special Tribunal for Iraq was not given jurisdiction of this crime in the context of the trial of Saddam Hussein and others, even though there were calls for prosecutions related to the Iraqi invasion of Kuwait in 1990.[84] The jurisdictional and procedural hurdles for future trials before the International Criminal Court will be considerable. But the inclusion of the crime of aggression within the Statute of the International Criminal Court will surely give some leaders cause to pause for thought before embarking on military adventures.

§ 5. International law in armed conflict

All parties to an armed conflict are bound to respect the applicable international law. Both the aggressor state and the state acting in self-defence will be bound by the laws of war, now often known as international humanitarian law. A distinction is drawn between

---

83. *Trial of German Major War Criminals* (1946) Cmd 6964 (London: HMSO) at 13.

84. The Statute did, however, refer to a provision of Iraqi national law that could be used to prosecute a similar crime. See C. Kress, 'The Iraqi Special Tribunal and the Crime of Aggression', 2 *JICJ* (2004) 347–52.

inter-state conflicts and other armed conflicts involving organized non-state armed groups fighting against a state or each other. Certain rules from inter-state armed conflict will be inapplicable to internal armed conflicts.[85] So for example, in internal armed conflict there is no concept of a prisoner of war who can be detained until the end of the conflict and then must be released. In an internal armed conflict the captured non-governmental forces from the rebel side will usually be considered criminals for having taken up arms against the state, and the state can prosecute and punish them for their actions. By contrast, in an international armed conflict a member of the armed forces of a state captured by another state is not only entitled to be treated as a prisoner of war, but cannot be tried for having used force, even lethal force, against the armed forces of the capturing state. Even where the captured soldier belongs to the forces of an aggressor state, the individual crime of aggression, as we have seen, is a 'leadership crime' limited to those persons in a position to control or direct the armed forces of a state. The members of the armed forces of a state enjoy what is called 'combatant immunity' protecting them from prosecution for having used arms against another state. Of course they will

---

85. The rules on international armed conflict have enjoyed much greater attention from states as they obviously understand the reciprocal advantage of limiting certain methods and means of warfare. States have been less enthusiastic about limiting their freedom of action in the context of internal armed conflicts. Compare the long list of war crimes in international armed conflicts with the shorter provisions related to internal armed conflicts in the Statute of the International Criminal Court (1998) Art. 8(2). See also the distinctions drawn in the ICRC Customary International Humanitarian Law Study (Henckaerts and Doswald-Beck, above). See further Y. Dinstein, *The Conduct of Hostilities under the Law of International Armed Conflict*, 2nd edn (Cambridge: CUP, 2010); L. Moir, *The Law of Internal Armed Conflict* (Cambridge: CUP, 2002).

remain liable to prosecution for certain violations of the laws of war (war crimes).

The laws of war have a long history and have been developed through a multitude of treaties as well as through customary international law.[86] The International Committee of the Red Cross seeks to bring a degree of clarity to this branch of international law which has recently taken on new significance with the increasing prospect of war crimes trials for violations of the law of armed conflict.[87] The topic is complex, and here we can only sketch a few fundamental principles and list some of the war crimes included in the Statute of the International Criminal Court.

In considering the legality of nuclear weapons the International Court of Justice distilled many of the rules down to two cardinal principles:

> The first is aimed at the protection of the civilian population and civilian objects and establishes the distinction between combatants and non-combatants; States must never make civilians the object of attack and must consequently never use weapons that are incapable of distinguishing between civilian

---

86. For an overview see M. Sassòli, A.A. Bouvier, and A. Quintin, *How Does Law Protect in War? Cases, Documents and Teaching Materials on Contemporary Practice in International Humanitarian Law*, 3rd edn (Geneva: ICRC, 2011) 3 vols; R. Kolb and R. Hyde, *An Introduction to the International Law of Armed Conflicts* (Oxford: Hart Publishing, 2008); F. Kalshoven and L. Zegveld, *Constraints on the Waging of War*, 4th edn (Geneva: ICRC, 2011); C. Greenwood, 'International Humanitarian Law (Laws of War)', in F. Kalshoven (ed.), *The Centennial of the First International Peace Conference* (The Hague: Kluwer Law International, 2000) 161–259.

87. See S.R. Ratner, 'Law Promotion Beyond Law Talk: The Red Cross, Persuasion, and the Laws of War', 22(2) *EJIL* (2011) 459–506.

and military targets. According to the second principle, it is prohibited to cause unnecessary suffering to combatants: it is accordingly prohibited to use weapons causing them such harm or uselessly aggravating their suffering. In application of that second principle, States do not have unlimited freedom of choice of means in the weapons they use.[88]

The application of the relevant rules is complicated. As to the first principle, there are multiple controversies surrounding who qualifies as a combatant, when do civilians lose their protection from attack through direct participation in hostilities,[89] what constitutes a military objective and hence a legitimate target, as well as how to apply the associated rule on proportionality which prohibits excessive damage to civilian objects and lives when targeting a military objective.

In times of conflict the answers to these questions depend on multiple factors which remain quite context-specific. So for example, as suggested in § 2(b)(v), a bridge can be considered a legitimate target depending on the circumstances, and, even where the bridge can make a contribution to the military effort of the opponent, any targeting will have to take precautions to avoid civilian casualties, while the eventual bombing must not result in disproportionate civilian casualties. In order to make such an evaluation one would

---

88. *Legality of the Threat or Use of Nuclear Weapons*, ICJ Rep. (1996) p. 226, at para. 78.
89. N. Melzer, 'Keeping the Balance Between Military Necessity and Humanity: A Response to Four Critiques of the ICRC's Interpretive Guidance on the Notion of Direct Participation in Hostilities', 42(3) *New York University Journal of International Law and Politics* (2010) 831–916.

need to know the likelihood of civilians being near the bridge at any particular time of day or night, as well as the strategic advantage offered by the destruction of the bridge. The weighing of civilian lives against an abstract future military advantage seems grotesque and unworkable, but the principle forms the basis for calculations related to the legality of targeting in all modern conflicts.[90]

Similar controversies arise with regard to the second principle. Although a number of treaties prohibit certain weapons in the context of the principle prohibiting unnecessary suffering to combatants, states have resisted seeing this principle as leading to a prohibition of weapons that have not been specifically outlawed.[91] The debate may then turn on how the weapons are used rather than on the fact they have been used.[92]

The principles just outlined, sometimes known as the law on the conduct of hostilities, are complemented by humanitarian rules for the protection of the victims of armed conflicts. Those protected by these rules include the sick, the shipwrecked, prisoners of war and other detainees, and civilians in occupied territories.

---

90. For the difficulties involved in applying the law to the facts in such situations see Report of the Independent International Fact-Finding Mission on the Conflict in Georgia (2009) vol. II at 321–51; Final Report to the Prosecutor by the Committee Established to Review the NATO Bombing Campaign Against the Federal Republic of Yugoslavia (2000) 39 ILM 1257; Report of the International Commission of Inquiry to investigate all alleged violations of international human rights law in the Libyan Arab Jamahiriya, A/HRC/17/44, 1 June 2011.

91. Consider the detailed listings of prohibited weapons in the International Criminal Court Art. 8(2)(b). For an overview of the international law in this field see W. Boothby, *Weapons and the Law of Armed Conflict* (Oxford: OUP, 2009).

92. See the discussion in the ICJ Opinion and the separate and dissenting opinions in *Legality of the Threat or Use of Nuclear Weapons* (above).

As we saw in previous chapters there may be specific provisions not only regarding the treatment of such persons but also prohibiting any reprisals against them. The provisions of this branch of the law of armed conflict cover several hundred articles mostly found in the four Geneva Conventions of 1949 and their Protocols. Any idea that some people fall outside this protection in times of armed conflict is now discredited.[93] A sense of the minimum guarantees can be gleaned from Common Article 3 to the 1949 Geneva Conventions which reads as follows:

> In the case of armed conflict not of an international character occurring in the territory of one of the High Contracting Parties, each Party to the conflict shall be bound to apply, as a minimum, the following provisions:
>
> (1) Persons taking no active part in the hostilities, including members of armed forces who have laid down their arms and those placed hors de combat by sickness, wounds, detention, or any other cause, shall in all circumstances be treated humanely, without any adverse distinction founded on race, colour, religion or faith, sex, birth or wealth, or

---

93. The minimum rules regarding the treatment of those in the hands of the enemy can be found in Common Article 3 to the Geneva Conventions (the Conventions have been universally ratified) and Art. 75 to Protocol I. The United States recently recognized that although it is not a Party to Protocol I 'The U.S. Government will … choose out of a sense of legal obligation to treat the principles set forth in Article 75 as applicable to any individual it detains in an international armed conflict, and expects all other nations to adhere to these principles as well.' The White House, Fact Sheet: New Actions on Guantánamo and Detainee Policy, 7 March 2011.

any other similar criteria. To this end the following acts are and shall remain prohibited at any time and in any place whatsoever with respect to the above-mentioned persons:

(a) violence to life and person, in particular murder of all kinds, mutilation, cruel treatment and torture;

(b) taking of hostages;

(c) outrages upon personal dignity, in particular, humiliating and degrading treatment;

(d) the passing of sentences and the carrying out of executions without previous judgment pronounced by a regularly constituted court affording all the judicial guarantees which are recognized as indispensable by civilized peoples.

(2) The wounded and sick shall be collected and cared for.

An impartial humanitarian body, such as the International Committee of the Red Cross, may offer its services to the Parties to the conflict.

The Parties to the conflict should further endeavour to bring into force, by means of special agreements, all or part of the other provisions of the present Convention.

The application of the preceding provisions shall not affect the legal status of the Parties to the conflict.

Not only are such provisions binding on the parties to the conflict, but violations can also give rise to individual criminal responsibility as war crimes under international law. These crimes are supplemented by a list of crimes relating to the conduct of hostilities, as well as a longer catalogue of crimes which apply in times of international armed conflict.[94]

Although crimes against humanity were included in the Statutes of the Nuremberg and Tokyo Military Tribunals, those courts held that they could not examine such crimes unless they were connected to the conflict. Today crimes against humanity can be prosecuted not only where the acts are committed during armed conflict, but also in the absence of an armed conflict. Under the Rome Statute for the International Criminal Court, in order for these violations of human rights to constitute crimes against humanity, the acts must be committed 'as part of a widespread or systematic attack directed against any civilian population, with the knowledge of the attack'. In turn this means 'a course of conduct involving the multiple commission of acts... pursuant to or in furtherance of a State or organizational policy to commit such attack'. The following acts are included: murder; extermination; deportation or forcible transfer of populations; torture; rape, sexual slavery, enforced prostitution, forced pregnancy, and enforced sterilization; persecution on the basis of political or other grounds; and enforced disappearance of persons.[95]

The International Court of Justice has confirmed that international human rights law and environmental law both apply in times of armed conflict in addition to international humanitarian law.[96] As we saw in Chapter VII, the work of the International Law

---

94. Art. 8(2) ICC Statute.

95. Art. 7 ICC Statute.

96. See *Nuclear Weapons* (above) at paras 25 and 29; see further E. Brown Weiss, 'Opening the Door to the Environment and to Future Generations', in Boisson de Chazournes and Sands (above) at 338–53.

Commission suggests a long list of the types of treaties whose sub-ject-matter implies that they continue in times of armed conflict. Most importantly, international courts, such as the European Court of Human Rights, have applied human rights treaties in situations of armed conflict and occupation providing a remedy to the victims of human rights violations.[97]

The precise interaction, however, between particular provisions of human rights treaties and the laws of war, has caused consider-able confusion and controversy,[98] with some states claiming that one branch of the law should operate to the exclusion of the other. Although there may be situations where only one of these branches apply, in many situations the different legal orders operate in a complementary rather than an exclusive way. So for example, whereas a provision of human rights law may prohibit the arbi-trary deprivation of life or arbitrary detention, in order to deter-mine what constitutes arbitrariness in the context of armed conflict there may be a need to refer to the special rules of armed conflict which explain, for example, what constitutes a military objective (as seen above). In the same way, as we have just seen, the Geneva Conventions refer to 'torture' without further explanation. The

---

97. See, e.g. *Al-Skeini and others v UK*, 7 July 2011; *Al-Jedda v UK*, 7 July 2011; L. Doswald-Beck, *Human Rights in Times of Conflict and Terrorism* (Oxford: OUP, 2011).

98. For a very thoughtful exposition of the interaction between human rights law and humanitarian law see M. Sassòli, 'The Role of Human Rights and International Humani-tarian Law in New Types of Armed Conflicts', in O. Ben-Naftali (ed.), *International Humanitarian Law and International Human Rights Law* (Oxford: OUP, 2011) 34–94; on the recourse to the laws of war in the post-September 11 world see M.E. O'Connell, 'The Choice of Law Against Terrorism', *Journal of National Security Law and Policy* (2010) 343–68, and P. Alston, 'The CIA and Targeted Killings Beyond Borders', 2 *Har-vard National Security Journal* (2011) 283–446.

definitions and interpretation of the term 'torture' in human rights law will have to inform the application of the laws of war.[99]

§ 6. The present role of international law

Throughout this book we have discovered tension between states' interests and certain values related to human dignity, we have also encountered emerging notions of international community. *Obligations owed* to the international community (*erga omnes*), *norms accepted and recognized* by the international community of states (*jus cogens*), and now an international community prepared to accept a *responsibility to protect* people from mass atrocities (*R2P*). Developing a community which is more than simply another name for a collection of states is essential to any future further development of international law. It is not enough to appeal to something called the international community, the community has to feel that everyone is included and that everyone's plight is a matter for concern and for action.

Law is not a kind of cement which, by some inherent force of its own, can firmly bind together human beings or states which are otherwise unrelated to one another and ready to fly apart; nor is it something to which methods of mass production can be applied. Its growth can be stimulated, in fact if it is to develop beyond a very rudimentary stage it needs to be stimulated, by the purposive creation of specialized institutions such as courts through which it

---

99. For further examples and a deeper reflection on the complementary and convergence developing between the two regimes see D. Thürer, 'International Humanitarian Law: Theory, Practice, Context', 338 *RCADI* (2008) 9–370, at 110–63.

can perform its functions; but in the main it is a by-product of the development of a community sense and of the wider, not purely juridical, but also social and political organization in which a feeling of community finds expression.[100]

There are two popular but opposite misconceptions about the role of international law. One is the view of cynics, practical people who have shed their illusions, and believe quite simply that international law is a sham. They point to the absence of sanctions, and without troubling to examine whether the facts support them, assume that a law without sanctions is never observed. They note that this or that treaty has been broken, and infer that therefore no treaty is worth the paper it is written on. At the other extreme there is the utopian view of the ultra legalist lawyer who deals in codes and formulas as though they contained a magic of their own, or of the enthusiastic non-lawyer who imagines that earnest aspiration after a better international order can take the place of patient study of the actual problems. And yet international law today is a system in being, and it is possible, though perhaps not very easy, to discover how it is working.

It is not enough to refer to books; the literary history of international law, as well as much that is contained in traditional treatises, is in many respects misleading. We must look for a true picture, not so much at what is being written, but at what is being done, and for that we must go to the courts in which international

---

100. This last paragraph was originally included by Brierly as part of an address to Chatham House in 1944, 'International Law: Its Actual Part in World Affairs' in *The Basis of Obligation in International Law*, 305–13, at 312; also published in 20 *International Affairs* (1944) 381–9.

legal questions are decided and to the legal departments of foreign offices in which they are discussed. Here we shall find an immense amount of legal business being transacted, most of it practical and (to the non-lawyer) as dull as the work of any other lawyer. It relates largely to matters that receive only cursory mention in books about international law, to the drafting or interpretation of treaties on matters of greater and lesser importance, to the protection of nationals who get into trouble abroad, to conflicts of state jurisdiction, and to a variety of other matters, most of which are remote from high politics and of little interest to the man or woman in the street.

But what is significant about all of this work is that it proceeds on the assumption that states do normally observe their treaties and do respect the rules of international law, and this assumption is justified by experience. The judges and the lawyers involved use the same technique as other lawyers, and nine tenths of their difficulties, like those of other lawyers, arise in the application of accepted general principles to particular facts which are complicated or disputed, and not from any peculiar uncertainty or abstractness of the principles with which international lawyers have to deal. Most of those popular arguments which prove the non-legal or the peculiarly abstract nature of international legal principles are the pseudo-realist arguments of the theorist who, if he or she has examined the subject at all, has seen it in books and not in action.[101]

---

101. The last three paragraphs first appeared in similar form in Brierly's 'Law, Justice, and War' *Czechoslovak Year Book of International Law* (1942), reproduced in *The Basis of Obligation*, 265–79 at 265–6.

INDEX